AWAKENING TO THE SPIRITUAL ARCHETYPES IN THE BIRTH CHART

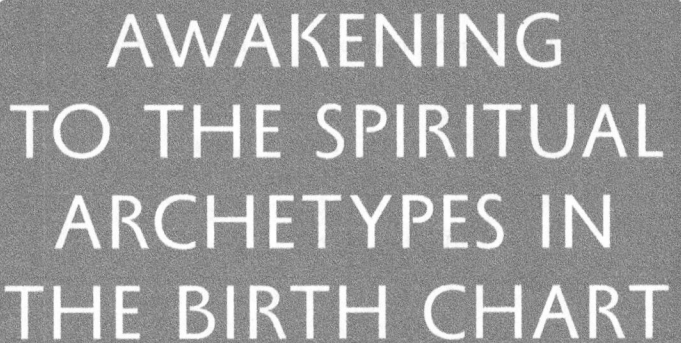

AWAKENING TO THE SPIRITUAL ARCHETYPES IN THE BIRTH CHART

FROM ASTROLOGY TO ASTROSOPHY

JULIE HUMPHREYS

Illustrations by Damijan Jerič

First published in English
by LogoSophia, an imprint of
Sophia Perennis 2023
© Julie Humphreys 2023

All rights reserved

No part of this book may be reproduced or transmitted,
in any form or by any means, without permission.

For information, address:
Sophia Perennis
PO Box 931
Philmont, NY 12565

978-1-59731-221-9 (pb)
978-1-59731-222-6 (cloth)

Typography and cover design: Michael Schrauzer
Cover image and text illustrations: Damijan Jerič

To my beloved husband for his sacrifices;
in grateful appreciation of Claudia Lainson,
who shone her lamp upon my path to the stars;
to my editor, Richard Bloedon, who was both
the stork and the midwife of this book; and
to the pioneers of astrosophy, whose work
has enriched my life beyond measure.

TABLE OF CONTENTS

INTRODUCTION by Claudia McLaren Lainson xi
AN INVITATION 1

PART I: What is Astrosophy? 3
  1 The Gaze of the Ancients upon the Starry Vault 5
  2 The Stars and Christ 8
  3 The Zodiac 10
  4 The Sidereal and Tropical Zodiacs 15
  5 The Circle of Twelve 18
  6 The Spatial Dominion of the Zodiac 36
  7 Stars within and without the Zodiac 39
  8 The Planets and the Moon's Nodes 40
  9 The Planets in the Signs 59

INTERLUDE: What is Christian Hermeticism? 101

PART II: The Celestial Wheel 105
  1 The Geocentric Chart 107
  2 The Heliocentric and Tychonic Charts 113
  3 The Ascendant-Descendant Axis 121
  4 The Vertical Axis 125
  5 The Quadrants 129
  6 The Houses 133
  7 The Planets in the Houses 143
  8 Elemental Balance in the Chart 174

PART III: Other Considerations 177
  1 Rulership 179
  2 Exaltation 182
  3 Retrograde Movement 187
  4 The Transposition of Mercury and Venus 189
  5 Let's Take a Breath 192

PART IV: Planetary Relationships 193
  1 Planetary Aspects 195
  2 The Meaning of Planetary Pairs in Aspect 200
  3 Cosmic Tempo 213

APPENDIX 1: Sidereal Longitudes of Important Stars 227
APPENDIX 2: Planetary Aspects within the
  Christ Chronology 229
APPENDIX 3: Geocentric Planetary Positions within the
  Christ Chronology 236

AN ABBREVIATED BIBLIOGRAPHY 247
ACKNOWLEDGMENTS 250

♈	Aries	☉	Sun
♉	Taurus	☽	Moon
♊	Gemini	☿	Mercury
♋	Cancer	♀	Venus
♌	Leo	♂	Mars
♍	Virgo	♃	Jupiter
♎	Libra	♄	Saturn
♏	Scorpio	♅ ♂	Uranus
♐	Sagittarius	♆	Neptune
♑	Capricorn	♇ ♇	Pluto
♒	Aquarius	⊕	Earth
♓	Pisces	☊	North Node of the Moon
		☋	South Node of the Moon

INTRODUCTION

THE TIME AND TEMPO OF THE WORLD ORCHESTRA

And God said, "Let there be lights in the firmament of the heavens to separate the day from the night; and let them be for signs and for seasons and for days and years."[1]

IN THIS REMARKABLE BOOK, JULIE Humphreys unearths the entombed wisdom of ancient Egypt as she deftly resurrects the spiritual archetypes of a lost cosmology. Setting the stage for our possible encounter with the language of symbols—which is both indefinite and constantly metamorphosing—she invites the reader to engage in the sacred dialogues that our ancestors once received clairvoyantly. This she does in such a manner that anyone, regardless of their familiarity with horoscopes, is able to begin a quest into understanding the moral-cosmic significance of houses, planets, constellations, and aspects.

In times long past, the stars spoke to human beings; and in this way, the rightful unfolding of history was guided. Over eons of time, however, the heavens fell silent, awaiting a time when we ourselves would learn how to speak to *them*. Many of us feel inspired to answer that call—although not as the priest/kings of old, but rather as sovereign individuals who have awakened from the *superficial*-world and are in search of the *depth*-world.

Our withdrawal from these lofty beings has resulted in an ever more dangerous plunge into a wilderness of materialistic assumptions. Astrology, too, has suffered such a fall. Through the magical, and initiating, domains of stellar archetypes, the cosmic script depicted in each birth chart reflects the journey into incarnation of one of God's holy children. And a horoscope *cannot* be contained within any kind of merely intellectual construct.

Considerations drawn from the Major Arcana of the Tarot weave throughout this book. As multivocal archetypes, they ask us to surrender what we *think* we know, so that knowingness itself may work through us. For, as Julie knows so well, nothing means anything if separated from the whole. Thus are we cautioned to tread carefully, lest we construct life-destroying systems that arrest the infinite in graveyards of ghostly forms.

The guiding arcana Julie specifically references are found in the 22 letter-meditations of Valentin Tomberg's *Meditations on the Tarot*. For example, a Magician begins it all (representing our Sun Self). He is one within himself, and he is one within the silence of the spiritual world. Representing the arcanum of "true spontaneity," he operates with ease, as if playing. To grasp what the Magician effortlessly experiences, it must be "reflected" within the soul—so that it becomes perceptible. Thus is the "pure act of intelligence" placed into an alchemical furnace that forges human thinking on the steel anvil of the High Priestess, after which it can be grasped and remembered. And as our Magician takes up his throne and opens the book of the High Priestess, we may find that the scepter of the Empress—the wand of sacred magic—is placed in our hand. It is a wand that initiates the action necessary if we are to harmonize our earthly biographies with our pre-earthly intentions. Thus speak the first three arcana of the Tarot. As we then accomplish the spiritual exercises they present, we gain self-mastery (The Emperor). Thereby do Saturn, Sun, Moon, and Jupiter prepare us to vanquish any ghosts we have dragged from the past—so that we may gain yet another octave on the spiral of our perpetual becoming. Where do we find these imperial signatures in our own birth chart? When wonder overcomes skepticism, our inquiry begins…

---

1   Valentin Tomberg, *Lazarus: The Miracle of Resurrection in World History* (Brooklyn, NY: Angelico Press, 2022), 40.

Our Magician longs to unite with our earthly consciousness, and to become both director and architect of the all-and-everything that our destiny has set before us. For in realms wherein we dwelled before we became the self we now know, he was known to us as our "higher Self." He guides us in deciphering the multivocal meanings in the language of symbols, discerning how they *specifically* speak to us. Symbols cannot be fixed and they do not judge; they *reveal*! They tether us not to constraining yokes, nor to burdens we no longer need carry. The lofty beings of the hierarchies are there to guide us, *and they are calling us all home*. Their imprints are *in* the horoscope. Can we find them?

Like archeologists rummaging through the dusty catacombs of antiquity, we seek the lost book of Thoth, which bears the sacred texts of Hermes Trismegistus. Has not this Hermetic Titan of old spread a rainbow across the millennia of history, one that stretches from Egypt to our time? If he could speak to us now, he would most certainly urge us to remember that "what is above, is also below." Communion!

The initiation secrets of the forgotten book of Hermes are breathed into life In Tomberg's momentous treatise on the Major Arcana of the Tarot. Invigorating our understanding of the heavenly world, these "letter-meditations" provide much-needed perspectives for our time. One such perspective — Astro-Sophia — draw nearer when the authenticity of sidereal astrology lives again. For the sidereal star chart "below" is in agreement with the stars in the sky "above." And when the horoscope thus aligns, we are able to liberate dead concepts that have withered into abstract enchantments.

As William Wordsworth noted so poignantly, we come to birth "trailing clouds of glory."[2] This represents the "positive karma" that is ours to develop anew. Hidden though these gifts may yet be, they are not to be ignored, for they represent the North Star within each birth chart. Do we not long to manifest the miracles gifted from the night side of our biographies (the inside)? Am I not myself the conductor who determines how I will perform the drama that shall be enacted on the stage of my life? I am! Symbols have scored the music; they are mine to follow...or not...for though the stars *incline*, they do not *compel*.

While invoking the presence of Love's enduring light, we can humbly approach the portals that are created through symbols, archetypes, and arcana. We may then find that "a veil is lifted"—thereby allowing us to fathom what otherwise might remain obscure. And so it is that Julie not only offers a ground from which our journey may begin, she also unceasingly encourages us to look even deeper, to bow ever lower. For she realizes that our concordance with star beings is born from a fusion of these multi-level realities. Such concordance engenders a Force—one that can permeate mystery with Reason.

What *is* this Force? It is Love: a force of mercy and forgiveness that permeates all creation. And in resurrecting the mummified corpse of the old astrology, we may gain a sense for this truth. Then may we gradually, or even suddenly, begin to see the cosmos from the *inside*. If we are looking only from the *outside*, we experience merely the cold and rigid moral impressions that reflect confining astronomical facts and limited astrological interpretations. Through *that* vantage, we bear witness to Snow White sleeping in her glass coffin. Looking from the *inside*, however, we experience the universe from within the ubiquitous field of Love. We perceive that it is filled with surging tides of wisdom, and that living beings are enthroned in the vaulted sky above us. Yet, *without* Love, we cannot assert ourselves as soul-beings in this sea of purposeful wisdom—and thus do we risk being swept away.

Love is the Force that gives us the strength to stand firmly within these surging tides, while also allowing us to become willing participants in the seeding of a new cosmos. Indeed, the destiny of all humanity is to bring Love into Wisdom, for this is how a new cosmology comes into being. The Mystery of Golgotha "turned time" as it birthed the Force of Love into the world.[3] And when our souls begin to love the Stars, we ourselves awaken from the frozen Copernican

---

2 "Our birth is but a sleep and a forgetting. Not an entire forgetfulness, and not in utter nakedness, but trailing clouds of glory do we come."
3 The Mystery of Golgotha comprises the Passion of Christ, his Descent into Hell, and his Resurrection. This indeed marked a "turning point in time."

machina coelestis—i.e., from seeing the universe as a kind of celestial machine.

Our confidence grows stronger when we dare to understand that Cosmic Beings watch over us as we approach their heavenly realms—where ideas, sentiments, and longed-for aspirations beckon us ever forward. In such a way do these mighty beings greet us when we turn to them—and as they call our souls into their light, we may inwardly hear their whispered secrets. How, we might wonder, do we begin? If we enwrap ourselves in a cloak woven from devotion's golden threads, we may find that our "inner Hermeticist" stirs within us, perhaps revealing a precious gem that proclaims the hidden message lying in the depths of our hearts: "You came from the stars, you live to remember that you *are* a star, and—as prodigal sons and daughters—you will return to the stars."

Julie's finesse with humor is one of her endearing signatures. Moreover, it suggests her willingness to be the Fool—for as she dances with the World of star beings, she is animated by the creative joy that lifts illusory mirages into the sphere of the Holy Spirit. Truth be known, only a Fool could write such a book: one that touches into the primordial realms of existence whence originates the purity of consecrated Idealism—the womb of platonic virtue. And as she makes rational what would perhaps otherwise be scorned, she indeed steps off a cliff. With temerity of spirit, courage of soul, and boldness (as well as brilliance) of mind, she delivers a manuscript that quite literally has been born out of the future.

Julie humbly acknowledges that what she sets before us is but a small part of much that is far too vast to be put into words. Although she directs a thunderbolt into the tower of the old astrology, she also readily acknowledges her own limitations. She therefore asks us to come into dialogue with her, uniting our *own* efforts with the explorations she initiates herein. In preparation for that dialogue, we will need the primal Force of sacrifice, lest the weight of our egoism drags us down; we will also need the Force of patience, lest our hurried pace leads us into limitation; and we will need the power born from the essential structure of our *immortal* being, lest we falter before the resurrecting Force of Love.

The cover image of this book invokes one of the three magi, reminding us that it is the destiny of each one of us to follow the star that is ours alone to follow. Our eternal Name is engraved upon our star. And as the resounding harmony of the World Orchestra reverberates throughout the starry firmament, we can imagine that one tone in this symphony belongs specifically to us—as it sounds the permanent memory of our unfallen divinity. Indeed, as citizens of a vast and wondrous universe, we remain irreplaceable. Thus is eternity incomplete without us. Verily, what the Alpha has set into motion, the Omega will bring into the silence of completion. Will we participate?

May you, dear readers, find your way to the stars—and may the stars, in return, find their way to you. The winged feet of Hermes are ours to don, so that together we may be carried into the cosmic dance of creation.

Claudia Mclaren Lainson,
Michaelmas, 2022

AN INVITATION

When I gaze upon the nighttime sky, I am astonished at the host of shining bodies—what we call suns and earths—that resonate within its bounds. My spirit then soars across all those stars, millions of miles distant, to the archetypal fountain of them all, from which flow all created things and from which new creations will continue to flow in all eternity.   Ludwig van Beethoven

No age has been as favorable to spirituality as this fifth [current] epoch. All that is needed is the courage to drive the money-changers out of the Temple.[1]   Rudolf Steiner

The heavens are telling the glory of God, and the firmament proclaims his handiwork.   Psalms 19:1

IN THE STARS, WE SHARE OUR spiritual home. This book is designed to make true star wisdom, or *astrosophy*, understandable to all.[2] To those already versed in astrology, as well as to those who can't identify a single star, your fellowship is sought by the growing "community of the cosmos" that longs to know what's really going on up there, and what it means to individual and human evolution. It is the author's hope that this book will serve as a reference and guide to all who wish to step upon this starry path. Together, we can learn a great deal more than we can alone—indeed, pilgrims who make this journey side by side will find *Sophia*[3] at their side. Not only do we benefit from each other's perspectives and wisdom when we take counsel with one another, but groups are increasingly becoming *vessels of revelation*. Tomberg wrote:

> Every insight that comes to [those that take counsel with others] is the result of a "council"—a consulting "together." In essence, before the knowledge ripens, a person must enter into various standpoints and cognitive levels. Not until one has identified selflessly with a series of different views and dispositions of mind does there arise out of these a *harmony*. This harmony is itself the newly gained insight.[4]

Though it could be said that all ancient astrological traditions flow from the same spiritual spring, it is *hermetic* astrology that provides the background for this work. Hermeticism refers to the Egyptian literature that communicated the divine science of astrology to the priests and disciples of Hermes. Clement of Alexandria (second/third centuries after Christ) attributed forty-two books to Hermes.[5] Most often quoted from this large body of work is the phrase, *As above, so below.*

As our current cultural epoch (Piscean/European) bears a special relationship to the Taurian/Egyptian,[6] it is incumbent upon us to follow—and eventually hold—the lamp of hermeticism. This is precisely the function of the anonymously

---

1 Rudolf Steiner, *Astronomy and Astrology* (Forest Row, UK: Rudolf Steiner Press, 2009), 230. See also CW Nr. 120. ("CW" refers *The Collected Work of Rudolf Steiner*, each volume of which has an assigned number. These numbers are helpful for locating specific lectures given by Steiner, regardless under what title it may have appeared in translation.)
2 Astrosophy is a spiritual account of the heavenly bodies and of our interaction with them.
3 Sophia, which means "wisdom," is regarded within astrosophy as a *divine being* who existed alongside the Word at the beginning of creation. *She is creation's wisdom.* In recent centuries (characterized by the advance of science), she has receded from human consciousness, but this has begun to change. As we approach the zodiacal age of Aquarius—during which Sophia will become more active in shaping our culture—she will appear to more and more human beings, thereby challenging any conception of her as being merely an "aspect" of the Divine.
4 Valentin Tomberg, *Russian Spirituality & Other Essays* (San Rafael, CA: LogoSophia, 2010), 44.
5 Robert Powell, *Hermetic Astrology*, vol. 1. (San Rafael, CA: Sophia Foundation Press, 1987), 1.
6 Steiner described seven great epochs within our current period of Earth evolution. (We are currently in the fifth of these, the Post-Atlantean.) Our great epoch, like the others, is in turn comprised of seven cultural epochs—wherein the seventh (the American) mirrors the first (the ancient Indian), the sixth (the Slavic) mirrors the second (the ancient Persian), and the fifth (our current so-called European epoch) mirrors the third (the ancient Egyptian). The fourth—the Graeco-Roman, during which Christ incarnated—stands alone.

written *Meditations on the Tarot*;[7] it comprises the *reincarnation* of the hermetic mysteries.

Much of modern astrology has been swallowed by intellectualism: It has been *materialized*. When it speaks of the forces that work through the planets and the zodiac, it typically does so only in terms of their effects. For example, we might be cautioned that a natal conjunction of the Sun and Saturn can indicate the likelihood of a rather melancholic individual, prone to self-doubt, whose successes must be hard-won. (If you were born under this aspect, take heart: Mozart was, too.)

Yet behind this aspect (and every other) one can discover *spiritual purpose*. In Mary's embrace[8] we find the proper measure of *restriction*, so that we are prevented from straying too far from our intended path. The true horoscope, Valentin Tomberg reminds us, will not be reached by a path of calculation but through a path of interaction with suprasensory beings.[9] In *Meditations on the Tarot*, Tomberg states further:

> The *original* of the "Sacred Book of Thoth [Hermes]" is to be found in the "transcerebral" region. For this reason it is necessary to seek for it not in crypts, manuscripts, or stone inscriptions, not even in secret societies or fraternities, but rather in the "sanctuary of the everlasting zones" belonging to Hermes. It is necessary to *elevate oneself* above the zone of cerebral intellectuality because the "sacred books" were written, according to the Hermetic treatise that we have quoted, *before* the formation of the brain.[10]

Since the cold and abstract nature of materialism has wrested control of human thinking in recent centuries, astrological influences tend to be considered in isolation, as *fragments* of a personality. Facts are added to facts—like bricks—constructing a sort of tower that is said to represent a unique individual. This approach can quickly devolve into an egoistic exercise of becoming intimate only with our feelings and desires, leading to *isolation within our own personality*—not to mention utter boredom! We know "ourself" but *not* the eternal Self that strings together the sum of our incarnations.

That Self calls to us from the future, elusive as a rainbow, whispering to us imaginations of who we might become. The practice of astrosophy gives us absolute faith in that future, for it brings us to the knowledge that our birth chart is the miraculous configuration of stars for which our individuality alone held—*and continues to hold*—the key. It brings us to the knowledge that this configuration, crafted by our own souls alongside choirs of Angel artisans, is the one best suited to the karmic work of a particular lifetime. Most importantly, it allows us to recognize the counterproductivity of feeling *aggrieved*. We can instead set about putting our own house in order, knowing that the karmic debts of those who brought us misery will be paid in time, as will all others. They are not our concern. We might even consider the benefits of forgiveness—which, like mercy, "blesseth him that gives and him that takes."[11] Karen Rivers wrote:

> Forgiveness functions on the level of personal karma mirroring Christ's forgiveness.... As a result of every act of true forgiveness, a liberated space, no longer filled with karmic substance, opens, into which Christ can enter and work, and to which the [adversarial] powers have no access. A new field of grace emerges under the guidance of Christ....
>
> Forgiveness creates a means of experiencing divine love.[12]

---

7 Although anonymously written and posthumously published, the author of *Meditations on the Tarot* is now known. It was Valentin Tomberg.

8 We'll find on pages 41–42 that there is a special relationship between Saturn and the Blessed Virgin.

9 Valentin Tomberg, *Christ and Sophia: Anthroposophic Meditations on the Old Testament, New Testament, and Apocalypse* (Gt Barrington, MA: SteinerBooks, 2006), 47.

10 Valentin Tomberg, *Meditations on the Tarot: A Journey into Christian Hermeticism* (Brooklyn, NY: Angelico Press, 2019), 262.

11 William Shakespeare, *The Merchant of Venice*, 4.1.185.

12 Karen Rivers, *Love and the Evolution of Consciousness* (Gt Barrington, MA: Lindisfarne Books, 2016), 171 and 173.

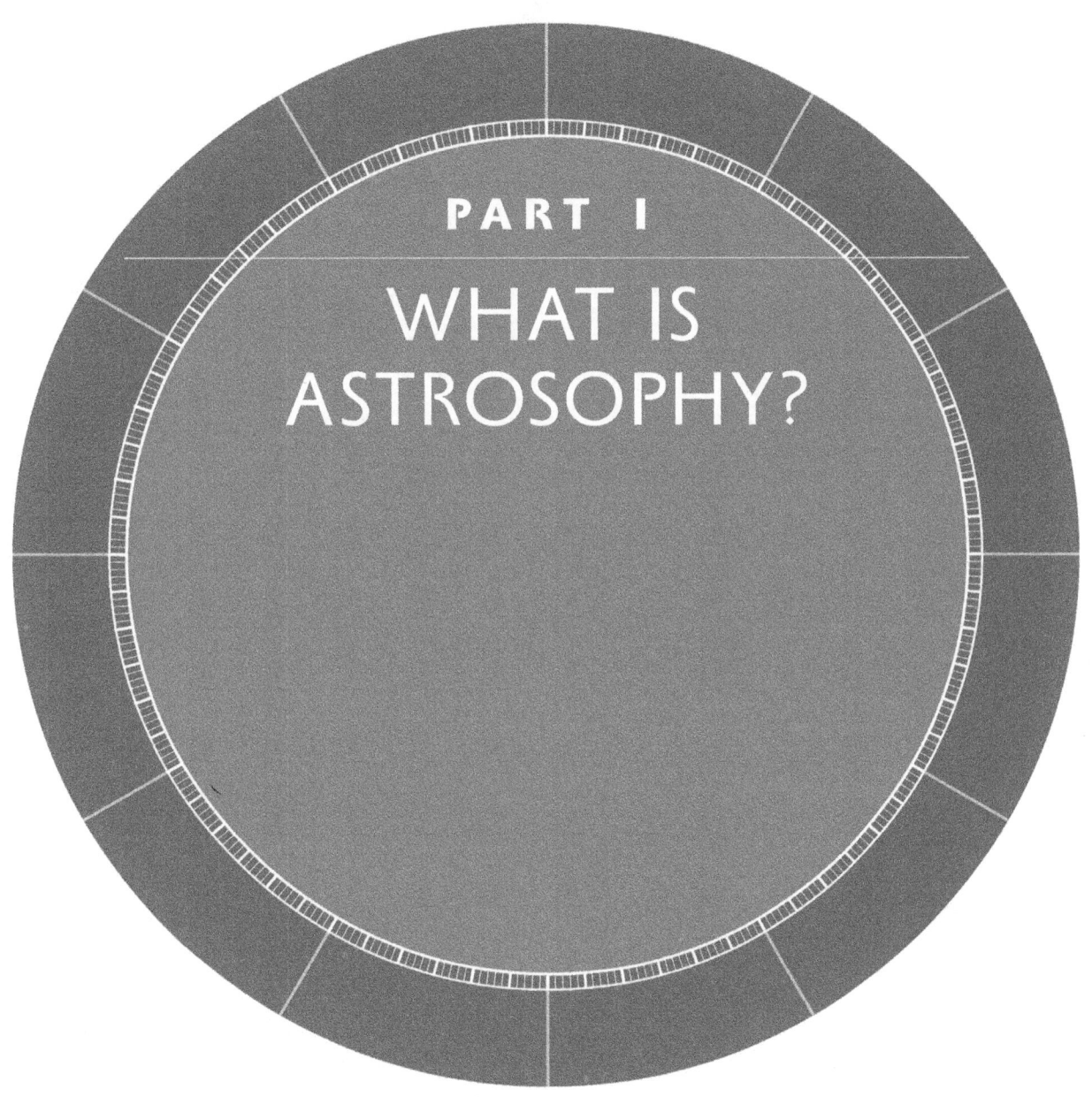

1

THE GAZE OF THE ANCIENTS UPON THE STARRY VAULT

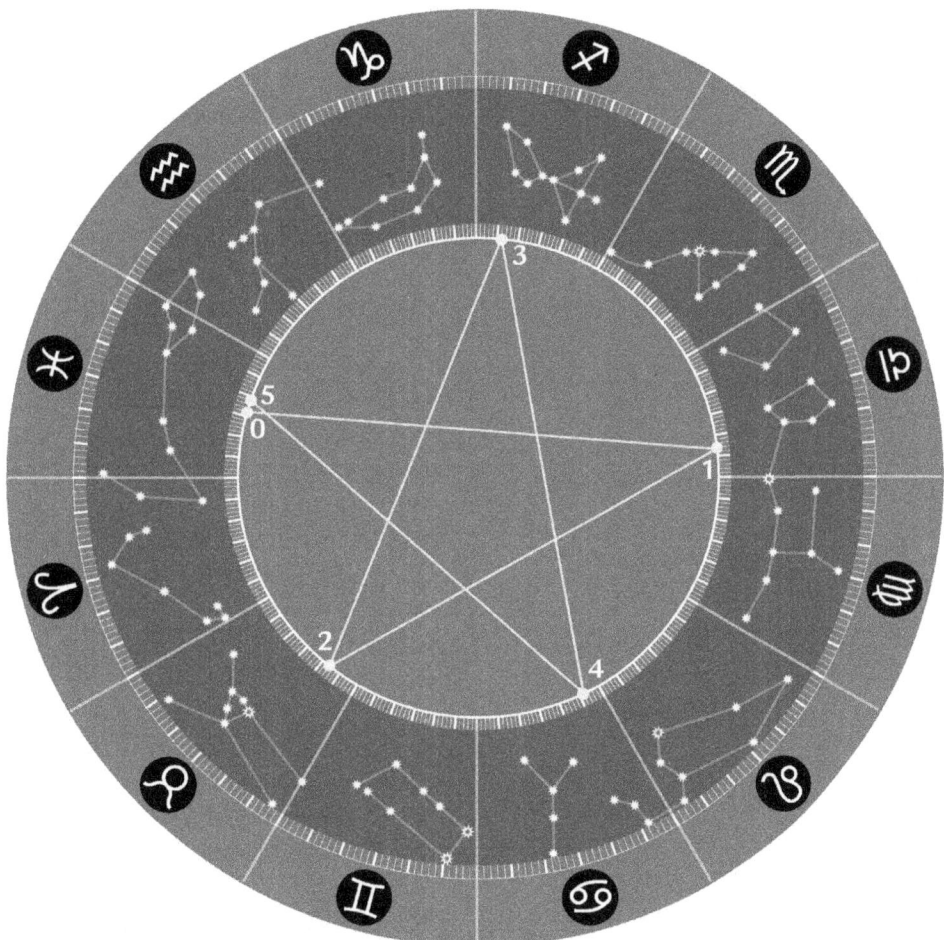

The superior conjunctions of Venus between Mar/2013 and Mar/2021

LONG AGO, WHEN WE EXPERIenced the majesty of the starry vault with an atavistic clairvoyance, it would have been inconceivable for us to have regarded ourselves as separate from the cosmos. Symbol and ritual had not yet devolved into superstition and habit. Within the cultural period of time identified by Steiner as the age of Taurus, during which the Egyptian culture held sway, humanity experienced itself as a child of the divine.[1] This was the same period of time within which the great patriarchs of ancient Israel lived.

The *vernal point*[2] then moved into the constellation of Aries, laying the foundation for the Graeco-Roman culture that would last until the onset of the Renaissance. Here we need to define the difference between a zodiacal age and a cultural age. (Both are 2160 years in length.) The zodiacal age begins when the vernal point moves backward across the cusp of a new zodiacal

---

1 Robert Powell, *Hermetic Astrology*, vol., 66.
2 The vernal point is the zodiacal degree of the Sun as spring begins. It moves backward one degree every 72 years.

sign. However, Steiner stated that the zodiacal impulse takes some time to work its way into the culture, and he defined the length of this intervening period as 1199 years. Each of these cycles can be thought of as a cosmic indication of a change in consciousness.[3]

The planet Venus brings us nearer to the significance of the 1199-year rhythm, for this is precisely the time required for the "Venus pentagram" to make its way around the zodiac. Although the movement of Venus around the Sun is nearly circular, we find that when we connect the zodiacal points of her conjunctions with the Sun over a period of eight years, a glorious cosmic star appears in the firmament: the *Venus pentagram*.

Approximately every ten months, Venus and the Sun convene at the same zodiacal degree. (This relationship is otherwise known as a conjunction.) This can happen in two ways: Venus can either stand on the near side of the Sun from the perspective of the Earth (this is referred to as an *inferior* conjunction), or beyond the Sun (this is known as a *superior* conjunction). The Venus pentagram is formed within the zodiacal circle by tracing all of the points of the inferior *or* superior conjunctions of Venus with the Sun. Within an eight-year period, five inferior and five superior conjunctions will occur.

If this cosmic star ended exactly where it began, the pattern would repeat endlessly over time, and there would be no 1199-year rhythm. When we look closely, however, we can see that this star does not finish (Point 5) *precisely* where it began (Point 0); it ends two or three degrees behind its point of origin. Over the course of 1199 years, the pentagram will *regress* though the zodiac, repeating about 150 times until it reaches Point 0 again. Robert Powell wrote:

> The ratio of the cycle of the Venus pentagram (1199 [years]) to that of the precession of the equinoxes (25,920 [years]) is a little less than the ratio of one to twenty-four, which is the ratio of one hour to one day. In other words, if the complete precession cycle is likened to a "world day," then the rotation of the Venus pentagram is akin to the passage of a "world hour." When a new astrological age starts, signified by the entrance of the vernal point into a new sign of the zodiac, a "world hour" still elapses before the new zodiacal impulse begins to register as a cultural phenomenon, and this lapse of time is measured by the rotation of the Venus pentagram. A new impulse starts to work on a spiritual level as soon as the vernal point enters a new zodiacal sign, but it has to filter through from cosmic realms, and *the rotation of the Venus pentagram serves to indicate the mediation of cosmic forces from the realm of the zodiac.* The Venus pentagram acts as a kind of cosmic transformer, stepping down the zodiacal impulse, which operates on a very high level, a religious level, to become a *social* impulse, which works on a more human level.[4]

Therefore, though the *zodiacal* age of Aries ended in 215, the *cultural* age of Aries continued until 1414. Throughout this period, humanity's fading clairvoyance was able to *coexist* with its quest for individual freedom and expression: Man knew himself to be an individual *in relation to* the divine. This worldview did not surrender completely when the cultural age of Pisces was underway; even the great scientists who kindled the natural science revolution in the late sixteenth and early seventeenth centuries did not doubt the spiritual origin of what they were observing. Johannes Kepler, who established the laws of planetary motion, said, "Science is the process of thinking God's thoughts after him."

In the more recent centuries, we've experienced ourselves above all as *free agents*. The wonder and awe that used to overcome us as we stood beneath the stars has given way to measurement, theory, and formulaic thinking. Rudolf Steiner put it this way:

> You know, indeed, what a great difference there is between the way a man felt himself to be within the whole cosmos in the Egyptian age, let us say, and even in the time of Greece, and how he feels since the beginning of the modern age — since the close of the Middle Ages. Picture to yourselves a well-instructed ancient Egyptian. He knew that his body was constituted not merely of the

---

3   Robert Powell, *Hermetic Astrology*, vol. 1, 61.
4   Ibid., 58–59. [My italics: JH.]

ingredients that exist here on earth and are embodied in the animal kingdom, plant kingdom, and mineral kingdom. He knew that the forces he perceived in the stars above also worked into his being as man; he felt himself a member of the whole cosmos. He felt the whole cosmos not only quick with life, but ensouled and imbued with spirit; in his consciousness there lived something of the spiritual beings of the cosmos, of the soul-nature of the cosmos and its life.

All this has been lost in the course of later human history. Today man gazes from his Earth up to the star-world, and to him it is filled with fixed stars, suns, planets, comets, and so on. But with what means does he examine all that looks down to him out of cosmic space? He examines it with mathematics, with the science of mechanics. What lies around the earth is robbed of spirit, robbed of soul, even of life. It is a great mechanism, in fact, only to be grasped by the aid of mathematical, mechanistic laws.[5]

The character of the zodiacal and cultural ages are cosmic imprints of the zodiac upon human evolution. *These epochs of time— and, indeed, our entire cultural life— depend upon the slow, circular movement of the Earth's axis.* If our polar axis were upright, twelve hours of night would follow twelve hours of day across the globe. There would be no seasons, and no vernal point to mark the beginning of spring. If our polar axis remained fixed in space,[6] there would be no sequence of cultural ages upon the Earth, and the cosmic door through which the hierarchies direct our evolution would not have been opened. One further thought to tuck away until we reach Part II: It is deeply significant that the direction of the movement of the vernal point through the zodiac is *contrary* to the advance of the zodiacal signs.

---

5 Rudolf Steiner, *The Ahrimanic Deception* (October 27, 1919), CW Nr. 193.
6 It does not. This will be discussed in Chapter 6.

2

THE STARS AND CHRIST

THE CHRIST IMPULSE, THAT OF divine love, is a moving current that fills and inundates all that exists. It has been the source of every religious inspiration across every age. Great churches like Chartres ring out the good news that the flame of the Christian ideal can still be found within their walls. Christ, like love, is everywhere, and is surrounding and permeating the Earth. Anyone can be moved by the Christ Impulse—anywhere and at any time. When we see the intertwined roots of redwood trees reaching out to each other in support, we are in the presence of Christ. When we see a new parents swaddle their infant, Christ is beside them. When we hear the joyful morning chorus of songbirds, Christ is smiling, too. If we sacrifice something—in love—for another, Christ remembers.

> It is a strange thing with those Christian impulses! It seems that intellectuality, learning, and erudition play no role at all in their spread.... What exactly is it that spreads? It is not the ideas or knowledge of Christianity.... [It] *is the moral feeling that has come with Christianity.*[1]

Nevertheless, the time has come to disentangle Jesus from the institutions that claim to represent him. Not all Christian institutions have upheld the ideals given to us by Christ. The uplifting sacred music and works of art that we seek out within the walls of our churches and halls sometimes seem overpowered by the growing rubble of all that has been done in Christ's name—and even in spite of it. As the tableau of these transgressions was beheld by Jesus in Gethsemane, he sweated blood. The conduct of many within the church's hierarchy has served Christ's eternal adversary, Ahriman (Satan), very well. The unfortunate result of this gross misrepresentation has been a growing abhorrence regarding "all things Jesus." This cynicism, which has reached the level of persecution in many parts of the world, will likely get worse before it gets better.

Having seen a "star" in the east, the three Magi traveled from Babylon to Bethlehem to honor the child who would be a new kind of king. The Magi were the last representatives of ancient star wisdom, thereby serving as a bridge between this spiritual tradition and Christ. So it was that the gifts borne by the three Kings—those of wisdom, piety, and strength of will—had their origin in ages past.

Why did Jesus incarnate in Palestine? As wise as Jesus was, why did he not grow up among the philosophers and academics of Greece and Rome? Why, instead, did he incarnate in Palestine, where he lived among a simpler people who had emerged from *within* this world of mature intellectuality? Steiner said that it was the unsophisticated folk of Palestine who were bearers of Christianity—uneducated people who loved Christ as though he were a much-loved member of their family.[2]

The answer is that the Christ spirit does not move between minds, but from heart to heart and from soul to soul, regardless of whether we have any intellectual understanding of it at all. Is this not exactly as love and affection weave among us?

It may seem strange to place astrology anywhere in the vicinity of Christ, *although this is precisely where it belongs*—for Christ's brief incarnation upon the Earth was the conclusion of a long, slow descent through the cosmos from the realm of the Father. More than 9000 years ago, the rishis of the ancient Hindu culture perceived this descent toward the realm of the fixed stars of the zodiac; they named the Christ spirit Vishvakarma. Christ's descent reached the level of our Sun during the ancient Persian

---

1 Rudolf Steiner, *The Fifth Gospel* (Forest Row, UK: Rudolf Steiner Press, 1995), 11. [My italics: JH.] See also CW Nr. 148.
2 Ibid., 5.

culture, and they called him Ahura Mazda. As the ancient Egyptian culture held sway, when Christ became known as Osiris, he was perceived within the phases of the Moon. Christ descended further to the elemental forces of the Earth during the time of the ancient Hebrews; Moses beheld YHVH in the burning bush.

Through the lens of the life of Christ, which continually illuminates our paths, astrosophy uplifts our understanding of the cosmos unto spiritual realms. Rudolf Steiner emphasized that the Christ always stood under the influence of the entire cosmos. We can do no better than to look to Christ's life for guidance—for this allows us to weave our stray threads into the vast cosmic tapestry. When we do so, every dilemma can find its resolution.

Astrosophy is sunshine and rain that quickens the seeds of a new spiritual culture. The door to this world has barely been opened—and yet, astonishing riches have already poured in through it, including a renewed and vital understanding of the planetary aspects. One can begin to comprehend, for example, the inferior conjunction of the Sun and Mercury not merely as a potential detriment to clear interpersonal communications (as Mercury is retrograde when this happens), but as an indication of *benediction*.[3] Is it a mere coincidence that the healing of the man born blind occurred on the day of an inferior conjunction of the Sun and Mercury? Or that Peter, James, and John witnessed the Transfiguration two days after the same aspect? Or that the changing of water into wine and the raising of Lazarus took place four and six days, respectively, after an inferior conjunction of the Sun and Mercury?

Our task now—and it is indeed a pressing one—is to attend to what is *looking down* to us out of cosmic realms. For the Earth, seen from the spiritual world, appears as a dark speck in space. It glimmers only in spots where human beings cherish selfless thoughts and feelings, freed from earthly gravity and directed toward the spirit.[4]

We are born of the stars, and to the stars we return, during sleep and after death. Through the stars, we discover the true context within which our lives unfold. Thus do we find the courage to move forward, as we know we must. And just as importantly, we also find humility within the epic scope of the Angels' human project.

---

3 An *inferior* conjunction of the Sun and Mercury occurs when a line projected from the Earth passes directly through Mercury *and then* through the Sun: Earth > Mercury > Sun > zodiac. This always happens when Mercury appears to us to be moving backward through the zodiac in a process that is called *retrograde movement*. When Mercury meets the Sun in *superior* conjunction, it is on the *far side* of the Sun: Earth > Sun > Mercury > zodiac.
4 Valentin Tomberg, *Christ and Sophia: Anthroposophic Meditations on the Old Testament, New Testament, and Apocalypse,* 223.

3

THE ZODIAC

THE SOURCE OF ALL THE STARS of the Milky Way, including our own Sun, is the Galactic Center (known esoterically as the Central Sun). Stars emerge from this nursery, arranging themselves in beautiful spiraling arms as they slowly move across eons of time.

Stargazers upon the Earth observe the zodiac as the great round of twelve constellations that appears to embrace the whole universe. Its stars are the outer manifestation of the highly evolved spiritual beings — the twelve holy living creatures — that work through these constellations; they adorn the twelve mantles of the Seraphim, Cherubim, and Thrones that partake in the guidance of humanity. Within the zodiacal circle, four of the holy living creatures hold fast the four directions of space: the Bull (Taurus), the Lion (Leo), the Eagle (Scorpio), and the Angel (Aquarius). In spontaneous obedience to God, the gaze of the twelve beholds both the Central Sun (the primordial source of love and creation) and the "sea of glass" that surrounds it. Thus does the circle of twelve reflect God's existence. Standing eternally in the presence of the divine, the twelve zodiacal creatures are themselves *sources* of the life and vivification that they mirror. We might thus regard the zodiac not only as the "circle of animals" (Greek: *Zoa*), but also as the "circle of life" (Greek: *Zoe*).

The zodiac is the cosmic temple of the spiritual origin of morality — the moral principles that await us at the end of our path to wisdom. The "I" of the human being journeys continuously around the circle, taking in the guiding forces of *the twelve virtues*, through which we draw nearer to that wisdom. These virtues speak to something that exists within our souls, to what Steiner described as "a divine heritage." There is thus an instinctive goodness that supports humanity until the time comes when we can fully understand the moral principles behind these virtues.[1]

The circle of twelve constellations holds the archetype of the human form; as our spirits dwell in the realm of fixed stars that lies beyond the planetary spheres, the seed of our next physical form is fashioned by the twelve holy living creatures.

Steiner taught us that each zodiacal sign is associated with a worldview that resonates in the human being through the activity of the "I." Just as each facet of a dodecahedron[2] is an equal part of the whole Platonic form, so does each sign of the circle of twelve represent *an aspect of the truth*. When we focus on just one worldview — as we naturally like to do — we regard our own perspective as the "right" one. *Everything would be so much easier if everyone else were more like me!*

In reality, each worldview is valid — and limited — to the same extent. There is profound wisdom in the zodiacal arrangement, within which each sign is adjacent to two others with which it has nothing in common, neither by element (fire, earth, air, or water) nor by quality (cardinal, fixed, or mutable). That's an amazing life lesson right there!

---

1   Rudolf Steiner, *The Spiritual Foundation of Morality* (Hudson, NY: Anthroposophic Press, 1995), 6. See also CW Nr. 155.
2   A regular dodecahedron is a twelve-sided three-dimensional form. "Regular" means that each side is exactly like all the others: in this case, a perfect pentagon. Three pentagonal faces meet at each of the 20 vertices. The regular dodecahedron is one of the five so-called Platonic solids.

The Zodiac

The twelve forms that are represented by the stars of the zodiac can be hard to discern if you attempt to see the creatures by "connecting the dots" in a logical fashion. Intellectual consciousness, in fact, takes you to a brick wall of sorts, not only because the pictures are difficult to form, but because it offers no existential explanation as to what lives *behind* these pictures. Clearly, the ancients saw something different — something that provided them inspiration, guidance, and nourishment.

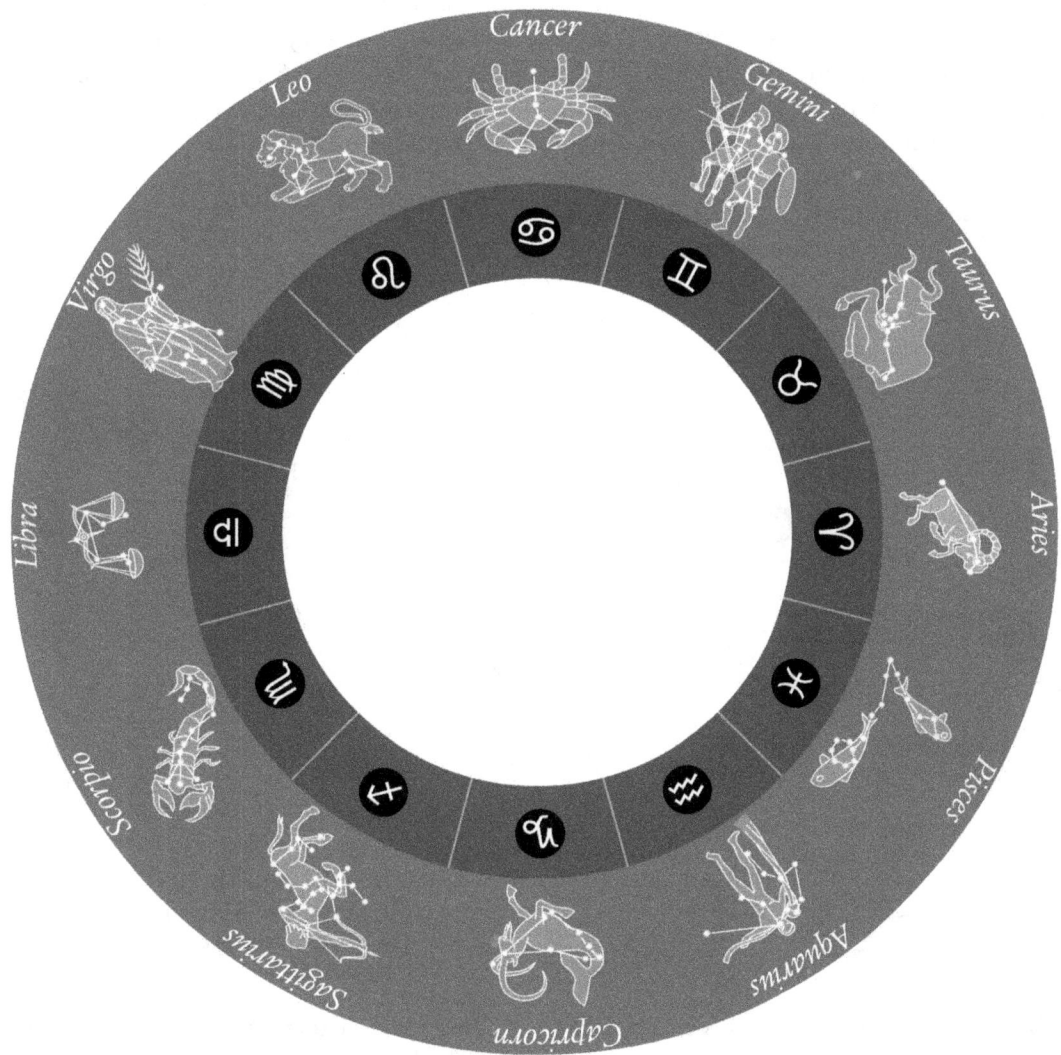

The clairvoyant consciousness of old beheld the spiritual archetypes behind the signs. These are the twelve facets of what might be called *divine animality*, to which humanity can aspire:

- Behind Aries they beheld leadership, individuality, and intensity of will.
- Behind the Bull, the power of productive concentration, a deep connection to Nature, and faithfulness of heart.
- The Twins revealed to them youthful joy, clarity of thought, and the ideal of true brotherhood.
- The Crab, the archetype of protective nurturing, faith in the power of self-sacrifice, and adaptability of will.
- Leo roared to them of an unquenchable love of life, moral courage, and warmth of heart.
- Virgo whispered the profound secrets of Nature, tenderness, and precision in thinking.
- From Libra they learned social artistry, scope of will, and the ability to justly weigh up possibilities.
- From the Scorpion, patience, depth, and vulnerability of heart.

- The stars of the Archer taught them self-control, a sense for the truth, and creative thought.
- Those of the Goat, in contrast, bestowed firmness of will, and led them to the woman who kneels eternally under the stars—at the bank of a river whose current flows from the past into the future.
- Behind the urns of the Waterbearer, Aquarius, the ancients beheld the breath of the spirit, magnanimity of heart, and the nature of our communion with our guardian Angel.
- Behind Pisces lived the force that weaves among all souls, as well as the fluid power of the will when it is connected to heaven.

the year, the Sun remains on the ecliptic as it appears—from the Earth—to circle through the constellations of the zodiac.

Now, if there were no tilt to the Earth, the Sun's orbit around it would follow the equator itself, and twelve hours of night would follow twelve hours of daylight the world over. Because of the 23½° tilt of the Earth, however, the orbit of the Sun is *oblique* to the equator, and crosses the equator just twice (at the time of the equinoxes).

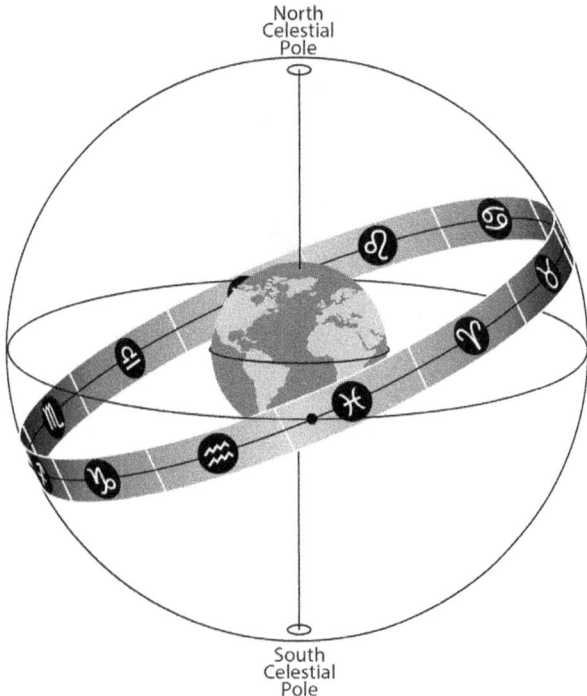

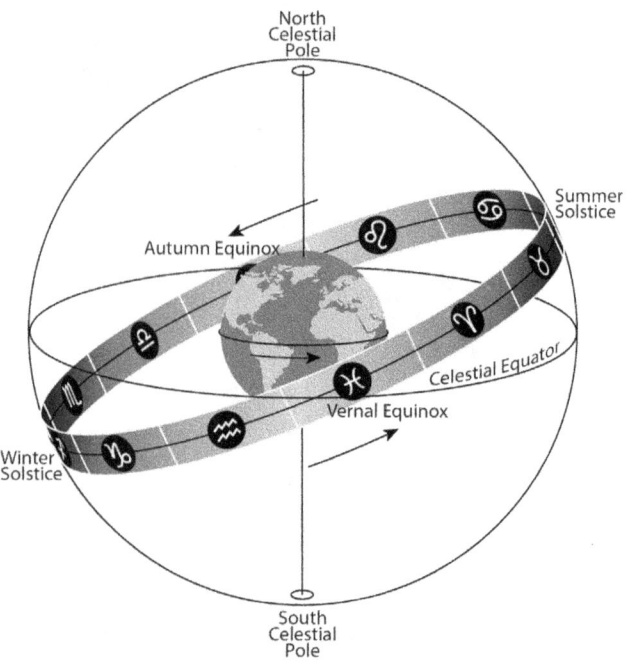

The upper and lower arrows indicate the direction of the orbit of the Sun from the northern perspective

Let's behold the circle of twelve constellations as a *unity*. Like all circles, the zodiac can be divided into 360 degrees. Although its stars are not anywhere near the same distance from the center of the celestial sphere, it's expedient to imagine the zodiac as a band (or a ribbon) of stars. The breadth of this ribbon is 16° from top to bottom. (This is approximately one sixth of a 90° arc.) With the exception of Pluto—whose orbit is eccentric—none of the planets strays beyond these sixteen degrees. The zodiacal band is bisected horizontally by a line known as *the ecliptic*.[3] Over the course of

An individual standing in the northern hemisphere gazes *southward* upon the zodiac; from this perspective, the zodiacal signs proceed anticlockwise, as does the Sun's path through them over the course of the year. From the northern perspective, the vernal point occurs when the Sun's path crosses the celestial equator *from below to above*. (This point could also be described as the Sun's *ascending* node.) Three months later, this "northern" individual would experience the summer solstice, which occurs when the Sun reaches 5° Gemini, the highest point of its journey at this time. The Sun then

---

3 The ecliptic is the path of the Sun around the zodiac—from the perspective of the Earth.

descends, crossing the celestial equator—this time *from above to below*—as it moves before 5° Virgo. (This point could alternatively be described as the Sun's *descending* node.) At this moment, we experience the autumn equinox. Lastly, when at the lowest point of its orbit, those in the north experience the winter solstice. At the present time this occurs when the Sun is before 5° Sagittarius.

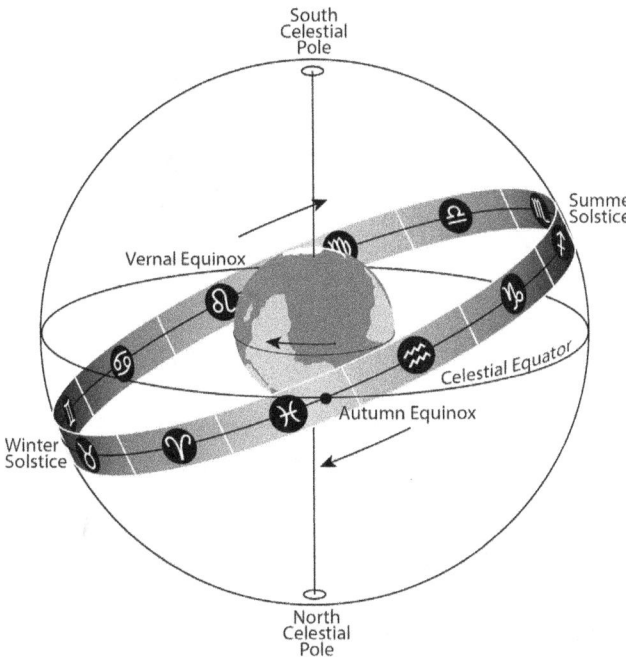

The upper and lower arrows indicate the direction of the orbit of the Sun from the southern perspective

How do those of us in the southern hemisphere experience the solar year? Gazing at the zodiacal band below the equator requires us to look to the *north*; hence the signs appear to advance *in the opposite direction* (i.e., clockwise). Since we know that Christmas day is often a sunny one in the southern half of the globe, we can readily understand that what is experienced as the winter solstice in the north is experienced as the summer solstice in the south. Furthermore, "above" and "below" have opposite meanings as well! *From the southern perspective*, the Sun crosses the ecliptic from below to above as it moves from north to south, and from above to below as it moves from south to north.

Ergo, from a strictly astronomical point of view, we might conclude that to our southern brothers and sisters the vernal equinox is in currently at 5° Virgo, while the autumn equinox is directly opposite at 5° Pisces.

Here we must depart from the astronomical reality and recall that the regression of the vernal point through the zodiac (as described by Steiner) influences both the cultural impulses experienced by humanity as well as the consciousness that underlies that culture. In this way, the vernal point is the same for the northern and southern hemisphere alike. For, surely, it's unimaginable that the great Arian cultural age, expressed primarily through the dominance of Ancient Greece and Rome, was accompanied simultaneously by a cultural age of Libra in the southern hemisphere!

If this sort of mental exercise makes your head hurt, you are part of a worldwide community of spatially challenged individuals like me! Do what I do: Have some Advil handy and set about making a zodiacal band with paper, pencil, and tape. Place at its center an orange marked with poles and an equator—and your tension should be eased considerably!

We can enhance our understanding of the Earth's relationship to the ecliptic if we imagine the zodiacal band *imprinted upon the Earth*. This gives us a visual representation of the Sun's apparent annual path around the Earth, as well as illustrating the four solar markers of the year: the vernal equinox, the summer solstice, the autumn (or autumnal) equinox, and the winter solstice.[4]

The four solar markers represent distinct turning points in the year; they are deeply relevant to our life on Earth as the heralds of the four seasons. To get a feel for this, we have to set aside the *daily* (diurnal) movement of the Sun resulting from the rotation of the Earth on its axis. Imagine instead that the Earth is completely still, and that the Sun is moving around the Earth as it passes before the twelve constellations of the zodiac over the course of the *year*.

---

4   The four solar markers announce the start of spring (the vernal equinox), summer (the summer solstice), fall (the autumnal equinox), and winter (the winter solstice). The Sun's degree at each of these points exactly divides the zodiacal circle into four equal arcs of 90°.

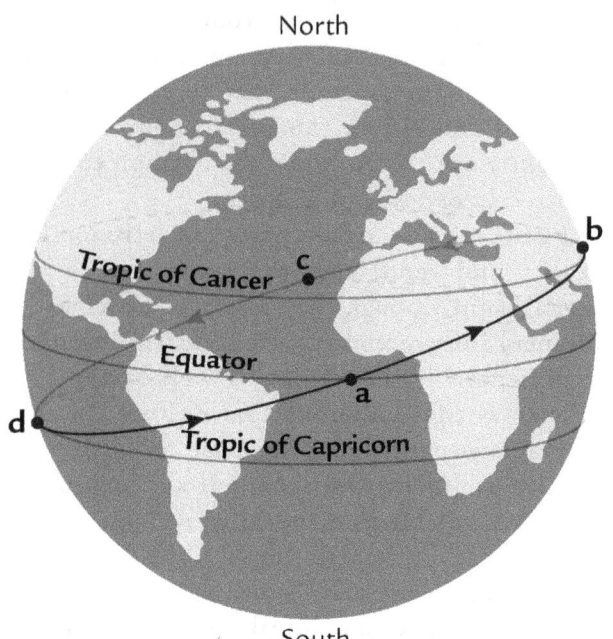

The imprint upon the Earth of the apparent yearly path of the Sun from the northern perspective

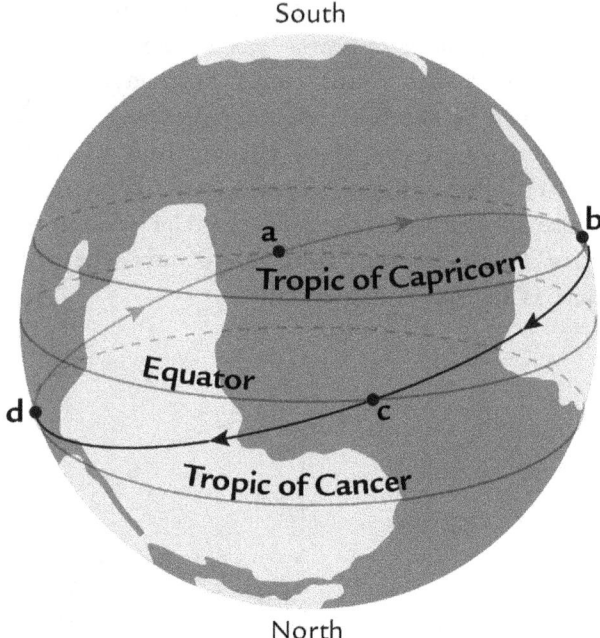

The imprint upon the Earth of the apparent yearly path of the Sun from the southern perspective

From either hemisphere, the Sun's path strays no farther than the Tropics of Cancer and Capricorn. When the Sun reaches the Tropic of Cancer, summer begins in the northern hemisphere, winter in the southern.

Let's start with the vernal point (a). At this moment, the Sun passes the equator from below to above; on this day the Sun rises and sets directly east and west, and night is as long as day. When the Sun reaches its degree at the summer solstice (b), we experience the longest day of the year. As it does so, it appears to "stop" in the sky—hence the origin of the word *solstice* (from the Latin for "sun stop")—before its gradual descent toward the equator again. The Sun reaches the autumn point (c) when it passes the equator from *above* to *below*; again, days and nights are of equal length, and the Sun rises due east and sets due west. Finally, when the Sun reaches its most southerly latitude, it appears to "stop" again—the winter solstice (d)—and we experience our shortest day of the year.

For followers of western (tropical) astrology, the Sun's zodiacal degrees at these four days of the calendar year *do not change*—they are fixed in time![5] This conception is *incontestably* at odds with astronomical reality. Practitioners of tropical astrology know this. Next, we'll delve into what is sacrificed when astrology loses its connection to the stars.

---

5 0° Aries at the vernal point, 0° Cancer at the summer solstice, 0° Libra at the autumn point, and 0° Capricorn at the winter solstice.

4

THE SIDEREAL AND TROPICAL ZODIACS
TWENTY-FIVE DEGREES AND COUNTING

THE BABYLONIANS CULTIVATED the earliest known culture to have left a record of the zodiac. They did so in the form of cuneiform tablets from around 500 BC. Though the Greeks were the first to apply geometry and trigonometry to astronomy, the Babylonians left behind a detailed star catalogue that identified their positions in relation to the axis connecting two opposing stars on the zodiacal wheel: *Aldebaran* at 15° Taurus, and *Antares* at 15° Scorpio. We can marvel that these ancient people knew *Aldebaran* and *Antares* to be precisely 180° apart—perfectly bisecting the zodiacal circle.

These tablets reveal that the Babylonians saw the zodiac as twelve signs of equal length, each 30°. It was known to them that the horizontal span of the zodiacal constellations varies, but they defined the influence of each constellation—its sign—by a 30° arc in space, one twelfth of the full circle. The 30° divisions reflect the clairvoyant perception of the exact extent of the influence of the spiritual beings underlying the twelve constellations of the zodiac.[1]

These signs were identified in relation to the fixed stars, defining a *sidereal* (from the Latin for "star") system of the zodiac. A stargazer in ancient Babylon, while looking up to the constellation of the Lion, would have known that he was simultaneously gazing upon the cosmic home of the spiritual beings at work in Leo. In sidereal astrology, the astrological signs will forever align with the constellations. *Sidereal astrology carries truth across time.* For that reason, it is this system alone that I use—though the aspects listed in a later chapter apply equally to the western (tropical) system of astrology.[2]

The sidereal system of the zodiac defines the planets' locations *spatially* (in terms of zodiacal longitude)—and we can therefore say that, through the sidereal zodiac, astronomical precision is maintained *eternally*. This is because the sidereal zodiac accounts for the phenomenon known as the *precession of the equinoxes*. Such "precession" entails the continual backward movement of the vernal point, the Sun's zodiacal longitude at the onset of spring, through the zodiac—which is caused by the slow, circular movement of the Earth's axis. Though the exact rate of precession[3] was not known before Newton, the *phenomenon* was identified by the Greeks before the time of Christ.

The validity of the sidereal system has been supported of late by the various star-finding applications that many of us have on our phones.[4] Because these apps clearly display the planets with sidereal accuracy, they also reveal to us the Babylonian eye-view of them. For the current year (2022), the dates of the Sun's ingress into the sidereal signs are:

April 15th — *Aries*
May 15th — *Taurus*
June 16th — *Gemini*
July 17th — *Cancer*
August 17th — *Leo*
September 17th — *Virgo*
October 18th — *Libra*
November 17th — *Scorpio*
December 17th — *Sagittarius*
January 15th — *Capricorn*
February 13th — *Aquarius*
March 15th — *Pisces*

The phenomenon of the precession of the equinoxes means that when we check our star apps on the first day of spring (March 20th), we'll see the Sun displayed near the *start* of Pisces—but

---

1 Robert Powell and Kevin Dann, *The Astrological Revolution* (Gt Barrington, MA: Lindisfarne Books, 2010), 6.
2 This is because a conjunction is still a conjunction, even if there is—sadly—disagreement about the zodiacal degree at which it occurs.
3 The exact rate is 1° per 72 years; 360° per 25,920 years.
4 StarWalk is excellent.

not at 0° Aries, as western (tropical) astrology would have us believe. The implication of the disparity between sidereal and tropical astrology is monumental. At the current time, for example, everyone born between March 20th and April 14th will do so under a *Pisces Sun*—not under an *Aries Sun*.

The effect of dropping this astronomical truthbomb upon the general populace is similar to that of a skunk wandering into a debutantes' ball: *The shift to sidereal astrology results in a whopping 83% of us learning that the Sun sign we've been identifying with is the wrong one—and this will not do!*

A deeper understanding of the zodiac—which leads us to the realization that the glory of one sign cannot outshine that of another—can soften the blow, although its impact seems to hit the dethroned Lions and erstwhile Aquarians the hardest. Alas.

To understand better the importance of the difference between the two systems, we can use the example of the healing of the nobleman's son, which occurred on 3/Aug/30, with the Sun at 10½° Leo. On this day, the illness suffered by the son on behalf of his father was healed. Each year, as the Sun passes this degree, memory of this miracle streams toward us: *Humanity was lifted out of its bondage to hereditary determinism.* Celebration of the cosmic date of an event is therefore *eternal* in its nature and in its effect: The same "current" is activated every time the correspondence is repeated in the cosmos. When we favor the calendar in lieu of the zodiacal degree, however, we overlook the relevance of the *zodiacal correspondence*. In other words, we can choose to honor this event on the 3rd of August this year (its "calendar birthday," when the Sun now stands before 16° Cancer)—*or*, we can wait until the Sun finds 10½° Leo on August 28th—and feel the cosmic wind at our backs. Powell wrote:

> The principle underlying Cosmic Christianity is that all historical events are "remembered" by the cosmos by being inscribed in the so-called "akasha chronicle" or "akashic record," whose outer expression is the sidereal zodiac. *Everything is recorded in the stars.* Of the multitude of memories imprinted in the starry heavens, however, some are more important than others. The most important memories of historical events are those connected with the life of Christ. This is because, to use a phrase coined by Rudolf Steiner, the incarnation, life, death, and resurrection of Christ signify the "turning point of time," the pivotal axis upon which the whole of history turns.[5]

The origin of the tropical zodiac—the system widely in use for centuries—lies with the Greeks. Through the work of Euctemon (fifth century BC), Hipparchus (second century BC), and Ptolemy (whose great star catalog, *Almagest*, was compiled in the second century AD), the Greeks put forth a variant of the zodiac in alignment with the four principle solar markers of the year: the spring equinox, the summer solstice, the autumn equinox, and the winter solstice. The tropical zodiac erroneously maintains an everlasting connection between these *points in time* and the constellations of the zodiac; as we know, it advances the idea that *forever and always*, the Sun enters Aries on the day of the spring equinox!

Conversely, the siderealist arrives at a different conclusion (that the vernal point is currently at 5° Pisces), acknowledging the constant, steady motion of this point around the zodiacal circle. The difference is currently *twenty-five degrees*, and it will continue to grow until the two systems are 180° apart. (In the year 13,175, the vernal point will be 0° Libra—*180°* from the static vernal point of the tropical zodiac! What then?)

The western (tropical) zodiac is, fundamentally, a *temporal* system: a "calendar" that maintains our connection to the wisdom of the seasonal rhythms. It must also be understood that, at the *birth* of the tropical system, the vernal point was at 1° Aries; it was thus a time when the entry of the Sun into Aries *did* nearly coincide with the start of spring. Whether or not it was the intention of Ptolemy that this seasonal connection remain immutable is not known—although it is clear that the Greeks were well-aware of the phenomenon of precession. At any rate, although Ptolemy was a brilliant academic, he lacked an understanding of the clairvoyant

---

5 Robert Powell, *Chronicle of the Living Christ* (Hudson, NY: Anthroposophic Press, 1996), 122-23. [My italics: JH.]

perception of the Babylonians of old. The last bearers of this faculty were the three Magi who traveled to the crib of the Redeemer in Bethlehem.

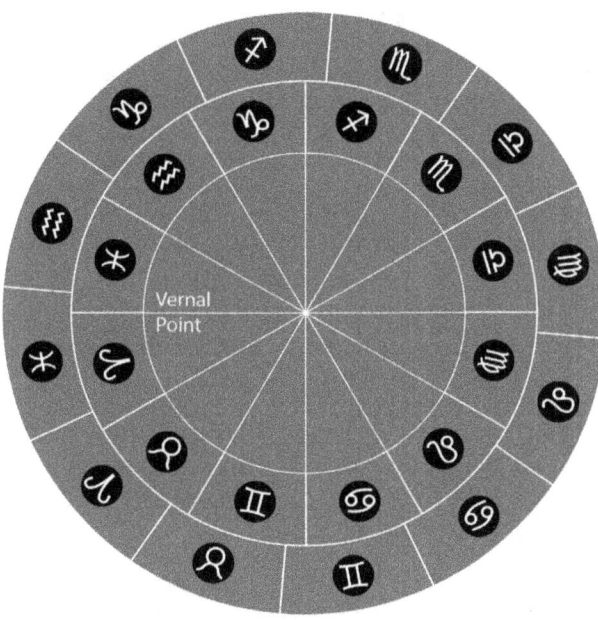

The current alignment of the tropical (interior) and sidereal (exterior) zodiacs. (To convert any tropical longitude into a sidereal longitude at the present time, we simply need to subtract twenty-five degrees. This number will grow by one degree every 72 years.)

One factor that has supported the continuation of the tropical system can be found on any map of the world. The Tropics of Cancer and of Capricorn, currently at 23°N26' and 23°S26', respectively, show the upper and lower limits of the Sun's apparent annual path around the Earth. Despite the fact that it was during the year 215 AD that they became, astronomically speaking, the Tropics of *Gemini* and *Sagittarius*, the names of these lines have remained unchanged over time. Take note: In 2375, when the zodiacal Age of Aquarius will be upon us, accurate cartographers will be required to refer to them as the Tropics of *Taurus* and *Scorpio*! By this time, *the five degrees of overlap that the sidereal and tropical zodiacs share will be g-o-n-e*: The two systems will be a full 30° apart, the length of an entire zodiacal sign. In other words, the year 2375 will mark the beginning of a long period during which the influence of the tropical signs of the zodiac will be completely severed from its stars!

We will invoke Steiner for our final argument in favor of the sidereal zodiac. While it is true that he did not explicitly favor the sidereal over the tropical, he was specific and definite in his assignations of the start of the cultural ages, which are based upon the astronomical reality of the sidereal system.

5

THE CIRCLE OF TWELVE
THE CONSTELLATIONS OF THE ZODIAC AND THEIR MEANING

JUST AS THE AIR AROUND US fills our lungs, permeates our blood, and makes our lives possible, so too are the twelve starry signs of the zodiac the source of our *cosmic nourishment*: the spiritual air that connects us to higher realms.

Mention of the four Royal Stars of the zodiac—the first to reveal themselves to the eye of the spirit—dates back to Zarathustra; these are *Aldebaran* (15° Taurus), *Regulus* (5° Leo), *Antares* (15° Scorpio), and *Fomalhaut* (9° Aquarius)—all shining from the four fixed signs of the zodiac. As the term implies, the fixed signs share a *stabilizing* quality. They have been described as pillars of the universe, and even as the "foundation stones" of the holy circle. To the left and the right of each fixed sign are two others; thus, the twelve are gathered. Within the zodiac we encounter three sets of four, and four sets of three; that is, the holy animals reveal both their *archetypal quality* (cardinal, fixed, and mutable) and their *spiritual archetype* among the four elements (fire, air, water, and earth).

The three qualities (also known as modes) make the most sense in the light of anthroposophy, for the cardinal signs concern foremost the will aspect of the human being, the fixed signs the feeling life, and the mutable signs the thinking aspect of soul.

Each quality is represented by a cross in space: the *cardinal* cross of Aries, Cancer, Libra, and Capricorn; the *fixed* cross of Taurus, Leo, Scorpio, and Aquarius; and the *mutable* cross of Gemini, Virgo, Sagittarius, and Pisces. "The law of the Cross" determines the interrelatedness of the four points.

The marriage of opposites—this traditional theme of alchemy—is the essence of the practice of the law of the Cross. For the Cross is the union of two pairs of opposites, and the practice of the Cross is the work of conciliation of four opposites.[1]

For example, a planet in Gemini requires study of Sagittarius; and three planets placed in Leo, Scorpio, and Aquarius immediately draw the eye to the wisdom of Taurus.

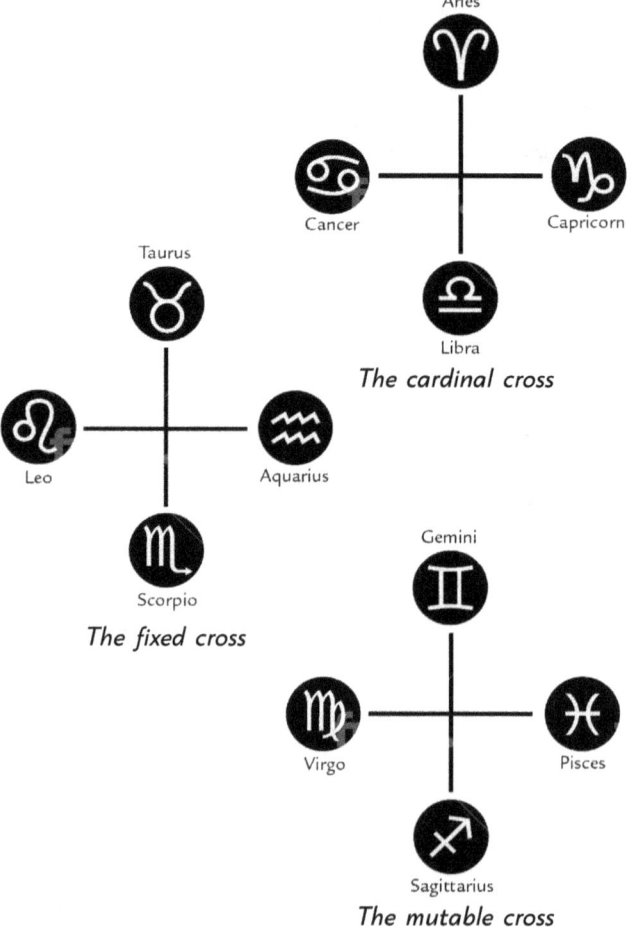

The cardinal cross

The fixed cross

The mutable cross

---

1 Tomberg, *Meditations on the Tarot*, 259.

The Circle of Twelve

Each of the four elements finds expression in one cardinal, one fixed, and one mutable sign of the zodiac; thus a triangle of *fire*, a triangle of *earth*, a triangle of *air*, and a triangle of *water* are formed within it.

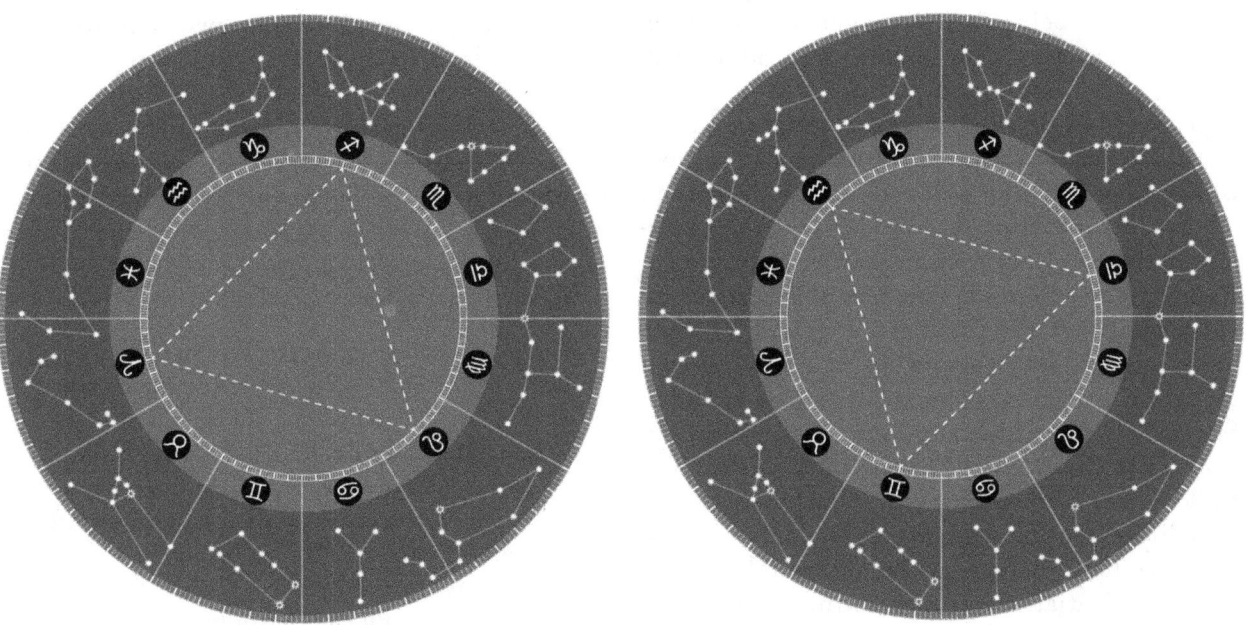

The triangle of fire: Aries, Leo, and Sagittarius

The triangle of air: Gemini, Libra, and Aquarius

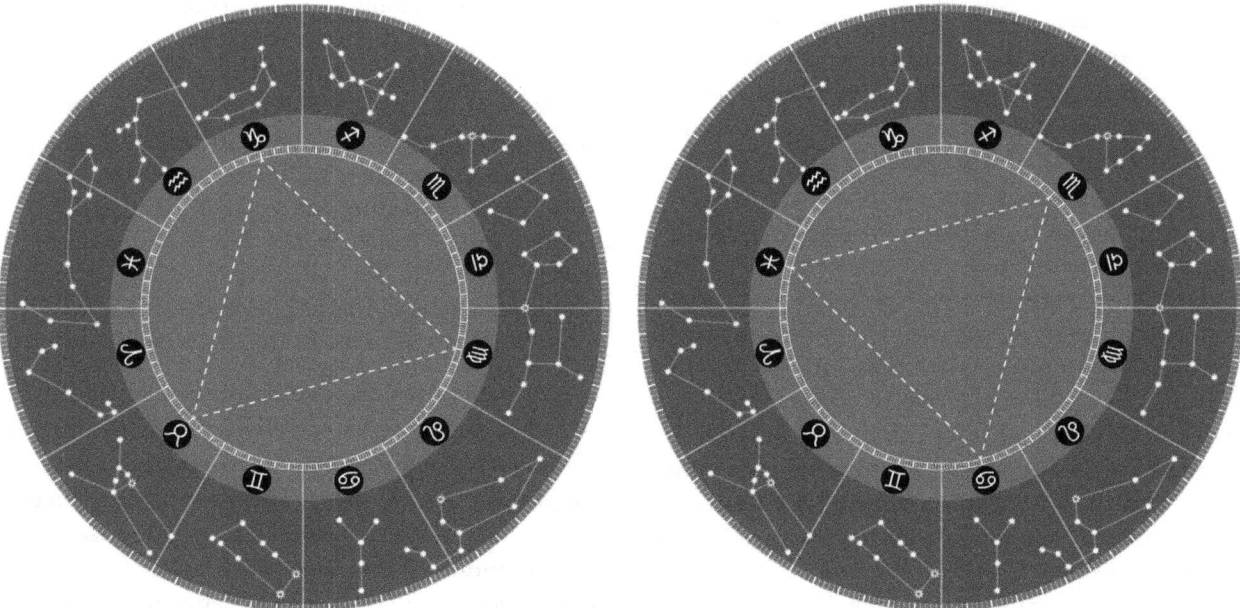

The triangle of earth: Taurus, Virgo, and Capricorn

The triangle of water: Cancer, Scorpio, and Pisces

Those signs that share an element have an easy association; furthermore, fire and air are compatible, as are earth and water. We carry within us the forces of all twelve zodiacal signs. By the time Earth evolution reaches its end, many millennia hence, humanity will have interiorized them all. For now, we find that the typical incarnation will call upon the individual to focus upon a few of them, represented by the zodiacal placement of the planets and other significant markers in the chart.

The zodiac constellations are the dominion of the three highest angelic hierarchies: the Seraphim (the spirits of love), the Cherubim (the spirits of harmony), and the Thrones (the spirits of will).[2] These beings are so elevated in relation to humanity that they cannot be understood through ordinary consciousness. Just as the appearance of Christ before him rendered Saul blind and unconscious for three days, we, too, would swoon in the presence of the Seraphim, Cherubim, and Thrones. In order that the inherent radiance of the zodiac may be received, it must first be "dimmed." One way this is achieved is by means of the intercession of the planets. Thus, as each planet passes before a zodiacal constellation, it receives the wisdom that radiates from the constellation behind it and sends it onward to the Earth. Mars, of course, interprets these forces differently than Venus does.

Achievement of some degree of consciousness of the zodiacal beings has been accomplished by the great initiates over the centuries *as a result of their spiritual-moral development*. So great is the risk of megalomania for spiritual seekers that Steiner and Tomberg both made it clear that spiritual development must be accompanied by an even greater effort in the moral realm. Zodiacal awareness is *necessarily* given to us in the form of spiritual exercises, and cannot be known solely by means of a scholarly approach. Tables and charts—of which many of us are so fond—might bring us to the door, but will ultimately leave us standing in a cold rain without a key!

One such collection of spiritual exercises is found in *Meditations on the Tarot*. The fact that the Tarot is now employed primarily as a fortune-telling device is suggestive of the degenerative work of adversarial forces that seek to sever our connection to the spiritual world. I will admit that when I was first introduced to Tomberg's letter-meditations on the Major Arcana, I was wary in the extreme.

The intent of this great work is to revive the hermetic tradition (which is inherent in the ancient wisdom of the Tarot), and to simultaneously immerse its readers in its spiritual current. And yet, *Meditations on the Tarot* is also permeated with the reality of the Christ Impulse. It has *Christianized* the Tarot.

The twenty-two letter-Arcana of *Meditations on the Tarot*—like the twenty-two letters of the Hebrew alphabet and the twenty-two pathways within the Sephiroth Tree of the Cabbala—serve as approaches to the gateways to the world of spirit: paradisiacal gateways that have been closed since the Fall. The Sephiroth Tree *is* the Tree of Life, perceived by the ancient Egyptians as dwelling within the stars of Orion and of Lepus below it.

From Joel Park:

> The Egyptian mysteries of Hermes Trismegistus—of Isis and Osiris—were once perceived within the constellations of Orion and Lepus. When Moses (who had been raised as an Egyptian and was initiated into their rites) left with the Hebrew peoples, he brought the "hidden treasures of Egypt" along with him. What was once perceived within the stars in the form of Hermeticism became codified within the Sephiroth Tree, with its ten Sephiroth, four planes, and twenty-two paths of wisdom (the twenty-two letters of the Hebrew alphabet). At the time of Christ, the reality of the Sephiroth condensed even further, and became the etheric body of Christ. This body was to be brought to the Mother in the depths as a seed, in order to grow once again the Tree of Life—reopening the gates of Paradise, the way to the Mother in the depths. It was this very Sephiroth Tree that began to radiate out of the center of the Earth at the moment of the Resurrection on Easter Sunday.[3]

It is, of course, no coincidence that the number of zodiacal signs (twelve) added to that of the planets (seven classical, three transcendental) totals twenty-two. The spiritual-intuitive research of Robert Powell has yielded definite correspondences between the letter-Arcana of *Meditations of the Tarot* and the constellations and planets that surround us.[4] These comparisons will be touched upon, in turn, as we move through the zodiac, and then through the planets.

---

2   These three hierarchies are also active in the affairs of humanity through their presence in the planetary spheres—the Seraphim in the sphere of Saturn, the Cherubim in the sphere of Jupiter, and the Thrones in the sphere of Mars.
3   Joel Matthew Park, "The Archetypal Language: Returning to the Origin of the Houses, Part III" (*Star Wisdom*, vol. 4. Hudson, NY: Lindisfarne Books, 2022), 103-4.
4   They are: Aries/The Fool; Taurus/The Judgment; Gemini/The Sun; Cancer/The Moon; Leo/The Wheel of Fortune; Virgo/Force; Libra/Justice; Scorpio/Death; Sagittarius/The Hermit; Capricorn/The Star; Aquarius/Temperance; Pisces/The Hanged Man; Sun/The

♈ ARIES

The letter-Arcanum entitled "The Fool" (XXI) brings our attention to an image of a wandering individual dressed in clothes that invite ridicule, as does the fact that he allows a dog to bite at his pants. Yet Aries is the domain of the formative forces of head—indeed, it was during the Age of Aries that human intellect reached its pinnacle. The fool depicted in the card does not appear to be a genius of any kind! And yet, the subject of this meditation is not intellect alone, but also *love*. Love is the fertile soil from which the Aries virtue of devotion can be cultivated.

What has The Fool renounced, and why? What has made him a vagabond in jester's attire? *He acts on behalf of the magic of love.* Due to love, the Fool has passed from personal intellectuality, moved by the desire for knowledge, to higher, *divine* knowledge. He stands for love in the face of every atrocity and injustice; and in doing so, he upholds the sovereign freedom of the individual.

> The twenty-first Arcanum of the Tarot is therefore that of the hermeticist's method of sacrificing the intellect to spirituality in such a way that it grows and develops, instead of becoming enfeebled and atrophied.... [It] is the alchemical work of the union of human wisdom (which is folly in the eyes of God) with divine wisdom (which is folly in the eyes of man) in such a way that the result is not a double folly, but rather a single wisdom which understands both that which is above and that which is below.[5]

(Hereafter within this chapter, references in this section to *Meditations on the Tarot* will be noted with the abbreviation MOT, along with the appropriate page number.)

The Ram, with a strong feeling for its own individuality, is the leader of the zodiac. His leadership is achieved and maintained by the moral worth of his ideas. The Ram is so decisive and adept at problem-solving that he can become annoyed with opposition, as well as with the slow speed at which everyone else is moving. Nonetheless, we see his backward glance—for he concerns himself with the well-being of the eleven who follow him. In Aries, the leader of the twelve, we feel the forces of creation as they are first set in motion: the power of love. The fool knows that love is the source, cause, and motivation of the creation of the world. [MOT, 618]

For the ancient Persians, the ram was the symbol and vehicle of Agni, the fiery principle of pure spirit. In ancient Egypt, the god Amon-Ra, the all-powerful Sun, was worshipped in the form of a ram, crowned with the solar disk—perhaps an intuitive perception of the Christ spirit, born of the Sun. Zeus, too, was portrayed with ram's horns.[6] For Christians, of course, Jesus is the Lamb of God, who sacrificed himself for the sins of humanity.

While within the constellation of Aries, we receive the formative forces for the creation of the head, the seat of our consciousness. In the glyph we experience uprightness, and indeed we can admire the moral uprightness of a Ram who tends the fire of the ideal—the highest of which is love—and longs to awaken others to it. Steiner assigned to Aries the worldview[7] of IDEALISM. The true idealist believes that material phenomena have no real meaning unless there is within them something to which the soul can aspire and direct itself. We must be careful not

---

Magician; Moon/The Empress; Mercury/The Pope; Venus/The Lover; Mars/The Chariot; Jupiter/The Emperor; Saturn/The High Priestess; Uranus/The Tower of Destruction; Neptune/The World; and Pluto/The Devil.

5   Tomberg, *Meditations on the Tarot*, 605.
6   Louis Charbonneau-Lassay, *The Bestiary of Christ* (Harmondsworth, UK: Penguin Books, 1991), 67-68.
7   Steiner spoke of particular worldviews associated with each zodiacal sign. Though they can be described simply as differing ways of looking at the world, they are in fact spiritual archetypes that find expression through the "I" of the human being. The worldviews exist on a higher plane than do temperament and character. See Mario Betti's book, *The Twelve Ways of Seeing the World* (Gloucestershire, UK: Hawthorn Press, 2019).

to separate an Aries from his ideals, for without them he can become a cynic—a most sad and unnatural condition for a Ram.

Aries's natural devotion to these ideals—abetted by the certainty characteristic of the fire element—can foster narcissism if the inherent self-confidence of Aries has fallen into arrogance. It can be "his way or the highway." This forms the image of the zealous battering ram that scatters all in its path. When Aries is instead motivated by love, he becomes the lamb (a willing servant of God), discovering victory in defenselessness. Only a Fool maintains the fountainhead of *idealism* despite assaults from the nipping dog of materialism.

♉ TAURUS

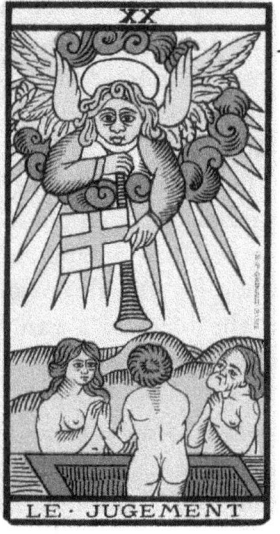

"The Judgment" (XX) depicts an Angel holding a trumpet above three individuals below. A youth, who has responded to the call of the trumpet from above and has been resuscitated, stands in a tomb as the father and mother look on. Within the stars of Taurus dwells an orientation to the utterance of sound—for it is the Bull that provides the archetype of the human system of speaking and listening.

The youth has heard the trumpet, has responded to it with effort, and has been *resurrected*. Resurrection is regarded by tradition to be identical to the last judgment: a single event seen from two sides. The resurrection body—the indestructible kernel of the physical body that is *active will* during life—grows and matures from incarnation to incarnation in preparation for the re-establishment of its unity with soul and spirit. [MOT, 583] Tomberg wrote:

The idea and ideal of resurrection [go] further than the negation of Nature... it signifies its complete transformation, the alchemical work on a cosmic scale of the transmutation of Nature—spiritual as well as material, "heaven" and "earth." There is no idea and ideal more bold, more contrary to all empirical experience, and more shocking to common sense than that of resurrection.... [It] presupposes... becoming a motivating spirit instead of a "moved" spirit; not only of participating actively in the process of world evolution, but also of raising oneself to conscious participation in the work of divine magic—the magical operation on a cosmic scale whose aim is resurrection. [MOT, 558]

...Just as the earthly father and mother give life to the child at his incarnation, where the Angel of life sounds the "trumpet" formed by his outspread wings is then turned above—so do the celestial Father and Mother restore the child to life at his resurrection, where the Angel of resurrection sounds the trumpet in order to call his soul and his body to resurrection—and the "trumpet" formed by his outspread wings is then turned below. [MOT, 560]

This letter-Arcanum concerns itself with memory and remembering—for just as forgetting, sleep, and death are three manifestations of a single thing, so are remembering, awakening, and resurrection. What are we to remember, to bring to consciousness? The answer is: *everything*, little by little. At the last judgment, our memory is restored and consciousness is awakened. And as we judge ourselves, Christ is there to comfort us.

The sound of the Angel's trumpet bears within it the entirety of the Akashic chronicle.[8] When we hear it, we *know*—we know when we have contributed to the suffering of others, when we have eased that suffering, and when we have been forgiven. Through the spiraling sculpture of his horns, the Bull listens; through his four stomachs, he digests; and through his larynx, he speaks that which has then become his own.

---

8   The Akashic chronicle, maintained and guarded by the beings of the zodiac, holds the memory of all that has transpired upon the Earth. It comprises, in fact, three different chronicles: the first consists of facts alone; the second reveals the ever-changing equilibrium between good and evil; the third—also known as the "book of life"—is a moral accounting of human deeds that can be "updated" through forgiveness and atonement.

Taurus is the last one standing when the winds reach seventy-five miles per hour: "the sequoia in the forest." As we might imagine, this stability depends upon a mighty force of will, a raw power that almost incomprehensibly breaks through from the invisible realm into the visible. In Aries we encountered uprightness, the first essentially human characteristic; in Taurus, we hit upon the second: the means by which sound—leading to our ability to speak—is born within us. Through speech, what exists in our consciousness can be shared with others.

Taurus stands firmly in the natural world; but with its horns, it seeks the spiritual aspects behind this world. The Great Pyramid of Giza, built during the age of Taurus, is representative of the qualities of the Bull: for its foundation is wide and strong—even immovable—and its apex points to the heavens. With its great eye, *Aldebaran*, Taurus keeps watch over the circle; its keen perceptions reveal to humanity what must be remembered and *transfigured*. To the Bull, the image of "one who works in the field of God," all life is sacred. As the Moon finds its point of exaltation among the stars of the *Pleiades*, we can intuit the ancient connection of Taurus (which Venus rules) with the divine feminine. Once the mother's milk is dry, we turn to the milk of the cow. In the horns of the Bull we remember the horns of Isis—by which cosmic thought can be ingested.

In the glyph, we can see the bottom of the great cosmic circle to which the thoughts of Taurus are directed. Bulls have an innate sense of concept that can enliven and resuscitate humanity. Sometimes, however, their thoughts can encircle their horns f-o-r-e-v-e-r, evading digestion by the greater organism and thereby fostering overthinking and an obsessive quality of thought. Alternatively, Bulls can easily muster the patience to "chew the cud" until the job is done. Digestion requires *stillness*—just as physical growth requires sleep.

But stillness in the absence of inner motion can lead to rigidity and the inability to move forward. When the Bull loses its interest in new concepts, it can become apathetic and self-indulgent: the sorriest imaginable state for a Bull!

Stability and *integrity* are the bywords of Taurus; Bulls are usually happy to serve as a "rock" for others. Steiner assigned the worldview of RATIONALISM to Taurus, which implies using logic and reason to reach conclusions. Additionally, it's important to Taurians that these conclusions have a practical application in the world—and "practical application" is the specialty of Taurus. The Bull knows that, through listening, we can participate consciously in the work of divine magic. Indeed, miracles are the alliance of the divine will (*above*) with the human will (*below*).

♊ GEMINI

The letter-Arcanum "The Sun" (XIX) is that of intuition. This image depicts two children, standing under the Sun, who entreat us to see ordinary and simple things in the light of day—and with the outlook of a child. One child touches the head of the other while the second child reaches for the heart of the first.

Intuition, Tomberg explains, is the alliance of active wisdom and active intelligence (intelligence *reunited* with wisdom), and it presupposes their cooperation. It leads us to identify our "star" in full clarity—the path that we know we must follow despite life's inevitable distractions and the efforts of others to take us off of this path.

> These two children thus represent intelligence endowed with childlike confidence with regard to the spontaneous wisdom of the heart.... One could hardly better represent the relationship of intelligence and spontaneous wisdom brought into play in intuition.... For this relationship presupposes such purity of intention as is found only with a child.... [This relationship] excludes tendencies to domination and authority. [MOT, 528]

> May those who follow the "star" do so completely and without reserve! May they not seek — once having the "star" before their eyes — scientific confirmation, approval, or sanction... or, what would be still worse, direction on the part of science! May they follow the "star" above them and *nothing else*! [MOT, 534]

The main stars of Gemini — *Castor* and *Pollux* — uphold the ideals of cooperation and of brotherly love that are revealed in the myth of the two half-brothers: one divine (Pollux), and one mortal (Castor). We can see the brothers standing side by side in the Gemini glyph; indeed, this glyph is a symbol of duality and symmetry: darkness and light, male and female, life and death. True brotherly love is not achieved by *ignoring* what we don't admire in another, but by *recognizing* the spark of the divine that lives within each of us. We can also identify within the Gemini glyph the channel that exists in all human beings between the lower ego (personality, tendencies) and the Ego (our higher Self). Tomberg referred to these two versions of ourselves as "eyes" — and our task is to engage them together. The Gemini channel linking the earthly and the divine is upheld by two pillars, known by many names: Jachin and Boaz, prayer and benediction, mercy and severity. Only when they remain erect, side by side, can the "eyes" see together.

In Gemini we encounter the worldview of MATHEMATISM, *or* HERMETICISM. This perspective presumes an open and upright channel between what is above and what is below; we must look to the spiritual world to find the true origin of order, measure, and number. Certainty in the *moral order* is what guides human intelligence to follow the "star" of wisdom — the "I" of each of us — and this makes it possible for Gemini to uphold its virtue of perseverance.

In Gemini we receive the formative forces for the development of the shoulders and arms. The playfulness of Gemini holds the archetype of the joyous youth: Gemini sees the world through a child's eyes. As it is with a young, sanguine child, Gemini can find it difficult to walk in a straight line — or even to remain tethered to the Earth (a trait that is evocative of Gemini's ruler, Mercury). What anchors the Twins is a persevering faith in the guiding star of individuals, and of humanity.

Versatility is Gemini's constant companion; but when thoughts and energies are scattered far and wide, the verticality of the hermetic channel cannot be maintained. Clarity of thought, the natural gift of this mutable air sign, will then remain elusive. Worse still, we'll lose our "north star." And not only will we find it difficult to commit to anything — we will also become vulnerable before the (perhaps dubious) certainty of others.

♋ CANCER

The letter-Arcanum "The Moon" (XVIII) brings to consciousness the problem of all that is contrary to life. The card depicts no greenery whatsoever — instead, we see two stone towers behind a stagnant man-made pond, within which is confined a crayfish. Above the scene, two canines bay at the fully eclipsed Moon. Although the Moon has the capacity to reflect the light of the Sun (as human intelligence can reflect the creative light of conscience), this capacity can be eclipsed by materialistic intellectuality. [MOT, 494] For materiality is to intelligence as the Earth is to the Moon.

> The sun, moon, and stars are — according to Genesis — lights "in the firmament of the heavens to give light upon the Earth"... Now, human consciousness is the field where *three* kinds of light are manifest: *creative* light, *reflected* light, and *revealed* light [the Sun the Moon, and the stars]. [MOT, 495]

Materialistic intelligence is always and only concentrated on the product (or result). This form of thinking is oriented toward facts, and therefore cannot focus on the process of becoming — what Tomberg refers to as *the intuition of faith* or *the principle of springtime*. Is not this principle the essence of the impulse to nurture?

Tomberg warns us against a particular state of consciousness — that of "knowing better." It plunges intelligence into a pond of stagnant water with an exact geometrical border; thereby, while demanding creative effort, it retreats in the face of all that is new.

In the face of "disquieting contradictions [or antinomies]," intelligence is ill at ease:

> Whilst retreating, whilst refusing to decide to leap or fly either over the "dog" of submission to authority ("credulous obedience") and the "wolf" of criticism denying all authority ("critical revolt"), or over the intellectual "tower of Babel" of theses and that of their antitheses, intelligence nevertheless remains ill at ease. [This is] because of the imperceptible drops [depicted in the card], emanating from the radiation of synthesis eclipsed by the projection of the shadow of arbitrary human will, which fall into its subconscious and constantly disturb it. [MOT, 517]

While the first three signs of the zodiac revealed characteristics of the human being that are directed outwards — uprightness, speech, and symmetry — the image of a crab offers something quite different. It brings to mind a creature that prefers to remain in the background, or to be completely hidden. Indeed, this creature is one that will fight only if its life depends on it. The Crab is happy staying put, finding what it needs in its immediate surroundings, which it tends with great care. It lights a fire in the hearth and keeps it burning.

Empathy and selflessness can be taken so far by the Crab that these qualities can morph into egoism (though the Crab would be loath to admit it). For, giving endlessly in the absence of individual Ego-strength results in a "false selflessness" — one that seeks to feed on the Ego-strength of others. This not only weakens the life forces, but can also render us burdensome in our interactions with others. Who does not resent gifts from one whose "I" lies flat, like a serving of Jello on the floor? Alternatively, we always feel gratitude for the sacrifices that have been made on our behalf by one whose sense of self and mission is absolute. From them come the deeds that can truly be our salvation.

MATERIALISM as a worldview implies a person's abiding interest in material life — i.e., in relation to the material world and its laws. Derived from the Latin for "mother," inherent in the term is the concept of participating in "that which is becoming"; in fact, the star cluster at the center of the constellation is often referred to as the Manger. The glyph of Cancer (the image of the ribcage) brings to mind enclosure — a loving embrace of what must be protected. She guards the inner temple of the human being, always listening for the heartbeat within.

We observe in the glyph that there is a break, an abyss, between the two arms of the spiral; and within this abyss, we can perceive humanity's lost connection to the spiritual world. This rent — this breach — where we see the stars known as the Manger — was redeemed by the one who was born in Bethlehem more than two millennia ago. *Humanity was thus given the potential to resurrect from the depths of the abyss into which it has hurled itself.* Earlier, the ancient Egyptians saw in the stars of Cancer the image of a scarab — an image that they added to many sarcophagi. These beetles, who are known for digging and burrowing into the Earth, were provided in this way to the dead as a means of guiding them through the underworld. The beetle laboring in the Earth, in the words of Willi Sucher, "became a symbol of the promise of resurrection after death, after earthly struggle."[9]

Cancer's ruler, the Moon, is the planet related to the human brain and, by extension, to human intelligence. Just as the Moon reflects the glory of the Sun, so can human intelligence be warmed by morality and conscience, whose origins lie in the spiritual world. (Does not a mother caring for her child mirror God's love of creation?) In contrast, a Moon that is *devoid* of reflected sunlight results in a Crab encased within itself — and who then resents the demands that are made upon it, while thereby robbing itself of the ability to care selflessly for others. For when the Crab retreats in the face of heaven, it is unable to bridge the abyss between matter and

---

9   Willi Sucher, *Isis Sophia: Outline of a New Star Wisdom* (Meadow Vista, CA: The Anthroposophy Research Center, 1985), 36.

spirit. Selflessness alone allows it to enter the cathartic waters of life. Then, and *only* then, does such progressive movement allow the Crab to ensoul matter with spirit. The Crab's movements are rarely direct and — when it is in a stressful situation — can even be described as frantic.

♌ LEO

"The Wheel of Fortune" (X) depicts a wheel in motion. There are two animals upon it: a dog (ascending) and a monkey (descending). On a platform above the wheel sits a sphinx with a white sword, representative of the unity of the human and animal kingdoms. If the sphinx were not there, the image would evoke eternal repetition — within which human hope and endeavor would be in vain. As it is, the monkey (being carried away from the sphinx) is a reduced being, whereas the dog appears to be aspiring toward a higher condition. In the descent, we can perceive the process of *in*volution; in the ascent, a path of *e*volution is revealed. Is evolution predetermined, or is it not?

Eternal repetition is suggestive, like the wheel itself, of a closed circle (we can also see this represented in the *ouroboros*: the serpent biting its tail). Indeed, the world of the serpent — in which we live — seeks to consign us to this eternal prison. Only when we understand evolution as both a cosmic tragedy and drama can perdition and salvation be understood.

Who is right? Those for whom evolution is an organically determined process in which descent and ascent are only two successive phases of a single cosmic vibration? Or those who see in evolution a cosmic tragedy and drama whose essence and *leitmotiv* correspond to the parable of the prodigal son? [MOT, 237]

However, it is characteristic of all advanced religions that there exists an exit as well as an entrance to this circle.

There is an entrance, which is why Christmas is a joyous festival. There is an exit, which is why Ascension is a festival. And that the world can be transformed, such as it is, into such as it was before the Fall — this is the "good news" of the festival of festivals, the festival of the Resurrection or Easter. [MOT, 243]

Who among us doesn't admire the boldness of the Lion? Even his ability, now and then, to let out a tremendous roar that captures the attention of all within earshot? SENSUALISM is the worldview Steiner associated with this constellation. The Lion's daring and enthusiasm are born of his abiding love of life, his need to gather as many experiences as he can — for he trusts above all his sense impressions. These, rather than reasoned understanding, provide him with his orientation to the world; they say to him: "You're alive!" The Leo glyph reveals its connection to the development of the human heart, for the glyph begins with a heart — just as *Regulus*, the star that marks the heart of the Lion, can be seen very near the start of the constellation. Emanating from this heart is a pathway that reaches outward, as compassion does from a heart full of warmth.

Though the human heart is enclosed within the protective structure of the ribcage, it is nonetheless in conversation with the outside world through its connection with the lungs. A heart that is noble conveys royalty, power, strength, and courage. Lions symbolize watchfulness; and in this image, Christ can be found as the good shepherd of us all.

As the only sign ruled by our Sun, Leo bears a connection to the "I" of the human being. When his willingness to do battle is transformed into moral courage, he is the ideal of the noble ruler: a servant. He is then compassionate and understanding of his own deficiencies and those of others. Recognizing the sovereignty and natural authority of the individual, he also has the courage to protect others when they are threatened. The wise ruler never seeks to usurp the authority of others — instead, he stands behind the boundaries of his *own*. The Lion looks at the great wheel of life, a symbol of eternal repetition, and fixes his gaze on the opening to the spiritual world. He holds open the door through which the dove may descend.

Now, it can happen that fiery Leo's (sometimes) brassy entrance into a room results in the consumption of all the oxygen within it, leaving the other occupants a bit overpowered. A Lion who is puffed up with his own importance might seek to dominate others, assuming he is in charge whether or not that right has been earned. The tyrant's roar is loud, but no one will follow unless coerced. And when he realizes that he lacks true authority, he descends into the realm he most dreads: the closed circle of egoistic repetition that signifies the loss of his freedom. This is a very sad state for our zodiacal King. The virtue of compassion thus enfolds upon itself, leaving in its wake a sucking force of compression. Endlessly seeking self-affirmation in the serpent's world, he fights all who refuse to yield to his roar.

♍ VIRGO

"Force" (XI), the letter-Arcanum that corresponds to Virgo, depicts a woman who appears to be of ordinary strength gazing off into the distance, having completely subdued a lion! How has she managed to do this? Force is power without effort and obedience to the divine. We can, however, identify two different forms of obedience. In the first, we obey out of fear of the power of another; our will has been subjugated. In the second, we obey when we stand in holy awe before the voice of truth.

Tomberg refers to this state of spontaneous obedience as *implicit* (or, *natural* religion). It implies the perception *of* and reaction *to* what is above. The Virgin's state of purity—her non-fallen nature—was our shared condition before the Fall. In the presence of what Tomberg calls "holy animality," the obedience of the lion in the card is instinctive. This quality is represented in the Apocalypse of St. John by the four holy animals, who surround the throne of God. (Their synthesis is the sphinx: the Bull, the Lion, the Eagle, and the Angel/Man.) We can arrive at a conviction with the serene clarity of the "waters" surrounding the throne, like a sea of glass, or we can be swept away by the waters that poured forth like a river out of the mouth of the serpent. One illumines, while the other sweeps us away.

> Scripture has two different terms in Greek for "life": *Zoe* and *bios*.... *Zoe* is therefore the source and *bios* is that which flows, having come from the source. It is *bios* which flows from generation to generation; and it is *Zoe* which fills the individual in prayer and meditation.... *Zoe* is vivification from above in a *vertical* sense; *bios* is vitality which, although it once issued from the same source above, passes in the *horizontal* from generation to generation. [MOT, 277-78]

The practice of the ten commandments—which are described in glorious clarity and depth in this letter-Arcanum—sets us on the path from *bios* to *Zoe*.

The Virgin is the holy living creature among the twelve who has the power to tame a lion in an instant. To the Virgin, compulsion and conquest are superfluous, as she is a friend to all; she possesses all the power of pure, non-fallen (or virgin) nature. Virginity in this context, of course, has nothing to do with the physical body, but instead is a state of soul that reflects purity and cooperation with the natural world, whose mysteries she holds close to her heart. Through the worldview of PHENOMENALISM, the Virgin eternally reveals the heavenly origin of nature.

The gift of Virgo, an earth sign, is precision in the realm of thinking.

Virgo bestows sobriety, and thus protects us from the excessive lure of our sympathies and antipathies. As Mary and her family fled to Egypt, springs welled up from the cool earth to quench their thirst. Likewise, the Sun, Moon, and stars lend their assistance to those who aspire to this state of being. One moves toward the state of virginity through observation of the ten commandments. The Virgin, accustomed to being underestimated, longs to serve others.

From Virgo we receive the formative forces for the digestive system: the true inside of the human being. Substance that is ingested herein is then worked upon—ultimately to be transformed into energy and nutrients for the body. This requires the basic determination of what is "friend" and what is "foe"—as well as just how much of the latter can safely be taken in. On the level of the soul, we can think of this as a clear sense of boundary for self and others. This boundary is not static; it moves with each new interpersonal interaction. When this boundary is known with clarity, the Virgo virtue of courtesy (or, grace) finds easy expression. If, instead, the boundary is misjudged, it can result in inappropriate intrusion as well as inappropriate withholding—a lack of tact—particularly in social settings.

Virgo is also the spiritual source of our musculature, which gives our thoughts and will the ability to set us in motion. Motion is the very nature of Mercury, the ruler of Virgo. She bestows upon us the formative forces of the womb, knowing as she does that life proceeds from a holy source. In so doing, she cradles in her embrace all that is in the process of becoming. She longs to nurture and protect until it is time to harvest. Her embrace, which encompasses the entirety of humanity, is mirrored in the Virgo glyph. Behind the stars of Virgo weave the forces of ripening—it could even be said that she has an innate sense of *readiness*. She knows when it is time, for her inner movement ebbs and flows with the seasons.

♎ LIBRA

In "Justice" (VIII) we observe a woman holding a set of scales and a sword, which she uses when she must. She is seated between two pillars; these can be imagined as will and providence, or as severity and mercy. Justice is the being who judges and weighs the relative merits of both "pillars."

In other words, she represents the function of the law. Tomberg wrote:

> Thus she says: "I am seated on the seat which is between the individual will of beings and the universal will of the supreme Being. I am the guardian of equilibrium between the individual and the universal. I have the power [through the sword] to re-establish it each time that it is violated. I am order, health, harmony, *justice*." [MOT, 174]

Within the capability of the human being is the ability to judge actions and phenomena; we do this all the time. This is as it should be, for we must name what is good and what is evil. However, we lack the authority to condemn *beings*.

We can look to the Sephiroth Tree for guidance on the execution of justice.

> The right pillar is often designated the "pillar of Grace (Mercy)," whilst the left pillar bears the name the "pillar of Severity." Now, these two pillars...correspond, from the point of view of justice, to *defense* and *prosecution*, whilst the middle pillar corresponds to *equity*. The system of the ten Sephiroth is based on mobile *equilibrium*, with the tendency to re-establish it in an instance where a momentary dissymmetry is produced. *It is a system of balance.* [MOT, 178]

To engage in impartial justice, we must weigh and judge *beyond* the limits of our character (our astral body) and our temperament (our etheric body). Conscience exists beyond—and above—these limits; and it is here that the domain of *freedom* begins and is found. [MOT, 196] This freedom—our free will—is the reason that an astrological chart, which is an "astral document," cannot be regarded as predictive; for although the stars incline, they do not compel.

In days of old, the ancients beheld within the constellation of Libra not only the scales, but also the being whom God trusted to hold them: the Archangel Michael. Weighing up for each of us the relative merit of our thoughts, feelings, and deeds is precisely what Michael, the Lesser Guardian of the Threshold, must do. Michael, of course, quite naturally stands for justice, as it is he who casts the dragon into the abyss each autumn. Though it might be hidden, a strong will impulse exists behind the refinement and sweet countenance of Libra (gifts of its ruler, Venus).

In Libra, we move from the interior (Virgo) to the human relationship with the world outside. Indeed, Libra needs to be in conversation with others. The Scales imply balance within (equanimity of soul) and balance without (the ability to stand and walk upon the Earth).

Steiner identified REALISM as the worldview of Libra — a perspective less concerned with how things *should be* than with the reality of what we actually perceive. Libra knows what he needs to do to be effective in the world, and his native charm assists him in his quest. If you long to know how to hone your social skills, Libra's the one to keep an eye on. And we'd all do well to remember what has never been forgotten by Libra: that the *wisdom of groups* is what allows the truth to manifest. At the same time, we must guard against putting more faith in that which is *general* at the expense of that which is *individual*.

Scales — as well as the hips of the human body, which develop under the direction of the Angels of Libra — imply balance. Whereas the Bull finds balance through rootedness to the Earth, Libra's balance is dynamic, ever moving — much like judgment itself, which we are called upon to summon without cease. The constant movement of the balance pans serves to convey this implicitly. The *quality* of our judgments, however, depends on conscience. Indeed, we may ask: does conscience guide our decisions, or do our personal viewpoints and positions hold sway?

When Libra freezes in the center, or cannot find center at all, there can develop a tendency to look longingly to the grass on the other side of the fence. We might add that the Venusian characteristic of avoiding conflict and decision is also not unknown. If Libra falls asleep at the fulcrum of the scales, however, equanimity is lost — and so, too, is its sense of *scope*, which is the proper blessing of the element of air upon the will.

The rounded portion of the upper part of the glyph is imagined as the altar of Christ, for it is he who took up the ultimate redress of the sins of humanity.

 SCORPIO

"Death" (XIII) presents us with an image of a skeleton working with a scythe — one who appears to reap scattered parts of the human body that are pushing up out of dark soil. Our empirical experience of death, writes Tomberg, is *disappearance*:

> Forgetting, sleep, and death are three manifestations of the same thing — namely the "thing" which effects disappearance.... [They are] three manifestations — differing in degree — of a sole principal or force which effects the disappearance of intellectual, psychic, and physical phenomena. [MOT, 342]
>
> Now, birth, awakening, and recall, on the one hand, and death, falling asleep, and forgetting on the other hand, constitute, so to say, the two "pillar-forces" of reality. They manifest in remembering and forgetting, in the rhythm of sleeping and waking, and in that of birth and death — as well as in the respiration of organisms, in the circulation of the blood, and in alimentation. They are the "yes" and the "no" in every domain — mental, psychic, and physical. [MOT, 354]

Why is the skeleton using the scythe?

> [Death] accomplishes *amputations* of sick members — "sick" in the sense that they have usurped a domain of existence which does not legitimately belong to them — before the sickness become irremediable. What Death does in this card is therefore to act as a guardian of the threshold between the two worlds.... Death corresponds to surgery in the "cosmic hospital." It is the last expedient to save life. [MOT, 370]

Simultaneously a disappearance and a call from the spiritual world, death accompanied incarnation as a necessary consequence of the Fall. Between lifetimes, our life among the stars and planetary spheres reminds us that it is *spirit* from which we were born, and *spirit* to which we will return!

The Scorpion holds the memory of the archetype of the Eagle, which was the ancients' clairvoyant perception of this sector of the zodiac. Within its stars we can seek the height and depth of perception—the insight—of the soaring Eagle. The patience of Scorpio (and the understanding it seeks) find expression in the reflection of the stars in heaven upon the surface of a deep, clear lake.

With its poison gland and dart, the Scorpion is also a symbol of death. We would all do well to understand the tender, vulnerable heart that dwells within her breast, for when she feels threatened, she can rush to judgment and *sting*. And yet poisons can also be delivered in small, therapeutic doses. Sometimes a "sting" can be an agent of transformation; how often does a dreaded piece of news result in the emergence of an opportunity that couldn't have been imagined earlier? Scorpio wonders: Must we always be *forced* to approach the threshold, beyond which lie the mysteries of the spiritual world? The Scorpion, in fact, *wants* to confront the darkness—for this is how she comes to know herself and the world.

The Scorpion understands a great deal, even having an intuitive sense of the "smell" of a situation. She is a stranger to superficiality, having an abiding need to understand what goes on *below the surface*. This is the worldview of DYNAMISM spoken of by Steiner; it implies *depth*. Through Scorpio's influence, we could spend hours on a park bench watching others, speculating about their lives with great interest, but might not feel any need to interact. Within Scorpio lives the ancient mantra: *To be silent*.

This brings us to one of the hazards of the influence of the Scorpion: antisocial behavior—for it holds no fear of darkness and solitude. When we consider the modern ruler of Scorpio (Pluto, god of the underworld) that has been added to the traditional one (Mars), we get a sense of how truly dark, how *anti-life*, things can get down there. When the stone is in front of the tomb long enough, the Scorpion is paralyzed by doubt and despair, and liable to turn its stinger onto itself. Then, only the radiance of love has the power to recall it to life.

From Scorpio radiate the forces necessary for the development of the sexual organs—the physical source of new life.

SAGITTARIUS

The letter-Arcanum "The Hermit" (IX) concerns the resolution of opposing theses, or antinomies. The peripatetic Hermit of the card is the figure of a spiritual father who walks the hard way, and is consequently able to pass through the "narrow gate." [MOT, 200]

The Hermit is the solitary man with the lamp, mantle, and staff. His lamp shines the light of truth into the darkness; his mantle brings consciousness of the *whole* truth that can be known only through the "collision of opposites," and his staff confers the power of intuition through immediate experience ("touching" the Earth).

The letter-Arcanum reveals three ways in which the "collision of opposites" can occur. The first method is to mix the opposites. This results in a descent into confusion: When we mix paints of any opposing colors, we end up with the same muddy brown. We might also call this *ignorance*. The second method involves a sort of compromise (or "finding the average") between the two opposites, whereby both are lost to "common ground of *human knowledge.*" Through the third method, opposites can be united on a higher level *after they have fully revealed themselves as opposites*.[10] *Wisdom* is their synthesis. Such synthesis presumes the ability to separate ourselves from personal and collective positions and beliefs.

This is difficult to do. For this reason, Tomberg suggests that we live under the sign of the cross:

---

10 Tomberg, *Russian Spirituality*, 45-46.

This means to say that one separates the quantitative ["horizontal"] and qualitative ["vertical"] aspects of the world in a clear way, and that one takes account of the precise difference between the function of a mechanism and the action of a sacrament. For the whole world has its mechanical side and its sacramental side. Moses describes the sacramental world in the book of Genesis; modern astronomy is in the process of describing the world-machine. The one speaks to us of the "what" and the other of the "how" of the world.... The mechanism is knowable through quantity; the essence is revealed by quality.

And the scientific creed? How does one reconcile it with the Christian creed?...

Crucify the serpent. Put the serpent — or the scientific creed — on the cross of religion and science, and a metamorphosis of the serpent will follow. The scientific creed then becomes what it *is* in reality: the mirroring of the creative Word. [MOT, 215]

The stars of Sagittarius long to fully awaken our creative capacity. Half horse, half human, the mythical centaur reminds us that we have within us a lower, *animal* nature, as well as a higher, *spiritual* one. Horses can be patient and wise, or wild and rebellious, thereby revealing the eternal human struggle. The centaur asks: *Which half is dominant?* How can we put the lower half — known for its strength and speed — in the service of the intelligence of the upper half? The answer lies in *self-control*. This implies a reining in of the thinking, feeling, and willing impulses that serve only ourselves. It implies *prudence*.

Sagittarius supports mobile, creative thought, which is the natural gift of the fire element to our thinking. The glyph is a dynamic one, depicting the Archer's arrow as it is about to fly off at great speed toward its quarry. The Archer's "wide view" is a gift from its ruler, Jupiter. The bow itself suggests readiness to vanquish and conquer in the name of righteousness; Christ, also, bears a bow (along with his sword) in the Book of Revelation. In imaginative vision, we can experience the archer as a seeker of the truth, and the arrow as his question as it's being sent out to the spiritual world.

The hunter resists confinement of any kind. This is an expression of the Jovian quality of *expansiveness*. The Archer wanders, but he does so with purpose; the Hermit, too, wanders the world. Hardly surprising is the fact that it is the thighs — the most powerful muscles in the body — that develop under the aegis of Sagittarius. They allow us to *run*.

The arrow in the Sagittarius glyph conveys the ability of the Archer to focus every ounce of his attention and energy on his quarry. And yet, if he falls prey to the Sagittarian peril of one-sided thinking, his arrow will find only falsehood. This can result in a moralizing, dogmatic individual who lacks discernment — in which case the smile that normally comes so easily to the Archer will be elusive. If, however, the lamp of the Hermit lights his path, his arrow will fly straight for the truth, moving easily through the dark clouds of distraction and lies.

Steiner's worldview for Sagittarius is MONADISM, which refers to the indestructible kernel of the human being (the "image") or of another entity. However, it is the task of the Archer to endeavor to hold in equal regard opposing persons or concepts, whereby the gradual transition from the one to the other can be revealed like the colors of a rainbow. The Archer is thus able to look upon two opposing ideals or concepts with *complete impartiality*, so that he might have consciousness of the *whole* truth — thereby gaining the qualities of a great teacher.

♑ CAPRICORN

"The Star" (XVII) is the letter-Arcanum wherein we might know the esoteric meaning behind the stars of Capricorn. This is the letter-Arcanum of growth and continuity, symbolized by the spiral. On the card, we find the image of a woman kneeling beside a stream. She kneels beneath eight stars;

the landscape is lush. And she pours water from two vases. Tomberg wrote:

> Just as there is Fire and fire, i.e. the celestial Fire of divine love and the fire of electricity due to friction, so there is also Water and water, i.e. the celestial Water of the sap of growth, progress, and evolution, and the lower water of instinctivity—the "collective unconscious," engulfing collectivity—which is the water of floods and drowning. Thus, the woman represented on the card of the seventeenth Arcanum pours water from *two* vases—held in her left and right hands—which blend into the same stream. [MOT, 469]

Continuous transformation is the essential manifestation of the agent of growth; growth *flows* and is therefore not revolutionary—for revolution necessarily requires shocks and upsets. The agent of this transformation is the current of hope:

> Hope is not something subjective due to an optimistic or sanguine temperament.... It is a light-force which radiates objectively and which directs creative evolution toward the world's future. It is the celestial and spiritual counterpart of the terrestrial and natural instinct of biological reproduction.... In other words, hope is what moves and directs *spiritual evolution* in the world.... [MOT, 471-72]

Hope is the essence of motherhood—for by the simple fact of being a mother, she professes the divine origin of the world ("the Alpha") and the divine aim of the world ("the Omega"). Hope is the blood of the spiritual world. Without hope, we are imprisoned in the closed circle of the serpent's world—the circle that separates the "higher waters" above the firmament (hope) from the "lower waters" beneath it (the continuity of life). A *miracle* is the descent of hope—which unites the actions of the two "waters."

The Goat, who reveres those facets of the past that are noble and good, longs to reanimate what is worthy of the future. Capricorn strives to maintain the golden thread that connects the past to the future, for it knows that progress without *revolution*—which treads upon the past—is the ideal. Courage is the virtue streaming from its stars.

Well-known to the Goat is that there are *two* currents which move together toward the future: the spiritual "sap" of evolution, and the water of instinctivity. The Goat entreats us to say *yes* to one, and *no* to the other, for it knows that hope—which directs spiritual evolution toward its future—cannot live within the second current alone.

With an innate devotion to order and hierarchy (courtesy of its ruler, Saturn), Capricorn is not one to "wing it," break ranks, or take a path without knowing the final destination—on which its eyes remain trained until its task is complete. Once the Goat is sure of its course, it will not waver. Capricorn stands as a great leader to those who wish to follow him.

The Capricorn constellation was known to the ancients as the *gateway of death* for the excarnating soul. Its worldview, as given by Steiner, is SPIRITISM: Indeed, the Goat kneels beneath the stars above its head. Like so many patriarchs and initiates of long ago, the Goat withdraws to solitary heights to be nearer to God, and is happy to deny itself in service of this purpose. *Capricorn strives to raise the material to the spiritual.* The harsh conditions and deprivation that are characteristic of such a climb are easily tolerated by the Goat: *It endures.* The knees are the part of the human body for which we can thank Capricorn—as these allow us to adapt, absorb shock, and bow in reverence.

The Star reveals the spiral as the pattern of growth—for growth (spiritual and biological) proceeds both vertically and horizontally.

The forces of Capricorn continually pour the living water of the spirit (which bears the principle of continuity) upon humanity. They uphold tradition—the "moral backbone of time"[11]—because the Goat knows that it is one of the agents of spiritual growth: It *flows* from the past to the future. This is not easy for one with such high regard for the past: and sometimes, when Capricorn abandons its mission, it can harden and rigidify as it clings to

---

11   Valentin Tomberg, *Proclamation on Sinai: Covenant and Commandments* (Brooklyn, NY: Angelico Press, 2022), 104.

what *was*—and to the safety of what is already known. The Goat can thus be imprisoned in a world without promise.

The earth element confers firmness upon the will—and during its life, the Goat must forge such firmness into iron. This quality is precisely what can turn a "fallen" Goat into such a ruthless adversary—one who will do everything it can to reach the top. This sort of Goat delights in exposing the weaknesses of those it regards as its opponents—and its list of these can be very long indeed. The Goat can then descend into paranoid self-pity.

♒ AQUARIUS

The letter-Arcanum "Temperance" (XIV) presents to us the image of an Angel pouring water horizontally between the two vases that she holds. Within "Temperance" we encounter the spiritual exercise that brings us into communion with our guardian Angel. The Angel remains with a single individual throughout the full sequence of lifetimes, and therefore understands (in a way that we cannot) the purpose underlying this sequence. When called upon, the guardian Angel offers counsel by way of our conscience. Although it is the wish of the guardian Angel to protect and defend us throughout our lives, it will never compromise our free will; nor will it remove temptation from our path. As to the water that moves between the vases, Tomberg wrote:

> The guardian Angel...watches over the functioning of the spiritual-psychic-corporeal circulation, i.e., the *health* and the *life* of the whole human being. This is why the card...represents [the Angel] engaged in the accomplishing of his office of regulating the system of circulation, or the human being's fluidic system. [MOT, 385]

He wrote further:

> The system in question comprises several active centers—the "lotuses," the nerve centers, the glands, to name only the principal ones—but the harmonious functioning of all these centers depends upon a single thing...the current which constitutes the relationship between the *image* and the *likeness* in man. [MOT, 385]

The image and the likeness coincided before the Fall. Since their separation, there has arisen with in us a contrast between the divine blueprint (the image) and how far we have descended from that ideal (the likeness). It is overwhelming to consider the vast chasm that separates the two. The relationship between them reveals itself through tears:

> The contrast between image and likeness is experienced as inner *weeping*. Weeping is the reality of the fact that the two sisters—the image and the likeness—*touch*. [MOT, 387]

Temperance is the spiritual exercise that enables us to know the difference between the two. It involves finding the current of inner life, and endeavoring to live in accordance with it.

Through the mighty first hierarchy of Angels that dwell within the constellation of Aquarius, we come to understand the nature of the communion between the individual and his guardian Angel. Indeed, Aquarius is the representative of the Angel among the four holy animals of Ezekiel and the Book of Revelation. Each Angel guards, cherishes, protects, visits, and defends its charge upon the Earth, providing to each of us what Tomberg described as *pure maternal love*. May this be known to all whose mothers fell short of this ideal! Christ, too, is often represented artistically with wings: an indication of his angelic character as the Father's messenger.

Aquarius, or the Waterbearer, is the realm of the zodiac through which cosmic etheric forces flow to Earth. Knowing as we do that intuitive thinking exists within the etheric realm, we can appreciate the connection between Aquarius and innovation: *thoughts not yet known to others*. This quality is well represented by Uranus, the secondary ruler of this sign. The realm of Aquarius bestows the capacity to take in the twelve points of view; this could otherwise be described as a *propensity for objectivity* or, alternatively, as *gnosis*—the planetary mood of Saturn, the Waterbearer's primary, ancient ruler.

However, without the warmth of morality, his thinking can become abstracted, leading to *an equal indifference to the twelve*. The freedom-loving Aquarius—to whom boundaries and limitations are not easily accepted—can then become an insufferable know-it-all. *Humility* alone allows Aquarius to bow before an intelligence surpassing his own.

The glyph is a representation of the hermetic axiom, *As above, so below*. In the ideal human—i.e., in the *angelic*—we recognize the universal longing to regain our place in the spiritual world. The future calls to Aquarius, and he feels its breath upon his cheek. The worldview of Aquarius is PNEUMATISM; the Greek word from which it derives refers to the *life force*, which is taken in with the breath.

The celestial-etheric current brings healing. Indeed, we find that the Sun was stationed before the stars of Aquarius at three of the seven healing miracles of Christ: the healing of the paralyzed man, the feeding of the five thousand, and the walking on the water. Additionally, the Sun at these events was aligned with megastars of the Northern Cross (which is referred to by Robert Powell as "the portal to the kingdom of the Father").

The Waterbearer willingly diminishes himself so that others within his circle may increase. He is a servant of the future. Furthermore, because of his magnanimity of feeling, and his embrace of the full round of points of view, Aquarius represents the circle of community. Opposite the Sun, whose physical counterpart is the human heart, Aquarius symbolizes the periphery—where the blood is sent forth by the gating mechanism within the heart. Through the beings of Aquarius, we receive the "formative forces"[12] for the development of the lower leg. Moreover, within these forces lies the ability to send the blood back to the heart.

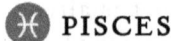 PISCES

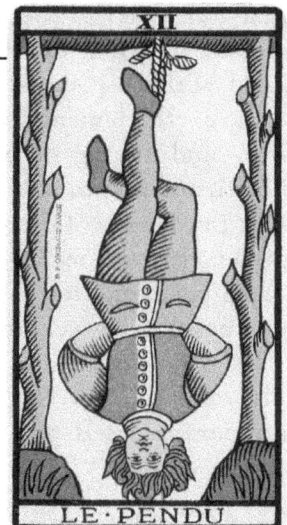

In the image of "The Hanged Man" (XII), an upside-down young fellow is suspended by one foot from a sort of crossbeam. He is not struggling in the least; thus do we enter into a meditation upon gravity. The Hanged Man cannot act; he can only be *acted upon* from above. His feet—organs of the will—find their "ground" in spiritual heights, while only his head—through perception—concerns itself with the ground below. The twelve zodiacal constellations thus become channels for his will. The Hanged Man is pulled toward solitude:

> It was in solitude that [the desert fathers] could *live*, i.e. develop spiritual temperature, breathe spiritual air, quench their spiritual thirst, and satisfy their spiritual hunger... [MOT, 308]

The soul of the Hanged Man experiences absolute solitude, suspended between heaven and Earth. (Tomberg refers to this as the "zero point.") This is at one and the same time a benefaction and a martyrdom. [MOT, 307] His soul is elevated by the contemplation of the divine, and is simultaneously inspired to descend to the world of terrestrial affairs in order to execute moral-spiritual deeds on behalf of humanity. Abraham *obeyed*; his head followed his feet.

Heavenly gravitation is so real that it can take hold of not only the soul but also, in rare cases, the physical body. Such was the case as Jesus walked upon the Sea of Galilee.

As we meditate upon this miracle, we can imagine Jesus walking upon the horizontal bridge of the Pisces glyph—the bridge that leads from the past to the future and separates the celestial above from the terrestrial below. Celestial gravitation is the force that kept him above water. In Peter we can observe something else:

---

12 From the beings of the zodiacal round, we receive the spiritual archetype for human body. Each zodiacal sign carries the formative forces of one aspect of our physical form. An illustration of these correspondences can be found on page 10.

The Circle of Twelve

Now, the words "I am; do not be afraid" spoken by the one walking on the water amount to the statement: "I am gravitation, and he who holds to me will never sink or be engulfed." Because *fear* is due to the menace of being engulfed by elemental forces of gravitation of a lower order, i.e. of being carried away by the play of blind forces from the agitated "sea" of the [serpent's] "electrical field" of *death*. "*I am*; do not be afraid" is therefore the message of the center, or Master, of celestial gravitation, demonstrated by the action of support with regard to Peter, who was saved from sinking.... This message contains... the solemn declaration of the *immortality* of the soul, in so far as the soul is capable of transcending the engulfing gravitation and "walking on the water." [MOT, 310]

Pisces is the starry realm of the point of exaltation[13] of Venus, whereby the planet of love is strengthened within the zodiac's citadel of love. The heart of Pisces makes room for all; under its sway we regard humanity as a unity, and we are happy to gather strays into our fold. This is an expression of PSYCHISM, the worldview that Steiner discerned through the stars of the Fishes. In this context, *psychism* refers to the *world soul* of which we are all a part. Through the forces of Pisces, we become fully engaged in our work upon the Earth.

With Pisces — the omega of the zodiac — we arrive at the feet of the human being, for the forces behind the Fishes are what hold their spiritual archetype. The Fishes bring us fully into earthly life: The feet support uprightness and allow us to achieve independence. But as we navigate the tides in this ocean of freedom, we must discover our unique place within humanity and within the cosmos — lest we be cast adrift forever by the currents of doubt and loneliness.

In Pisces, we hold the image of having brought our consciousness fully down to Earth, where we feel the Mother beneath our feet and long to know her mysteries. And yet, we know that we must turn our gaze once more to the spiritual world and to the long, gradual inbreath of the cosmos that will take us back to it. Pisces is the bridge that spans the abyss between past and future, between this world and the heavenly world. Since antiquity, this duality has been expressed by the silver cord between the two starry fish — between the one that swims horizontally, with humanity, and the one that swims toward heaven. This duality, like all others, needs to find a balance within us. When the "upper fish within" seeks heavenly realms, Pisces is ideally suited to living a spiritual life, even to having the ability to hear the divine call. When the "lower fish" (i.e., swimming horizontally) exerts the stronger pull on us, we can be tossed about in the current of lies and delusion, our trusting nature easily exploited. This is one expression of the lower influence of the Neptune, the secondary ruler of Pisces.

Pisces conveys a profound moral impulse. Within its stars there exists a "longing to belong" to the whole world (a legacy of its primary ruler, Jupiter) and to see humanity as a single organism. Yet another gift of the Fishes is the quality of *fluidity* in our thinking, which often finds an artistic or other creative path.

The fish was an image of divinity long before Christ — the celestial "fish" of them all, although what made the fish primarily a Christian symbol was the onset of the zodiacal age of Pisces (in AD 215), together with the ascendancy of Christ in the West. Pisces portends a time when, through our faithful devotion to humanity's evolution, the weight of our past transgressions will be lifted. It guards the mystery of *celestial gravitation*: the force that impelled Noah to build his ark, led Abraham to Canaan, and allowed Jesus to walk upon the water.

---

13 For more information about exaltations, see Part III, Chapter 2.

6

THE SPATIAL DOMINION OF THE ZODIAC

THE AREA IN SPACE THAT IS influenced by a given zodiacal sign extends all the way to the Earth (from the geocentric perspective) or to the Sun (from the heliocentric perspective). This is essential to understand. *But this is not all.* Each sign also holds sway over the area of space *above* and *below* it.

the firmament; it divides the celestial sphere into a northern and a southern hemisphere. The equator and poles of this sphere are exact projections of those of the Earth:

The second perspective from which we can locate stars and planets uses as its foundation the *ecliptic plane*, where the zodiac is found. The ecliptic plane bisects another sphere of stars—

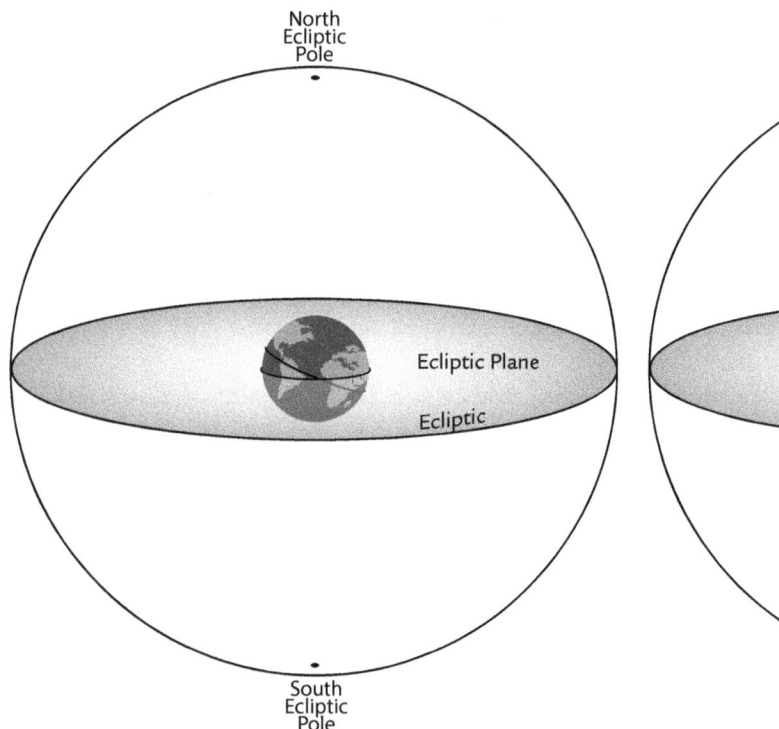
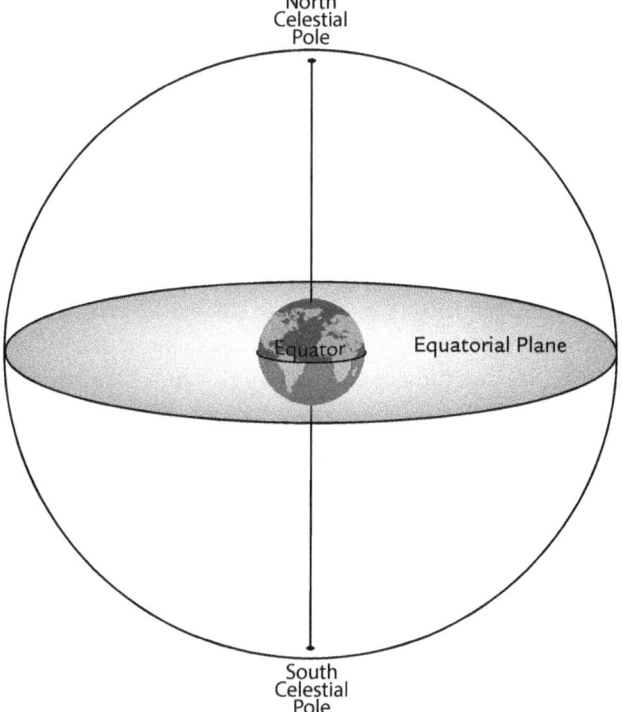

There are two perspectives from which we can identify the locations of heavenly bodies. They arise from two different imaginary planes. The first is the plane upon which the equator—as well as its extension into space, the *celestial equator*—lie. From this orientation, we measure the position of a planet or star in terms of how far above or below the equatorial plane it is,[1] as well in terms of its corresponding location along the Earth's equator.[2] The equatorial plane must be imagined as extending infinitely into

the one that bears the zodiac as its "equator." Its poles are known as the north and south ecliptic poles. Again, the *foundation* of the ecliptic plane is the zodiac.

It must be borne in mind that the celestial sphere that is bisected by the equator is *not* in alignment with the sphere that is bisected by the ecliptic. The equator and the ecliptic (as well as their corresponding polar axes) are offset by 23½°.

---

1   Its *declination*.
2   Referred to as *right ascension*. Both declination and right ascension are geocentric in nature.

The Circle of Twelve

Let's imagine placing the center of a bow compass at the North Pole. We'll then extend the arm with the marking device to the point at which the North Ecliptic Pole meets the Earth, and proceed to draw a circle upon the globe. We'll do the same around the South Pole.[3] (On any globe or map of the Earth, the equator is identified as 0°; the North and South Poles are at 90° north and 90° south, respectively.) The two circles that we've drawn extend 23½° from the poles, and are otherwise known as the Arctic and Antarctic Circles.

As the Earth spins on its axis each day, the ecliptic pole "inscribes" these same circles upon surface the Earth. For locations on the Arctic

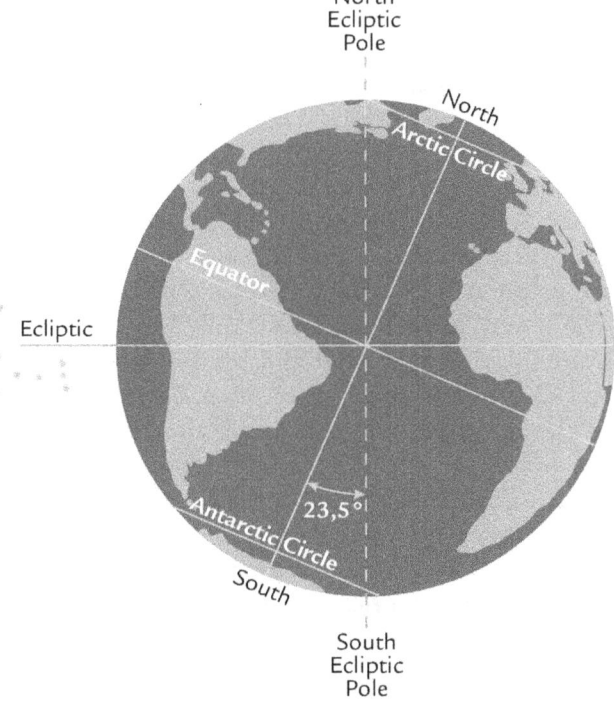

and Antarctic Circles, there is no darkness on the day of the summer solstice (the "midnight sun"), and no daylight on the day of the winter solstice (the "polar night"). The closer a location is to the poles, the more "midnight suns" and "polar nights" will occur.

As navigators have done for millennia, we can think of the celestial poles — which are direct extensions of our North and South Poles — as *stars*: our North and South Pole Stars. However, *the Earth's polar axis is not stationary*; over the course of many thousands of years, it rotates like a spinning top, inscribing — when we extend them into space — two circles in the firmament, one in the north and one in the south. At the center of these starry circles in the sky are the north and south ecliptic poles. This means that at any given time, the celestial poles and the ecliptic poles are *also* offset by 23½°.

This "gyration" of the Earth's axis is usually chalked up to the gravitational forces of the Moon, although there have been challenges to this notion. Whatever its cause, we simply need to know that *it happens*. One full rotation of the Earth's polar axis occurs over a period of 25,920 years, which is otherwise known as a Platonic year. (Steiner referred to this period of time as "a great day in the heavens.")

The movement of the polar axis has two implications. Firstly, *our pole stars change over time*. At the moment, *Polaris* guides our northern navigators. But in about 8000 years' time, *Deneb* will do so, as will *Vega* 4000 years after that! Secondly, *this movement is the origin of the precession of the equinoxes*. Indeed, if the polar axis were stationary, there would be no sequence of cultural ages!

Now, when we use the ecliptic plane as a reference, the *zodiac* is the background against which we determine the positions of the stars and planets. A star's position in relation to its corresponding zodiacal degree is its *celestial longitude*[4]; its distance above or below the ecliptic is known as its *celestial latitude*.

We can visualize this starry sphere in the image of an orange that has been cut into twelve equal lunes, each representing the domain of one zodiacal sign. The Earth and Sun can be thought of as tiny dots in the general region of the center of this sphere. Before Copernicus, this starry sphere was not thought of as infinite, but was instead imagined as defining *the limit* of the firmament. To the stargazers of old, each star seemed to be woven into this sphere; in other words, it was thought that all the stars in the heavens were equidistant from the Earth.

---

3   In this two-dimensional illustration, these circles appear to be straight lines.
4   The frame of reference for celestial longitude is the zodiac; therefore celestial and zodiacal longitude are the same.

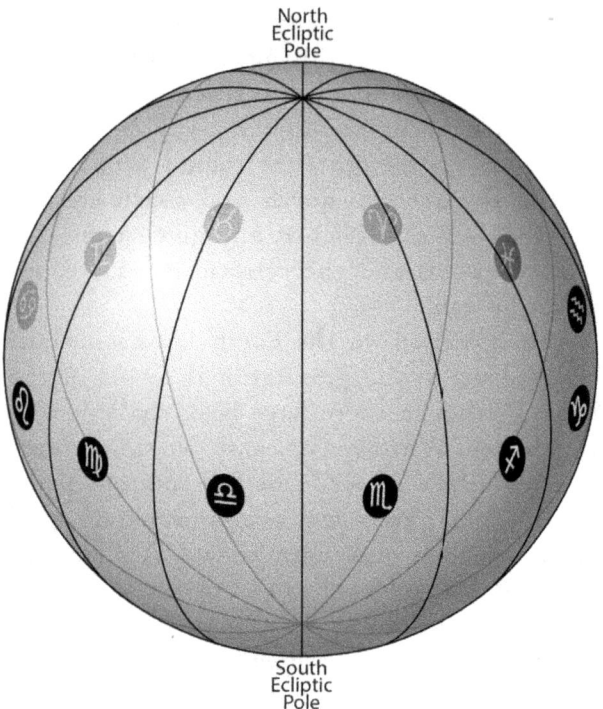

The ecliptic is deeply relevant to humankind—so much so that Robert Powell refers to it as the *heart meridian* of the cosmos.[5] If we can further imagine this sphere as a globe with its own "lines of longitude" that connect its poles, then it becomes clear that each meridian crosses the ecliptic at one of the 360 zodiacal degrees.

The influence of any heavenly body, moving or stationary, exists along the full length of its zodiacal longitude—all the way to the ecliptic poles, as well as all the way to the center of the celestial sphere. To my knowledge, Laquanna Paul was the first to liken these lines of longitude to *energy meridians*. In this way, we can think of each zodiacal degree as part of a *zodiacal meridian*—within which exists *a unique etheric current*. The nature of this current can be known through an acquaintance with the mythology of the stars—for within these ancient tales, Sophia's wisdom resounds.[6]

Moreover, through the remarkable work of Robert Powell, we can come to know the etheric currents that live within the zodiacal meridians by way of the life of Christ. (The planetary positions during and surrounding Christ's life are detailed in Appendix 3.) A birth chart might reveal, for example, the Sun at the same degree as it was when Jesus performed a miracle. Immerse yourself in the biblical account of this event, as well as that of Anne Catherine Emmerich. These correspondences have the power to set us on a new path.

We can use the example of the megastar *Deneb* (also visualized as the head of the Northern Cross), to understand this better: *Deneb* is aligned with the meridian that intersects the ecliptic at 10½° Aquarius. Though *Deneb* lies about 60° north of the zodiac (thousands of light years away), its stellar influence follows this meridian down to the ecliptic, whence it can flow into human hearts. In the case of *Deneb*, we know that the Sun passed before 10½° Aquarius at the feeding of the five thousand and the walking on the water. Each time the Sun passes this degree of the zodiac, the cosmic memory of these miracles is awakened.

---

5 Powell and Dann, *The Astrological Revolution*, 147.
6 In addition to the traditional sources of mythological tales that we might have studied in school, I can highly recommend the following: Scott's *The Christos Sun Meditations*, Sucher's *Isis Sophia*, and Paul and Powell's *Cosmic Dances* duo.

7

STARS WITHIN AND WITHOUT THE ZODIAC

WHAT IS A MEGASTAR? Astronomers distinguish between *intrinsic* brightness, or luminosity, and *apparent* brightness. Defined as a star whose luminosity is 10,000 times that of our Sun, a megastar—if it is far enough away—may not appear very bright at all! So, why do they matter to astrosophers? *Because the Sun, at every one of the seven archetypal miracles of Christ, was situated under the influence of a megastar.*

Additionally, the firmament is filled with other important stars with which planets aligned during and around the life of Christ. One of countless examples of this is *Regulus*, the heart of Lion, at 5° Leo—which was the zodiacal degree of Venus at the death of Lazarus, and that of Mars at the death and Assumption of the Virgin. We can say, then, that the forces of *Regulus*—which can be held in imagination as a source of compassion and moral courage—wove between these two individuals during the ministry of Christ and beyond it.

The sidereal longitudes of many of the stars relevant to our study—along with their names and the constellations to which they belong—can be found in Appendix 1. Knowledge of these stars gives us a deeper sense of the reality of the "spiritual currents" that run through their sidereal longitudes. When you identify a planet in a chart at the same degree as one of these stars, take a moment and familiarize yourself with the myths associated with its constellation—for the stars speak through these stories.

The ecliptic—the path of the Sun from the perspective of the Earth—serves as the connection between these currents and humankind. How exactly do these currents reach us? The answer (as intimated above) lies with the *planets*. As they move through the sidereal longitudes before the background of the zodiacal stars, the planets serve as our *interpreters* of the twelve holy living creatures.

8

THE PLANETS AND THE MOON'S NODES

COSMIC "WORDS" ARE CREATED through the interweaving of the planets and the zodiac. To the clairaudient, the planets bring vowels—bearers of qualities of *soul*—to the consonants, which are expressive of the *spirit*. Only together do they create a language.

Seven "classical planets"—Moon, Mercury, Venus, Sun, Mars, Jupiter and Saturn—are visible to the naked eye and have therefore been gazed upon since the dawn of humanity. Though the Sun and Moon are not planets at all (and are often referred to as "luminaries"), their status, as such, has been maintained over the centuries by their importance to human existence.

These seven planets are intimately connected, on several levels, to each human being. The classical planets serve as the backdrop to the unfolding of the seven-year periods in each life.[1] Their forces are incorporated into the human astral body through the seven chakras, and into the etheric body through the various human organs. The Angels who work within their "spheres"—their spiritual domains—assist us, after death, in the review of the life we've most recently lived (as well as in the forging of karma for the life to come). Furthermore, as described by Steiner, these same planetary spheres mark the seven stages of Earth evolution.[2]

Uranus, Neptune, and Pluto (the three outermost planets) work upon us in a very different way. They came into being *outside* of Earth evolution, and therefore bear no association to the human chakras or to our system of organs.

Uranus, Neptune, and Pluto have a gargantuan effect on individuals and humanity that could never be denied; but they are *transcendental* planets, and therefore need to be considered separately from the seven classical planets. They hold within them not only the highest spiritual qualities—Imagination, Inspiration, and Intuition—but also forces of *hindrance*, through which the anti-Christ seeks to find a way into human souls.

When unaspected[3] by the Sun, Moon, Mercury, or Venus (those planets closest to the Earth) or to any of the main axes in the chart, the effect of the transcendentals is more *collective*. This means that their influence will be felt largely "out there," and less so within ourselves. When there *is* such an inner connection, however, we will find ourselves tempted again and again in the favored manner of the transcendental in question; one of our life tasks will then be to bring this temptation underfoot. If we fail to do so, the higher spiritual faculty associated with it will remain out of reach.

Lastly, each of the ten planets has an *ennobled* (or higher) nature, as well as a *fallen* (or lower) nature. As to which of them manifests in the individual—this depends upon our moral development!

---

1 There periods are described in Chapter 3 of Part IV.
2 These are also known as the *manvantaras* in Hindu cosmology.
3 This means that there exist no astrological aspects (particular geometric alignments) between the transcendental and the other planets mentioned.

THE CLASSICAL PLANETS

 SATURN

In *Meditations on the Tarot*, Tomberg wrote,

["The High Priestess" (II)] is the [letter-Arcanum] of the twofoldness underlying consciousness — spontaneous activity and its reflection; it is the [letter-Arcanum] of the transformation of the pure act [or, the breath of the Holy Spirit] into representation, of representation into memory pictures, of memory pictures into the word, and of the word into written characters of the *book*.[4]

(Hereafter, references in this section to *Meditations on the Tarot* will be noted with the abbreviation MOT, along with the appropriate page number.)

The card bears the image of a woman in a three-layered tiara holding open a book on her lap. She is the sacred guardian of that book. Tomberg wrote:

The tiara is [three-layered and is] laden with precious stones, which suggests the idea that it is by way of three stages that the crystallization of the pure act descends through the three higher and invisible planes before arriving at the fourth stage — the book. [MOT, 40]

Gnosis is the subject of this letter-Arcanum: the descent of revelation that ends in its expression in "the book." The High Priestess is seated; she is listening attentively in silence. Her stillness is indicative of the reflective method demanded by higher knowledge. She is wisdom itself. Tomberg wrote:

[The gnostic sense] is the *contemplative* sense. Contemplation — which follows on from concentration and meditation — commences at the very moment that discursive and logical thought is suspended. Discursive thought is satisfied when it arrives at a well-founded *conclusion*.... The gnostic sense begins to operate when it is a matter of a new dimension in the act of knowledge, namely that of *depth*.... How does one arrive at this? By listening in silence.... But there is an essential difference between the "listening silence" of contemplation and the silence arising from the effort to recall. In this second situation, it is the *horizontal* — in time, past and present — which comes into play, whilst the "listening silence" of contemplation relates to the *vertical* — to that which is above and that which is below. [MOT, 44]

The twofoldness underlying our consciousness is reintegrated within the soul by way of "listening in silence." This listening is the "water" that reflects the "fire" of the spontaneous activity of the spirit.

Placed at the outermost boundary of the classical planets, Saturn is the slowest by far, requiring twenty-nine and a half years to orbit the Sun. With the loving concern of a parent, its orbit embraces the whole of the classical solar system. In fact, Saturn fulfills the role of the good parent — one who protects, discourages recklessness, and strives to keep us on our true path. This necessitates a certain narrowing of focus, but is ideally accompanied by an attentiveness to the dangers of rigidity and inhibition.

Saturn's cool exterior belies a deep inner warmth. At its best, its influence confers endurance and determination. Saturn's intent is truth, depth, and thoroughness. As such, it resists rushing of any kind. Furthermore, Saturn brings all unpaid bills to our doorstep; although it can sometimes have a sobering — even a melancholy — effect on self and others, it is simply urging us to align with reality and to acknowledge our responsibilities. To be sure, this is something we often do reluctantly, because it requires that we vigilantly

---

[4] Tomberg, *Meditations on the Tarot*, 40.

maintain and upgrade the underlying structure of our lives. The purpose of Saturn's "scythe" is to cut back what no longer serves our higher resolves. When this is accomplished, new seeds can spring to life.

Inner reflection and introspection—which can sometimes demand isolation from others—are the natural inclinations of the "Saturn" individual. The Seraphim within Saturn's sphere enable cosmic memory that is felt deep within our bones—for it is the memory of our individuality across time. Saturn also brings to us the certain knowledge of our individual mission for the present lifetime. Tomberg wrote:

> A true mission on Earth serves the cause of the ennoblement and spiritualization of *that which is*, i.e. of what lives as tradition. It brings an impulse effecting the rejuvenation and intensification of tradition. Arbitrary missions, on the contrary, aim at revolutionizing the course of mankind's history and substituting specific innovations for what lives in tradition. [MOT, 353]

In *Meditations on the Tarot*, we read that, for the soul turned toward the spirit, Saturday is the day of the Holy Virgin (458). The Virgin protects our holy covenant with the Father; indeed, it is she who guards our spiritual mission until the time when we are ready to be anointed. Saturn in the birth chart enlightens us as to the nature of that mission. We will find that the matters of its house[5] will demand a great deal of our attention.

Saturn's influence can be imagined as Mary's mantle holding us near, providing us warmth and guidance. Rejoice and be glad! We raise our "star" to the zodiac as we pursue our mission and devote ourselves humbly to the missions of others. Saturn fosters resolve, discipline, and allegiance to duty and responsibility. It shows us where we can find inner strength. Negative Saturn qualities include grumpiness, negativity, and rigidity. The lower forces of Saturn can render us demanding—and even cruel.

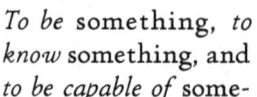 JUPITER

The letter-Arcanum "The Emperor" (IV) leads us in a meditation upon the nature of true authority, which is in the domain of every individual to differing degrees. Authority is the completely manifested divine name:

> *To be* something, *to know* something, and *to be capable of* something is what endows a person with authority. One can also say that a person has authority in proportion to what he unites within himself of the profundity of mysticism, the direct wisdom of gnosis, and the productive power of magic.... It is authority alone which is the true and unique power of law. Compulsion is only an expedient to which one takes recourse in order to remedy a lack of authority. [When authority is present,] compulsion is superfluous. [MOT, 77-78]

Therefore, the subject of the card is unarmed, for weapons are not necessary. In his right hand is a scepter, while his left hand is around his belt, which serves the function of holding impulses and personal will in check, so that he is not diverted from his post. He is leaning against his seat with legs crossed. The context of this card is *active renunciation*.

The Emperor has therefore renounced *movement* by means of his legs, and *action* by means of his arms. Furthermore, his crown signifies that he has renounced the freedom of intellectual movement. Lastly, he has renounced his personal mission in favor of the throne upon which he is qualified to reign over free beings. He is anonymous.

> The formula: *verum, sine mendacio, certum et verissimum* ["true it is, without falsehood, and certain"] therefore states the principle of epistemology (or "gnoseology") of hermetic

---

[5] The system of houses will be discussed in Part II, Chapter 6.

philosophy, with its triple touchstone. This principle can be formulated in several ways. Here is one: "That which is absolutely subjective (pure mystical experience) must objectivize itself in consciousness, and be accepted there as *true* (gnostic revelation), then prove to be *certain* by its objective fruits (sacred magic) and, lastly, prove to be *absolutely true* in the light of pure thought based on pure subjective and objective experience (hermetic philosophy).... In hermetic philosophy something is absolutely true, therefore, only when it is of divine origin and bears fruit in conformity with its origin. [MOT, 88-89]

God bless Jupiter, the lord of expansion and opportunity! One of Jupiter's greatest gifts is the ability to take the broad view—to evaluate all of the aspects of a situation from a distance, as if from Zeus's chariot—and to make the necessary connections between these aspects. Jupiter is the domain of higher thought and philosophical thinking: When something hits us "right between the eyes" (the location of the third-eye chakra), it signifies that we understand it fully. And it is the *desire to understand* that sets the Jupiter lotus flower in motion.

"Jupiter" individuals are natural leaders who take charge and delegate easily: We convey authority that inspires others. Jupiter inclines us toward risk and the defiance of boundaries: exuberance and generosity abound. Through the influence of Jupiter, we lean toward optimism and good cheer; we're interested in everything that doesn't drag us down.

The Angels of Jupiter, the Cherubim, guard sacred places; and it is indeed the Jupiter chakra in which the divine "I" of the individual is felt most strongly. Bearing a natural connection to lawfulness, Jupiter dislikes chaos. Jupiter moves around the zodiac in an orderly fashion, spending one year in each sign.

Known among stargazers as the "great benefic" for its positive influence as "the helping hand of the cosmos," its blessings can only be undone—with the speed of a lightning bolt—by unbridled egotism accompanied by a lack of gratitude. In the birth chart, Jupiter reveals in what way we exercise instinctive judgment. It shows us where, and in what manner, support will be readily available to us.

In *Meditations on the Tarot*, the author writes that Thursday is no longer the day of Jupiter, but is instead the day of the Holy Spirit (458): the force of love that weaves between creator and created. The Holy Spirit is at once the bearer of Sophia's wisdom and the Comforter spoken of by Jesus:

> But the Comforter, the Holy Spirit, whom the Father will send in my name, he will teach you all things, and bring to you remembrance of all that I have said to you. (John 14:26)

When heeding the call of fallen Jupiter, we might find ourselves out on a limb if our optimism does not align with reality. We can become bossy—even tyrannical—as self-indulgent egotism eclipses the radiant wisdom that could otherwise be our guide.

♂ MARS

"The Chariot" (VII) is the letter-Arcanum of self-mastery. It presumes as its starting point that the individual has already taken up the sacred vows of obedience, poverty, and chastity. We must first wonder: What else is there to master?

The answer lies in another more subtle temptation that is both the root and the synthesis of the other three: the temptation of *pride*—of acting "in one's own name," as master instead of servant. Mastership is not the state of being moved, but rather that of being able to set in motion. [MOT, 147-48] Jesus provides us with the archetype of mastership, for his refusal to be moved by the temptations in the wilderness is what set in motion the response from above, in the form of the ministering of Angels.

The charioteer in the card is standing in a horse-drawn chariot with a canopy; he is holding no reins and appears to be a passive occupant. He seems to be meditating. Tomberg wrote:

> The charioteer... is the victor over trials, i.e. the temptations; and if he is master, then it is thanks to himself. He is alone, standing in his chariot; no one is present to applaud him or to pay homage to him; he has no weapons—the scepter that he holds not being a weapon. If he is master, his mastership was acquired in solitude. [MOT, 152]

The failure to overcome the temptation of pride leads us by the hand toward an inflated opinion of ourselves, whereby we necessarily set others "below" us. When we seek experience of what lies behind the veil of the senses, subjecting ourselves to such inflation becomes our primary risk.

> Monasteries and spiritual orders have always known this, thanks to the immense pillar of experience which they have accumulated over millennia in the domain of the *profound life*. This is why their whole spiritual practice is based on the cultivation of *humility*. [This is because] spiritual megalomania is as old as the world. [MOT, 156, 159]

Worship and work are its remedy.

A tremendous energy pulses within the sphere of Mars, the domain of the Thrones. The glyph itself is a dynamic suggestive of forward motion and *drive*. Through the energy of Mars, we *make things happen*, in no small part due to its force of will. In fact, through the "eyes" of Mars we regard the whole of reality as a manifestation of will. Never one to laze dreamily on the couch, Mars is *always* champing at the bit—sometimes even becoming somewhat of a hothead! Although "Mars" people can lack sensitivity to the feelings of others, who can fail to admire their ability to get things done? Or their strength and courage to *not back down*? Or their pioneering spirit? Mars shows us how to remain calm in the face of turmoil, so that we aren't distracted from what we need to do.

Mars in the birth chart tells us what we put our weight behind, what we'll stand up for. It reveals the fire in our belly, and the willingness to protect others from harm. Mars is *bold*, as well as *brave*, even when wisdom might caution otherwise. Impulsiveness, aggression, hurtful speech, and a tendency to foment conflict are characteristics of Mars that we encounter in those of us who lack self-mastery. Though the typical "Mars" individual eschews diplomacy as an utter waste of time—believing as he does that a roomful of diplomats is unlikely to get anything done—he must nevertheless acquaint himself with its virtues. He will thereby gain in strength and in righteousness.

It can be difficult to have a neutral reaction to "Mars" individuals. We either admire them or we don't—although sometimes our tendency to shun our own dynamic capacity engenders our antipathy. Mars is the planet associated with the throat chakra—and therefore with the capacity for speech—through which we reveal our inner life to others (we can speak to hurt others, or to love and support them with our kind words). Mars holds the mystery of the Word: *love, made manifest*. We need the forces of Mars in order to maintain a clear perception of the material world—so that we may work within it.

The Thrones of the Mars sphere bestow upon us the willingness to battle for righteousness. Indeed, when Mars speaks the truth, it resounds throughout the cosmos. In *Meditations on the Tarot*, the author writes that Tuesday, to suprasensory perception, is no longer the day of Mars, but of the Archistrategist Michael (458), the crusader for truth who keeps the dragon underfoot.

Mars requires two years to make its way around the zodiac. He teaches us how to develop, through self-mastery, not only a *positive attitude* toward the tasks of others but also a *tactfulness* in all communications. With Michael at our side, we thirst for the truth and for humility.

Mars's negative influence can make us combative, selfish, argumentative, and domineering.

⊙ SUN

"The Magician" (I) is the letter-Arcanum of the essence of mysticism. We become mystics when we dare to elevate ourselves toward the divine creative fire. This letter-Arcanum is the first, because the exercises within it are the key to all the others:

> ["The Magician"] reveals that which is necessary to know and to will in order to enter the school of spiritual exercises whose totality comprises the Tarot.... In fact, the first and fundamental principle of esotericism ... can be rendered by the formula: *Learn at first concentration without effort; transform work into play; make every yoke that you have accepted easy and every burden that you carry light!* [MOT, 7-8]

Tomberg wrote further:

> "Concentration without effort" is burning without smoke or crackling fire. On the part of the human being, it is the act of *daring* to aspire to the supreme Reality, and this act is real and effective only when the soul is serene and the body is completely relaxed—without smoke and crackling fire. [MOT, 41]

This form of concentration—characteristic of a juggler or a tightrope walker—is a matter of bringing the consciousness from the head to the heart—from the brain to the rhythmic system. When the consciousness is thus *elevated* to a perfect calm, we can see the unity of all things through the immediate perception of their correspondences; this is the method of *analogy*. The subject of the card is a young man (standing at ease behind a table) who seems to be playing a game effortlessly. Tomberg wrote:

> [He] who makes use of the method of analogy on the intellectual plane must have worked much...before attaining the faculty of immediate perception of analogous correspondences, before becoming a "magician" or "juggler" who makes use of the analogy of beings and of things without effort, as in a game. [MOT, 19]

In our solar system, the center that holds the periphery in place is the Sun; in our chakras, it is the heart; and in the human community, it is Christ.

As the Sun rests at the center of our solar system, it works selflessly to maintain order around it. In fact, the Sun sphere—through the work of the angelic hierarchies within it—is the origin of the laws of planetary motion. The Sun exerts the necessary gravitational forces to prevent the other planets from flying off into chaos. The same can be said of the influence of the heart chakra in the human being, which has a mediating effect between the three chakras above it and the three below. The Sun confers upon us order, creativity, and direction. It quietly harmonizes polarities. Of course, the Sun also brings us warmth, morality, goodness, and integrity—shining on the good and the wicked alike. One who is "heartless" is a stranger to these qualities. The Sun bears the qualities of righteousness, mercy, and purity. It implies a state of lucid awareness.

The Sun is the regent of the impulse of freedom. It bears vitality—for the beating of its human counterpart, the heart, defines life. Just as the rhythm of the Sun is regular and unrushed, so are we in our best health when our heart does the same. People with a strong Sun influence eschew recognition and seek to maintain harmony within the group. "Sun" people quietly accept whatever it is that an experience may offer. Just as we may take for granted the glory of a sunny day, we may not readily notice the workings of the "Sun" person. When the "Sun" in our midst—or within our souls—is absent, disorder soon follows.

The Sun in the astrological chart represents our eternal divine nature and higher will, as well as the actual source of the "I" of the human being. Indeed, the sign in which the Sun is positioned is the *mantle* of the individual's "I" for that particular incarnation. As the Sun beckons us toward self-realization, its zodiacal sign sheds light upon the ideal path for our quest. When contemplating the Sun's placement in a birth chart, we can ask ourselves: *What sublime qualities are seeking expression through this individual?* We can further say that the house in which the Sun finds itself at birth further clarifies the "department" of life wherein our earthly ventures will best assist in this expression.

In *Meditations on the Tarot*, the author writes that, while it is true that Sunday is the day of the Sun with respect to the human psycho-*physical* organism, it is the day of resurrection with regard to our psycho-*spiritual* life. [MOT, 458]

Fallen Sun forces can make us egotistical, self-centered, and full of false pride. If the glory of our divine "I" is encapsulated in egotistical self-centeredness, we can easily become pawns in unrighteous agendas that mercilessly serve immoral ends.

♀ VENUS

The card that represents "The Lover" (VI), the subject of our meditation on Venus, features a young man flanked by two women, one of whom is touching his shoulder while the other points to his heart. The young man seems oblivious to the presence of the cherub above them, armed with a bow and arrow directly aimed at his shoulder. Herein, we witness how the infant archer has found the one for whom he'd been searching.

All three sacred vows (obedience, poverty, and chastity) are discussed in this letter-Arcanum, along with their corresponding temptations. Its main them, however, is *chastity*: loving with the totality of our being. The temptations and their vows can be imagined as two overlapping triangles that form a hexagram. Thus does the seal of Solomon carry the memory of paradise and the Fall.

The three vows are, in essence, memories of paradise: when man was united with God (obedience); where he possessed everything at once (poverty); and where his companion was at one and the same time his wife, his friend, his sister, and his mother (chastity).... [Total] communion between two, between one and another, which comprises the entire range of all possible relationships of spirit, soul, and body between two polarized beings, necessarily constitutes the absolute wholeness of spiritual, psychic, and physical being, in love.

[Chastity] is *living unity*. [MOT, 124]

When we are chaste, the heart becomes the center of gravity; we are then free of envy as well as indifference. Tomberg describes the second temptation in the wilderness (when the Devil said to Jesus: *If you are the Son of God, throw yourself down!*) as the "groping trial," against which chastity is our bulwark. When we are unchaste, we seek experience *in order to dispel doubt.*

Because evolution proceeds gropingly from form to form, trying and rejecting, then trying anew.... [the world of evolution] is neither the accomplishment of absolute wisdom nor absolute goodness. It is rather the work of a really vast intelligence and a very resolute will pursuing a definite aim determined by the method of "trial and error."... It is therefore the serpent... that the world of biological evolution reveals to us, and not God. It is the serpent who is the "prince of this world," and who is the author and director of the purely biological evolution following the Fall. [MOT, 142]

The flaming arrow of the cherub conveys the memory of paradise and the condition of chastity. When the arrow finds us, "trials" and "groping" are no longer necessary; we simply ask, seek, and knock—and await revelation.

You'll want to be around Venus—everyone does. Naturally happy, Venus exudes warmth and love; she is the receptive soul in every group, the *listener* to Mars's *arguer*. Her interest in the affairs of humanity is absolute. A natural diplomat, she has the ability to weave others together by showing them what they share in common. Not a wonder, then, that the Archai of the *Venus* sphere are the beings who ensure that our lives are strewn with opportunities to connect with the karmic group proper to each incarnation.

Venus is not terribly interested in what we are thinking—for she longs instead to understand what lives in our hearts. This, however, leads us to one of her downfalls, namely weighing too heavily on the sympathies and antipathies of herself and others. Venus stands for love and beauty, and supports artistry of all kinds. She bestows upon us refinement and sociability.

Venus orbits the Sun in 225 days (i.e., in about seven and a half months), but the time between superior *or* inferior conjunctions is much longer—nineteen and a half months (583 days) on average. The time that passes between superior or inferior conjunctions is known as its *synodic period*. We'll choose the superior conjunction for our example.

During a superior conjunction, we find the Earth, the Sun, and Venus in precise alignment:

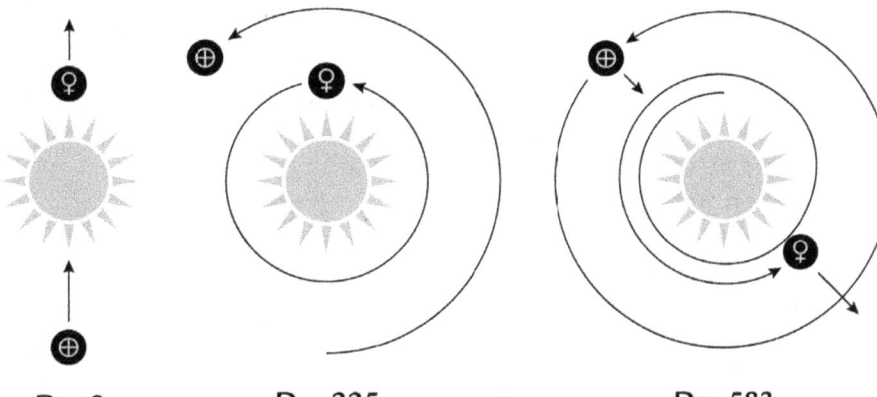

Day 0   Day 225   Day 583

Venus completes her solar orbit two hundred twenty-five days later;[6] however, because the Earth hasn't had time to complete *its* turn around the Sun, alignment with the Sun and Venus is impossible: Another *year* must pass before this occurs!

This discrepancy explains why Venus requires eight years (five conjunctions × 583 days) to inscribe her pentagram in the cosmos—despite the fact that she orbits the Sun in 225 days. (The same principle applies to the conjunctions of the Sun and Mercury, but Mercury's orbital and synodic periods are much shorter—88 days and 116 days, respectively.)

Venus is also considered a *benefic*, meaning that she brings blessings and ease. But when expressed through poor moral judgment, these qualities can result in a sort of indolence—a lack of get-up-and-go and a willingness to allow others to take the lead too readily. Of course, Venus is foremost the planet of artistry and beauty in all its forms, bearing also the qualities of equanimity, peace, and balance of soul—the latter defined by Tomberg as "spiritual health." Venus in the chart shows us *what we love*, and how we enjoy ourselves.

Traditional astrology would have us guard against Venus's potential for laziness and jealous envy, but through the study of astrosophy we learn that Venus has a higher connection to all that transpired during the Passion of Christ. In *Meditations on the Tarot*, the author notes that Friday's long association with Venus has given way to Calvary, to Christ crucified (p. 458).

We can see it in the glyph: a human being upon a cross. Therefore, in order to reap Venusian rewards, we must accept the righteousness of karmic necessity (the cross that we must carry)—an acceptance that leads to both joy and sorrow. Until we bear our personal cross, we will lack a certain freedom in the matters of the house where Venus is found. Through our personal Calvary experience—as our hands and feet are nailed to our destiny—our hearts open to receive Christ.

Negative Venus traits can manifest as idleness and a tendency to be wishy-washy. When our hearts are unchaste, we might project our own lack of peace onto others, whereby our rivalrous jealousy nails them to accusations born of our hidden envy. In the obsessive accumulation of material possessions, vanity can mask our lack of self-love.

---

6   This is presented here from the perspective of the *northern* hemisphere. (Remember: from the perspective of the *southern* hemisphere, both the zodiac and the orbits of the planets proceed *clockwise*.)

☿ MERCURY

In the card representing the letter-Arcanum "The Pope," (V) we observe a man with a white beard seated before two pillars. He is in the process of conferring a blessing upon a small group kneeling before him. He wears on his head a large diadem and holds a staff topped with a triple cross.

We are directed immediately toward an act of benediction. Tomberg wrote:

> Now, benediction is more than a simple good wish made for others; it is also more than a magical impress of personal thought and will upon others. It is the putting into action of divine power transcending the individual thought and will of the one who is blessed as well as the one who is pronouncing the blessing. [MOT, 100]

What has occurred before the scene in the card is *prayer*. Prayer and benediction are the phases of our spiritual respiration that move in different directions; we "breathe out" our prayers to the spiritual world — with hope and humility — and "breathe in" the celestial response to these prayers. We can liken this to the circulation of the blood, in which we can identify a phase of "prayer" (after the red cells have offloaded their oxygen in the capillaries) and a phase of "benediction" (when the blessed oxygen — bestowed by the spiritual world — can be taken up by the red cells, to be circulated again).

The Pope guards the equilibrium of our spiritual respiration — between prayer and benediction, between day and night, and between human effort and divine grace:

> The Pope is always at the middle of a conflict between ideal truth and actual truth.... And this conflict is a *wound* — namely the fifth wound, *the wound of the heart*. For if the Emperor has four wounds, the Pope has five. [MOT, 105]

To clairvoyant vision, the Mercury chakra is seen as two overlapping pentagrams. Tomberg explained:

> The pentagram as the sign of *intellectual autocracy*, i.e. the emancipated human personality, is *good* when it is the expression of the personality whose will is united and bound to the fullness of the manifestation of Unity (the decad); and it is *evil* when it expresses the will of the personality separated from this Unity....
>
> It is only the *pentagram of the five wounds* which is the effective sign of personal sacred magic, whilst the *pentagram of the five currents of personal will*,[7] no matter how the points of this pentagram are turned, is the effective sign for the imposition of the personal will of the operator on beings weaker than him — it is always a fundamentally tyrannical act. [MOT, 108]

The "gates" of the five currents of personal or arbitrary will can be closed through the acquisition of the five blessed wounds; this entails the practice of obedience, chastity, and poverty. Once closed to the forces *below*, they can then be filled from *above* by the absolutely pure will of the divine.

Swift, joyful Mercury brings us *levity* in body and soul. The Mercury influence is essentially sanguine; when we watch happy children move about among their peers, we witness Mercury spin its magic. Mercury delights in social interactions, communication, and fun; moreover, it is the "Mercury" individual who can be seen trying to draw others into the social mix with what might be termed a healing art. However, Mercury's need for change — the next bit of excitement — can cause us to become both fickle and easily bored. Because no grass grows under Mercury's feet, conscious effort is required to develop loyalty and the ability to bring tasks to their conclusion.

Mercury also bears the *light of awakening*, forming the basis of our human intelligence: logical thinking, along with flexibility and speed in making mental connections. Our Mercury forces coordinate the assimilation of sense impressions,

---

7   These are otherwise known as "gates of hell." They are: the desire to be great, the desire to take and to keep, and the desire to advance and to hold onto at the expense of others.

thoughts, and motivating impulses. Mercury also reveals to us the nature of our interpersonal relationships, as well as the warm interest in others on which such connections depend. The challenge for "Mercury" people is that of achieving stillness and rest. (The Mercury mind can spin at such speed that cosmic thoughts can find no purchase!) Its house position in the chart tells us of where our minds will find both sustenance and challenge. As the two pentagrams come into harmony, consciousness increases—thus does that which was previously fleeting gain depth. Moreover, through an interest in all things, our minds gain autonomy of consciousness in both day and night worlds. Mercury shows us where forgiveness can bring healing.

The Archangels of the Mercury sphere bestow us with adaptability and inventiveness. In Mercury we find an ancient association with the healing arts—within and apart from the practice of medicine. Healing, which is accomplished through cooperation with the wisdom of nature, requires that our judgment remains unaffected by the currents of our personal will. Such healing, in itself, offers a description of the Mercury chakra—the 10-petalled lotus flower—which appears before clairvoyant vision as an *upward*-pointing pentagram of thought superimposed upon the *downward*-pointing pentagram of will. Without the subjugation of the personal will, the Winged Messenger is unable to bring cosmic wisdom to human deeds.

Although only 88 days are required for Mercury to circle the Sun, it has a synodic rhythm of about four months—meaning that four months separate *superior* conjunctions as well as *inferior* conjunctions. Thus, within a year, three sets of conjunctions (inferior and superior) will occur.

In *Meditations on the Tarot*, the author reveals that Wednesday is no longer the day of Mercury, but of the human pastors of mankind (458). This suprasensible perception is an expression of the highest qualities of Mercury: interconnectedness and healing.

The impulses from lower Mercury can make us restless, flighty, nervous, and superficial. If we become ensnared by all the "noise" in our surroundings, our will is rendered incapable of autonomous action—we are then tossed hither and yon, lacking the ability to bring order to our thinking.

 MOON

"The Empress" (III) is the letter-Arcanum of sacred magic—magic performed by one who has become an instrument of divine power. All magic owes its execution to the power of the subtle over the dense; and in the case of sacred magic, it is the divine (the "subtle") that rules over our consciousness (the "dense").

On the card is the image of a crowned woman who holds a scepter and a coat of arms emblazoned with an eagle. Tomberg wrote:

> The crowned head indicates the power of the Divine over consciousness; the right arm (according to the viewer of the card), which bears a scepter topped by a cross mounted on a globe of gold, represents the power of consciousness over force; and the left arm, which carries a shield bearing an eagle, signifies the power of energy over matter....
>
> The crown is the *divine authorization* of magic. It is only magic crowned from above that is not usurpatory. The crown is that which renders it legitimate. The scepter is *magical power*.... The shield bearing an eagle shows the *aim* of magical power; it is its emblem and its motto, which reads: "Liberation in order to ascend." [MOT, 54]

Sacred magic—whose archetype lies within the ministry of Christ—never encroaches upon freedom, but instead seeks to restore the freedom to see, hear, walk, live, and to be ourselves. In addition to freeing us from our infirmities, sacred magic liberates us from doubt, fear, hate, apathy, and despair. [MOT, 61] We need only imagine ourselves present at one of Christ's many miracles to know this must be so. Sacred magic was the essence of life before the Fall.

Behold, I am the handmaid of the Lord. This is the prerequisite attitude of soul in order to be the instrument of sacred magic—which manifests by way of *miracles*:

> Yes, the miraculous does exist, for *life* is only a series of miracles, if we understand by "miracle" not the absence of cause (i.e., that it would not be caused by anyone or anything—which would be more the concept of "pure chance"), but rather the visible effect of an invisible cause, or the effect on a lower plane due to a cause on a higher plane. [MOT, 67]

The ability to eclipse the Sun is a power that belongs to the Moon alone. This depends entirely upon its proper distance from the Earth; were it any closer or farther away, eclipse of the Sun would not be possible. We experience an eclipse of the Sun inwardly when we leave open the "gates of hell" of the root chakra, which serve as evil's points of entry into our souls. In contrast, the *spiritual intention* of the eclipse is to call forth the higher, moral forces of will—the creative light of consciousness within ourselves—in order to overcome the personal (or "lower") will, which resides primarily in subconscious realms. The Moon symbolizes the orientation of this lower will in the human being: that which stands between us and the Father, the Son, and the Holy Spirit. In *Meditations on the Tarot* it is stated that, with respect to the soul turned toward the spirit, Monday is now the day of the Holy Trinity. [MOT, 458]

Because the Moon suggests obscurity, our meditations on its nature lead us to the following question: *In what ways does our soul eclipse our spiritual light?* And yet, the Moon also reflects the divine light of the Sun—thus muting a radiance that would otherwise be unendurable to look at. Similarly, it is *reflected* sunlight that has the capacity to make visible what lies in the darkness of the subconscious, whereby it might be evaluated with reason and conscience.

The Moon's sidereal orbit is defined as its 360° journey around the zodiac; this requires 27.3 days—exactly one tenth of the average human gestation. However, the time between Full Moons—its *synodic orbit*[8]—is 29½ days. This is because the Moon, in addition to the 360° of the full circle, must also cover the distance of the *Sun's movement* since the last Full Moon. (Those who don't mind calculations will note that the Moon travels 12° each day, requiring two and a half days to move through one zodiacal sign.)

Though we tend to think of our will-forces as emerging from the conscious mind, Steiner explained that the opposite is true—that it is actually the subconscious force of will that engenders the *thought* (or, *idea*) of wanting something! As such, the Moon represents the way we react to the world "without thinking"; it points to where our deep, unexplained sensitivities lie. These behaviors are rooted in the past through karma. As we develop spiritually, and the darkness of the subconscious is thus diminished, "doing what comes naturally" gradually gives way to behavior that is morally inspired. This is the meaning of "having the Moon under our feet."

Through the Moon, we encounter the forces of generation and heredity—i.e., the horizontal bloodline (the "false vine"). This is another tug from the past. Familial heredity has the power to anchor us there, leading to stagnation: *Am I destined for substance abuse? Or for an unhappy home life?* Some of these hereditary challenges might be yours to take up and overcome, while others can be properly passed over and discarded. Sorting these attachments is part of our "Moon work."

The Moon in the birth chart indicates where we may encounter self-doubt, and where we feel the least comfortable. *This discomfort is a reflection of the karmic work that is yet to be accomplished.* Shedding light on our tendency to nurture, it echoes the early relationship with our mother. Moreover, it not only shows us where we will experience frequent changes—it also confers the flexibility to adapt to these changes with grace.

Perhaps most noticeably, the Moon is reflective of *outer* life that is visible to others—our "comfortable" behaviors that stem from past experiences. The fallen instincts of the Moon tether us to behaviors that simultaneously chain us to the past—and mask the higher nature that is the true essence of each human being. Indeed, an overattachment to the past is at the same time a renunciation of growth.

---

8 The synodic orbit of the Moon refers to the completion of a full cycle of phases, e.g. from Full Moon to Full Moon. This orbit is greater than 360° because the Sun has been moving, too, and the Moon must "catch up." In the autumn of 2021, the Full Moon shone from 3° Pisces in September and from 2° Aries in October; therefore, the distance the Moon had to travel to complete its synodic orbit was 389° (360 + 29 = 389).

The Moon's *lower* forces can make us moody, insecure, and needy. In contrast, *higher* Moon forces reflect the Sun of our "I"; they awaken intuition — our immediate recognition of this reflection. When we bring the sunlight down to our feet, i.e. when we "stand upon the Moon," we are able to do what the gods need us to do. *This is sacred magic.*

THE TRANSCENDENTAL PLANETS

Chapter 8 of Robert Powell's second volume of *Hermetic Astrology* is not to be missed. Every once in a while you read something that gives you the impression that the tilt of the axis of the Earth has changed. This chapter is one such something!

Two aspects of Chapter 8 will be discussed here. Firstly, Powell links the dates of the discoveries of Uranus, Neptune, and Pluto to disruptive world events that perfectly characterize the nature of these planets. Secondly, he makes it clear that the transcendental planets speak to humanity of invisible worlds and of the spiritual hierarchies within them. However, there is an attendant warning: When we remain ignorant of these forces, or are morally unprepared to receive them, they can cause tremendous destruction. We ignore them at our peril.

In contrast to the earthly metals long identified as associated with (or, as "remnants of") the classical planets,[9] vestiges of Uranus, Neptune, and Pluto are trapped in the Earth as *subearthly* forces:

Uranus: trapped/fallen light.
Neptune: trapped/fallen sound.
Pluto: trapped/fallen life.

These forces can also be characterized as the manifestations of the thought, feeling, and will nature of the anti-Christ — *and through our encounters with them, we come to know evil.*

Were we perfect individuals, these rising subearthly forces would find no one to adhere to. As it is, we attract them when we place the earthly above the spiritual through *doubt*; when we are led to *hatred* by instincts that originate in the darkness of the subconscious; and when we seek to subjugate, through *fear*, the will of others to our own. These are the temptations of Uranus, Neptune, and Pluto. If a positive spin can be put on these personal and collective trials, it is that *they serve to challenge our attachment to the material world*, for the transcendentals have the power to bring us to our knees — the position in which we often find ourselves when we turn to the world of spirit for help.

Because there exists a collective influence of the transcendentals, they can engender historic events. Given the collective state of humanity, we can well imagine that many of these events have been destructive. For those moved by the study of history, Richard Tarnas's *Cosmos and Psyche* offers a rich and engaging chronicle of world events that have fallen under their sway.

The personal and collective antidote to these temptations lies in the practice of the three sacred vows. *Poverty* is not only a thirst for the truth, but also a consciousness of the spiritual world as superior to all that exists in the material realm. *Chastity* allows us to bear witness to the eternity of love; consciousness that is guided by conscience and the clear light of reason is *chaste*. *Obedience to the will of God* entails absolute humility. When these temptations are overcome — which thus presumes moral development — the blessings of cosmic intelligence (Uranus), cosmic harmony (Neptune), and cosmic life (Pluto) are within reach.

⛢ URANUS

In "The Tower of Destruction" (XVI), we enter the school of humility. The bolt of lightning that blasts the stone tower to smithereens represents a celestial *intervention*. It functions as an encounter with reality for those who have "constructed" a closed and absolute system — an

---

9 These are as follows: Saturn/lead, Jupiter/tin, Mars/iron, Sun/gold, Mercury/quicksilver, Venus/copper, and Moon/silver.

intellectual apparatus — that endeavors to be self-sufficient — and is thereby at odds with divine law. Whoever creates a *structure* not in harmony with heaven is creating a *cloud* in heaven — and thereby *seeds a thunderstorm*.¹⁰ From Tomberg:

> One can neither build it [truth] nor possess it as a finished and completed structure: It must be created unceasingly by the '*fire* from above' — this is the *orientation* in all problems and tasks, but not a personal *possession* at one's own disposal.¹¹

The tower is reminiscent of the Fall. It represents a shift from a *vertical* attitude of soul to a *horizontal* one that is characteristic of the world of the serpent — wherein humility is scorned:

> [The] dawn of humanity did not take place either in a *desert*, where nothing happens, or even in a *jungle*, where everything sprouts forth and grows without the regulating and directing control of the Spirit, or, lastly, in the conditions of a city or *town* where nothing sprouts forth and grows but where everything is caused and done through the regulation and direction of the Spirit. A "garden" is thus a state of the world where there is cooperation and equilibrium between Spirit and Nature....
>
> The primordial and eternal mission of mankind is thus to cultivate and maintain the "garden"; i.e. the world in a state of equilibrium and cooperation between Spirit and Nature. [MOT, 439-40]

Let us resolve not to substitute the *fabricated* for the *revealed*!

The Uranian blend of freedom, originality, and humanitarianism has the power to change the world. Uranus encourages us to go our own way, to think independently, and to know the truth. Uranian thoughts can come to us on the charged tail of a lightning bolt (the "Aha!" moments) or in tiny floating sparks that capture our attention and set us on a new path of inquiry. Each one of us — even those of us who are not thinkers of great stature — is capable of receiving a flash of imagination that, when joined by those of others, makes possible the revelation of larger ideas and concepts.

The natural adversary of all things stodgy, Uranus has the unique ability to blow away the cobwebs — those that have collected on the outdated structures of our lives, and on familiar thoughts that we have allowed to become rigid and counterproductive. Gusts of fresh air can do wonders — but sometimes they are not enough.

The lightning bolt perfectly describes the sudden action of Uranus. It's not only shocking, it's also exciting, unexpected, and *upsetting*! At its most benign, the bolt of lightning can jolt us into a state of heightened attention. This might be all we need to set us on a path of natural growth, one that requires patience and humility. The humble understand that there is no earthly system of thought or system of governance that can set itself above the light of World Thoughts: They will never mistake stones for bread. Happy to toil anonymously, they have no need to seek recognition for their work.

If, however, humility remains elusive and we feel a longing to exalt ourselves — to build a "tower" above others (such as the Tower of Babel), lightning has another function entirely. In *Meditations on the Tarot*, in the letter-Arcanum titled "The Tower of Destruction," the charged bolt is described as *the means* of the inevitable humiliation that will be experienced by those who have "built a tower" to replace revelation from heaven. *The lightning bolt is divine reality from above that is brought to bear upon the questionable activity from below.* The tower reduced to rubble is the symbol of this humiliation. [MOT, 444] When we are able to recognize this humiliation for what it is, we are enlightened: Our thoughts are then freed from the tower we have constructed for them.

Robert Powell has established a link between subearthly Uranian forces and the thought life of the anti-Christ, which is *electric* in nature. If we imagine divine light as the companion of divine truth, we must think of the trapped light (known as "electricity") as *the accomplice of abstract, materialistic intellectualism*. Light that

---

10   Tomberg, *Meditations on the Tarot* (2022 edition), 670; and *The Wandering Fool* (San Rafael, CA: LogoSophia, 2009), 84. *The Wandering Fool* has been integrated into the 2022 edition of *Meditations on the Tarot* in a section titled "Early Studies on the Fourteenth through the Twenty-Second Major Arcana of the Tarot."
11   Tomberg, *Meditations on the Tarot* (2022 edition), 672; and *The Wandering Fool*, 86.

is thus trapped is enchained by personal positions and ideas; it can be likened to an eclipse of the Sun, seen imaginatively as the occulting of divine light by human intellectualism. We can become vehicles of cosmic light[12] only if we free ourselves from this perverted intellectualism. This can be achieved through the vow of poverty, which can be understood outside of the materialistic construct as *a thirst for the truth*.

Uranus in the astrological chart signifies where we will experience sudden and unexpected changes, as well as flashes of brilliance and originality. This will require agility and an open mind toward the future, for sometimes it happens that Uranus takes from us — or calls upon us to leave behind — something we hold very dear.

Negative Uranus traits include agitation, contrariness, nervousness, and a lack of warmth. Under its influence, we can make hasty changes — without thinking through the consequences!

♆ NEPTUNE

"The World" (XXII) sets before us an image of the world as a work of art. In the card, a naked woman is dancing. She holds a wand and a philter, and is surrounded by the four holy living creatures: the Bull, the Lion, the Eagle, and the Angel — which are representative of the four elements. Tomberg wrote:

> [The] fifth essence — at the center of the four elements — is Joy: By dancing, the naked woman directs with her magic wand the circle of blossoming life whose manifestation is the four elements which surround it.[13]

What has this to do with the modern conception of joy, which is more or less the pursuit of "feeling good"? Very little, it would seem! "Feeling good" implies satisfaction, whereas joy is the result of the quest for *truth*. From Tomberg:

> [Just] as there are ecstasies and illuminations from the Holy Spirit, so there are intoxications from the spirit of mirage — which is named the "false Holy Spirit" in Christian Hermeticism. Here is a criterion for distinguishing them: If you seek for the *joy* of artistic creation, spiritual illumination, and mystical experience, you will inevitably more and more approach the sphere of the spirit of mirage and become more and more accessible to it; if you seek for *truth* through artistic creation, spiritual illumination, and mystical experience, you will then approach the sphere of the Holy Spirit, and you will open yourself more and more to the Holy Spirit. The revelations of truth issuing from the Holy Spirit *bring with them* joy and consolation (consolatory spirit = *Paraclete*), but are only *followed* by the joy which *results* from the revealed truth...whilst the revelations that we have called "mirages" follow the joy — and are born from the joy. [MOT, 629-30]

Applying the criterion above confers the sobriety necessary to avoid inundation by the "stolen water" of illusion. The dancer in the card reminds us that illusions always contain some measure of truth, and therefore have the capacity to be very persuasive.

The negative forces of Neptune have the ability to *immerse us* in the darkness of our instinctivity with the power of the Niagara River. Neptune's subearthly deposits bear the temptation of feelings that are magnetized. Such feelings move endlessly — as if moving from magnetic pole to magnetic pole — between our sympathies and antipathies. There can develop a *self-satisfaction* in this polarization of the feeling life, for our preferences — even hedonism — are at the center of every decision; reason and conscience no longer hold sway. Within this magnetic field, truth can no longer be discerned, and we become susceptible to the "intoxication" of sweet lies. Once we become confused, the inundation of delusion soon follows. *Mass consciousness*

---

12 This is referred to on the path of inner development as the stage of *Illumination*. The further stages are *Inspiration* and *Intuition*.
13 Tomberg, *Meditations on the Tarot* (2022 edition), 692-93; and *The Wandering Fool*, 112.

can be considered as a current in this river of deception.[14]

Powell describes the negative subearthly forces of Neptune as an expression of the feeling life of the anti-Christ, which is magnetic in nature. This entity carries a hatred (or, antipathy) for all that is good, loving, kind, noble, and charitable — as well as an attraction (or, sympathy) to cruelty and to the triumph of the strong over the weak. "Magnetized feeling," based on any number of arbitrary factors, encourages us to hate whole groups of people: *We become unable to see them as individuals*. Powell's primary example of Neptunian illusion is communism. Lenin, he states, lived under the illusion that he was working for the betterment of mankind.

> That this was an illusion is evident from the fact that he allowed the perpetration of monstrous and inhuman deeds to be executed in the accomplishing of his aims. The true Good, on the other hand, cannot do otherwise than spread goodness.[15]

Magnetized feeling renders us unable to discern truth from illusion. This is because our primary reason for everything is based upon our personal sympathies and antipathies. It's almost as if our feelings create a barrier around us that conscience and reason cannot penetrate; we thereby "cast ourselves from the pinnacle." The practice of *chastity* (in its deeper, spiritual sense) bears the power to resist such illusions. Taking up this vow enables us to distinguish truth from intoxication. Temperance, or *balance of the soul*, underlies chastity and engenders *purity* — which can make us receptive to the inflow of Inspiration from the spiritual world.

For prepared souls, Neptune opens us to the spirit. It brings about a rending of the temple veil, making possible the faculty of spiritual communication (*spiritual hearing*) on a very high level; thus does feeling become permeated with cosmic sound (Inspiration). Neptune bestows upon us ideals of all sorts, and those of a *spiritual* nature have the ability to sustain us throughout all of the sorrows of our lives. Neptune encourages us to care for the weak and needy — the "strays" among us. She reminds us that human souls are woven together.

In order to push us closer to spirit, Neptune's unique method is *dissolution*: What we have established and built here on Earth, and within ourselves, can be carried away in an instant as if by rising floodwater. Sometimes, we are left with no choice but to start over — whereupon the "real world" might seem to us more illusory as the grip of material possessions and of public honors loosens a bit.

The house of Neptune in the birth chart will reveal the domain in life in which we will have the most tenuous hold — the one in which we might have to reinvent ourselves repeatedly. It also indicates where we are encouraged to be guided by spiritual ideals.

When heeding the call of lower Neptune, we can find ourselves unable to "come down to Earth." We can be deceitful, easily manipulated, and impractical.

PLUTO

Meditating on evil — the subject of "The Devil" (XV) — can lead to *identification* or even *communion* with it. The study of "The Devil" thus poses a grave danger, that of immersing ourselves in its toxic juices. This danger can be avoided through the practice of *naming* evil and then giving it what Tomberg refers to as the "knowing glance." He wrote:

---

14 Mattias Desmet, author of *The Psychology of Totalitarianism*, articulated the phenomenon of "mass formation" that emerged during the recent pandemic. This term takes us beyond "mass consciousness" (what the majority thinks and believes, whether true or not), into the realm of totalitarian control — in which dissent is actively punished by those in power. Desmet cites *loneliness* as one of its causes; indeed, the disruption of family and community bonds are fundamental to all who aspire to totalitarian control. Moreover, every tyranny offers benefits to those who comply: access to cultural events, purported superiority over others, protection from losing one's livelihood, freedom from persecution, etc. It's very difficult *not* to conform to these ideologies — so much so that even those who previously rejected them might eventually embrace them as their own.
15 Robert Powell, *Hermetic Astrology*, vol. 2. (San Rafael, CA: Sophia Foundation Press, 1989), 321.

One ought not to occupy oneself with evil, other than in keeping a certain distance and a certain reserve, if one wishes to avoid the risk of paralyzing the creative élan and a still greater risk—that of furnishing arms to the powers of evil.... One can understand [evil] only at a distance, as an *observer* of its phenomenology. [MOT, 403]

The image on the card brings before our eyes a large figure with horns and wings. The wings are nothing like those of an Angel; they resemble instead the wings of a bat. The figure is naked and has the features of both man and woman: It is androgynous. Below him stand two small figures, one male and one female, that are chained to the pedestal on which the devil stands. It does not inspire; *it enchains and directs*. The he-devil and the she-devil have forfeited their freedom!

What is the significance of the androgynous nature of the devil? It represents the perversion of sufficing unto ourselves:

> The smaller he-devil and she-devil... are chained to his pedestal: *He* is their *ideal*, and the one does not seek the other in order to find the *other*, but to make the other a part of *itself*....
> [The devil] is free of the universal attraction, being attracted to oneself through oneself in oneself.[16]

The devil is the model of self-absorption; it is a closed circuit. How are we to protect ourselves? Tomberg wrote:

> Good does not combat evil in the sense of destructive action. It "combats" it by the sole fact of its *presence*. Just as darkness gives way to the presence of light, so does evil give way before the presence of good....
> Light drives out darkness. [MOT, 421]

The will-forces of the anti-Christ find expression in the subearthly remnants of Pluto. They can be defined by the longing for power over others: *My will be done.* Mad dictators—becoming too numerous to count—serve as ready examples of this impulse. Though initially able to somehow convince the masses that their intentions are righteous, all dictators eventually rule by fear and violence. Pluto instills fear, which inhibits our proper relationship to the future and to the spiritual world. Moreover, it seduces us with endless justifications for our questionable deeds. Sex and money have long been associated with Pluto, as both are easily put into power's service.

Pluto confers ambition. "Pluto people" have a penchant for getting to the bottom of things. Being both perceptive and brilliant, they are experts in strategy.

Tomberg described the vow of obedience *not* as the subjugation of one's will to another, but as *the faculty of knowing and recognizing the voice of truth*. This sacred vow of obedience to God—*Thy will be done*, or acting in accordance with conscience and reason—can thwart will-to-power in the human being. Of course, as there are few among us who live exclusively by this precept, earthquakes abound—the earthquake being a physical manifestation of Pluto's hold on the human being. Like an earthquake, Pluto—once set in motion—is relentless and unstoppable. It upsets the notion of a stable world beneath our feet.

Pluto's negative influence can make us antisocial and unforgiving—even spiteful. This can cause us to seek out (and even delight in) power struggles.

Powell connects the discovery of atomic power and the negative forces of Pluto, describing them as *trapped life*. Indeed, the will-life of the anti-Christ comes to expression in the human will in the manner of atomic power; it emerges from the subconscious depths, the residence of our lower will-forces. Uncontrolled will-impulses lead to violence—even sexual violence—and reveal a rejection of the sacred foundation of all that lives: They are essentially *anti-life*, leading to union with evil.

Yet Pluto also holds the key to union of another sort—with the *divine*. Those who practice obedience will find within the forces of Pluto the primal life-will of the cosmos, through which cosmic love and Intuition may be cultivated in the human being. Thus may will-to-power be transformed into will-to-service.

Pluto's effect upon humanity as a whole can lead to *revolution*; its position in the birth chart will reveal where in our lives "a personal

---

16 Tomberg, *Meditations on the Tarot* (2022 edition), 666-68; and *The Wandering Fool*, 80.

revolution"—or, at the very least, very challenging crises—might occur. Pluto shows us—if not where power will tempt us—where we'll need to wrestle our personal will-forces into submission, to the extent that this is necessary. But it is also true that Pluto can bestow upon us the power to regenerate, to transform what is dead and useless into *new life*. This is dependent, however, on our ability to courageously face all that fills us with dread.

THE MOON'S NODES

The Moon's path around the Earth forms a great circular plane that is not precisely aligned with the great circle of the ecliptic. Although the center of these two circles is the same (it is the Earth itself), the path of the Moon and the path of the Sun cross in only two places. These crossing points are deeply significant for a number of reasons. Known as the Moon's North and South Nodes, they represent (according to Steiner) *portals to the astral world*. By way of these two points, our world is opened to the starry realm.

Eclipses of the Sun and Moon can happen only when the luminaries and the Earth are aligned at one or both of the Nodes; therefore, the Nodes can also be characterized as "places of eclipse." The Babylonian stargazers were keen chroniclers of eclipses—without the aid of telescopes, slide rules, or computers (!)—they observed that eclipses occurred in predictable sequences.[17] Whether or not they also recognized the regression of the Nodes through the fixed constellations, they nevertheless beheld them clairvoyantly as they experienced eclipses of the Sun and Moon.

The Moon's Nodes, always 180° apart, are joined by an axis that runs through the astrological chart. To better form an imaginative picture of the Nodes, we look to the annual path of the Sun around the Earth. In addition to a high point (which occurs at the summer solstice) and a low point (at the winter solstice), the Sun's path crosses the equator twice (at the equinoxes, or vernal and autumn points). If we were to make an analogy between the orbits of the Sun and Moon around the Earth, the North Node of the Moon could be called the "vernal point" of its orbit: the point at which it crosses from below the ecliptic to the space *above* it. Likewise, the South Node of the Moon could be imagined as its "autumnal point": the degree at which the Moon crosses from the space above the ecliptic to the space *below* it.

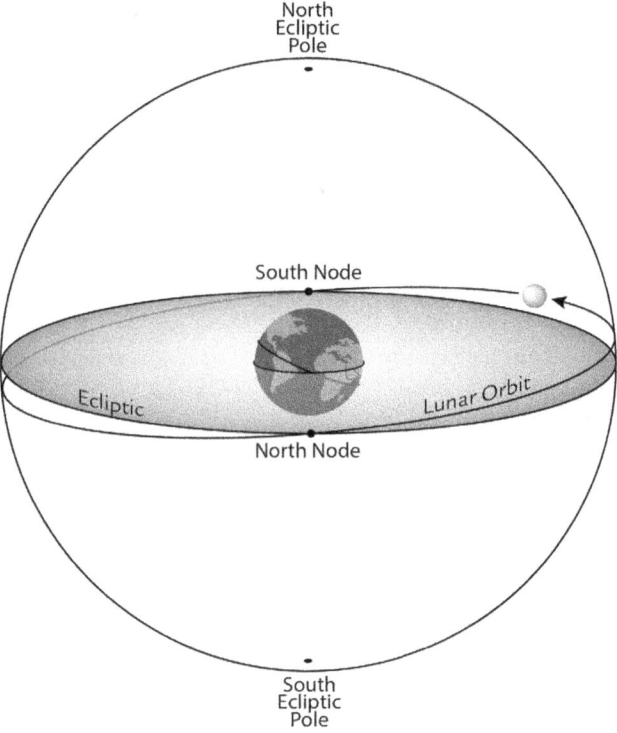

The orbit of the Moon around the Earth

Since the Moon sphere is the *repository of our karma*, we can be sure that the Nodes spin a karmic thread and represent an important indication within the astrological chart. Any planet that is within a few degrees of either Node will exert a powerful influence during the incarnation. Put another way, the forces of that planet will be tied up inextricably with our karma.

There exist many different conceptions of the relative influence of the two Nodes—enough to fill a small library. One theme that seems to weave through them all is their association to *karma*—and, I would add—to *karmic connections*. This, of course, is supported by Steiner's

---

17   This is now known as the *saros period*, which is just over 18 years. An eclipse "repeats" when the Moon next returns to the same phase, the same Node, and the same distance from the Earth. Modern astronomers have given each eclipse a *saros number*—which it shares with all the other eclipses in the same series. A *saros series* has a "life" that averages some 1400 years; it is "born" at one of the poles, moves north or south across the equatorial region, and finishes its "life" at the opposite pole.

description of the nodal axis as an opening to the angelic realm, wherein our karma is determined (and guarded) until the next incarnation begins. Returns and transits [18] that involve the Nodes can have profound consequences, as they represent "openings" to this portal.

Fundamental to most conceptions of the Nodes is the difference between them; in general, the North Node is connected to the future and to growth, while the South Node represents what is in our best interest to move beyond. Vedic astrology refers to them as the dragon's head (Rahu, the North Node) and the dragon's tail (Ketu, the South Node). These characterizations illuminate the importance of remembering that they are *"one dragon"* and must — like all opposites — be considered together. Sometimes we can gain a sense of the two Nodes' importance in our biography by simply look at the two zodiacal signs, as well as the two houses that they link. But in my experience, this is not always the case.

If we were to put an anthroposophical spin on the Nodes, we might look to the North Node for *Sun karma*, and to the South for *Moon karma*. We can begin to get a sense for this by way of a comparison of the North and South Nodes to the vernal and autumn points of the Sun. On the first day of spring (when the annual path of the Sun crosses the equator from below to above), new impulses *descend* from the starry realm, reaching to us from the future. In the natural world, leaf buds form and reach *upward*. Will we respond in kind? The efforts that we exert in service of this future form our *Sun karma*. Our Sun karma bears the thoughts, words, and deeds that have the power to influence the future; *the North Node is its gateway*. The path offered by the North Node is one of growth that is elucidated by both its zodiacal sign and its house placement.

At the South Node, we experience the "autumn point" of the orbit of the Moon. Just as trees begin to shed their leaves when fall arrives, the nodal autumn point heralds a time of letting go. Many astrological traditions posit that the South Node is irrevocably attached to past karma — known in astrosophy as *Moon karma*. In contrast to Sun karma, Moon karma *ascends* from below. It comprises both karmic debt (our unfinished business) and habitual, comfortable patterns from the past. In the latter case, the South Node might be imagined as the favorite pair of sweatpants that we hesitate to give up, long after the elastic has given way. You might have worn them as you watched every episode of all fourteen seasons of *Dallas*.[19] If you happen to pass a mirror when you're wearing those sweatpants, *you know for certain that you can do better*. In other words, we can "fall into" the South Node behaviors unconsciously. The zodiacal sign and house placement of the South Node (always directly opposite those of the North Node) illuminate the characteristics of our Moon karma.

But is this really relevant? Steiner made no distinction between the North and South Nodes. Could it be said that his reference to them as portals to the angelic realm is *dispositive* — in other words, that it supercedes the myriad distinctions between them? I recommend that you first study them as a united pair. And remember: Each of us "exists" at the midpoint of the nodal axis of the Moon!

Furthermore, it's worthwhile to take note of all planets that aspect the Nodes in a birth chart — keeping in mind that planets cannot be in aspect to just one of the Nodes.[20] Carefully observe the effects of the return of the Nodes to their zodiacal degrees at this birth; also observe the planetary transits — particularly of the transcendentals — across the Nodal axis. You will then have gained enough insight to conclude whether there is anything to be gained by distinguishing between the two Nodes.

Of course, the direction of the Moon's movement across the nodal points is relative to the location of the observer. Let's return to our discussion of the vernal and autumn points of the Sun — but this time from the perspective of the southern hemisphere. We can observe that the

---

18   These subjects are taken up in Part IV, Chapter 3.
19   I actually did this!
20   A planet that is conjunct the South Node is simultaneously opposite the North Node. A planet in square aspect to one Node is in square aspect to the other Node. The same principle applies to the four *angles* of the chart: specific points that establish the four quadrants therein. Known as the Ascendant, Descendant, EZ, and EN, these points define the horizontal and vertical axes in the chart. They are always 90° apart. If, for example, the EN is conjunct the North Node, the EZ is conjunct the South Node, and both the Ascendant and Descendant are square *both* of the Nodes.

perception of the Sun's movements above and below the equator are reversed; it could thereby be posited that the North and South Nodes of the Moon must be reversed for southern hemisphere events. This is, in fact, the *astronomical* reality. But once again, physical certainty collides with spiritual truth! For just as the influence of the vernal point (from the northern perspective) is uniform across the globe, so is that of the North Node. This is the position taken by Jacques Dorsan, who practiced astrology for many decades in both hemispheres of the globe.

For those who remain unconvinced, imagine two souls as they descend through the planetary spheres on their approach the Earth. One is born in Oslo, the other near Melbourne. Are we to assume, therefore, that these two individuals will fall under the influence of different North Nodes?

The nodal axis moves regressively through the zodiac at a rate of about 19° per year; the full revolution around the zodiac requires eighteen years and seven months. The return of this axis to its position at birth can be regarded as "a moment in time when the starry realm projects into and permeates our own." This explains why the *returns* of the Nodes to their respective degrees at birth—which we will examine later—are so important.

⑨ THE PLANETS IN THE SIGNS

AS THE PLANETS MOVE through the zodiacal signs, they interact with the forces that stream through the stars of the twelve holy living creatures. Each planet is guided by its own rhythm. In our solar system, the orbits of the various planets in our solar system follow the zodiacal circle from Aries to Taurus, from Taurus to Gemini, and so on. Stargazers in the northern hemisphere observe the zodiac displayed in an anti-clockwise direction, while those in the southern hemisphere (who view the "zodiacal plane" from its "other" side) see a clockwise arrangement of the signs.[1]

The spiritual forces of any of the zodiacal signs are brought closer to us through the presence of any planet moving before its stars. Much as the angelic hierarchies "step down" the radiance of God to a "wattage" that can be safely received by humanity, so the planets—each in its own way—serve to make understandable the lofty mysteries of the twelve holy living creatures. Indeed, we could say that *the planets act as beacons to the living spiritual beings of the zodiacal signs.*

The zodiacal placement of the transcendentals can be thought of as collective. Everyone born within a given seven-year period will have Uranus in the same sign; for Neptune it's 14 years, and for Pluto, 21 years. This means that you and your contemporaries will feel the planets' influence in a similar way. (For example, those born under Neptune in Aries will likely be devoted idealists—even to the point of zealotry—because both planet and sign support this. Neptune in Libra might give us a deep longing for justice, however impractical it might be to achieve.)

The following content is offered as a brief overview that is intended to assist readers in taking some initial steps toward the interpretation of a birth chart. The various letter-Arcana within *Meditations on the Tarot* contain the lost language of imaginative consciousness. Immersion in this language allows us to penetrate the guiding spiritual archetypes that seek our recognition—and may thereby lead us to the full measure of what a star chart can reveal. For example, if Saturn is in Aries, the combination of "The High Priestess" (II) and "The Fool" (XXI) form a significant "lens" through which we may ponder the meaning of this stellar placement. Our immersion into the archetypes of these particular Arcana will be greatly enhanced if we also take up the moral-spiritual exercises depicted in these letter-meditations.

The interrelatedness of all of the various indications within each chart warns us that *nothing means anything if held in isolation from the whole.*

THE CLASSICAL PLANETS

 SATURN

The zodiacal placement of Saturn indicates the nature of an individual's spiritual mission. As the sphere of Saturn is the first planetary sphere we enter on our path to rebirth, we can imagine the Holy Virgin gathering up all the resolves to which we pledged as we journeyed through the great school of cosmic night. The memory of these promises will lie in the depths of our being, awaiting a time when our consciousness quickens them into the light. The Seraphim, the spirits of love, dwell within the realm marked by the orbit of Saturn, and they have set into us the rhythm and tempo of time. Our individual mission might be carried out independently of our profession: it is a calling from the Seraphim, who illuminate how we might participate in the evolution of ourselves and of humanity. The time at which our mission reveals itself to us can vary.

---

1 Please refer to the illustrations of the zodiac from the northern and southern perspectives on pages 12–13.

SATURN IN *ARIES*
The High Priestess (II) meets The Fool (XXI)

Saturn in Aries can be seen as a commission to fully develop as individuals. Our spiritual mission will most likely entail developing initiative and independence; perhaps we will even need to learn how to "go it alone," exercising a boldness that may, at first, seem foreign to us. When leadership opportunities present themselves—particularly when they are unwelcome—we might regard them as being *guidance from Mary* that provides us a means of stepping into our given destiny. Because leadership can satisfy an urge for power, we do well to remember that, in its highest form, leadership requires no coercion. Collaboration with others serves as a bulwark against the Aries dangers of zealotry and narcissism. The mission of those of us born under this placement will, in some form, be tied to *idealism* and to serving a higher purpose. Navigating situations in which we must take a moral stand, regardless of the difficulty in doing so, enlivens our quest. When we bow before the needs of evolution, even at great personal cost, we emulate the kings of ages past who prostrated themselves before the Child—for Saturn was in Aries at the adoration of the Magi.

SATURN IN *TAURUS*
The High Priestess (II) meets The Judgment (XX)

The spiritual mission of those of us born with Saturn in Taurus will most likely require steadiness of purpose and thoughtful reasoning—for this is not a placement that will favor whimsical changes. Overcoming inconsistency supports our efforts to live into our mission; alternatively, however, the Bull's inclination toward stubbornness can act as a restraint against progress. A practical approach to life will offer us much assistance—for one of the Bull's strengths is the ability to establish practical applications for ideas seeking form on Earth; Taurus, the first earth sign, is the signature of buliders. Taurians are the deepest of thinkers, and they long to pursue something of abiding interest. Because Venus rules the Bull, it is often the case that those of us born with this placement will have an attachment to all that is guided by the planet of love: the arts (particularly music), as well as everything beautiful—including the natural world. Saturn in Taurus encourages the fine-tuning of the horns so that we might *hear* the mighty thoughts of spirit coming into time, and *digest* them. The greatest example of this lies in the Nathan Jesus, whose entire being listened to the creative force of love resounding through the world—for Saturn was in Taurus at his conception.

SATURN IN *GEMINI*
The High Priestess (II) meets The Sun (XIX)

The spiritual mission (unless we are hermits!) cannot easily be accomplished without cooperation with others. After all, the stars of Gemini shine on behalf of brotherly and sisterly love! The spiritual mission benefits from the talents of Gemini's ruler, Mercury: communication, mediation, and quick thinking. Gemini's versatility brings something lovely and light-hearted to Saturn, often resulting in the ability to pursue many things at once. However, perseverance must remain the watchword, as "too many irons in the fire" can cause us to lose sight of our guiding star. This loss compromises the integrity of the hermetic channel (between *above* and *below*)—rendering it too wide, too narrow, or even closed in silence. Throughout the temptations in the wilderness, Saturn was in Gemini. If Jesus—in open communication with worlds above—had not been true to his star, he could not have endured the intensity of these torturous trials. Saturn in Gemini asks us to follow our star and no one else's, and to faithfully recognize the stars of all others.

SATURN IN *CANCER*
The High Priestess (II) meets The Moon (XVIII)

The spiritual mission requires selflessness, supported by a clear sense of our own value as individuals. Cancer naturally protects and nurtures what it knows to be precious. This can occur *within* the family—which might indicate weightier than usual family responsibilities—or *outside* of it (caring for the health and viability of an organization, for instance). Saturn in Cancer asks us to listen for the sounding of the beating heart within all living things, so that we might regard matter as a vessel for the soul. Under its influence, we yearn to tread upon the bridge between the material and spiritual worlds—a bridge that can be imagined at the center of the spiraling arms of the Crab. When Saturn is before the stars of the Crab, the spiritual mission may ask us to sacrifice a great deal — for it suggests that we work on behalf of something we deem greater than ourselves. Thus does it lead us from the confines of the present to the freedom found in the world that is becoming. Nelson Mandela (1918–2013), born with Saturn in Cancer, is exemplary of our theme, as he spent twenty-seven years in prison for his efforts to eliminate apartheid in South Africa. His vision of the future of his country led to his presidency between 1994 and 1999.

SATURN IN *LEO*
The High Priestess (II) meets The Wheel of Fortune (X)

The spiritual mission will likely involve coming into our proper authority: We are being asked to strive to fill the unique "star" of destiny that awaits us. Perhaps initially unwelcome to individuals who prefer anonymity, Saturn in the Lion usually demands *visibility*. And while it is true that Leo has a flair for the dramatic (or even a love of the spotlight), moral uprightness implies that our authority and recognition should be put in service of others. Such service presumes compassion for human failings — compassion that is based upon the acknowledgment of our own missteps. This placement asks that we take risks in full consciousness: not in the manner of a gambler down to his last chip, but with *certainty* of the good that can be accomplished if the bet pays off. Those of us born under this combination are asked to take responsibility for the course of our lives and to pursue this course with creative fire. Once we have summoned the courage to understand our karma, we are drawn to the certain knowledge that, beyond the isolation of the "eternal repetition of the wheel of life," *freedom* exists. Steiner's large body of work on the cosmic law of karma stands as a leading example of these impulses — for Saturn was in Leo at his birth in 1861.

SATURN IN *VIRGO*
The High Priestess (II) meets Force (XI)

The spiritual mission asks that we take part in providing nourishment to what is "striving to become." When born under this placement, we want to know that our efforts are of service to others; however, it is important that we never allow ourselves to be "used." Nutrition — and other mysteries of our well-being — may influence the life path. Virgo beckons us to know the Earth intimately: her life forces, and her powers of growth and healing. The Saturn-in-Virgo individuals among us are called to protect all that is *innocent*. Before the stars of Virgo, Mary-Saturn guards purity within the folds of her mantle; she reveals that doubt can be overcome when we call upon our spiritual and earthly orientations to work in unison — and that her rejuvenating life-force knows no obstacles. Sophia, who makes known the divine origin of the natural world, uplifts our hearts and souls through nature, art, and religion. Peter Deunov (1864–1944), who was born with Saturn in Virgo, founded an esoteric school in Sofia, Bulgaria in 1922. This school was devoted to the nurturance of the future Slavic culture that will be founded upon brotherly and sisterly love.

SATURN IN *LIBRA*
The High Priestess (II) meets Justice (VIII)

The spiritual mission will be influenced by the quality of our associations with others — therefore, working alone may be at odds with our quest. These associations will be strengthened by diplomatic efforts that create a peaceful milieu — one in which diverse individuals can identify common ground. Because Venus rules Libra, the arts and all things beautiful may play a role in our endeavors. Those born under this combination might be inspired by two images of the Archangel Michael: one, keeping the dragon underfoot (which allows goodness to prevail, as does the ideal of justice); the other, holding the scales in balance (representative of fairness). Saturn's exaltation in Libra brings to mind the ideal of law that is administered fairly, but also mercifully. The study of justice (which is properly the province of Libra) requires that we explore the balance between freedom and providence, and between the individual and the universal. Saturn in Libra asks that we strive to mend the differences that span the apparent chasm between opposing sides. This cannot be accomplished without equanimity of soul, whereby personal preferences are set aside.

The Solomon Mary, whose conception and birth occurred when Saturn was in Libra, will stand for all time as an example of equanimity — for, she was willing to walk the stations of the Cross in order to bear witness to the suffering of her Son.

SATURN IN *SCORPIO*
The High Priestess (II) meets Death (XIII)

The spiritual mission will ask that we take a deep dive into whatever it is we pursue. Skimming the surface (or jumping from one thing to the next) limits our ability to receive spiritual insights — for these insights are repelled by souls who have not experienced *silence*. When in Scorpio, Saturn is well-disposed to suspend logical thinking in favor of the study of what exists behind the veil of the senses. Those born under this placement might thus be uniquely qualified to discern the hidden dynamics that exist in this realm, which includes the mysteries of death and rebirth. The natural tendency toward secretiveness that may accompany this placement can support these efforts — as long as our silence is a reflection of Scorpio's love of introspection, and not of a distrust of others. Saturn's scythe here conveys the "cutting and pruning" of what is no longer vital, on which transformation relies. The High Priestess reminds us that the absence of faith, hope, and love are descriptive of the extent to which we are "dead." She knows — as did the Nathan Mary, who was conceived and born under this astral signature — that doubt and a lack of faith block our ability to remember our divine origin and our divine purpose. Indeed, these hindrances can all too easily become "the stone placed before the tomb."

SATURN IN *SAGITTARIUS*
The High Priestess (II) meets The Hermit (IX)

The spiritual mission will require that we focus all of our attention on the matter at hand, in the manner of an archer whose arrow is trained upon its quarry. Herein lies the danger of this astral signature, for this level of focus can engender dogmatism, whereby we can lose perspective of the wider reality. Truth must be the ultimate the aim of our hunt — for it is the task of those born under this placement to be able to discern truth from mere falsehood (which often bears the *appearance* of truth). When Saturn is situated before the stars of the Archer, the self-control that Saturn so often demands is especially relevant, for he is the "archetypal wanderer." Although we might sometimes need to wander in solitude, Saturn in Sagittarius asks us to walk purposefully from concept to opposing concept, from ideology to opposing ideology — bearing only our staff (whereby spirit speaks to us through intuition), our mantle (through which faith fills our heart), and our lamp (which illumines cosmic truth). Those willing to walk in the manner of the Hermit might find the wisdom that radiates *from the heights* above every "unsolvable" problem — for Saturn was in Sagittarius at the birth of Valentin Tomberg (1900–1973).

SATURN IN *CAPRICORN*
The High Priestess (II) meets The Star (XVII)

When Saturn, the planetary ruler of Capricorn, is before the stars of the Goat, it evokes the connection between memory and the fully activated crown — expressed through the image of the Goat's horns. Indeed, an extraordinary faculty of memory is often observed among those born under this placement. The spiritual mission of those of us born beneath this astral signature will find assistance in a firm will; we might also cultivate endurance, a Capricorn specialty that makes possible the Goat's ability to take the long view. These qualities are enhanced by the Goat's inherent ability to quickly adapt to changes of circumstance without losing composure — or losing sight of its dearly held aim, no matter how long it takes to realize that aim. Those born under this placement often have a deep longing for respect, although the resulting load of responsibilities that we are willing to take on in order to gain that respect may be heavy. The mission that does not disrupt *tradition* will be the most successful, for the Goat knows that it bears one of the currents that moves humanity from its past to its future. And while it is laudable to revere those aspects of the past that are moral and just, we must also be prepared to meet the changes that the future brings with courage and good will. When Saturn is positioned before the stars of the Goat, we can envision hope radiating from the center of the galaxy—bearing the promise of the future. Our mission might require us to climb the mountain alone. Winston Churchill (1874-1965), who was born with Saturn in Capricorn, was a pariah for a significant part of his political career, labelled a warmonger and alarmist for voicing his assessment of enemy aggression in both World Wars. And yet, even when England's predicament was most fraught with apparent hopelessness, his leadership never wavered.

SATURN IN *AQUARIUS*
The High Priestess (II) meets Temperance (XIV)

Strength of community will likely be foundational to the success of our mission. Therefore, cultivating warmth and magnanimity of heart (a concern for all) will guide us toward this success. Aquarius reveals itself as the source of the flow of etheric forces in our world; and for this reason, Saturn's presence here can stimulate the exploration of these formative and creative forces in nature. As Aquarius bears the impulses of humanitarianism, personal grandstanding will not advance our quest, nor will any desire for individual power and recognition. Saturn so-placed invites us to warm the chilly corners of the intellect with the breath of the Holy Spirit, which can lead us beyond the limits of our intelligence. Those of us born under the influence of this placement long to know what is striving to manifest from the future—for it is *this* that nourishes our souls! Therefore, the spiritual mission may well seem "out there," and might be greeted by incomprehension. This is of no consequence. We (and our peers) have the opportunity to serve as vessels for the revelations that can lead humanity forward into new territory. Saturn was in Aquarius at the birth of Ita Wegman (1876-1943), trailblazing physician and the first head of the Medical Section of the Anthroposophical Society.

SATURN IN *PISCES*
The High Priestess (II) meets The Hanged Man (XII)

In Pisces we come to the end of Saturn's journey around the zodiacal belt. In a certain sense, Pisces releases Saturn from some of its rigor—thus, the spiritual mission that beckons from the Fishes might be pursued in a less-structured way. Indeed, our journey might well meander a bit, as this is a path that tends to ask that we "move this way and that" when we follow our inspirations. However, this method must be distinguished from aimlessness—for when others are allowed to determine our course, success will be hard-won. Through the stars of the Fishes, we might experience *celestial* gravitation, whereby our will can be oriented toward heaven. However, like the two fish swimming in different directions within the constellation, those of us born with Saturn in Pisces also feel *earthly* gravitation through our abiding love of humanity and our desire to serve its evolution. Saturn was in Pisces at the birth of Elisabeth Vreede (1879-1943), who served as the first head of the Mathematical-Astronomical Section of the Anthroposophic Society. Having met Steiner in 1903, Vreede was at his side when the first Goetheanum was built. Following Steiner's death, she supported the work of Tomberg, identifying him as critical to the future of the Anthroposophic Society; this ultimately contributed, however, to her ouster from the Society's leadership in 1935.

♃ JUPITER

The zodiacal placement of Jupiter illuminates the wisdom that seeks expression through each individual. We can imagine ourselves descending into Jupiter's sphere with the spiritual resolves that were bestowed upon us in the Saturn sphere. Once among the Cherubim (who dwell within Jupiter's sphere), we are given a sense of the wisdom that gives form to these resolves. The character of this wisdom can be revealed by Jupiter's zodiacal sign; we are thereby given a precious gift that can assist us throughout our incarnation—provided that we make an effort to understand it. The zodiacal sign of Jupiter is also suggestive of the worldview and virtue that might be of particular help to us. Jupiter asks us to step into our "natural" authority, which can be imagined as *the space we are meant to fill*. The extent of this space is well-known to the Cherubim, the spirits of harmony, who protect it until the time that we are ready to take our places. The Cherubim respond to human effort.

JUPITER IN *ARIES*
The Emperor (IV) meets The Fool (XXI)

What can an emperor learn from a fool? He may come to realize that justice is best upheld only through the respect for the sovereign freedom of the individual. And what can a fool learn from an emperor? Perhaps that wisdom can sometimes be found through the renunciation of our freedoms—when our mission requires this of us. Jupiter, when before the stars of Aries, asks us to strive to develop qualities of leadership—even if such ability remains elusive. The self-confidence of Jupiter finds an easy home here, and reminds us of its power when accompanied by moral uprightness. Those of us born under this configuration are encouraged to decide what deserves our wholehearted devotion—and to then strive to inspire others who might kindle the same love within their hearts. Fallen Jupiter-forces can incline us toward recklessly doing whatever we please; we can avoid this temptation through the practice of humility. Both of Mary Magdalene's conversions occurred when Jupiter was in Aries. Raised in an affluent family, she was what might today be called a "party girl." Her first conversion followed Jesus's words ("Do penance, believe, and share the kingdom with me!"[2]), which moved her deeply; however, she quickly returned to her old habits. Six weeks later, as she watched Jesus speak of sin and God's mercy, she lost consciousness three times and asked if her salvation were still possible. He forgave and blessed her.

JUPITER IN *TAURUS*
The Emperor (IV) meets The Judgment (XX)

Who better to judge than the Emperor, who renounced his personal freedoms in order to fill his post? When before the stars of Taurus, Jupiter will bear the wisdom of the necessity of "chewing the cud," so that our thoughts and experiences can be fully digested in the four stomachs of the Bull. It is this digestion that allows for the Taurus ideal of *inner balance*—for all that is "undigested" can render us "top-heavy," and therefore unstable. Those of us born under this placement might be inspired by the spiritual archetype of the divine feminine, which is intricately bound up with the stars of Taurus as well as with the great Egyptian age that developed under its influence. While the stars of the Bull ask us to hold high the torch of *rationalism* (the ability to understand through sound reasoning and logic), the upwardly turned horns of the Bull suggest an attunement to spiritual realms. Jupiter was in Taurus at the birth of St. Teresa of Avila (1515–1582), who was well-known for her religious ecstasies. (According to Tomberg, she was in spiritual communication with Jesus.) Taurus confers the power of *productive concentration*—and St. Teresa indicated that the concentration necessary for spiritual prayer is the fruit of the moral purification of the will.[3]

JUPITER IN *GEMINI*
The Emperor (IV) meets The Sun (XIX)

What combination could better represent the union of reason and faith? And of super-human wisdom and human intelligence? Wisdom descends from heaven to earth; our ability to receive it depends upon the integrity of our connection between above and below. The vertical channel between them is maintained by faith in the love between Creator and created. When we seek the sacred guidance of the spiritual world, we can know the world below. Those of us born under this placement are invited to develop *perseverance*, the virtue Steiner applied to Gemini. Should we ignore this invitation, we risk scattering our energies in such a way that we are unable to commit ourselves to anything. This is a sad state of affairs—for, in truth, flightiness betrays a lack of faith in our higher Self. The stars of the Twins radiate the wisdom of cooperation and love among our fellows. Such love is based upon a certain knowledge of the divine nature of each of us; if we lose sight of this, the light of our "guiding star" will remain occluded by clouds of doubt. Our star is one that can be followed by no one else. We can imagine Jupiter in Gemini as *radiant wisdom before a background of purity of intention*, a purity that reflects the spontaneous wisdom of the heart that is so

---

2 See the account of Anne Catherine Emmerich for 8/Nov/30.
3 Tomberg, *Meditations on the Tarot*, 9.

characteristic of children. Maria Montessori (1870-1952) was born with Jupiter in Gemini. One of the first female physicians in Italy, she developed educational practices based upon her experiences in working with children who had learning disabilities, thereby revolutionizing their care at the time. Her legacy stands as a shining example of the virtue of recognizing the divine in each of us.

JUPITER IN *CANCER*
The Emperor (IV) meets The Moon (XVIII)

The forces of Jupiter, when in Cancer, carry an innate sense of creating surroundings that nourish the soul. Jupiter's exaltation in Cancer—signifying the height of Jupiter's power of expression—can be imagined as human intellect (the domain of Cancer's ruler, the Moon) offered in service of Jovian wisdom. Within the stars of the Crab exists a concern for humanity—a warning against allowing our intellect to remain encased within the confines of our skull. The presence of Jupiter here can *either* magnify our inclination toward materialistic thinking, *or* incline us to reject "facts" as the boundary of truth. Cancer's virtue, selflessness, implies acts of kindness that are freely given *in full consciousness*, whereby there is no compromise of our own Ego strength. Each gift of selflessness that we bestow upon others serves to purify the soul; this knowledge enables us to lovingly bear any personal sacrifices thereby entailed. Jupiter was in Cancer at the birth of Rudolf Steiner (1861-1925), whose extraordinary biography reflects such selflessness. Steiner embraced his mission early, devoting his life to the evolution of humanity through spiritual science. Although his work was tireless, exhaustive, and broad, he never sought recognition for his work.

JUPITER IN *LEO*
The Emperor (IV) meets The Wheel of Fortune (X)

When before the stars of the Lion, Jupiter's influence brings warmth and compassion, traits that are exemplified and idealized in the wise ruler—for such a ruler leaves his citizenry in complete freedom. Both Jupiter and Leo signify authority and certainty; therefore, those of us born under this placement will likely be offered many opportunities to develop these qualities. Jupiter reminds us that, by bowing spontaneously before the true Self, we gain the means to step off the "world mill" (i.e., to escape from eternal repetition). Cosmic law demands that we accept our shortcomings, so that we can begin to "knead the dough" of our karma. The reach of the intensity and creativity of Leo's fire (which lives within its ruler, the Sun) is expanded by Jupiter; however, we must be willing to build a fortress against both egotism (a puffed-up sense of our own importance) and egoism (self-centeredness)—which incline us to prefer self-enrichment to performing deeds on behalf of others. The finest example of this lies with the Nathan Jesus, whose conception occurred when Jupiter was in Leo—for his every deed reflected the will of the Father, the tenderness of the Mother, and the wisdom of the Holy Spirit.

JUPITER IN *VIRGO*
The Emperor (IV) meets Force (XI)

When before the stars of Virgo, Jupiter radiates the wisdom of Nature and her phenomena, leading us straight to the garden of the Mother upon the Earth. In what ways can the natural world lead to understanding of the starry cosmos above? What life-giving forces are held therein? As Virgo brings *precision* to our thinking and *sobriety* to our souls, endeavors that lack these qualities are less likely to find a foothold for those born under this configuration. Virgo, as the starry representative of non-Fallen Nature—the condition humanity experienced before the Fall—stands as the promise of our eventual return to our lost harmony with Nature. The Emperor's obedience to higher worlds reveals the wisdom of the ten commandments as our path back to our primordial condition. When we pray, and when we sacrifice, the Virgin fills us with rejuvenating life. This combination carries the imagination of the arms of the Mother around the whole of humanity; through her influence, we long to provide tenderness and comfort to the needy. Mother Teresa (1910-1997), whose life was a demonstrative example of these qualities, was born when Jupiter was in Virgo.

JUPITER IN *LIBRA*
The Emperor (IV) meets Justice (VIII)

We might posit that Libra's influence is the most objective of the zodiac. For, in order that a peaceful resolution can be achieved, those under its sway typically wish to hear the full scope of any circumstance. *Through listening to the wisdom of others*, our spiritual quest is supported and rewarded. Jupiter and Libra are united in upholding the *ideal* of justice, represented by the dynamic motion around the fulcrum of the scales of Justice. (Justice represents equilibrium and harmony between all opposing principles—e.g., will and providence, the individual and the universal). Although Libra's ruler, Venus, can mollify the dictates of the law (both human and cosmic) with the quality of *mercy*, the equilibrium of the scales (and of the Archangel Michael himself) depends equally upon the principle of *severity*. Equilibrium—or spiritual health—eludes us when we surrender to our personal positions and our temperamental inclinations. Jupiter in Libra seeks peace. Peter Deunov (1864–1944), who was so active in promulgating peace in Bulgaria during WWII, was born beneath this astral signature.

JUPITER IN *SCORPIO*
The Emperor (IV) meets Death (XIII)

Jupiter in Scorpio may confer a great interest in what lies beyond the sense world. For those of us who do not fear it, this includes death. By means of our trials and suffering, such interest holds the promise of inner transformation. As Jupiter expands the already mighty will-forces behind the Scorpion's rulers, Mars and Pluto, we might call upon the ancient formula that corresponds to the Eagle/Scorpion: *To be silent*. Within silence, we have the opportunity—through our impulses, illuminations, and insights—to *mature*. Silence creates a natural emptiness (which the Emperor achieves through his renunciation of freedom), allowing the spiritual element to manifest. However, those born under this signature should guard against any antisocial tendencies, or an affinity to the darker aspects of humanity. For when Jupiter heeds the fallen Scorpion, judgments can lack mercy—thereby rendering us apt to lash out. Jupiter before the Scorpion's stars inclines us to seek wisdom in worlds unseen. Jupiter was in Scorpio at the birth of Valentin Tomberg (1900–1973), who endeavored ceaselessly to explore these worlds.

JUPITER IN *SAGITTARIUS*
The Emperor (IV) meets The Hermit (IX)

When Jupiter and Sagittarius are working toward a common purpose (as they easily do!), Jupiter supports a higher order of thinking. Moving before its stars, Jupiter—ruler of the Archer—inclines us to know the wide world and the full breadth of its ideas. But this knowledge depends upon the radiance of the lamp that we carry as we walk, our willingness to know the whole truth (which requires the "collision of opposites"), and the power of our intuition. The *ignoble* forces of the Archer, on the other hand, can push us toward dogmatism—rendering us crazed about a single concept. Those of us born under this placement are asked to keep our arrows trained upon truth; this demands discernment: the ability to identify the abstractions that obscure divine reality. With Jupiter's help, the Sagittarian arrow can go a little farther. Jupiter was in Sagittarius at the birth of Jawaharlal Nehru (1889–1964), the Cambridge-educated lawyer who was one of the central figures in support of Indian independence, which ultimately came about in August of 1947. A close friend of Gandhi, Nehru spent three years in prison for his (then radical) support of Home Rule in India. Throughout his adult life, he remained focused on the ideal of an India independent of the British, with its own place in international affairs. He served as Prime Minister for seventeen years.

JUPITER IN *CAPRICORN*
The Emperor (IV) meets The Star (XVII)

When before the stars of the Goat, Jupiter bestows the wisdom and essential nature of *tradition* and its life-blood, *hope*. These are the agents of continuity and of spiritual growth which effect the transformation of the ideal into the real. Tradition is thus revealed as a bulwark against revolution. Jupiter in Capricorn urges us to take on pursuits that are structured, well-planned, and carried to their conclusion. Jupiter here says, "Don't give up!" and leads us to the means (our *knees*) to dodge and weave around life's inevitable obstacles. Alternatively, endurance and agility can play into the fallen Capricorn tendency for success at any cost, and Jupiter can exaggerate this dysfunction. Capricorn draws us to the knowledge that the fatigue and aridity of terrestrial life can be rendered fertile in the silence of the starry world—as is exemplified by the fact that Jupiter was in Capricorn at the births of both Tycho Brahe (1546–1601) and Willi Sucher (1902–1985). Brahe upheld the spiritual reality of the cosmos through the Tychonic system, whereby the Earth-centered experience of the cosmos is taken into account. Willi Sucher established the practice of astrological biography, through which the spiritual forces at work during gestation are shown to manifest at consistent stages throughout our lives.

JUPITER IN *AQUARIUS*
The Emperor (IV) meets Temperance (XIV)

The living water that moves between the Angel's urns (as depicted in the fourteenth card of the Tarot) bestows upon us the quality of *temperance*: tranquil, light-filled enthusiasm that is prone to neither ecstasy nor despair. Alternatively, our consciousness can be drowned in the turgid "lower waters" of the subconscious. Jupiter in Aquarius warns against the egotism that is betrayed by any effort to "come in our own name," and asks instead that we serve without renown. This placement supports the revelation of wisdom within communities of friends, whereby we can learn to "think on our knees," in humility. It bears the mystery of our communion with our guardian Angel, the wise being unique to each of us who, through our conscience, shows us wisdom's path—but leaves us in complete freedom to take another. The wisdom of Jupiter before the stars of Aquarius tends to be ahead of its time; those of us born under this placement tend to have a sense of the future that is reaching toward us, across time. Jupiter was in Aquarius at the birth of Florence Nightingale (1820–1910), who singlehandedly transformed nursing—which, until that time, was assigned to those from the lowest stations in life—into a *profession*. This she did through her revolutionizing approach to the care of soldiers in Constantinople. Born into a wealthy British family with humanitarian inclinations, she felt called to nursing, even avoiding marriage in order to do so. She rejected the constraints that were put upon women.

JUPITER IN *PISCES*
The Emperor (IV) meets The Hanged Man (XII)

When before the stars of Pisces, Jupiter (its primary ruler) asks us to remember that *the divinity of each of us is but one part of the divinity of the whole organism of humanity.* Indeed, knowledge of our interconnectedness often leads to a willingness to help those in need, a trait frequently observed in those born under the influence of this placement. Jupiter emphasizes the compassionate and charitable tendencies of Pisces; neither the Emperor nor the Hanged Man serves his own personal interests. The downfall of Pisces lies in a lack of self-discipline, which can lead us to become unduly dependent upon others. The imaginative capacity of Pisces is magnified by the presence of Jupiter before its stars, as is fluidity in our thinking (the gift of the water element upon our intellect). This flexibility is implied by the presence of two fish within the constellation. Comprising the bridge between past and future, as well as the "zero point" between earthly and celestial gravity, even the duality within the sign is twofold! "The Hanged Man" is shown upside down, with his feet (as the means of his deeds) facing upward; he has replaced the terrestrial domain of freedom with *spiritual* life, toward which there is often a strong attraction. The cleansing of the temple is a glorious example of "the head following the feet"—for as Jesus overturned the vendors' tables in the temple, his feet responded to a commandment from heaven, *and his head obeyed.* Tomberg wrote:

> The will is an active force.... In order for it to be able to perceive, it should not—it *must not*—become passive, for then it would fall asleep or fade away. This is because its very nature is activity, and in ceasing to be active it would cease to *be* will; no, it should... transform "*my* will" into "*thy* will."[4]

---

4 Tomberg, *Meditations on the Tarot*, 317.

♂ MARS

Within the sphere of Mars dwell the Thrones: the spirits of will. These Angels bestow upon us the ability to act in the world. This implies encountering a barrier (or a conflict) and breaking through it by way of our own force of will. The zodiacal placement of Mars reveals how drive and desire will manifest in our lives: where we tend to have get-up-and-go. Where will we take a stand to protect what we hold dear? Mars will show us, for it is "the warrior within." When we live with a sense of security, we tend to discredit Mars energy. But this is unfortunate—for, in doing so, we turn our backs on a *spiritual archetype*. Because of its association with the astral body,[5] Mars might also reveal to us the way in which we will have to develop self-control. When Mars goes rogue, we can run "hot"—looking for a fight and ready to blow a gasket at any moment.

MARS IN *ARIES*
The Chariot (VII) meets The Fool (XXI)

Mars—particularly when in Aries—dislikes being idle. Those of us born under this placement might be inspired to develop courage and leadership, so that we can become active participants in the world. As the ruler of Aries, Mars works easily when before its stars; this placement suggests support for any efforts made to strengthen confidence and initiative, however difficult this may seem. Mars in Aries can portend the need to fight for and defend what is important to us—and such defense might well demand personal sacrifice of some kind. Indecision works against the blessings of the Thrones, although it is also true that acting on behalf of righteousness requires that we temper any inclination toward recklessness and aggression. Becoming intoxicated by the power that can be associated with taking the lead can be prevented by examining which of our actions spring from devotion to our convictions, and which might be merely self-serving. May our ideals be the power behind our chariot! The Archangel Michael, cosmic representative of Mars, is the guardian of the threshold, the being who reveals to us the nature of our double (or shadow); his strength assists us in finding the courage to bear our confrontation with our lower nature.[6] Our double effectively chains us to the Earth; *it opposes levity*. Because Jesus bore no double (he and his mother, the Nathan Mary, are the only two individuals about whom this can be said), he was able to walk on water. Mars was in Aries at the time of this miracle.

MARS IN *TAURUS*
The Chariot (VII) meets The Judgment (XX)

When before the stars of Taurus, Mars encounters a calming stream of Venusian energy, rendering anger more difficult to arouse; however, once the fuse is lit, it's best to get out of the way! Mars before the stars of the Bull illuminates the human larynx, for this is the location of the Mars chakra as well as the region of the body attributable to the forces of the Bull. (In the larynx we find the capacity to speak, whereby we can communicate our thoughts and feelings with others.) Initiatives relating to the land (Taurus) and to the arts (the Bull's ruler is Venus) are supported by this combination. This is a great placement for building of any kind! It can be said that a practical, steady approach to life is most likely to support our success. The greatest pitfall of this combination is *resistance to change*, which has the potential to cause a great deal of inconvenience to others. Not everyone can wait the way the Bull can! Mars in Taurus implies the expression of divine will through human deeds. We can see this impulse working behind the sacrifice of the Solomon Jesus at the union in the temple (when Mars was in

---

5 Steiner described great seven periods of evolution known as "planetary conditions." At the center of the seven is our current "Earth" condition. The first of the great periods, known as Ancient Saturn, occurred within the current orbit of Saturn. At this time, when the human body was a body of *warmth* (fire), the seed of the physical body lived as a spiritual archetype. This condition was followed by Ancient Sun, which occurred within the current orbit of Jupiter. During the Sun period, when the physical body condensed into a gaseous state (air), the archetype for the etheric body of the human being was born. During the planetary condition Steiner referred to as Ancient Moon (which took place within the current orbit of Mars), when the astral body was seeded, the physical body condensed further into a state that was comparable to what we know as *liquid* (water). Solid matter (and our human physical form) did not exist until the Earth condition. A thorough accounting of these and subsequent stages can be found in Chapter 4 of Steiner's *An Outline of Esoteric Science*.

6 The human double comprises the transgressions, accrued over time, that exist as "deposits" in the subearthly realm.

Taurus)—at which time the great knowledge of the Solomon Jesus was bestowed upon the pure, simple being of the Nathan Jesus.[7] Once the sacrifice was made, the Nathan Jesus was able to give voice to the wisdom formerly held within the "I" of the older Jesus child—whereby all who gathered around him were astonished and filled with holy awe.

MARS IN *GEMINI*
The Chariot (VII) meets The Sun (XIX)

Those of us born with Mars before the stars of Gemini are encouraged to develop a willingness to cooperate with others and to cultivate a tolerance for having a good number of "balls in the air." Indeed, those of us who tend to focus on one thing at a time are amazed at what the Mars-in-Gemini friends around us are capable of! Though this tolerance rightly implies resourcefulness—learning to juggle a number of pursuits at the same time—fickleness and impatience will limit our ability to concentrate on the matters at hand. The beings of Gemini bring *levity* to all they touch, calling to mind an image of Mars sharing a few jokes from time to time. Mercury's rulership of Gemini supports communications of all kinds, suggesting success in endeavors that rely upon these talents. Perhaps most importantly, those of us born under this placement must keep in mind the lesson of Castor and Pollux: that love of our "brother" sometimes requires us to allow another's star to shine more brightly than our own. Indeed, among the twelve senses identified by Steiner, the one attributable to Gemini is the sense for the higher nature of others. The greatest example of this sense lay with the Nathan Jesus, whose sacrifice upon the Cross was given so that the sins of humanity could be lifted—whereby the "I" of each of us could be known. Mars was in Gemini throughout the Passion of Christ.

MARS IN *CANCER*
The Chariot (VII) Meets The Moon (XVIII)

The protective reverence that Cancer holds for the force of life—such as that which lives within a beating heart—can be directed toward human deeds when Mars is before its stars. These efforts must be freely given in the way of a loving mother working on behalf of her child. The stars of Cancer bear the instinct of purification (catharsis), which can be expressed as the movement from the confines of the "shell" of our lower selves toward the house of the Father: the dwelling place of our higher Selves. Mars in Cancer implies selflessness; indeed, the need for personal sacrifice might be a theme in our lives. We must remember, however, that selfless deeds are no longer "selfless" when they leave behind a residue of resentment. The Crab's natural sensitivity to criticism (courtesy of its ruler, the Moon) might need to be worn down a bit, although this can occur naturally when our focus turns from self to others. The Crab's quick movements from side to side exhibit its adaptability. The tenacity and determination of Mars when in Cancer is not to be underestimated: Among the twelve, Cancer would be the one to put your money on as best able to lift the full weight of a car in order to save a child—and she can do it with one claw behind her back! Mars was in Cancer at the birth of John the Baptist, who devoted his life to preparing for the Messiah. (Even when in utero, he leapt for joy when in proximity to the Nathan Jesus, who was gestating within the womb of Mary.) It was John the Baptist who led by the hand the first penitent from the ancient world [for he was the "son of penitence" on his father's side and the "son of innocence" on his mother's] to the altar of grace of the new world.[8]

MARS IN *LEO*
The Chariot (VII) meets The Wheel of Fortune (X)

When Mars is before the stars of Leo, creative energy enlivens our deeds. In ever-ready Mars, our imagination can effortlessly intuit the influence of the fire element upon our celestial warrior! Actions might be bold, and they are usually carried out with great certainty of purpose. When in Leo, Mars easily steps into leadership roles. This can be a high-visibility placement for Mars, one that typically confers a good measure of freedom in the realm of chosen

---

[7] This event is described as the "union in the temple." A spiritual accounting of this even can be found within Steiner's *The Fifth Gospel*. See also CW Nr. 148.
[8] Tomberg, *Meditations on the Tarot*, 484.

activity. This describes a gift that is best not abused by self-serving actions aimed at consolidating our power at the expense of others. A readiness to fight—usually evident in those born under Mars in Leo—must be distinguished from *moral courage*, which does not exert force over others. And for those of us who are (by nature) inclined to shy away from conflict, the roar of the king of beasts might serve as our inspiration. The Mars-in-Leo individuals among us tend to be protective of our young, for whom we have a special affection. Pride, however, is the downfall of this placement—one indication of the effect of *astral instability*. Mars was before the stars of Leo at the birth of French Emperor Napoleon (1769-1821). His fiery boldness, the certainty of his actions (whether honorable or not), and his unwillingness to back down from any fight he regarded as righteous are uniquely characteristic of this placement.

MARS IN *VIRGO*
The Chariot (VII) meets Force (XI)

When Mars is before the stars of Virgo, he's putty in her hands—for aggression, compulsion, and conquest (natural Mars tendencies) must bend to Virgo's greater force. This force of the Virgin is based upon obedience to—as well as harmony and cooperation with—the divine. Those of us born under this placement might find that the Virgin softens any tendency of Mars toward sharp, impulsive speech. We are often naturally oriented toward service to others—including ministering to those in ill health; in fact, the health of the natural world, including the human body, are often of interest. Abundant energy for work (and other duties) is usually evident. Because of the natural precision within the forces of the Virgin, pursuits that are less defined in nature are unlikely to meet with success. However, we might point out that a related downfall of this placement is an inclination for excessive criticism. As the cosmic defender of the Virgin, the Archangel Michael (who, to the clairvoyants of old, stood beside the Virgin, holding the Scales) longs to protect all that is innocent and pure. The Virgin represents humanity before the Fall; she cannot be conquered. When before the stars of Virgo, Mars finds self-mastery through the practice of the ten commandments. Mars was in Virgo at the onset of the forty days in the wilderness, during which Jesus, hungry and alone, was faced with near-constant temptation. The tempters were rendered powerless by his serene humility.

MARS IN *LIBRA*
The Chariot (VII) meets Justice (VIII)

The conciliatory influence of Libra's ruler, Venus, can incline those of us born with Mars in Libra toward *diplomacy*—which can be called upon to great effect, and may be even be fundamental to our success. Those of us born under this placement tend to have an intuitive sense that direct confrontation may not be the most productive course; also evident is an appreciation for the power of peaceful resolution. Although the courage of Mars when in Libra tends to be less brash than when in Aries or Leo, it need not be any less powerful. This placement summons the imagination of Michael battling injustice on behalf of humanity; our armor and sword are often taken up for the benefit of others. Additionally, equanimity of soul—Libra's higher gift—will depend upon our humility and self-mastery. Mars was in Libra at the birth of Mohandas Gandhi (1869-1948). Gandhi was a peaceful warrior for human rights in both South Africa and in India, despite having been imprisoned frequently. A British-educated lawyer, he spent decades engaged in non-violent resistance to British rule as well as to injustices within Indian culture. His simple garment, the dhoti, signified his identification with the suffering of the poor. Gandhi was assassinated while attending a prayer meeting. It might also be noted that he was against the partition of India following the achievement of its independence, as he foresaw the violence that would ensue.

MARS IN *SCORPIO*
The Chariot (VII) meets Death (XIII)

Scorpio, said to be the birthplace of Mars (its classical ruler), is the temple of transformation within the circle of twelve. It holds the promise that—by way of our trials—"lead" might be forged into the "gold" of higher consciousness. When among the stars of the Scorpion, however, Mars must learn patience; when this is understood, strategy can be raised to the level of an art form. The arrows that are part of both glyphs are suggestive of the strong force of will that dwells within this placement. Our understanding of this comes further into focus if we consider the Scorpion tendency to do nothing in half measures. Because Scorpio leads us to what "lies beneath," Mars's placement in it often manifests through activities and endeavors that are "under the radar," or even occult in nature. One downfall of this placement is a tendency to nurture resentment—for our sense of loyalty is strong, and we expect the same from others. Pride, too, can cause us to stew in our own juices and to judge others harshly. (Indeed, our words can thereby inflict a great deal of pain.) Mars was in Scorpio when the changing of water into wine took place during the wedding at Cana, which healed humanity's fall from the loving union that existed between God and the world. As the wedding guests drank the new wine offered by Jesus and Mary, they were able to remember their existence alongside God—and their remoteness from the Father was thereby healed.

MARS IN *SAGITTARIUS*
The Chariot (VII) meets The Hermit (IX)

The Chariot of Mars will travel a great distance when before the stars of Sagittarius. Our travels, however, must be guided by the quest for *wisdom*. Because the Archer's arrow is poised to arc above the breadth of the whole world, we can often observe in those of us born under this placement a marked adventurousness and love of wide-open spaces: the cowboy on the open range, with no love of standing still for very long. This placement brings to the forefront the benefits of self-control, particularly as it relates to our verbal expression—for our inclination to speak the truth might lack tact. We are usually able to give whatever we pursue every ounce of our effort and attention—provided we fully believe in what we are doing. However, we might also guard against becoming overzealous, whereby we can descend into dogmatism and a tendency to moralize. The Archer supports philosophical thinking and other endeavors of the human mind that necessarily rely on reason and conscience. Creativity of thought—the gift of the fire element upon human thinking—brings warmth to otherwise abstract topics. Mars was in Sagittarius at the birth of Theodore Roosevelt (1858–1919), the paragon of the tireless, exuberant adventurer in both his public and private life. His love of the outdoors developed into the creation of the National Park system in the United States.

MARS IN *CAPRICORN*
The Chariot (VII) meets The Star (XVII)

Mars's exaltation in Capricorn suggests that it is supercharged by Capricorn's extraordinary ability to endure hardship (which can be visualized in the Goat's ability to adapt to changes in terrain). The firmness of resolve that characterizes the Goat—the gift of the element of earth upon the human will—adds ambition and focus to the already formidable force of our celestial warrior! We cannot fail to add that Capricorn might be pleased that its virtue (courage) is so easily summoned by Mars. However, this placement might also incline us to disregard the views and feelings of others along our way. At its worst, Mars in Capricorn can compel us to be overly critical and to spend a good deal of energy trying to thwart our enemies—both real and imagined. Because the Goat is ruled by Saturn, its gaze looks not only toward the future—which it dares to face with courage— but to the past as well. Dwelling within Capricorn's stars is *a reverence for tradition*, for the Goat understands this to be the agent of continuous transformation—or, *growth*—whose action is propelled by *hope*. Tradition stands in contrast to revolution, which must topple and upset in order to bring the future into being—often leaving the past behind like so much rubble! Mars was in Capricorn at the healing of the nobleman's son.[9] The archetype of heredity, however, is vertical: This archetype was distorted at the Fall—thereby adding to the "image and likeness of God" the possibility of the transmission of the *characteristics* of ancestors. Through the intercession of Jesus, the son was brought into connection with the archetype of the father-son relationship—and so he was healed.

---

9   The sins of the father of the child manifested as illness in the boy. The nature of this sin involved the renunciation of the nobleman's "I" to his king—for it is said that the "I" of the father influences the physical health of the child.

MARS IN *AQUARIUS*
The Chariot (VII) meets Temperance (XIV)

When Mars is before the stars of Aquarius, our respect and love for our community can direct the course of our chariot. We might be asked to do battle against anything that threatens our society, our community, or our friends; indeed, we may already be inclined to rattle our swords in response to what we regard as an injustice. This is an independent duo that invites us to develop our uniqueness. Those of us born with Mars in the Waterman tend to defy limitations imposed by others and may do everything in our power to work beyond them. When before the stars of the Waterman, Mars favors measured actions that defy an inflated consciousness of the self. This placement confers *an allegiance to the future*, which means that our work may be unappreciated—or even actively opposed—in the present. Through its association with Michael, Mars in Aquarius is highly attuned to life's inevitable *unfairness*. Indeed, conversations can feature many an exposition upon the ubiquity of this grievance, and our actions might strive for its resolution. Mars was in Aquarius at the birth of Jacques Lusseyran (1924-1971), who—although blinded in childhood—became a leader of the French Resistance during WWII. (Afterwards, he became a brilliant academic.) In 1941, at the tender age of seventeen, Lusseyran put together a Resistance group among his Lycée friends; their primary goal was to print and disseminate the truth about the progress of the war. He was captured by the Germans in 1943, and, as if by a miracle, survived his two-year imprisonment at Buchenwald.

MARS IN *PISCES*
The Chariot (VII) meets The Hanged Man (XII)

When Mars is before the stars of Pisces, we are invited to meditate upon the apparent conflict between Mars (along with its great force of will) and the Hanged Man, who is suspended in such a way that he cannot act at all. In the image of the Hanged Man, the organs of his will—his feet—are oriented toward heaven. Although inspired by the divine, he does not forget the world below his head; and for this reason, he seeks to accomplish spiritually inspired deeds on behalf of humanity. The nature of Mars's work when in Pisces can be solitary, far from the prevailing current of everyday life. These tasks can be made easier by way of a love of humankind as well as a receptivity to the realm of the spirit. For some of us born under this placement, the attraction to the spiritual world is so strong that there can exist an indifference to worldly matters. Effort might also be required to avoid drifting into (rather than consciously choosing) situations that arise through the might of others. Many of us will experience the inclination to help and defend those who seem unable to fend for themselves. Those born under this signature might be willing to sacrifice for a greater good and might ask the same of others. Mars was in Pisces as Jesus stilled the Sea of Galilee. Following his ordeal in the wilderness (and by way of his practice of the three sacred vows of poverty, chastity, and obedience), Jesus became master of the elements of fire, earth, air, and water. As the violent tempest raged around their boat, Jesus slept. When he did nothing to help them, the disciples became more fearful and agitated. Then, as he arose, he said, "Peace! Be still!"—and the sea was quiet again.

SUN

The Sun, as representative of our higher nature, signifies the spirit that draws us forward toward humanity's destiny. The Sun shines as the golden chain—the "I"—that links together each individual's successive incarnations. It represents dignity, character, vitality, and self-reliance. It imbues all it touches with goodness and morality, and therefore seeks to bring to expression within the human being the highest teachings of the zodiacal beings. The Angels of the Sun sphere—the Spirits of Form (Exusiai), the Spirits of Movement (Dynamis), and the Spirits of Wisdom (Kyriotetes)—act as intermediaries between destiny and freedom within each life. If we think of the zodiacal constellation behind our birth Sun as the starry mantle proper to our incarnation, we might then resolve to understand and express the noble characteristics of our Sun sign. Additionally, we can intuit that *neglecting* to discern the development of these characteristics is akin to riding a horse—although one that is headed in the wrong direction!

SUN IN *ARIES*
The Magician (I) meets The Fool (XXI)

The Sun's exaltation in Aries suggests that the highest ideals of the hierarchies of the Sun can gain strength of expression through this configuration. Both the Sun and Aries share the qualities of confidence, morality, and power of will. When in our birth chart, this placement invites us to strive to develop these traits so that we are able to assert our (often radical) ideas in the world; additionally, the Sun-in-Aries individuals among us often possess the ability to get initiatives off the ground. The strength of intellect that manifested among the great thinkers of Greece (in the age of Aries) depended upon the power of *effortless concentration*, effected through the transposition of the brain to the domain of the Sun-heart within: the rhythmic system. The Sun in the midst of our solar system, like love itself, is the gravitational force that stands between order and chaos. Narcissism, impulsiveness, and an indifference to the views of others are potential downfalls of an Aries Sun. Those of us born under this placement must make every effort to devote ourselves to others and to moral causes of our choosing, no matter how foolish we may appear—for the Fool has no interest in personal claims to authority or power. Did not Jesus renounce all claims to earthly power as he endured absolute immobilization at the hands of his persecutors? For the Sun was in Aries throughout the Passion of Christ.

SUN IN *TAURUS*
The Magician (I) meets The Judgment (XX)

Those of us born with the Sun in Taurus are encouraged to explore the proper limits of *personal will*. Meditation upon this theme is predicated upon the practice of silence, which hones our ability to *hear*. Typically, Taurians are very deep thinkers and excellent practical problem solvers; they are often able to readily identify which actions are needed, and are enthusiastic about executing their advancement. In other words, the Bull knows how to make things work in the material world—believing as he does that an idea without a practical application is of little use to anyone. Just as the digestion of thoughts, food, or experiences cannot be rushed, hurrying about for the sake of change and stimulation might work against the natural gifts of this placement; a fickle nature can even hinder development. To wear the mantle of the Bull, we must strive to allow reason and logic to guide our thinking process. Our eyes must be open. When we direct our "horns" toward the totality of the cosmos, we seek to understand the creation of the material world out of the Word. A love of the natural world and a sense for its divine origin are often present. The Sun was in Taurus at the birth of Ralph Waldo Emerson (1803–1882). Emerson recognized that nature was permeated by the divine; and he warned of the distractions that existed (even in the early nineteenth century!) to draw us away from its solace and beauty.

SUN IN *GEMINI*
The Magician (I) meets The Sun (XIX)

The celestial Twins will remain side by side for eternity—and the Sun before the stars of Gemini extols the diurnal principle of cooperation as an evolutionary force. Loving cooperation presumes that we cherish a sense for the intrinsic worth—the immortal light—of others. Gemini bestows upon the Sun a childlike wisdom that speaks in the language of the heart. This placement invites us to think in the way of a child at play: *with concentrated seriousness, but without burden*. Gemini bears a natural sense of symmetry: between left and right, between darkness and light, and between heaven and Earth. The stars of the Twins stand for the principle of thinking in the light of faith as a means to develop intuition—for it was intuition alone that drew the Magi to the crib of the Redeemer. When in Gemini, the Sun commands that we follow our own "star" to the ends of the Earth. The Sun was in Gemini at the birth of John the Baptist, who was innocent of the ways of the world. Whereas the Magi bestowed upon the Child the wisdom of the ancient world, the gift of John the Baptist to Jesus was a pure heart that could see the Divine.[10]

---

10   Tomberg, *Meditations on the Tarot*, 485.

SUN IN *CANCER*
The Magician (I) meets The Moon (XVIII)

When the Sun is in Cancer, our higher nature seeks expression through the virtue of selflessness. The impulse to nurture — usually in evidence in those born with this placement — is represented within the glyph itself, sometimes seen as an image of the human breasts, source of nourishment to our newborns. When, however, this impulse is not attended by a strong sense of Self, it can result in the sort of sacrifice that leaves us (and our intended beneficiaries) depleted. The shell of the crab is suggestive of the Cancerian danger of *materializing the intellect* by assuming the attitude of one who "knows better" than others — thereby consigning us to our shells, whence we no longer see or expect anything worthwhile. When the fallen forces of Cancer take hold of us, there can even exist a tendency to flee (or to hide) when under stress. Those of us born under this placement might remember that it is in our power to *reflect* the pure light of cosmic objective truth as well as to *obscure* it. We are encouraged to emerge from the security that we find in the past — our "old shell" — and to instead, with faith and courage, participate in what is becoming. If we imagine ourselves embraced by the two starry arms of the Crab, we are asked: Will we stagnate, or evolve? The Sun was in Cancer at the birth of the Nathan Mary (who experienced the immaculate conception following the Annunciation), at which she spoke the words, "Behold, I am the handmaid of the Lord. Let it be unto me according to your word." Although the Nathan Mary was just fourteen years old when she was visited by the Angel Gabriel, she faithfully took part in the miracle that was unfolding.

SUN IN *LEO*
The Magician (I) meets The Wheel of Fortune (X)

When the Sun is in Leo, hear it roar! The Sun, as ruler of the Lion, is most "at home" before its stars. Those of us born under this placement are invited to strive to stand before the world, unafraid and certain of our abilities. Righteous authority, however, cannot be maintained without compassion for others — for without it, we disdain weakness and we "rule" by compulsion alone. The Sun in Leo confers *vitality*, seen imaginatively in the Lion's mane. "The Wheel of Fortune" brings before us an imagination of the dangers of submitting to the confinement of the closed circle of the serpent's world. In the letter-Arcanum, this circle is represented by the endless, repetitive turning of the wheel of life, thereby creating a prison for the spirit. The spinning of the closed circle of the scientific and material world creates a downward suctional force like that of a whirlpool, whereby we can find ourselves lost in the world of the senses. The "I" of each of us, knowable since the Mystery of Golgotha, enables us to find an opening in the circle that leads us to salvation: *an eternal connection to the cosmos and to its evolution.* Through this opening, the order and wisdom of the universe can be known. The Sun was in Leo at the healing of the nobleman's son; through the father's rejection of his own sovereign authority, the boy had become ill. The vertical heredity that was distorted at the Fall was restored when the father — through his faith in Jesus — brought the child into a direct relationship to the divine archetype.

SUN IN *VIRGO*
The Magician (I) meets Force (XI)

The Virgin awaits her coronation on Earth — when brain-bound intellectuality will bow in the presence of wisdom, and unite with it. When positioned before the stars of Virgo, the Sun reveals to humanity the true power that always appears as powerlessness — as was the case when Jesus Christ hung upon the Cross — for true power cannot be gained at the expense of others. Although many of us born under this placement don't advertise our strengths (due to our inherent modesty), there can exist an ability to make a friend of every enemy, and to overcome all manner of obstacles. The Virgin upholds our hope and faith that life proceeds from a holy source — the throne of God — and flows toward an end of supreme worth.[11] Innocence, too, comes from this same source, and the Virgin is its eternal standard-bearer. The Sun before the stars of Virgo radiates the force of purity, for the Virgin guards what humanity lost at the Fall:

---

11 Tomberg, *Meditations on the Tarot*, 270.

an existence in harmonious cooperation with the divine. Our path homeward is lit by the ten commandments. Those of us born under this placement are encouraged to cultivate an attunement to what the hearts of others are longing to hear, for this is true courtesy. However, the natural humility and modesty of Virgo can also lead to confusion about boundaries both in the social realm and between the inner and outer self—so these must be clearly understood. Any planet in Virgo has the potential to carry a tenderness that finds its archetype in the Son cradled in the arms of the Virgin; therefore, it is all the more unfortunate when we allow ourselves to be swept away by the electrifying flood of the serpent's waters. The Blessed Virgin remains the highest example of this placement (the Sun was in Virgo at her birth), whose many appearances across the centuries have bestowed upon us the hope for our eventual return to the holy source above us.

SUN IN *LIBRA*
The Magician (I) meets Justice (VIII)

When the Sun is in Libra, the quality of diplomacy—whether hard-won or innate—might have a profound effect on our relationships with others. Diplomacy implies possession of the ability to observe events from the standpoint of the fulcrum of the scales, whereby we weigh up the merits of opposing views and ideas judiciously. When we do so, we judge not by our inclinations and personal positions, but by conscience alone. The planetary ruler of Libra, Venus, reveals to us the art of seeking common ground. (This is the basis of the social skill so often apparent in those of us born under this configuration.) The tendency to seek harmony by way of avoidance of conflict and all manner of messiness—to "fall asleep"—can also be in evidence. The Angels within Libra's stars strive to teach us the value of equilibrium of soul, a hallmark of spiritual well-being. Through the sacrifice of Jesus Christ, we can find equanimity throughout all of our trials and suffering; as the Lord of Karma, it is he who has shown us our path forward through the understanding of our karmic burdens. Through karma's laws, we learn that judgment of others is beyond our competence as human beings. The Sun was in Libra at the birth of Fyodor Dostoyevsky (1821–1881), whose novels wrestle with the themes of justice, crime, punishment, and remorse. His character Ivan Karamazov is the source of the oft-quoted phrase, "If there is no God, everything is permitted," thereby revealing the spiritual foundation of morality.

SUN IN *SCORPIO*
The Magician (I) meets Death (XIII)

When before the stars of Scorpio, the Magician finds an easy association with the ancient precept *To be silent*—for the concentration without effort that is the foundation of the Magician's work requires a state of consciousness in which thought, feelings, and the will are brought to a state of perfect calm. The insights—or divine inspirations—that thereby find us can reveal what lies beyond the threshold. Many of us born under this placement have a knack for going straight to the hidden heart of the matter in all its depth—and yet, in truth, this is not always welcome! Although we are typically keenly interested in our fellow men, we frequently fly below the radar, preferring instead to observe goings-on from behind the scenes. The Scorpion bears the power of transformation, whereby suffering and loss can be spun into gold within the soul. Those of us born when the Sun is in Scorpio might do well to attend to the vulnerability of others and to maintain faith in their ability to change—for this alone will disarm our harsh judgments of them. The Sun was in Scorpio at the first conversion of Mary Magdalene. Having first been deeply moved by Jesus's invitation to share the kingdom with him through penance, the once-profligate woman was rendered a servant of Christ by his words of consolation for her inner agitation.

SUN IN *SAGITTARIUS*
The Magician (I) meets The Hermit (IX)

The Sun before the stars of the Archer enables us to hone our ability to focus all of our will and attention on our chosen target. Together, they inspire a boundless quest for the totality of truth that might lead us to the ends of the Earth—for the Sagittarian gift of *breadth of thinking* inclines us to think beyond borders. However, this cosmic blessing, like all others, comes with a warning:

We must guard against wandering without aim, restless and full of doubt — for the fallen Archer's weak self-discipline has the power to take all of the tension out of our bows. The Sun before the stars of Sagittarius unites day consciousness (Sun) with that of the night (Sagittarius). Our luminary of the day bears the mood of empiricism — by way of which we gain knowledge through the senses: We believe what we see with our own eyes. The Hermit's knowledge is achieved in three ways: through his intellect (his lamp), through the harmony found through analogy (his mantle), and through immediate experience (his staff). Most Sun-in-Sagittarius individuals express themselves honestly and do not stand on ceremony; in the absence of self-control, however, these qualities (though often refreshing) can incline us to unleash our honest remarks like so many darts. This is less likely to happen when we are honest with ourselves. The Sun and Sagittarius (our third fire sign) share a creative force: *the Archer's fire bearing special significance due to its alignment with the Central Sun.* The Sun was in Sagittarius at the birth of Beethoven (1770–1827), who was able to hear the harmonies that proceeded from this holy source. He was deeply disappointed that there wasn't time to transcribe all that he heard!

SUN IN *CAPRICORN*
The Magician (I) meets The Star (XVII)

When born under a Capricorn Sun, we are invited to look beyond the physical, biological, and intellectual laws that determine the current of the "lower waters" of humanity — the laws that create a prison for the spirit. The worldview of *spiritism* permeates the Sun when before the stars of the Goat, allowing for the intercession of the divine *when we kneel before it*; and the horns of the Goat signify the fully activated crown. This placement asks that we recognize continuity as the foundation upon which the future must rest — we revere *growth* (the universal sap of life) over *revolution*. The Sun in Capricorn reveals hope as the force that directs evolution; we can thereby acknowledge both the divine origin of the world and its divine aspiration. The constellation of Capricorn bears the cosmic gift of firmness upon the human will, which is one reason that leadership can so often be observed in those born with the Sun in Capricorn. This resolve of will allows us to maintain our focus on the "prize" that we seek — even when it lies on the distant horizon, perhaps even lifetimes away. Indeed, Capricorn blesses willing souls with the power to endure. The lofty beings of the Goat provide the etheric shaping for the skeleton and knees, as well as for the eyes. The Sun was in Capricorn at the adoration of the Magi, who knelt before the Child whose life signified the beginning of what Steiner referred to as the "turning point of time." The course of humanity's future was thereby changed.

SUN IN *AQUARIUS*
The Magician (I) meets Temperance (XIV)

The magic of the Sun in Aquarius is often expressed as an uncanny sense of the way the future is seeking to draw us forward. Because of this orientation, we can find ourselves a bit out of step with the rest of our cohort, but this should not (and usually doesn't) concern us. Typically unencumbered by an allegiance to convention, those of us born under this placement tend to be the reformers of the zodiac, who seek change on behalf of the well-being of the human community. We long to bring a fresh breeze into every room, so that stale ideas might be cast to the winds. When the Sun is before the stars of Aquarius, we might discover the role of the guardian Angel, who acts as a counterweight to the ignoble inclinations that we have acquired since the Fall. Our guardian Angel accompanies us throughout all of our incarnations; we may imagine this Angel holding both ends of the golden thread of spiritual purpose that connects the individual's incarnations. Through this Angel, each of us is able to experience pure maternal love; for it works tirelessly on behalf of the human being it is tasked to guard, cherish, protect, defend, and (perhaps) visit.[12] The Aquarius impulse for community radiates from the Sun when before the Waterman's stars; we can thus discover that individuals across the world — individuals who will never meet — can unite in community by

---

12   Tomberg, *Meditations on the Tarot*, 375.

way of shared *inspiration*. The Sun was in Aquarius at the births of both Steiner and Tomberg,[13] great teachers of humanity whose spiritual missions to establish international spiritual communities (through anthroposophy and Christian Hermeticism) were linked through their direct experiences of the Christ.

SUN IN *PISCES*
The Magician (I) meets The Hanged Man (XII)

The Magician, who has raised consciousness to the level of the heart, finds himself upside down when before the stars of Pisces. Suspended between heaven and Earth, he is given the spiritual task of orienting his will upward, toward the spiritual world. Those of us born under this configuration are thus presented with the following quandary: How might we execute spiritual deeds upon the Earth? The Pisces heart hovers between above and below, attuned to the world of spirit but equally devoted to earthly obligations. This is represented by the silver cord connecting the two fish in the starry ocean of the cosmos, who are swimming in different directions — one vertically (connecting heaven and Earth), and one horizontally (connecting human hearts). The "bridge" in the Pisces glyph spans the abyss between the past and the future, and those of us born under this placement are being asked to find our way across it. This can lead us to an abiding need to understand the Mother beneath our feet and the forces that exist within the subearthly layers that surround her. It is the spiritual freedom characteristic of Pisces — and our independence from old dogmas — that will guide humanity toward the future. The Sun in Pisces inspires us to regard the whole world as a work of divine art — one that reveals the goodness, truth, and beauty of the divine. However, it simultaneously warns us against being at odds with reality — against being deceived by apparent goodness, imagined truth, and virtual beauty — which offer intoxication, but never *joy*. Those of us born under this placement tend to be deeply moved by the suffering of others. The Sun was in Pisces at the conception of the Nathan Jesus, whose life upon the Earth was devoted to the alleviation of humanity's suffering.

 VENUS

The placement of Venus in a chart reveals to us what we love and *listen to*. She is happy wherever she is! The planet of love creates a chalice for our soul and reveals to us what is held within it. We look to Venus to learn of the characteristics of the "personal cross" we must carry, and of the good that might flow through us, into the world, once we accept this cross as the spiritual blessing that it is. When we turn to the image of "The Lover" in the sixth letter-Arcanum of *Meditations on the Tarot*, we see the nature of this cross in the image of the hand of one individual being placed upon the heart of another: *loving sacrifice in service of others*. Venus also leads us to our karmic group, for it is the Archai (the Angels of the Venus sphere) that are responsible for coordinating individuals in this manner. And because Venus is the planet of beauty, she reveals to us the way in which our artistry might be expressed.

VENUS IN *ARIES*
The Lover (VI) meets The Fool (XXI)

Venus before the stars of the Ram (ruled by Mars) can harden the usual conciliatory quality of the planet of love. Alternatively, Aries might also inspire Venus to develop the necessary "backbone" to stand her ground, which may not be her habit. And who can deny the blessing of the ability of gentle Venus to soften the Ram's tendency toward impulsivity and argumentativeness? When before the stars of Aries, Venus can confer warmth of affection and devotion to all she loves; she draws the intellect toward the heart — whereby we are able to distinguish between mere intellectuality and cosmic truth. And yet, this placement simultaneously warns against allowing intellect to *wither* before our deeply held feelings — for our intellect must be *elevated* toward the wisdom of love, but not *abandoned*. (Would not turning our backs on intellect constitute an affront to Aries, our cosmic representative of the upright, thinking individual?) Within this placement, the image of "the fool for love" arises before our eyes. Venus in Aries upholds the ideal of *divine* love, whose torch she will carry for all time. Venus was in Aries at Pentecost, when

---

13 The birth charts of Steiner and Tomberg can be found on page 221. The Sun in both charts is not only in the same zodiacal sign, but in the same *degree* of Aquarius.

Christ entered the souls of the disciples through the intercession of Mary-Sophia. Following the Ascension, the disciples had been united in their suffering and grief at the loss of Jesus. Then, following Pentecost, Jesus's "flock" of disciples became eternally united through his love.

VENUS IN *TAURUS*
The Lover (VI) meets The Judgment (XX)

As the ruler of Taurus, Venus—with its inherent artistry, musicality, sense of harmony, and sensitivity to beauty—finds a supportive embrace among the stars of the Bull. Those of us born under this placement typically find it easy to enjoy life in a way that inspires others. The legendary force of will that dwells within the stars of the Bull might be disguised in velvet and lace by gentle Venus—and it is sometimes the case that it is squandered altogether through indolence. This placement usually confers a deep love of nature, as well as the peace and revitalization that it provides. The Bull's influence upon the planet of love is *constancy*—allowing affections to be enduring and faithful. We might also observe an affinity for comfort and ease, accompanied by an aversion to change. On a higher plane, we can think of Venus—our finest planetary representative of the art of listening—as fine-tuning the Taurian faculty of "spiritual hearing" (which is beautifully expressed in the horns). Venus in Taurus resounds with the message that the spoken word can be the bearer of love, and thus may be a force of healing and of awakening to life. Venus was before the stars of the Bull at the union in the temple. Separated from his family for three days during their annual Passover trip to Jerusalem, the twelve-year-old Nathan Jesus was found teaching in the temple with unparalleled erudition. This was made possible through the sacrifice of the Solomon Jesus, who had freely given his "I" to the loving, simple-minded boy who, twenty-one years later, would die upon the Cross.

VENUS IN *GEMINI*
The Lover (VI) meets The Sun (XIX)

When Venus is in Gemini, artistry can be expressed with versatility. Those of us born under this configuration are being asked to interact—and to cooperate—with a wide variety of individuals. Venus and Mercury (planetary ruler of the Twins) create the warp and weft of our human tapestry. In those of us born under this placement, we might therefore expect to find a faculty for communication that is born of a love of others (like a bee moving from flower to flower). Those who prefer solitude might have their work cut out for them—and yet, what a lovely assignment this would be! The Twins are the consummate representatives of effective communication, and Venus among its stars can confer an artistic quality to our expression through speech and the written word. Language itself can be an artform with this placement. Those of us born with Venus in Gemini must keep in our hearts the myth of the love between Castor and Pollux—so that we might be inspired to sacrifice for our "brothers and sisters." (This will serve to diminish any tendency toward superficiality.) The Gemini virtue of *perseverance* might best be understood as *a willingness to shoulder responsibility in order to help those we love*. Venus was in Gemini at the birth of Novalis (1772–1801), the German romantic poet known for the tender and loving way that he expressed himself. *Hymns to the Night* and *Sacred Songs* reveal an intimate understanding of Christ and Mary-Sophia.

VENUS IN *CANCER*
The Lover (VI) meets The Moon (XVIII)

When in the constellation of the Cancer, Venus warms the interior of the Crab's shell with selfless love. This is a sensitive combination that draws us toward the nobility of what Tomberg referred to as the *intuition of faith*, or the *principle of springtime*[14]—whereby we turn our attention away from the hoped-for results of our efforts. (This is so that we might find satisfaction in participating in the creation of what is *becoming*.) The color green that is associated with Cancer is thus easily understood. (Green is Venus's color, too; she is often depicted in nature's embrace.) Within the starry arms of the Crab lies a cosmic womb in which life is protected and nurtured. And although motherhood and breastfeeding (associated with this constellation) are archetypal examples of this principle, nurturance can take many more forms

---

14 Tomberg, *Meditations on the Tarot*, 501.

than freshly baked bread and honey from the backyard hives — for there are as many ways to give of ourselves as there are human souls. Those of us born under this signature often find that it is *selflessness* that lights our path to redemption. Venus in Cancer sets our intelligence on a path of sympathy, thus rescuing it from the limits of thinking that we "know better" than others — however, when our thinking lacks warmth, so will our heart! Cancer's characteristic attunement to the feelings of others might compel us to go out of our way to make others feel that they belong. Venus was in Cancer at the birth of Mother Teresa (1910–1997), whose missionary work on behalf of the dying and destitute in India remains one of the greatest examples of joyful, selfless giving.

VENUS IN *LEO*
The Lover (VI) meets The Wheel of Fortune (X)

The naturally compassionate planet of love finds warmth among the stars of Leo. Being lion-hearted implies a deep compassion for the failings of others — but this is predicated upon being intimately aware of our own shortcomings. This placement exudes warmth, generosity, and the ability to enjoy life to the fullest. However, the lower forces of Venus can speed Leo toward a life of pleasure-seeking — a sad state of affairs for the king of beasts, who would thereby give up his right to wear a crown. Alternatively, if we strive for equanimity of soul, the balance and harmony for which Venus is known can support the steady rhythm of the heart, which is Leo's domain. A profound love of children is often evident, as is loyalty toward those whom we love and admire. The creative impulse within Leo can easily find expression through the arts when it streams through the planet of love. Though Leo's willingness to brawl is subdued by the presence of Venus (our cosmic peacemaker), those of us born under this configuration tend to admire daring in others. One pitfall of this pairing is the need for attention — which can sometimes be the motivation behind our abundant charms. Venus was in Leo at the birth of the Blessed Virgin; her compassion for others was boundless, her moral authority was absolute, and her equanimity in times of suffering remains a guiding force for humanity.

VENUS IN *VIRGO*
The Lover (VI) meets Force (XI)

When in Virgo, Venus puts before our imagination the cosmic archetype of a daughter embraced by her mother. And just as there is no limit to what a mother will do to protect her child, so does the cosmic Mother embrace the whole of humanity within her robes. She loves us as we are. Venus in Virgo upholds the ideal of purity of heart, whereby — having achieved consciousness of the full distance of humanity's fall from the "image" of God — we have the "eyes" to see within humankind its *divine archetype*. The Virgin loves us without reserve. The stars of Virgo bear the formative forces for the development of the womb, the symbol of the nourishment and the protection of all that is innocent and powerless. We can thus intuit within this placement an innate sense of readiness, or ripeness, in both the human being and in nature. Venus, while within the embrace of the Virgin, seeks to identify what is *needed* and to endeavor to fill that role. This is a pairing that gives rise to an admiration for those who approach work with care and love. Typically a combination that confers modesty, Venus in Virgo might act as a refreshing rampart against self-promotion. This placement brings to mind a garden — representative of the fruitful result of the cooperation and equilibrium between spirit and nature. May we tend our gardens with care! Venus was in Virgo at the conception of John the Baptist, who spent much of his childhood alone in the desert, for he had become an object of Herod's fear (and thus, of his hatred). John's solitude enabled him to protect the promise of his mission to baptize the pure One who would bear the "I" of Christ.

VENUS IN *LIBRA*
The Lover (VI) meets Justice (VIII)

As the ruler of Libra, the planet of love easily finds expression in the social milieu. Venus in Libra suggests a love of interacting with others, for both of these contribute to happy alliances. Indeed, we could interpret in this placement the faculty of "social artistry," for human interactions have her full attention. The "weaving" impulse of Venus has the ability to mitigate conflicts between us by revealing what positions and attitudes might bind us together: *Venus, before the stars of Libra, comes in peace and longs to maintain it!* Seeking to bring empathy and mercy to the balance pans of the Scales, she has no interest in "taking sides." When plagued by doubt and indecision, however, Venus loses the ability to see the full scope of the reality before her—and her dislike of all forms of unpleasantness can sometimes engender a tendency to "fall asleep" in the presence of conflict. Sadly, this constitutes a setting down of a heavenly commission. When moral development is wanting, those of us born under this pairing can succumb to laziness and envy—for the grass might always seem greener on the other side of the fence. Venus in Libra fosters refinement and an interest in the arts. This combination was present at the birth of Jane Austen (1775–1817), regarded as one the finest novelists of her (or, indeed, *any*) time. Her heroines never abandoned their forbearance, tolerance, and compassion when they were subjected to the casual cruelties of others. The caustic wit and irony that she wove into her prose has delighted the underappreciated for over two centuries.

VENUS IN *SCORPIO*
The Lover (VI) meets Death (XIII)

When Venus is before the stars of the Scorpion, feelings tend to run very deep. Scorpio's vulnerable heart longs for *loyalty*—and those of us born under this placement prize this virtue highly and offer it wholeheartedly to those we deem worthy of it. The trusting nature of Venus acts as a breath of fresh air to Mars-ruled Scorpio, which sometimes bestows a tendency to view everything in terms of rivalry and power struggles. The combined lower aspects of this pair can create "a dark soup of soul," whereby we can easily fall prey to suspicion and jealousy. On a more elevated plane, those of us born when Venus is in the midst of the Scorpion's stars tend to be drawn to the mysteries that exist behind the veil of the material world. This placement thereby allows us to perceive the alchemical heart of the zodiac, wherein our trials, temptations, and suffering might be spun into the gold of transformation. Venus—in this placement—can bring equanimity and peace. (In fact, many born under this combination hold no fear of death.) There might even exist an intuitive sense of the spiritual world as our true home. Venus was in Scorpio at the Baptism, precisely aligned with the star that marks its heart: *Antares*. Tomberg wrote that the moment of the Baptism is the boundary, in what is depicted historically, between the Old Testament and the New Testament. In the Baptism, the living consummation of the past absorbed into itself the living seed of the future.[15]

VENUS IN *SAGITTARIUS*
The Lover (VI) meets The Hermit (IX)

Venus before the stars of the Archer suggests an expectant outlook, as well as the ability to find joy in life—no matter the circumstances. The Archer, well-known for adventurousness, might bring to Venus an all-embracing perspective, such that experiences are sought from many sources and cultures, whether or not we have the luxury of travel. The objects of our affections might also have the effect of opening a door to another world. Venus in Sagittarius implies a feeling for the truth—while simultaneously softening any inclination (at the expense of kindness and love for those around us) to say what is "true". An interest in religious or philosophical matters may set us on the path to knowledge of the full breadth of opposing ideals. Moreover, those of us born under this configuration might strive to understand the *moral foundation* behind every idea. This requires that we separate ourselves from any collective positions—and seek guidance instead from the light of consciousness, from awareness of the *whole* truth, as well as from intuition derived from direct experience. This placement can engender restlessness when we lack a quest that stirs the soul. The image of the centaur (half-animal and half-human) is suggestive of humanity's struggle to overcome its lower nature—which makes us vulnerable to temptation. Venus was in Sagittarius as Jesus stilled the Sea of Galilee. Having overcome the temptations in the wilderness, Jesus had mastered the elements; thus, as the sudden storm raged, he slept against the mast. Disturbed by Jesus's apparent indifference to their plight, the disciples were overcome with fear as well as anger. Jesus reproved them for their lack of faith and their susceptibility to fear.

---

15 Tomberg, *Christ and Sophia*, 142.

VENUS IN *CAPRICORN*
The Lover (VI) meets The Star (XVII)

When before the stars of Capricorn, Venus directs our soul toward the spiritual world—the luminous source of hope that directs creative evolution toward the future. Hope draws us from one life to the next, from the past to the future, from potential to reality. "The Star" is the letter-Arcanum of Eve, and of all mothers across time. Thus, when in communion with "The Star," Venus listens for continuity—knowing that what has already occurred prepares us for what will be. Those among us born with this placement tend to have a certain nobility of heart—a no-nonsense demeanor—owing to Saturn's rulership of the Goat. A natural poise (we might even say "unflappability") and strong work ethic (which accompanies Venus while in this sector of the heavens) often puts those of us born under this configuration "in control"—where we prefer to be! This proficiency is also supported by the Capricorn trait of endurance. However, it is best to remember that the ambition associated with Capricorn can appear as a need to be well-thought-of. (This can sometimes devolve into envy of those of higher stature.) When Venus is before the stars of Capricorn, the soul's stance is firm—and yet we still possess the ability to navigate changes in terrain as the future demands. It was Jesus's unwavering devotion to his mission that allowed him to endure the temptations in the wilderness before the Angels ministered to him—for Venus was in Capricorn during these ordeals.

VENUS IN *AQUARIUS*
The Lover (VI) meets Temperance (XIV)

Venus before the stars of Aquarius suggests an eagerness to engage with those of different walks of life, for the Aquarian heart is magnanimous. The sense that Steiner attributed to this region of the zodiac is *warmth*; Venus in Aquarius is therefore an astute judge of the "temperature" of others, and she seeks warmth in their company. However, being perhaps the most objective sign of the zodiac, Aquarius can sometimes engender a cool demeanor, whereby we can seem equally remote from *all* points of view. (This might be imagined as a bee that has strayed far from the hive for too long.) When before the stars of the Waterman, Venus usually derives a great deal of happiness through friendships and community—groups that she will ideally serve with love and care. The need for freedom for which Aquarius is known might find a stronghold in the soul when Venus is in this sector of the heavens. In consequence, we may not look kindly upon our constraints, whether imposed by circumstances or by others—and thus, as we listen for what is striving to be heard from the future, we know that freedom will grant us the necessary agility to meet it. Venus was in Aquarius at the healing of the paralyzed man, who was able to walk after enduring thirty-eight years of the limitations imposed by his paralysis. The healing properties of the waters of the pool—depicted on the "Temperance" card as pouring forth from the vases of an Angel—were activated by the stirring of an Angel's wing.

VENUS IN *PISCES*
The Lover (VI) meets The Hanged Man (XII)

In Pisces we reach the feet of the human being, by which we are able to move in freedom upon the Earth. Through the Angels of Pisces, we are able to take spiritual impulses into our whole being. The exaltation (and, therefore, strength) of Venus in Pisces might simply be imagined as Venus (who bears the gift of *listening*) within the boundaries of the sign of spiritual hearing (Pisces). This placement often confers an openness of heart that can attune us to human suffering—the universal language of humanity. The somewhat dreamy and idealistic nature of this combination—though it bears the power to lift the weight of our cares—can also lead to a dysfunctional passivity, a lack of backbone. We can then drift without purpose, letting the currents of mass consciousness (or, of our *feeling* life) carry us where they will. And yet, Venus before the stars of the Fishes can make possible profound inspirations in all aspects of the arts. Because this placement invites us to experience the connectedness of all in the human family—like a tapestry created from the golden threads spun by each individuality—we recognize that human evolution depends upon our earthly deeds. Venus was in Pisces at the birth of Tomberg, a Hanged Man in human form. The epic scope of his spiritual deeds on behalf of humanity expressed the condition of having replaced earthly gravitation with that from above.

☿ MERCURY

Within the sphere of Mercury dwell the Archangels, the "folk" spirits. Groups of individuals who share the same values are guided by these beings in matters of their true mission and their spiritual progress as a group. Therefore, Mercury in the birth chart implies cooperation and enlightens us as to the nature of our interactions with others. Moreover, while stimulating our intelligence and promoting healing, it brings a youthful levity to all that it touches. *It guides us toward the ideal direction of our thinking.* However, Mercury can also bring mental agitation—implied by its agility and speedy pace—thereby reminding us that serenity stimulates prayer.

MERCURY IN *ARIES*
The Pope (V) meets The Fool (XXI)

When before the stars of Aries, Mercury asks that our minds be set ablaze by the flame of our ideals, the highest of these being *love*. Those of us born under this configuration are encouraged to direct our minds to what we regard as being of enduring moral value; this implies initiatives that benefit others—our "flock." To be in the presence of an Aries intellect is to feel rather slow on the uptake! Indeed, those of us born under this placement are typically clear and decisive thinkers—who can become impatient when others take their time "arriving at the point," or (heaven forbid) when they *never* do. Sometimes, however, the thoughts of Mercury-in-Aries individuals can disappear as quickly as they catch fire, for Mercury usually does not stay put for long. This placement begets a directness of expression that can sometimes appear aggressive to the unprepared; coupled with a reluctance to hear others' points of view (not unknown to this placement), arrogance can ensue. We can head this off at the pass if we heed the warning of this placement to beware any endeavor of which we are the sole beneficiary. This placement was present at the birth of Raphael (1483–1520). He remains unsurpassed in his conveyance, through his brushwork, of the love between Mary and Jesus.

MERCURY IN *TAURUS*
The Pope (V) meets The Judgment (XX)

The Angels of Taurus typically engender a love of thinking—"chewing the cud"—which, at its highest expression, serves our moral development. Steiner indicated that *rationalism* is the worldview that streams from Taurus; this suggests that our thinking is most productive if supported by reason and logic. When Mercury is in Taurus, speech often forgoes flourish in favor of simplicity and directness. This placement is often indicative of an excellent memory. Furthermore, the faculty of hearing might play a predominant role in our learning process. Decisions are typically arrived at with care and deliberation, which can sometimes come to expression as a refusal to give up an old idea, *no matter what.* For those of us born under this placement, the Mercury "hum" can often be calmed in the presence of natural beauty. What is of value to us—in any realm—will occupy a good deal of our thoughts; when we lack a spiritual sensibility, however, our minds can be mired in an endless quest for security. Mercury was in Taurus at the cleansing of the temple. When Jesus overturned the tables of the vendors and money changers—whose reverence for money had led them to engage in commerce within the temple—he sought to awaken them from their materialistic slumber.

MERCURY IN *GEMINI*
The Pope (V) meets The Sun (XIX)

Mercury's status as ruler of Gemini contributes to the strength of the intellect inherent in this placement, summoning the imagination of the mind of a joyful "multitasker." While this level of adaptability might be admired by the rest of us, it can also leave us in possession of merely superficial knowledge of a given assortment of topics. Furthermore, Mercury in Gemini reminds us to develop a solid grounding upon the Earth, lest our swiftly moving thoughts be scattered to the winds. If we ignore this warning, however, we might renounce the Gemini gift of seeing clearly in the present, as if through the eyes of a child. The awareness of the "star" that is uniquely ours to follow can elude us if we heed the modern-day "scribes" and "priests" who seek to disturb the needle of our compass through the art of distraction. May it never be so! Those of us born under this configuration recognize that we stand to learn something from everyone we meet — and, in this way, we uphold the ideals of brother- and sisterhood, as well as of cooperation. As the planet of healing, Mercury before the stars of Gemini invokes the following words of Tomberg: "There is no healing if it be not for all."[16] Mercury was in Gemini at Pentecost, when the Holy Spirit streamed directly upon Mary — while tongues of fire shot up above the twelve gathered around her. This event represents the ideal of a vertical channel between above and below (as depicted in the Gemini glyph), free of distraction and mental clutter.

MERCURY IN *CANCER*
The Pope (V) meets The Moon (XVIII)

Within Cancer, we encounter the need to delve into the essence of matter — for the worldview of *materialism* radiates from its stars. Matter is everything that we can see. All that is created through the Word is matter: a granite massif, a redwood forest, an alpine field of wildflowers, a cub, a newborn. Matter is also what humanity has created: Michelangelo's David, money, houses, cars, weapons, satellites. Cancer's glyph reveals two spirals separated by a breach; one spiral draws us toward the center, while the other draws us outward. The breach is the abyss that has developed between the material world and that of the spirit. It had been humanity's task to remove itself from its connection to spirit in order that freedom — and the developing "I" — could be experienced; we must now embark on the return journey. When Mercury moves before the stars of Cancer, thoughts turn to matter, calling us to recognize the spiritual origin of the natural world, and of humanity. It asks that we warm all that we cherish with our soul-breath, our "touch." We can often observe in this combination a tendency to tend the home fires and (at its best) thinking that is selfless. However, Mercury in Cancer also stands as a warning; for a purely materialistic intellectuality — whereby we regard the brain *alone* as the domain of our thought-life — can eclipse our ability to *reflect* the creative light of conscience. The connection between the Crab's ruler (the Moon) and the subconscious suggests that feelings might intrude upon thinking in ways of which we are unaware. We can typically observe an interest in the past, but we must fight any inclination (however compelling it might seem) to stagnate there. Mercury was in Cancer at the raising of Lazarus. His yearning for the realm of the eternal was so strong that he lost interest in everyday life. Jesus's call ("Lazarus, come forth!") was one of remembrance for the suffering of humanity.

MERCURY IN *LEO*
The Pope (V) meets The Wheel of Fortune (X)

Although Mercury in Leo can engender great warmth of expression that is born of an abiding compassion for the weaknesses of others, it asks that we also seek Leo's "kingly" and "queenly" qualities. The Lion brings the gift of creativity to thought, and (usually) an ability to express ideas with confidence. This placement invites those among us who have not yet found our authoritative voice to strive to develop it, inwardly, to the degree that is proper to each of us. Leo's worldview is *sensualism*; at its highest expression, this can manifest as a love of life's earthly experiences — an urge to enjoy life the fullest. But sometimes the natural courage and confidence of the king of beasts can take us a step too far, thereby knocking us off of our throne. Mercury was in Leo at the birth of Herman Melville (1819–1891), whose great work *Moby Dick* explores the consequences of unbridled instincts — in this case, revenge. Ahab was captive in the closed world of the serpent — the "world mill" — and was subject to the influence of powers far greater than he. Had Ahab sought an exit from the "eternal repetition," he might have found — through a connection to the cosmos beyond — an understanding of his karma before the mighty force of the great whale.

MERCURY IN *VIRGO*
The Pope (V) meets Force (XI)

When Mercury is before the stars of Virgo, our thinking might be oriented toward the power of renewal that permeates all living things; in the presence of this superior force, we bend spontaneously in holy awe — for we know that it proceeds from a sacred source — and

---

16 Tomberg, *Meditations on the Tarot* (2022 edition), 682; and *The Wandering Fool*, 99.

our thoughts might thereby reflect the serene clarity of the "sea of glass" that surrounds this source. This placement suggests that we seek within the phenomena of nature the secrets of healing. Does our thinking occur in harmony with these phenomena, or does it merely serve the currents of our personal will, which so often work against them? The thoughts of those of us born under this configuration often turn to the subject of health and how to maintain it; perhaps Virgo, as the sign in which Mercury finds rulership and exaltation, can be understood as the constellation in which healing and movement find communion. The virtue that streams from this region of the zodiac — courtesy — can be expressed (by way of Mercury's intercession) through all of our communications when we seek to meet the needs of others. Although this placement can confer tact in verbal exchanges, it can sometimes lead us to midjudge what should be said and what is best kept to ourselves — such as when we are distracted from our higher purpose. The Mercury-in-Virgo mind is usually able to penetrate complex and intricate subjects and evaluate them objectively; it is typically detail-oriented. Mercury was in Virgo at the birth of Mother Teresa (1910-1997), who faithfully devoted her life to the care of the ill and the suffering. Perhaps her most enduring legacy is her ability to attend to her duties with such joy.

MERCURY IN *LIBRA*
The Pope (V) meets Justice (VIII)

Mercury in Libra bears the gift of scope in our thinking, whereby we resist subjectivity. We can behold in the fulcrum of the Scales the ideal of justice: the ability to assess relative merit and harm in the light of *conscience*, which exists high above personal convictions and sympathies. Mercury in Libra might set the compass of the mind toward peacemaking, cooperation, and diplomacy; our minds thereby turn to how reconciliation can be achieved in the face of conflict. When before the stars of Libra, Mercury often engenders an aptitude for weaving others together on behalf of a shared interest. We might even observe among those of us born under this placement a knack for creating the impression that we agree with whomever we're speaking to! Others often find us persuasive — although under the influence of this placement, we sometimes find ourselves in need of hearing the ideas of others in order to achieve clarity of thought. When the less admirable tendencies of Mercury in Libra are evident, we can observe a reluctance to weigh in for one side or the other — which is an expression of a disinclination to "rock the boat." Mercury was in Libra at the birth of Mohandas (Mahatma) Gandhi (1869-1948). His adherence to the ideal of non-violence was the core principle of his valiant (and successful!) endeavor to maintain peace within the context of the political and religious shifts that were afoot in India before its partition from Britain in 1947.

MERCURY IN *SCORPIO*
The Pope (V) meets Death (XIII)

Shining as a beacon toward the bottom of every deep well, Mercury before the stars of Scorpio engenders a desire to look beneath the surface in order to uncover what is hidden. This might lead us to seek to understand the dynamic forces that originate behind the veil of the senses, to unearth what lies within the subconscious of the human soul — or, alas, to enter into the heart of darkness. (Joseph Conrad was born beneath this placement.) At the center of the constellation is *Antares*, the star that guards the secrets of death — secrets that can only be known through the practice of silence, at which Scorpio excels. We could even say that, among those of us born under this configuration, we can usually observe a preference for saying very little — and when we do speak, we favor the discussion of topics of substance. Mercury-in-Scorpio people don't spend a lot of time thinking or speaking about trivialities! *Pride and jealously can stoke a need to wield power over others.* Indeed, Mercury was in Scorpio at the birth of Stalin, who is said to have communed regularly with the demonic realm, wherein his evil and treachery found sustenance. Moreover, the ideas set into motion by Stalin are still wreaking havoc upon the world — for, the legacy of his cruel tyrannies continues to weaken the family, the society, and the church.

MERCURY IN *SAGITTARIUS*
The Pope (V) meets The Hermit (IX)

Sagittarius bequeaths upon Mercury an *aim*, whereby — not content to merely dip its toes in the waters of knowledge—it seeks to know wisdom through the totality of truth. Using the Hermit's staff, Mercury gains the "bone speech" of immediate, intuitive experience. Alternatively, the Mercury impulse to illumine and awaken might enable the Hermit's lamp to shine a little brighter, thus illuminating the problems that are before us with *clarity*. Because this placement of Mercury implies the continued expansion of our thinking, a love of exploration (through both study and travel) can often be in evidence—sometimes developing into relationships with those from different cultures. Mercury works well here, in that it brings joy and a youthful outlook to the (usually) highly focused demeanor of the Archer; it demands control of thought, such that our thinking remains impartial and is thus unable to work in the service of the five currents of the personal will (the desire to be great, to take, to keep, to advance, and to hold onto at the expense of others). Sagittarius grants upon human thinking the fire of creativity. Mercury was before the stars of the Archer at the births of Tycho Brahe (1546–1601) and Johannes Kepler (1571–1630), the two astronomers who brought together entirely different conceptions of the heavens in an era when the world seemed ready to replace the geocentric (Ptolemaic) system. (During the last year of Brahe's life, Kepler worked as his assistant in Prague.) Each was intent on revealing the true nature of our solar system. Brahe conceived of a geo-heliocentric system within which the Earth ceded none of its importance to the Sun "in the midst"; Kepler, on the other hand, established the laws that formed the basis of modern astronomy. Either system without the other lacks the *totality* of the truth, for the Tychonic system provides a context for *spiritual* reality, while the Copernican (which Kepler advanced) provides the same for the *physical* reality.

MERCURY IN *CAPRICORN*
The Pope (V) meets The Star (XVII)

The stars of the Goat confer upon Mercury the ability to concentrate for long periods of time. "Capricorn thinking" values order and structure. Its ruler, Saturn, brings seriousness and purpose to Mercury; but while the focus of thought and the gravity of intent can be a great gift to sometimes-flighty Mercury, our cosmic messenger can also be weighed down with pessimism, like a child struggling with a bag that's too heavy. Our way out of this frame of mind lies with an understanding of the spiritual purpose of our suffering, and of the unique mission for which we incarnated. Steiner identified *spiritism* as the worldview of Capricorn, perhaps because the constellation was regarded in ancient times as the gateway to the gods. The letter-Arcanum "The Star" reveals *tradition* as the spiritual current that draws us forward toward the future on the wings of hope. (This is the origin of the time-honored observation that "Capricorn reveres the past.") The Mercury-in-Capricorn individuals among us are ordinarily careful about what we say, lest we lose the respect of others that we value so highly. Mercury was in Capricorn at the birth of Charles Dickens (1812–1870), whose great works nurtured the hope for a future in which the suffering of children and the poor could no longer be overlooked by the industrial society that had perpetuated their vulnerability.

MERCURY IN *AQUARIUS*
The Pope (V) meets Temperance (XIV)

Mercury in Aquarius engenders minds that await the breath of the Holy Spirit. The placement is suggestive of an objective, original mind that thinks "ahead of the curve," toward the uncharted future—one that is naturally devoted to the truth and is typically unafraid to oppose the mainstream currents of thought on its behalf. It could almost go without saying that this capacity might not always be embraced among those who are content-with-how-things-are. It is characteristic of those of us born with Mercury in Aquarius that we shine our light upon what is seeking our notice from the spiritual world. Indeed, we long to shine this light into every dark corner of the mind that needs a bit of housekeeping. Mercury in Aquarius beckons us to think in a new way:

> We can try *to think with the flood*—i.e., no longer to think *alone*, but rather *together* with the anonymous "choir" of thinkers above, below, yesterday, and tomorrow. "*I think*" then gives way to "*it thinks*."[17]

---

17 Tomberg, *Meditations on the Tarot*, 393.

While the winged messenger is in Aquarius, his job is to nourish the minds of others with the promise of the future; this is an inventive placement that also carries with it an interest in the exchange of ideas within friendships and within community. Indeed, without the feedback of others, our ideas can become abstract and fixed, devoid of warmth. "Temperance" reveals the work of our guardian Angel, who guards our *image*—our perfect Self—as our *likeness* does its work upon the Earth. Mercury was in Aquarius at the birth of Valentin Tomberg (1900-1973), who wrote extensively about the fundamental necessity, in spiritual life, of *meditation*. He stated that definite times should be set aside for the practice—which requires us to be fully conscious—so that our openness to everyday life does not become lost.

MERCURY IN *PISCES*
The Pope (V) meets The Hanged Man (XII)

At the end of our zodiacal journey, we stand upon the Earth as spiritual beings who can partake wholly in the substance of *life*. While we fully engage in material life, holding fast to our steps upon the Earth, we simultaneously keep one ear open to the whisperings of the divine world. Equilibrium between the two worlds requires what has been described as "a constancy of conscious, active choosing."[18] The gift of Pisces upon human thinking is *fluidity*, easily imagined as a fish darting this way and that, impossible to catch. The Pisces mind sometimes flows with the current, and sometimes swims against it. In doing so, it *adapts* and listens for what is coming. Those born under this configuration are familiar with the struggle that is sometimes required to emancipate ourselves from old concepts. Among those of us born under this placement, we might encounter inspired thinking (courtesy of Neptune, the secondary ruler of Pisces); but this faculty is accompanied by a warning against "magical" ideation that is at odds with the day-to-day demands of material reality. Alternatively, we might also observe within this placement a tendency toward a scientific-materialistic cast of mind. (Both of these elements have flourished during the age of Pisces.) Mercury in Pisces typically inspires deep empathy for the suffering of others. This configuration was present at the birth of Steiner (1861-1925), who provides for us the sublime example of simultaneously grasping the past *and* the future, while also giving us insight into humanity's task of achieving equilibrium between the loss of the one and the promise of the other.

MOON

The zodiacal sign of the Moon is one of the most important indicators in a birth chart. It reveals the texture of our karma within a lifetime (and the virtue that might support it)—but it can also obscure the reasons behind that karma. The sign of the Moon describes our inherent behaviors, whose origin lie in the subconscious. The Moon represents heredity: the horizontal stream that connects generations, *as well as the bonds to this stream that might be better left behind*. The placement of the Moon is also remarkably descriptive of our relationship with our mother (or other primary caregiver)—which, as we know, many of us spend our entire lives trying to untangle. The Moon's zodiacal sign shows us how we tend to nurture others. It can be an uncomfortable fact that, according to Steiner, *we all choose our parents*. This we do in order that the ideal "table" be set for our incarnation.

MOON IN *ARIES*
The Empress (III) meets The Fool (XXI)

When the Moon is in Aries, it reflects the fiery light of *idealism*. This is a Moon that is willing to sacrifice for what it loves! Idealism—which reveals how things *ought* to be—can, however, incline us to set aside other considerations, such as the ultimate effectiveness of our actions and the viewpoints of others. Representing thinking (Aries) and the brain, the organ of thought (Moon), this pair illuminates the role of human intellect. As a result, *either* the personal self (the ego) can remain the author of the act of consciousness, *or* the "thinking self" is quieted before a greater intelligence (and can thus be prepared to receive it.) This is an independent Moon that usually gives us drive and

---

18 Laquanna Paul and Robert Powell, *Cosmic Dances of the Zodiac* (San Rafael, CA: Sophia Foundation Press, 2007), 100.

initiative, but this can sometimes be accompanied by rushing headlong into the unknown. It is a placement that typically expresses impatience, a wide competitive streak, and the tendency to take things personally. Quickness to anger is characteristic, though not necessarily visible. We take care of others by making it known that we will stand up for them. The Moon was in Aries at the birth Albert Schweitzer (1875-1965), who had achieved expertise in several subjects, including music, philosophy, and medicine. His medical missionary work in Africa (in what is now Gabon) was undertaken as a Christian endeavor, offered as atonement for what he regarded as the sins of colonialism. His first hospital, created in 1913, fell into disrepair during WWI. Throughout his long life, he worked intermittently at the hospital that ultimately rose from the ashes of the first. He died in Gabon at the age of 90.

MOON IN *TAURUS*
The Empress (III) meets The Judgment (XX)

When together, the Moon and Taurus (its sign of exaltation) reveal the possibilities that derive from the alliance of divine will and human will. Although the demeanor of many with this signature might be described as easygoing, the will tends to be very strong indeed. The spiritual task of this placement is this: to elevate the personal will from our astral body (the seething hotbed of our likes and dislikes) to our *conscience*, which dwells above it and receives its direction from heaven. Perhaps the Moon finds its exaltation here due to the Taurian capacity for the restoration of memory—whereby our past (the source of our karma) might be recalled and brought to light. Those born with the Moon in Taurus bear a sensitivity to the divine (or, archetypal) feminine; through her influence, we *listen*, and then *digest* what we have heard. This can take time! Therefore, while the deeds of those of us born with a Taurus Moon are usually endowed with a stable, practical character (steadfast and realistic, we tend to finish what we begin) we might also be *wary of change*. When we lack a sense of the true value of things, we can rely too heavily on material comforts. We long to make those we love feel the security that we value so highly. The Moon was in Taurus at the birth of Johannes Kepler (1571-1630), who believed the starry heavens to be a manifestation of God that is accessible to humanity through the natural light of reason. Kepler's "horns" were attuned to the cosmic truth of the physical reality of the heavens.

MOON IN *GEMINI*
The Empress (III) meets The Sun (XIX)

The Moon in Gemini suggests *motion*; those of us born under this placement might be interested in so many things that moving with agility among them is often characteristic. We might observe the gifts of youthful joy and purity of intent within this placement, which simultaneously confers a genuine interest in others. This is one of the strongest astral signatures for cooperation and for communication; underlying these qualities is the ability to bring others together through shared purpose. This combination bears a warning, however, and its name is *Inconstancy*. Therefore, those who continually move from one thing to the next—never giving anything the attention it deserves—risk losing the clarity of thinking that is the natural offering of Gemini. *The Gemini Moon bears the teachings of the union of faith and intelligence, which are the alchemical substances of intuitive certainty.* Those of us born under this placement are advised to follow the "star" above us, and to assist others in doing the same. The Gemini glyph bears the image of a vertical channel between heaven and Earth, by way of which what is *below* can finds its reflection in what is *above*. The Moon was in Gemini at the birth of Sir Isaac Newton (1642-1726/27), whose discoveries in the realms of motion, gravitation, and optics (among other subjects) revealed the divine origin of our planetary system. Newton, concerned that his work might cause us to think of planetary movements as mechanical (akin to great clock), reminded us that it was divine creation that set them in motion in the first place!

MOON IN *CANCER*
The Empress (III) meets The Moon (XVIII)

When in the sign that it rules (Cancer), the Moon bestows the impulse to nurture and protect life: the beating heart within material substance. Just as the ribcage protects the heart from harm, the gesture of the Crab is one of enfolding what it deems precious; hence, its virtue can be understood as the essence of selflessness. However, this impulse is best predicated upon a strong sense of Self, lest we dissolve into the requirements of others. The Moon in Cancer takes us straight to the manger—which is at the same time an imagination of the starry cluster within the center of the sign, as well as the alpha and the omega of the world—for therein lay the Heart that is at the center of all hearts. When in Cancer, the Moon bears the danger of materialistic intellectuality—*thinking that occludes the creative light of conscience.* Furthermore, when we lack the humility and willingness to learn from others, our intelligence can be relegated to a pond of stagnant water. There can exist a tendency to hide when under stress. The Moon was in Cancer at the birth of Dr. Karl König (1902–1966), founder of the Camphill movement, which continues to provide a therapeutic and educational environment to children and adults with developmental impairments. His work exemplified a belief in the value of a loving, nurturing environment in which all participants have the opportunity to become the best that they can be.

MOON IN *LEO*
The Empress (III) meets The Wheel of Fortune (X)

In Leo, we come to the region of the zodiac that carries the forces which build up the human heart. As our "inner Sun," the heart is the center of our entire rhythmic system, whose rhythms mirror that of the cosmos: 72 heartbeats per minute, the same number in *years* for the vernal point to move one zodiacal degree; and 25,920 breaths per day, the same number in *years* in a Platonic year—the time required for the vernal point to move all the way around the zodiac. When before the stars of Leo, the Moon confers an inherent nobility (our "inner regent"), boldness, and warmth. There is usually a confidence to this Moon—a sense of our intrinsic worth—for the Lion bestows certainty of purpose and a tendency to step in and take charge when necessary. (Never mind that others might disagree with our timing!) The innate dignity of this placement can devolve into pride and self-importance when we deem ourselves superior to the more humble among us. A Leo Moon asks that we experience the world in full, and that we claim our proper place within it. This implies that those of us born under this configuration might need to "wrestle with ourselves" in order to bring our unique individuality to expression. The Baptism occurred when the Moon was in the center of Leo, providing for us a beautiful imagination of the Leo gesture given to us by Steiner (also born under a Leo Moon). As our arms are outstretched like the radiant rays of the Sun, we stream our love upon the whole world—and as we bring our fingertips to the top of our crown,[19] we bring expression to the raying in of the spirit, which found its highest expression at the Baptism in the Jordan.

MOON IN *VIRGO*
The Empress (III) meets Force (XI)

I have observed a consistent tenderness among those born with the Moon in Virgo—a disinclination to be unkind that is reminiscent of the Mother (Mary-Eve-Sophia) of us all, whom we associate with this constellation. Also observed among those of us born under this placement is a deep connection to the forces of the natural world, which played a part in every one of Christ's miracles; the plant alone offers a "manual" in which we can find innumerable laws of spiritual discipline.[20] This placement suggests a willingness to serve the needs of others, of which we can have a keen sense. This, however, does not require that we recede into the background with a vague sense of inadequacy. Instead, we might consider renouncing the need to force anything, in favor of "modesty that is born of illumined serenity." We thereby avoid what we might otherwise feel drawn to do if we were to be swept away by the river of our will—for the Virgo Moon bears the knowledge that true power lacks the hallmarks of a tyrant. Sometimes, this placement can engender excessive doubt and worry that can undermine our health. Additionally, we might need to

---

19 This movement forms part of the eurythmy gesture for the "t" sound that Steiner associated with Leo. Eurythmy is a form of movement introduced by Rudolf Steiner in 1912. Its patterns and gestures effect etheric movement, and thereby support health. Eurythmy is at the same time a spiritual practice.
20 Tomberg, *Meditations of the Tarot*, 258.

overcome any tendency to be overly critical of others. The Moon was in Virgo at the birth of Peter Deunov (1864–1944), who in 1932 created a form of movement known as paneurhythmy, which is usually done to violin pieces written by Deunov himself. Intended to support inner balance, these movements are circle dances that are ideally performed with the soles of the feet touching the Earth.

MOON IN *LIBRA*
The Empress (III) meets Justice (VIII)

When before the stars of Libra, the Moon typically imparts a distaste for unpleasantness, as well as a noted longing for peace and harmony. This can have two different effects: in the first case, we avoid conflict, preferring to "fall asleep" at its feet (i.e., simply avoiding making waves); in the second, we seek to build a bridge between the "warring" parties or concepts. Sometimes the Libra glyph is imagined as an altar; indeed, the eurythmy gesture for the sound Steiner gave for Libra[21] seems to create a current from below to above, whereby our prayers might be carried heavenward. In this sense, the fulcrum of the scales can be imagined as a doorway to the light of heaven. The Moon before the Scales of Justice implies deeds that serve the ideal of social justice — *as well as* the necessity to strive for inner balance, which is predicated upon self-mastery. A strong desire to be with others is often evident with this placement, and there can be an ease in the social milieu that rests upon natural grace and diplomacy. *Impartiality* is one of the great strengths of this combination. Additionally, we often find that Libra's ruler (Venus) confers charm and the ability to make others feel understood. The Moon was in Libra at the birth of Nelson Mandela (1918–2013), who sought to effect racial reconciliation in South Africa through the abolition of apartheid.

MOON IN *SCORPIO*
The Empress (III) meets Death (XIII)

When in Scorpio, the Moon confers intensity, whether apparent or hidden beneath a veneer of insouciance. Patience is often a strong suit. We are typically keen judges of the "moral smell" of a situation. The Moon-Scorpio combination summons before the mind's eye a deep lake with a surface as smooth as glass — on which all the stars above it are reflected! Those of us born under this configuration prefer to "go all-in and go deep" regarding whatever we pursue, which can even result in an aversion to what passes for polite conversation (and, sometimes, *any* conversation at all). This Moon longs for loyalty from others. (All the same, we keep our stinger ready in the event of a betrayal: Why has God given the Scorpion a deadly stinger — if not to protect its marshmallow-soft heart!) That having been said, forgiveness is one lesson that must be learned. Usually evident is a habit of keeping inner thoughts, feelings, and plans close to the vest; for Moon-in-Scorpio individuals, trust must be earned. Because Scorpio is a fixed sign, feelings can be hard to release. The Moon was in Scorpio during Jesus's conversation with Nicodemus, during which Nicodemus experienced a nocturnal initiation. Each initiation is a sort of death experience, followed by a "birth" into higher consciousness. The consciousness of Nicodemus was completely changed; he was "reborn" to the state of consciousness before the Fall — when Spirit was divine Breath and where this breath was reflected by virginal Nature ("water") — and he could then see the kingdom of God (John 3:3).

MOON IN *SAGITTARIUS*
The Empress (III) meets The Hermit (IX)

This is an adventurous placement that inspires the same quality in others. Those of us born under it typically exude warmth and generosity, preferring a casual atmosphere to a more formal one. The Moon before the stars of the Archer confers a strong allegiance to the truth, and the Moon in Sagittarius individuals among us are usually *searchers* who highly value freedom. Not only must the Archer run to remain in the hunt, and not only does Jupiter (the ruler of Sagittarius) defy limits of all kinds, but the Hermit "wanders the Earth":

---

21   Steiner associated each zodiacal sign with an archetypal gesture *as well as* a sound that could also be expressed eurythmically. For Libra, the sound is "ts" (as in prance), which is executed by way of bringing the palms, facing upward, from below to above in small feather-like gestures; the elbows move in and out as the palms seem to move through etheric clouds as they guide our prayers toward heaven.

The Hermit maintains the movement inherent in true freedom, which is a state of being that is experienced when we surrender all personal prejudices, opinion, and partiality.... [We] walk in servitude before the wonder revealed to us.... We move! Nothing is nailed down, and there is nothing to protect. There is nothing to have but what is necessary for humble servants of the good.[22]

The typical cheerfulness found in this placement rests upon a good deal of faith in humanity and in the moral order of the universe. Sagittarius compels us to take the broad view; therefore the Moon's presence before its stars suggests tolerance for (and an interest in) diverse points of view and different cultures. However, it can also be the case that the fallen forces of the Sagittarian Moon can lock our minds in dogmatism—causing us to adhere to ideas like a dog unwilling to give up a bone. Alternatively, the Moon in Sagittarius can awaken the capacity for *creative imagination*. It was before the stars of the Archer at the birth of Charles Lindbergh (1902-1974), who was one of the greatest adventurers of all time. Lindbergh birthed a new era of global travel when he succeeded, at age 25, in flying solo across the Atlantic in May of 1927—in a plane (the *Spirit of St. Louis*) that had just a single engine and no windshield through which to see ahead of him.

MOON IN *CAPRICORN*
The Empress (III) meets The Star (XVII)

When before the stars of Capricorn (ruled by Saturn), the Moon often confers a somewhat "cool-and-in-command" exterior that eschews histrionics and other effusive displays of emotion. (These are traits that we can place squarely at the feet of Capricorn's ruler, Saturn.) However, it is best not forgotten that this demeanor is just that: an *outward* appearance that belies *inner* warmth. Focus, endurance and a tolerance for isolation are gifts of the Capricorn Moon, which serve to keep our "eye on the prize"—whatever that might mean to us. "The Star" asks us to honor the currents—both cultural and spiritual—that nourish the soul and serve evolutionary growth across time; indeed, many a Moon-in-Capricorn individual has an affinity for tradition, as well as a respect for lawfulness and hierarchy. And although we tend to apply the same high standards to others as we do to ourselves, we can become severe and unforgiving when we judge stature by earthly metrics alone. The Goat brings to the Moon the gift of a firm will; our task, of course, is to use it in a way that benefits others. Those among us born under this placement long for respect and (usually) dread the exposure of any personal weakness. When the fallen forces of the Goat are heeded, we might, alternatively, be tempted to expose any and all weaknesses in *others*. The Moon was in Capricorn at the birth of Charles Darwin (1809-1882), who put forth a theory of evolution characterized by the nightmare of the survival of the fittest: *evolution without the directing principle of cooperation*.

MOON IN *AQUARIUS*
The Empress (III) meets Temperance (XIV)

The Moon in Aquarius suggests independent, reform-minded individuals who don't hesitate to defy convention (and, on occasion, give it the heave-ho altogether). *Humanitarianism* is also commonly expressed through this combination. Due to Saturn's rulership of Aquarius, those among us born under this configuration often exhibit a somewhat detached exterior; inwardly, however, those who bear this astral signature usually have a genuine and warm interest in others, and an ability to relate to those from different walks of life. After all, Aquarius is the "kingdom" to Leo's "king"! The greatest danger of this placement is abstract, materialistic thinking—for although there can be an encyclopedic knowledge of an impossible number of topics, we can sometimes observe an overreliance on *facts* as *truth*. The living water of the firmament pours forth from the stars of Aquarius! How might we receive its blessings of the sustenance of life? By finding Temperance, who is neither intellect nor subconscious drives:

> She is equable and tranquil enthusiasm, prone neither to ecstasy nor despair. She

---

22 Claudia McLaren Lainson, *The Hermit, the Minotaur, and the Shadow of Evil* (self-published, 2020), 8.

is the continual flow of living and life-bestowing water from one vessel to the other—never exceeding due measure—which is joyous serenity or peaceful and light-filled adoration.²³

The Moon was in Aquarius at the birth of Johann von Goethe (1749-1832), whose extensive study of botany (e.g., *Metamorphosis of Plants*) revealed the life force at work within the plant kingdom. Metamorphosis is effected through contraction and expansion—the vertical tendency (pushing up) alternating with the horizontal (blossoming out).

MOON IN *PISCES*
The Empress (III) meets The Hanged Man (XII)

When before the stars of Pisces, the Moon suspends us between heaven and Earth. With a profound hunger and thirst for the spirit, we can be drawn by way of spiritual gravity to the world above. And yet, those among us born under this placement will also know that we incarnated in order to engage fully in earthly life—for Pisces signifies the unity of human souls through love. Neptune, the secondary ruler of Pisces, can add an ethereal quality that might sometimes devolve into vacillation, or wishy-washiness; in this case, the spiritual orientation felt by most of us with the Moon in Pisces can sometimes be little more than "unicorn thinking." When our attraction to the celestial world loosens a bit, we can be engulfed in the *lower* gravitational forces of the subearthly realms, where we encounter the mystery of evil. Authentic faith—whereby we acknowledge the value of righteousness over strength, as well as of the sanctity of goodness—is what allows us to set our personal will "high above our heads," where it can find guidance from divine will. This is a very sensitive Moon that tunes our soul's "strings" so that they vibrate in the presence of pain and suffering; we long to bring lost sheep back to the fold, and ease their distress:

> If a man has a hundred sheep, and one of them has gone astray, does he not leave the ninety-nine on the hills and go in search of the one that went astray?... So it is the will of my Father who is in heaven that not one of these little ones should perish. (Matthew 18:12, 14)

A noble desire to sacrifice for others can sometimes take us too far from our own responsibilities. The Moon was in Pisces at the birth of Alphonse-Louis Constant (1810-1875), who was later known by the Hebrew rendering of his name: *Eliphas Lévi*. Though he left the priesthood at an early age, his lifelong study of esotericism led him back to Christ, with whom he had contact in later years.²⁴ A true man of the spirit, he sought to bring the Cabbala and the Tarot to Catholic teaching.

THE TRANSCENDENTAL PLANETS

 URANUS

Uranus reaches a new zodiacal sign every seven years, thereby moving at the same pace as the planetary periods in human development.²⁵ It draws us toward cosmic intelligence, finding solutions to problems that seem monolithic, unsolvable. As it moves through the signs, Uranus awakens humanity to new imaginations and to all of the blessings that this implies; its technique is usually *shock*. Uranus stimulates reform—consequently, we might tend to throw off the old as our attention becomes trained on the future. To minds that are filled with doubt, however, Uranus can facilitate the entry of the anti-Christ into our souls. Therefore, we could say that the imaginations of Uranus can be characterized by *genius* or by *electrified thinking*. In the first case, these imaginations stream from the Central Sun; in contrast, imaginations of an "electric" quality bear thoughts from the abyss: stones disguised as bread.

---

23 Tomberg, *Meditations on the Tarot* (2022 edition), 662; and *The Wandering Fool*, 72-73.
24 Tomberg, *Meditations on the Tarot*, 193.
25 These periods will be discussed in Chapter 3 of Part IV.

URANUS IN *ARIES*
The Tower of Destruction (XVI) meets The Fool (XXI)

When before the stars of Aries, Uranus helps our ideals take flight; thus, our imagination might turn to the ideals that can bring about radical changes in the world. Although decisiveness is a valuable asset, the Ram runs the risk of trying to "ram through" whatever stands in the way of these ideals. This can leave us wishing that some of the relics of the past had remained standing. Narcissism born of egotism is another danger. Uranus in Aries suggests brilliant thinking that has the capacity to upend the way we see the world—so that we might then see it through the lens of *divine love*. Simultaneously, Uranus in Aries warns of constructs of thought that undermine the rights of the individual. Uranus was in Aries at the birth of St. Francis (1181 / 1182), as well as during the coronavirus lockdowns of the 2020s.

URANUS IN *TAURUS*
The Tower of Destruction (XVI) meets The Judgment (XX)

When Uranus is in Taurus, our "horns" are attuned to the revelation of the spiritual aspects behind material existence. (Uranus was in this position at the birth of Rudolf Steiner.) Uranus in Taurus listens for the thoughts of creation. Because of the Bull's firm stance upon the Earth, any imaginations that are received are given the practical means of realization when Uranus is before its stars. The Uranian impulse for sudden change can experience some resistance when in Taurus, as the speed at which lightning operates can be at odds with the favored slower pace of the Bull. The challenge, therefore, lies in developing the soul quality of *flexibility*, which might allow us to adapt more quickly to the demands of evolution. Uranus in Taurus warns of the construction of human "towers" that defile the Earth, our home born of the cosmic Word. Uranus was in Taurus as American nuclear weapons were dropped upon Japan in 1945.

URANUS IN *GEMINI*
The Tower of Destruction (XVI) meets The Sun (XIX)

When before the stars of Gemini, Uranus finds the support of quickly moving Mercury, the ruler of the Twins. Whereas the thunderbolt *releases* energy, the Twins can *diffuse* it, bouncing from one thing to the next like a kite lost to the wind. Gemini stands for duality and cooperation; the pillars of the glyph—which can represent light and darkness, male and female, mercy and justice, east and west—are side by side, working together cooperatively. When these pillars remain upright, Christ can dwell between them. The task of the thunderbolt (when before the stars of the Twins) is to cast down any human endeavors that seed division within the brother- and sisterhood of humanity. Uranus was in Gemini shortly after the Battle of Gettysburg (1863). Although the battle was the bloodiest of the American Civil War, the decisive Union victory served to draw the conflict nearer to a close.

URANUS IN *CANCER*
The Tower of Destruction (XVI) meets The Moon (XVIII)

In the Cancer glyph, we experience the ebb and flow of etheric forces; at its center, the material and spiritual worlds collide—for the stars at its center were thought to be the gateway from the spirit to human, material life. Uranus before the stars of Cancer brings imaginations that might illuminate the spiritual origin of all matter—thereby creating a bridge between the starry spirals. Although at odds with the watery element, Uranus can counteract the Cancerian tendency to stagnate in the past. The fallen, materialistic impulse of Uranus (when before the stars of the Crab) might seek to deny spirit altogether, thereby reducing humanity to a collection of organisms, and motherhood to a biological function. We might then care for nothing outside of our own shells. Uranus was in Cancer at the start of Robespierre's Reign of Terror (1792–1794), as well as between 1954 and 1960, when in the West there began the cultural rumblings that would weaken the nuclear family.

URANUS IN *LEO*
The Tower of Destruction (XVI) meets The Wheel of Fortune (X)

When Uranus is before the stars of Leo, those who are ensconced in immoral authority are subject to the eventual hurling of the heavenly thunderbolt of *humility*. Leo stands for *moral* leadership, which is necessarily based upon compassion for those in the kingdom who are living at the bottom of the hill. Because of Leo's connection to creative endeavors, we may conjecture that Uranus can bring shocking innovative imaginations as well. (Uranus was in Leo at the births of the telephone and of the Edison Light Company, as well as during Tesla's early experiments.) In this placement, however, the danger of self-importance tends to lurk—*and this can lead us to engage in bold, ill-advised actions at the expense of others*. Uranus presided over the death of Christ, the King of kings, whose mission was somewhat of a thunderbolt to humankind. It was he who revealed to us the true nature of freedom.

URANUS IN *VIRGO*
The Tower of Destruction (XVI) meets Force (XI)

Uranus in Virgo is suggestive of illuminations of genius regarding the natural world and the life forces that lie within it. It simultaneously warns us against any constructs of thought that are in essence anti-life. Whereas the Virgin stands for purity and spontaneous obedience to God, the woman of Babylon actively seeks to destroy life. Uranus was in Virgo between 1967 and 1973; while many associate this time with a release from outdated cultural structures, it cannot be denied that the so-called sexual revolution has had many adverse consequences that we can regard as bold strikes against purity and life itself. Additionally, the uptick in drug use that was characteristic of these years continues to damage humankind. Although this period of time can be remembered for the notorious Mai Lai massacre and the Tet offensive (1968), it might also be regarded as the peak of the efforts of Mother Teresa (1910–1997), who abhorred violence because of her respect for *all* life.

URANUS IN *LIBRA*
The Tower of Destruction (XVI) meets Justice (VIII)

When among the stars of Libra, Uranus might suggest illuminations regarding not only the administration of justice, but also the *mood* of the culture to accept it. The concept of a twelve-individual jury (mirroring the twelve worldviews of the zodiac) might date back to William the Conqueror (1066). Moreover, it represents a human approximation of divine justice. Although we know that the judicial system is capable of grave failure—because it is a *human* system—it nevertheless once strove to reflect its spiritual archetype. However, we could say that there are two methods (or directions) of weighing: the "horizontal" and the "vertical." In the case of the former, we weigh according to weight, measure, and number—like the rider of the black horse in Revelation; in the case of the latter, we weigh according to *moral merit*. And when a justice system is no longer guided by moral choices, the jurors wield an improper amount of power that is easily abused. Uranus in Libra might call attention to these abuses. Uranus was in Libra at the birth of Abraham Lincoln, who freed enslaved African-Americans in Confederate states. Some northern states were not compelled to do so until the passage of the Thirteenth Amendment in 1864, one year after Lincoln's Gettysburg Address and the Emancipation Proclamation.

URANUS IN *SCORPIO*
The Tower of Destruction (XVI) meets Death (XIII)

Uranus in Scorpio is suggestive of imaginative insights into what lies beneath and beyond sense perception—including the life between death and rebirth. Tomberg was born when Uranus was in Scorpio; indeed, "genius esotericist" is one imagination of this combination. However, the association between the Scorpion and the subearthly realms (which can lure humanity into perversity and immorality) leads us to conclude that Uranus before the stars of the Scorpion can influence the unprepared to adopt different imaginations altogether—imaginations born of black magic, violence, and sex. This placement carries the danger of instilling a "wallowing in the illicit." Uranus was in Scorpio as AIDS was coming into focus; and although there still exists disagreement about its cause, it acted as a thunderbolt of sorts against promiscuity.

URANUS IN *SAGITTARIUS*
The Tower of Destruction (XVI) meets The Hermit (IX)

When in Sagittarius, before the stars of the Archer, Uranus brings revelations of cosmic truth. It can then be "the lamp of the hermit." However, we must ask where we've poised our collective arrow—for if it is trained on falsehood, it is falsehood that we will find. It is intriguing that the birth of the internet occurred under the aegis of Uranus in Sagittarius; its original motto was "Let's Share What We Know." Its distinction now is as the largest tower of Babel in world history! Tomberg wrote:

> At the root of the building of the tower of Babel is the collective will of "lower selves" to achieve the replacing of the "true Self" of the celestial hierarchies and God with a superstructure of universal significance fabricated through this will.[26]

This superstructure now defines the lives of millions who have chosen the amusements and conveniences of the electronic world at the expense of their sovereignty. Within the Sagittarian *tower*, truth is irrelevant. Only "correctness" matters. As Christ is the way, the truth, and the life, Ahriman offers wandering, falsehood, and death.

URANUS IN *CAPRICORN*
The Tower of Destruction (XVI) meets The Star (XVII)

When Uranus is in Capricorn, we can find that traditions and existing hierarchy are being challenged and upended. Equally possible are insights into how to reform those structures in order to avoid their downfall; in the case of both the Solomon Mary and the Nathan Mary (both of whom were conceived and born under this placement), we can recognize the awakening impulse of Uranus working on behalf of the continuation of spiritual evolution. Because Capricorn and Uranus are so opposite in nature, the saturnine Capricorn might resist the sudden reforms longed for by Uranus. If Uranus is able to prevail in spite of the Goat's cautions, revolutionary actions might shake us to our core. Uranus was in Capricorn at the October Revolution and as the Twin Towers dissolved into dust on 9/11.

URANUS IN *AQUARIUS*
The Tower of Destruction (XVI) meets Temperance (XIV)

It's a veritable lightning storm when Uranus is in Aquarius; due to this placement's shared outlook toward the future and its impulse for reform, limitations can seem to vanish. It entreats us to "think *with* others" in humility; we thereby willingly diminish ourselves so that others might increase. In its highest expression, Uranus in Aquarius engenders reforms that *uphold* community. However, we must distinguish between those reforms that truly do so and those that merely claim to represent "unity" while actively working behind the scenes to sever such connections. Uranus was in Aquarius during the 1830s, during which time the Parliament in Great Britain passed reforms that abolished slavery, dramatically curtailed child labor, and gave representation to more subjects. Soon after World War I (1914-1918), Aquarius saw Uranus again—at the formation of the League of Nations. The League gave control to a global elite that had the power to determine which nations of the world were subject to "international supervision," and which nations were not.

URANUS IN *PISCES*
The Tower of Destruction (XVI) meets The Hanged Man (XII)

Uranus was in Pisces at the conceptions and births of the two Jesus children. Uranus before the stars of the Fishes can be imagined as the light that will assist us in steadfastly remaining on the bridge between heaven and Earth. Like a tree, our "roots" must reach toward the Mother while our "branches" stretch toward heavenly realms—so that we remain fully engaged in earthly life as we try to understand what the divine world is asking of us. While encouraging us to avoid the enticements of excessive materialism (lest our hearts become mere instruments of our will), Uranus before the stars of Pisces warns us against succumbing to inspirations from lower worlds. This placement occurred when Stalin and Hitler came to power. It also presided over the stock market crash of 1929—when a thunderbolt struck the heart of the American financial system.

---

26 Tomberg, *Meditations on the Tarot*, 443.

The Planets in the Signs

♆ NEPTUNE

Neptune moves through a zodiacal sign in about fourteen years, whereby its placement is shared by a wide cohort.[27] Neptune in each zodiacal sign reveals the source of inspiration and spiritual ideals to that group. The character of the influence of Neptune depends upon our moral development. *Indeed, the highest ideals and inspirations can only be reached if our worldview is not clouded by illusion.* Neptune speaks to us through our feeling nature; hence, it represents Ahriman's point of entry into the feeling aspect of our souls. We can thereby be led to a world of illusory joy (even debauchery) in which the dissolution of the "I" can occur. If we fall prey to mass consciousness—abandoning the inner guidance of our individual conscience, we "plunge from the pinnacle."

NEPTUNE IN *ARIES*
The World (XXII) meets The Fool (XXI)

When Neptune is in Aries, we might avidly seek inspiration from new social concepts striving to be brought forward. Acts of pure love (which can make us seem very foolish indeed) can inspire us to learn of the power behind sacrificing on behalf of the object of our devotion. Although the Ram encourages the development of the unique personhood of each of us, Neptune in Aries challenges us to renounce *self-importance* so that we can act on behalf of others. When we neglect to do so, Neptune in Aries can amplify the hatred in our hearts, and we can then find ourselves isolated in the prison of self-servitude. Stalin (1878–1953) was born under this astral signature.

NEPTUNE IN *TAURUS*
The World (XXII) meets The Judgment (XX)

When Neptune is before the stars of the Bull, we listen for the cosmic harmony that uplifts the soul and draws us together as voices in a single choir. We might explore new ways to tend the Earth. Neptune in Taurus draws the mind toward the totality of the cosmos, which reveals the spiritual foundation of all that we see. By way of this placement, the human soul finds inspiration in the way that the faculties of listening and speech enable us to know one another. Indeed, it is thanks to Taurus that sound was born within us. While Neptune in Taurus challenges our attachment to our possessions—urging us to seek security in what is eternal—it might also bring to our attention the exploitative environment in which many must earn their pay. Neptune was in Taurus during the 1890s, when there occurred a great spate of labor strikes in the United States (among miners, railroad workers, and others).

NEPTUNE IN *GEMINI*
The World (XXII) meets The Sun (XIX)

When before the stars of Gemini, Neptune is well-disposed toward brother- and sisterhood. Indeed, the human community of souls, although it exists in the "horizontal realm," can be seen as an earthly expression of the vertical alliance between heaven and Earth. Neptune in Gemini inspires our faith in mankind as the image and likeness of the divine; it also reminds us of the "star" that shines above each human soul. Alternatively, we can heed the murmurings of the woman of Babylon, who entices us to sacrifice our brothers and sisters for the sake of personal gain. Neptune was in Gemini at the birth of Valentin Tomberg. As the herald of the coming age of brotherly and sisterly love, he revealed to us what will be possible when we take Christ into our hearts.

NEPTUNE IN *CANCER*
The World (XXII) meets The Moon (XVIII)

Neptune in Cancer seeks to draw the mind *beyond* the material intellect—which would otherwise lead us to look upon matter without troubling ourselves about the life-force that created it! Because Cancer implies nurturing and protecting life—just as the ribs protect the human heart—our cohort might place the need to protect and nurture all life above our own interests. We would thereby invoke the ideal of *selflessness*. Inversely, under the weight of our responsibilities, we can stagnate in a pool of resentment and self-pity. Neptune in Cancer radiates the

---

27 Neptune last moved into Pisces in 1859, into Aries in 1872, into Taurus in 1885, into Gemini in 1898, into Cancer in 1911, into Leo in 1925, into Virgo in 1939, into Libra in 1953, into Scorpio in 1968, into Sagittarius in 1982, into Capricorn in 1996, and into Neptune in 2009. It returns to Pisces in 2023.

principle of springtime, by which we cherish process (the drama of living!) over and above the eventual result of that process (the "harvest"). Neptune was in Cancer during the First World War—which engulfed the world with its apparent senseless disregard for young life.

NEPTUNE IN *LEO*
The World (XXII) meets The Wheel of Fortune (X)

In Leo we find an exuberance for experiencing all that life has to offer; through the interference of fallen Neptune, however, our joy for life can lead us to dissolution, whereby we give precedence to the satisfaction of our feelings *above all else*. When Neptune is before the stars of Leo, we are inspired to look beyond the world of vanity, where there is nothing new under the sun.[28] Through such inspiration, our inner instinctivity (animal nature) might seek spontaneous obedience to the divine, as represented by the four holy creatures: the winged Bull, the winged Lion, the winged Eagle, and the winged Angel.[29] The regal nature of Leo asks us to contemplate how our authority—howsoever great or small—can *inspire* rather than *coerce*. Neptune was in Leo when the etheric Christ appeared within the ether of the Earth.

NEPTUNE IN *VIRGO*
The World (XXII) meets Force (XI)

When Neptune is in Virgo, the natural world is our source of inspiration. We listen for the rhythms of nature's "songs," and long to sing them for others—for they reveal to us the magical forces of transformation that are active in our own souls. Here Neptune inspires us to tend the "garden" of the world, representative of a state of cooperation between spirit and nature. When before the stars of Virgo, Neptune might engender an impulse to protect innocence from all that seeks to corrupt it. Alternatively, we might listen to the murmurings of the anti-Sophia: the one who willingly defiles life, and who leads the soul to powerlessness through sterile enjoyments. Neptune was in Virgo at the height of the Third Reich. This was also the case when American atomic bombs were dropped on Hiroshima and Nagasaki.

NEPTUNE IN *LIBRA*
The World (XXII) meets Justice (VIII)

When Neptune is before the stars of Libra, the moral harmony that can be achieved between two people is regarded as a reflection of the shared rhythm of heaven and Earth, of above and below. Just as individuals strive for equilibrium (spiritual health) through the practices of contentment and empathy, so must two companions seek a harmony of soul between themselves. This can be achieved when we come together in order to find the truth. Will we take our sacrament at Michael's altar of truth—or will we seek communion at the altar of illusion? When Neptune is in Libra, we might seek to protect society's outcasts from injustice, but we must first find the courage for righteous action. Neptune was in Libra at the conceptions and birthd of the Solomon Mary and the Nathan Mary—exemplars of inner equilibrium and concern for others.

NEPTUNE IN *SCORPIO*
The World (XXII) meets Death (XIII)

When Neptune is in Scorpio, we look for inspiration in the mysteries of death and rebirth, as well as in the alchemy of transformation in the human soul—whereby our trials might be transformed into self-mastery. As we do so, we seek the "excision" of all that is unusable. Alternatively, we can be drawn helplessly into the dark world of all that is forbidden by society, thus isolating ourselves from the good and the beautiful. Neptune so-placed might allow us to be permeated by the divine breath, which reveals that death exists on two planes: physical death (defined by the presence of a corpse), and spiritual death (characterized by *remoteness from the Father*). Neptune was in Scorpio at the conception and birth of both the Solomon Jesus and the Nathan Jesus.

NEPTUNE IN *SAGITTARIUS*
The World (XXII) meets The Hermit (IX)

When before the stars of the Archer, Neptune might incline us to seek inspiration from the four corners of the globe—for Neptune here is able to move freely beyond the confines of our native culture. The quest itself is exhilarating! Through

---

28 See Ecclesiastes 1.
29 Ancient wisdom perceived within the Sphinx four fundamental rules of human conduct: to will (Taurus / Bull), to dare (Leo / Lion), the be silent (Scorpio / Eagle), and to know (Aquarius / Angel).

this combination, we might experience the joy of the ideal. May we follow the Hermit's lamp to the ends of the Earth! When Neptune is in Sagittarius, we are asked to discern the totality of truth from within the vast cacophony of *mass consciousness*. This requires a collective reining in of instincts, so that the will is better able to discern falsehood. Neptune was in Sagittarius at the creation of the "World Wide Web."

NEPTUNE IN *CAPRICORN*
The World (XXII) meets The Star (XVII)

When Neptune moves before the stars of the Goat, we seek *growth* over *revolution* (and other forms of upset), finding inspiration in the spiritual current of tradition. This current bears hope for the future and provides nourishment to our souls; it also refutes determinism of all kinds, leaving us free to dream on behalf of all we love. Capricorn favors long-term efforts (straight to the mountain top!), in part due to the Capricorn gift of flexibility, which allows us to make course corrections as needed. When we heed the siren call of the anti-Sophia, however, we might harbor hatred for others, thereby justifying "any means necessary" in the execution of our goals. Neptune was in Capricorn as Jesus performed the seven archetypal miracles, as well as during the events of 9/11.

NEPTUNE IN *AQUARIUS*
The World (XXII) meets Temperance (XIV)

When Neptune is before the stars of Aquarius, we listen for inspirations streaming from the future. Through Aquarius, we encounter the role of the guardian Angel—the being who stands between our immortal, divine nature (the "image") and what we have become since the Fall (the "likeness"). Tears are the gift that we receive when we come to an awareness of the distance between *image* and *likeness*. Temperance—which engenders health—is the state of the soul that allows us to establish the just measure of relationship between the two, whereby they *cooperate*. Temperance allows us to distinguish between truth (which has a moral quality) and intoxication (which does not). Inherent in both Neptune and Aquarius is the impulse for community; when we listen to the whispers of the anti-Sophia—who seeks to thwart evolution by destroying the loving bonds inspired by her counterpart—our highest goal becomes the mere satisfaction of our feelings. Neptune was in Aquarius throughout the Passion.

NEPTUNE IN *PISCES*
The World (XXII) meets The Hanged Man (XII)

In a gift of faith, the somewhat ethereal nature of Neptune (the secondary, modern ruler of Pisces) inclines the cohort born under this signature toward the world of spirit. When Neptune is before the stars of Pisces, we are inspired by righteous actions that might "lift all boats," for we understand that mankind is an ocean of souls—and that one person's experience is meant to help and serve others. Our hearts are often attuned to the sufferings of others and of the Earth. Alternatively, when we abandon our conscience—seeking joy instead of truth—we can be strangers to remorse and responsibility. Neptune in Pisces asks that we confront the mystery of evil so that it might be overcome in human hearts. Neptune was in Pisces at the birth of Steiner (1861–1925), who identified a primary task of our current age as the need to identify and name evil.

PLUTO

The zodiacal placement of Pluto is shared by a generation; it must therefore be considered in the light of *collective* influence.[30] Pluto draws us to cosmic life, and each sign reveals to us the qualities that a given generation is meant to bring to expression in order to sustain this life. As we may recall, however, the transcendental planets can take us to the heights as well as to the depths of human experience. Therefore, when a generational tendency to resist the lure of the lower forces of Pluto does *not* exist, we can be overcome by fear and led to revolution. For it is through the will of the human being that the anti-Christ can find his foothold, seeding a desire among us to become "princes of this world." Pluto rumbles beneath our feet like magma—looking for a path to the surface!

---

30 Pluto last entered Aquarius in 1793, Pisces in 1817, Aries in 1844, Taurus in 1876, Gemini in 1906, Cancer in 1933, Leo in 1953, Virgo in 1969, Libra in 1982, Scorpio in 1993, Sagittarius in 2005, and Capricorn in 2021.

PLUTO IN *ARIES*
The Devil (XV) meets The Fool (XXI)

Pluto in Aries can engender profound thinking. Indeed, the devotion of Aries to the ideal of higher thought is absolute. Furthermore, those of us born under this placement are set upon a quest for the fulfillment of our individuality. This requires courage, for it takes us onto the path of the *Fool*—which invites *ridicule*. So be it! Alternatively, when our focus turns away from a higher ideal, and focuses instead on our earthly personality (with all its predilections), narcissism rises from the shadow world, leaving us indifferent to the concerns of others. Steiner (1861–1925) was born when Pluto was before the stars of the Ram.

PLUTO IN *TAURUS*
The Devil (XV) meets The Judgment (XX)

When Pluto is in Taurus, the generation in question must intuit how the spiritual ideals of the time can best be made to work upon the Earth. It asks how that which we create upon the Earth might reveal the spiritual aspect behind existence. We are encouraged to nourish our speech with a *moral quality*. This requires that we listen "vertically." Alternatively, when we listen only "horizontally," we can be filled with indigestible information that loops endlessly within us. Valentin Tomberg (1900–1973), author of *Meditations on the Tarot*, was born under this placement. The spiritual exercises within each letter-Arcanum of this great work invoke a moral quality. Tomberg himself described this work as a reincarnation of the Egyptian mysteries.[31]

PLUTO IN *GEMINI*
The Devil (XV) meets The Sun (XIX)

When Pluto is in Gemini, the generation must maintain an upright channel to the spiritual world (*As above, so below*). Through this channel, the lower nature of the generation can meet—and be uplifted by—the higher. We must maintain a faithfulness in the higher nature that lives in all of us; this is the essence of true brotherhood. Inversely, when our intelligence does *not* seek cosmic light—wisdom—we lose that faith and are left to the vagaries of the material world, where we might be prone to fanaticism instead. Neptune was in Gemini during the whole of World War I (1914–1918), when brother fought against brother to profoundly horrible effect. The clarity of mind that is characteristic of Gemini was intentionally obscured by certain individuals who, working behind the scenes, encouraged this conflict for personal gain. Many of them made their fortunes at this time.

PLUTO IN *CANCER*
The Devil (XV) meets The Moon (XVIII)

Those of us born under this signature must strive to eradicate self-absorption. When Pluto is in Cancer, we must penetrate *matter*—its form and substance—within which the lawful principles of the Mother and the Father can be found. Inversely, we can sink into the abyss of abject *materialism*, which leads us into the currents of anti-life—such as eugenics, atomic warfare, and transhumanism. These currents form a vortex at the center of the Cancer glyph, between matter and spirit. Conscience is the door between the two. In both Pluto and Cancer, we encounter the hidden power of the subconscious, whence our will-impulses originate; Pluto can intensify their influence. This placement therefore asks that what dwells beneath the conscious mind be brought to consciousness—lest it drag us down at a time of its own choosing. Pluto was in Cancer during WWII (1939–1945).

PLUTO IN *LEO*
The Devil (XV) meets The Wheel of Fortune (X)

When Pluto is in Leo, the forces of the heart are ignited, and warmth and compassion might flow from *between* hearts. Humanity is thus presented with the image of the ideal ruler—one who gets no pleasure from his power over others, but who is instead revered and relied upon because he or she is *loved*. Alternatively, Pluto in Leo can compel us to overpower others and to "rule" by fear. The generation born under this placement is tasked with understanding what

---

31   The Egyptian culture flourished during the age of Taurus, defined as the 2160-year period in which the vernal point moved through that zodiacal sign. The spiritual exercises within *Meditations on the Tarot* defy intellectual characterization and exposition—for the Egyptians came to know the world through an imaginative picture consciousness.

King Solomon referred to as "vanity": the *emptiness* of the world of the serpent (i.e., that of fallen humanity). It was Mary-Sophia who—after the Fall—guarded the memory of the world that had been opened toward the Father. The Blessed Virgin was born when Pluto was in Leo.

PLUTO IN *VIRGO*
The Devil (XV) meets Force (XI)

When Pluto is in Virgo, the generation is disposed to intuit the phenomena of the natural world; this is so that we might live in harmony with spiritual law. So-placed, Pluto celebrates and protects every living thing, and demands that we nurture all that is worthy of "becoming." Inversely, we can be lured by the treachery of the Virgin's counterpart in the lower world, the woman of Babylon—who seeks to defile all innocence and enslave others through the power of compulsion. This placement summons before the imagination mighty Pluto, who bears the power of the underworld, kneeling before the purity of the Virgin. The highest expression of this astral signature can be found in the lives of the Solomon Jesus and the Nathan Jesus, both of whom were conceived and born when Pluto was in Virgo.

PLUTO IN *LIBRA*
The Devil (XV) meets Justice (VIII)

When Pluto is in Libra, it asks how the generation can imbue all of its judgments with mercy. For if we judge without it, we condemn individuals; and if we are merciful without judgment, we condemn nothing. It is the supremacy of love that holds the balance between the two, across time and within the individual. Love thus maintains the health of the individual and of humanity as a whole, *in equal measure*. The generation is tasked with upholding the rights of all people in such a way that the rights of the individual are not unduly compromised. The fall of the Berlin Wall (1989), which occurred when Pluto was in Libra, was an event that was expressive of this impulse.

PLUTO IN *SCORPIO*
The Devil (XV) meets Death (XIII)

When Pluto is in Scorpio, the generation must endeavor to see the dynamic forces that move behind appearances. Especially powerful due to its secondary rulership of Scorpio, Pluto here can incite power struggles. Pluto in Scorpio emphasizes our exposure to fear and shame—which can make us run for cover, or (when faced squarely) become the foundation of a "rebirth." This placement might instill in us a willingness to transform institutions and structures that no longer serve the good of humanity. The generation intuits that it must venture into the darkness in order to understand the mysteries of transformation and of death—in other words, of the threshold between worlds. We can soar like eagles, seeking divine inspiration, or else remain isolated in the darkness: proud, resentful, and ready to strike out at those whom we regard as "other." Pluto was in Scorpio when apartheid as a national policy ended in South Africa (1994); these efforts culminated in the establishment of the ANC (African National Congress), with Nelson Mandela as its first president.

PLUTO IN *SAGITTARIUS*
The Devil (XV) meets The Hermit (IX)

When Pluto is in Sagittarius, the generation is tasked with the resolution of antinomies so that the *fullness* of truth can be known. As opposing concepts and ideas, antinomies appear to be unreconcilable. This is a weighty task indeed—and one that must be guided by *truth alone*, whether or not it is in agreement with individual positions, but the Archer's starry arrow is trained at the Central Sun—the creative source of existence, as well as the origin of goodness, truth, and beauty! Inversely, we might be inclined to actively obscure the truth in order to ensnare others through lies and false dogma—for Pluto intensifies both the longing for truth and the inclination to be subsumed in monomaniacal dogmatism. Pluto was before the stars of the Archer throughout the ministry of Christ.

PLUTO IN *CAPRICORN*
The Devil (XV) meets The Star (XVII)

When in Capricorn, Pluto venerates tradition as a spiritual current: the sap of evolution. If the generation remains flexible and proceeds with order, lawfulness, and an unbending will, productive change—even productive *revolution*—is possible. Pluto in Capricorn says: "I revere God and I serve the future. My actions must be consistent with moral law." Inversely, the fallen forces of Capricorn can inspire cruelty, violence, and a craving for exposing the weaknesses of others; we are then, consequently, unable see beyond the time in which we are living. When we fail to stand on the shoulders of giants, revolution can rise like a putrid steam from the depths, inspired by destruction alone. Pluto was in Capricorn during the American Revolution.

PLUTO IN *AQUARIUS*
The Devil (XV) meets Temperance (XIV)

When Pluto is in Aquarius, the generation must find inspiration in what communities (large and small) might accomplish. *Aquarius is the zodiacal realm of etheric formative forces.* As a symbol, the imaginative picture of this constellation (with the Angel and the urns) suggests a cosmic source that never runs dry. *Conscience* expresses the influence of our guardian Angel — and when we fail to heed our conscience, we no longer see ourselves and others as beings created in the image and likeness of God. The lower forces of Pluto in Aquarius seek to sever human bonds, destroying community and family in order to amass power. The Reign of Terror (1793-1794) in France transpired as Pluto was in Aquarius. This campaign of death revealed the brutal fiction behind the revolutionaries' stated quest for liberty, equality, and fraternity.

PLUTO IN *PISCES*
The Devil (XV) meets The Hanged Man (XII)

When Pluto is in Pisces, the generation must endeavor to intuit Earth's mysteries. The last sign of the zodiac signifies that we have brought our consciousness down to our feet — yet we are nevertheless suspended between heaven and Earth, between the Father and the Mother. Through Pisces we learn of spontaneous obedience to the spiritual world, whereby our personal will is muted by the demands of evolution. Inversely, excessive materialism can chain us to the Earth (like Andromeda) — without the only defense against the rising subearthly forces: *Christ*. Pluto was in Pisces throughout the latter part of Beethoven's life (1770-1827). His choral Symphony No. 9, which was first performed in Vienna in 1824, extols joy and brotherhood. In the final movement, the chorus sings,

> *Do you not bow down, you millions?*
> *Do you not sense the Creator, World?*
> *Look for him above the starry firmament!*
> *There, above the stars, he must live!*

INTERLUDE

WHAT IS CHRISTIAN HERMETICISM?

CHRISTIAN HERMETICISM:
Finding the Extraordinary in the Ordinary

CHRISTIAN HERMETICISM, THE spiritual stream inaugurated by the Russian mystic and esotericist Valentin Tomberg, has a flavor of the deeply occult to those who are unfamiliar with it. This spiritual path was, after all, first described in detail in Tomberg's *magnum opus* (published anonymously), *Meditations on the Tarot: A Journey into Christian Hermeticism*—a title which itself conjures an aura of mystery and magic.

Yet, I would argue, Christian Hermeticism is *not* a path shrouded in the mysterious, bizarre, or arcane—but rather, it is a path that finds extraordinary magic in the ordinary experiences of life.

EXPECT THE UNEXPECTED

To those fearful of anything esoteric, the mere mention of the word "Tarot" is enough to cause them to thrill with terror, tossing *Meditations* into a bonfire and calling for the nearest exorcist. Those who *are* familiar with esoteric teachings, however, may have quite the opposite reaction, opening the book in eager expectation of arcane and obscure explications of ancient mysteries. The interesting thing about *Meditations on the Tarot*, however, is that it rather disappoints both those expectations, offering an altogether different spiritual vision than anyone expects.

To those fearful of the occult, it offers a surprising affirmation and defense of ordinary religious practices, such as the rosary, novenas, the Our Father, and other familiar prayers. It also appeals to aspects of Catholic faith and practice well-known to all, such as the spiritual office of the papacy, St. Benedict's famous dictum *ora et labora*, and the three vows of poverty, chastity, and obedience. Put another way, it defends simple Christian piety and devotion—something surprising to Catholics or other Christians who may expect anything occult to be a dangerous threat to their faith.

To an occultist fascinated by all that is obscure, strange, and mysterious, the book may offer a surprising lack of excitement. This is not to say that there are not many occult teachings within it. Many who are familiar with esoteric knowledge agree that *Meditations on the Tarot* is one of the most profound occult texts written, and copious mentions of such topics as alchemy, Cabbala, the Emerald Table, and magic abound within it.

What *is* unexpected, however, is that *Meditations* does not revel in or cultivate occult strangeness for strangeness' sake, something which I have found to be true of some other occult texts I have encountered. For it is, unfortunately, true that some occultists seem to disdain the ordinary or exoteric, eager as they are to bathe everything in the shadowy half-light of secretiveness, oddity, and obscurity. This type of esotericist revels in an atmosphere of mystery, seeing himself as a wiser-than-ordinary mage and proud possessor of secret knowledge inaccessible to the masses.

What makes Valentin Tomberg, and thus *Meditations on the Tarot*, unique is that he flatly rejects any cultivation of this pseudo-magical ethos. Of course, Tomberg was highly knowledgeable and experienced in nearly every occult stream, including Tantra, Tibetan Buddhism,

Rosicrucianism, Alchemy, Anthroposophy, Cabbala, and, of course, French Hermeticism, to name a few. But his project was not to plunge one into a bewildering whirlpool of esoteric currents, but rather to *marry* these esoteric currents in all their depth to the exoteric dimension of ordinarily life and religious practice.

WHAT IS CHRISTIAN HERMETICISM?

Christian Hermeticism is many things, some of which I hope to explore in future reflections, but it is in its essence a spiritual *way of peace* that seeks the reconciliation of opposites, the neutralization of binaries, through the dimension of depth. It is a work of love and healing that seeks a marriage between all that is seemingly conflicted and opposed, culminating in the ultimate reconciliation and re-union of Above and Below, God and fallen Creation.

And this way of peace encompasses all dimensions of life, not the least of which are the esoteric and exoteric, the extraordinary and the ordinary. *This* is why Tomberg refused to indulge in mystery for mystery's sake. This is why he refused to flaunt his esoteric knowledge, vast though it was. This is why Tomberg infused ordinary practices of Catholic piety with a degree of depth that had previously been overlooked.

Tomberg was not interested in fostering a new antinomy between the esoteric and the exoteric, a conflict that had been growing in intensity for centuries. Rather, he was interested in *healing* the deep wound in the Western soul which had relegated all magic, all mystery, and all spirituality to an occult domain in which it never really belonged, and which had in its place exalted Reason to an idolatrously divine state—a pathology which led to the untold destruction of the 21st century, and which, today, continues to destroy.

Yes, Tomberg's project was to *heal* the divide in the Western soul; and to do this, he sought to marry the ordinary and the arcane, the prosaic and the mysterious.

In his own words:

> Esotericism is not a collection of extraordinary and unknown things, but it is above all a less ordinary and less known way of *seeing* ordinary and known things—of seeing their profundity (*Meditations on the Tarot*, p. 51).

Christian Hermeticism, then, is emphatically *not* a cultivation of the bizarre or unusual, or a reveling in an aesthetic of strangeness. Much less it is an inflated and arrogant confidence that one has unlocked all the secrets of the universe.

(Incidentally, this is why Tomberg refuses dogmatic interpretations of the symbols of the Tarot arcana. Symbols, such as those on the Tarot cards, are stimulants to thought, not fixed or limited containers of only one truth. A dogmatic interpretation of the Tarot Arcana would lead to a doctrinaire attitude that would be the death of true hermeticism.)

Rather, Christian Hermeticism is about seeing *all of life* as an Arcanum, a mystery on which to meditate. It is thus a mystery which contains depths of infinite profundity to be discovered. The way of Christian Hermeticism is the way of *humility* and *wonder*, the way of perceiving the oceanic depths beneath the undulating surface of the experiences of ordinary life. It is a way of love and healing, of reconciling that which is opposed, so that once again reality may become transparent to spirit, and the glory of God may shine forth in all that is.

SAM GUZMAN, 2022

CHRISTIAN HERMETICISM:
Learning the Art of Learning

IN A PREVIOUS ARTICLE, I WROTE about how Christian Hermeticism—the unique spiritual tradition inaugurated by the Russian mystic Valentin Tomberg—united the exoteric and the esoteric, the extraordinary and the ordinary, the hidden and the well-known.

Contrary to popular preconceptions, Christian Hermeticism is not about immersing everything in a shadowy half-light of secret knowledge. It is quite the opposite: It is about bathing the quotidian and mundane in the radiant splendor hidden beneath the surface of things. It is about learning to see the profound mystery hidden in the depths shining forth in ordinary experience.

Today, I want to explore another dimension of the multifaceted reality that is Christian Hermeticism—learning the art of learning.

LET EVERYONE BE YOUR TEACHER

In the early pages of *Meditations on the Tarot*, Tomberg relates an anecdote from the life of St. Anthony the Great, one the most noted of the desert fathers of early Christianity. After his initial conversion, Anthony, it was said, sat at the feet of every monk, hermit, and holy man he could find and learned everything they had to teach. After this intense period of learning, St. Anthony spent the rest of his life interiorizing and assimilating all he had learned. In other words, the knowledge he obtained was not merely factual or conceptual. He labored to integrate it into his very being so that it became part of his soul.

Tomberg then goes on to emphasize that this should be the attitude and approach of every true Christian Hermeticist—for Christian Hermeticism is nothing else than *learning the art of learning*. Unlike a saint who focuses exclusively on the knowledge that pertains to salvation alone, however, no domain of human knowledge is excluded from the hermeticist. The true hermeticist seeks to learn *all* and *everything* from *everyone*. In short, all who find themselves called to this path—no matter how much they have already learned—live in a perpetual state of "beginners mind."

And significantly, unlike the mystery schools or secret orders that emphasize the value of enlightened Masters and Initiators who bestow secret knowledge, no Christian Hermeticist should pretend to be a Master who is "better than" any ordinary human being. Tomberg describes this vocation as a path of *servanthood*, not one of egoistic inflation or presumption to greatness.

Knowledge, then, is for the work of healing and service, not for feeling oneself a power-wielding mage in possession of the secrets of the universe. Those who look for dogmatic certainty with which to berate others, or for secret knowledge that will make themselves mighty, are missing the point of this spiritual path.

THE TOTALITY OF TRUTH

The path of the Christian Hermeticist, then, is a path of seeking and continual learning. It is a path of humility that eschews egoistic opinions and the all-too-satisfying group identity that comes with parties, factions, or various movements. The hermeticist feels an inner restlessness that is not content with easy answers or exclusive affiliations, and this restlessness impels him to walk from one end of the earth to other, assimilating the light of knowledge wherever he goes.

But what, ultimately, does the hermeticist seek? The answer, as presumptuous as it may sound, is knowledge of Everything. The hermeticist seeks nothing less the totality of Truth about reality, and will not rest until he obtains it.

Knowledge in the Western world has grown more and more specialized, with fields of research growing increasingly compartmentalized from one another. Many are satisfied with immersing themselves in one field of expertise only—say, for example, one aspect of the natural sciences. A scientist may spend his entire life studying the migration patterns of specific whales, while another researches genetic markers that predispose us to various illnesses. And in a lifetime of work, these two researchers will rarely, if ever, encounter one another.

Moreover, the likelihood of a scientist being well-versed in philosophy, literature, art, or music, in addition to his or her specialized discipline, has become increasingly rare. The Western mind has splintered knowledge into a thousand disparate pieces which never touch one another, each person holding a shard of truth with no one bothering to put the pieces together into a coherent whole.

The true hermeticist, on the other hand, is content with no less than the knowledge of all and everything. He is a generalist *par excellence*, confining himself to no exclusive discipline. Rather, he seeks to recognize the visage of Truth in ten thousand places—philosophy, psychology, history, literature, theology, natural science, geometry, music, and any other field of human endeavor. In all these places, the hermeticist incessantly seeks the totality of Wisdom, both exoteric and esoteric. He sees value in *all* fields of human striving, and in all of them he intuits a deeper underlying reality that binds many disparate fields of knowledge together.

A WORK OF HEALING

The work of the Christian Hermeticist, is, as I have said, the work of healing. And the word healing is intimately related to the word "whole." While others would *divide* human knowledge into ever more segregated parts or specialties, the Christian Hermeticist seeks to heal the mind by *uniting* opposing fields of knowledge. For the more the true hermeticist studies, the more he sees connections between various disciplines—accompanied by ever more flashes of insight which illumine the underlying union between seemingly disparate truths and fields of study. In the many, he sees the One. In the multiple, he sees the unity. In this way, the Christian Hermeticist is truly catholic, *katholikos*, universal and "of the whole." For the hermeticist knows that reality is not built upwards from the bottom, from the part to the whole, but rather from the top down—the whole giving coherence and meaning to the parts.

Ultimately, however, the greatest opposition the hermeticist seeks to heal is that between mind and heart, thought and feeling. For, knowledge of the head alone can never give life. Indeed, intellectual knowledge severed from a deeper knowing of the heart can unleash the greatest destruction, as the 20th century demonstrated all too tragically. Imbuing thought with the warmth of feeling, and feeling with the light of intelligence—this is the ultimate and final work of the Christian Hermeticist.

This feeling-thought of married head and heart is the doorway to a higher knowing. It is the real work we must all undertake, and one that is only beginning. And the end of it is nothing less than the New Jerusalem—reality both transfigured and resurrected.

SAM GUZMAN, 2022

These and other articles by Sam Guzman can be found at wayoftheheart@substack.com.

PART II
THE CELESTIAL WHEEL

1

THE GEOCENTRIC CHART

AT THE DAWN OF ASTROLOGY, WHICH TOOK PLACE IN ANCIENT Babylon, the Earth was experienced as the center around which the other planets revolved. To the Babylonian priests, the movement of the seven classical planets around the Earth created *nested spheres*, and the orbit of each planet signified the distal boundary of its influence. Though it might seem odd in the context of modern cosmology, this geocentric arrangement of concentric spheres around the Earth was fundamental to the astronomy of Ptolemy and persisted until the sixteenth century.

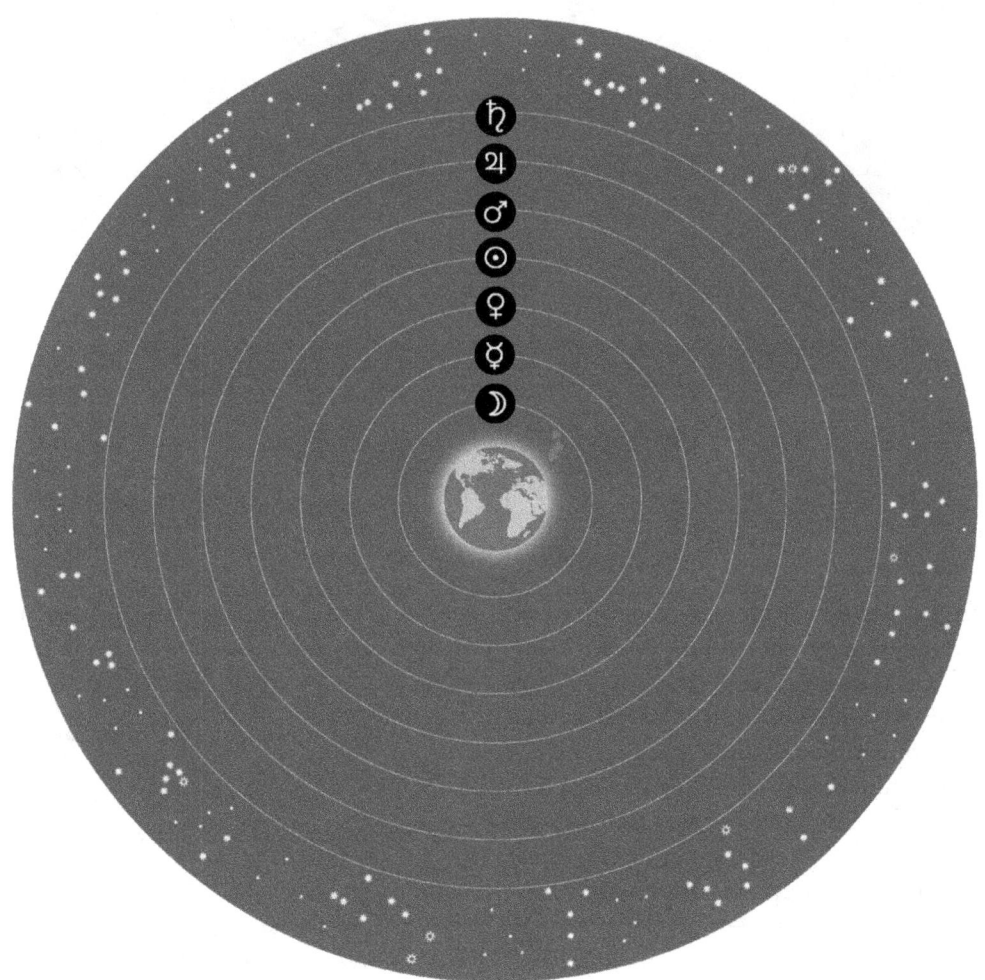

The geocentric (Babylonian/Ptolemaic) system

There is no evidence that the Babylonians had any notion of the physical reality of the Sun at the center of our solar system. As a result, their conception of the universe might seem quaint and archaic. But we would be deeply misguided to dismiss it as outdated—and outperformed—by the physical reality of the heliocentric orientation of our solar system as described by Copernicus in the 1500s.

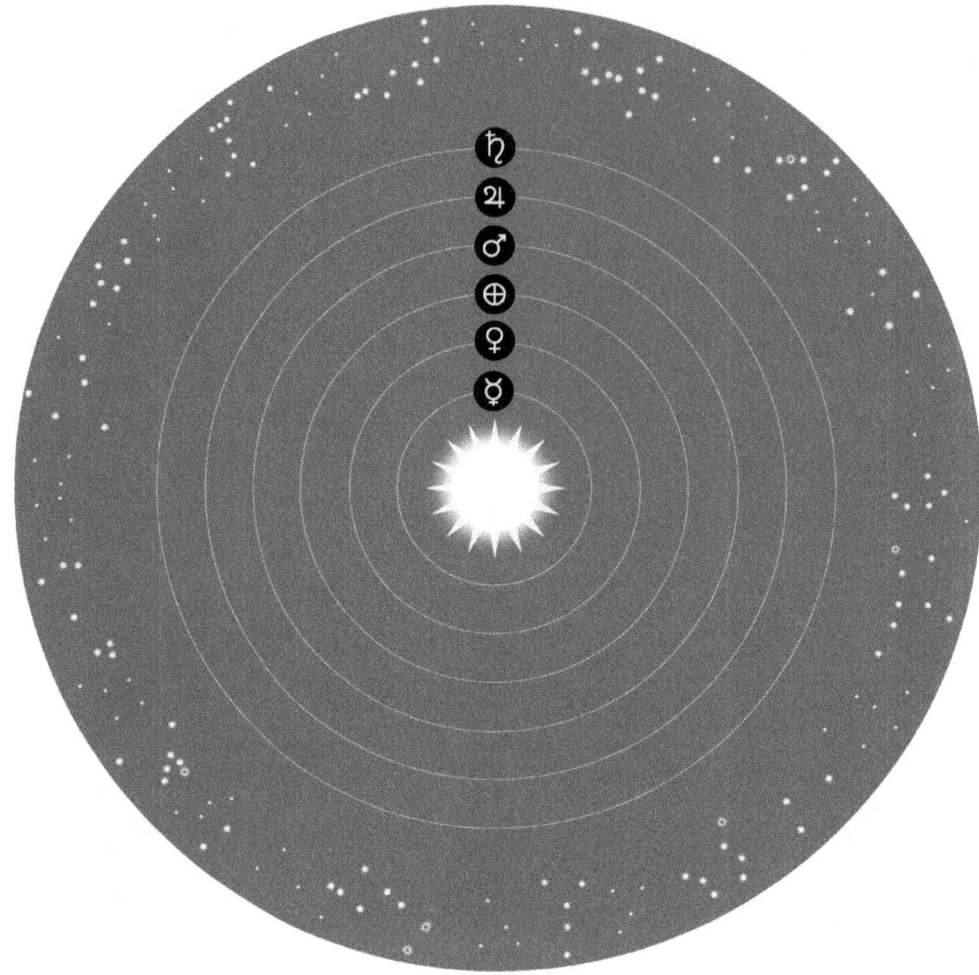

The heliocentric (Copernican) system

For example, we now know for certain that the Sun is stationary at the center of our solar system, and that its apparent motion is the result of both the rotation of the Earth on its axis as well as our annual loop around the Sun. Our intellect can measure the Sun's changing latitude above the horizon, or the number of hours of daylight that it shines upon us on a given day. But it cannot explain the joy that fills us as we watch the Sun rise—nor the warmth and faith that permeates our souls as it journeys across the sky each day. Intellect is powerless to present before our mind's eye the vision of the Sun asleep in the arms of the Mother as it travels below the horizon each night. As denizens of the Earth, the geocentric perspective allows us to partake in the rhythms of the natural world. Every evening, the glittering stars rise in the east after sunset. Can we or can we not trust what we see? Steiner said:

> When Copernicus explained that what we see is *maya*, illusion, and that we should rely on what we cannot see—that was the moment when science as we know it today began.[1]

If we dismiss the geocentric arrangement as untenable, we also discard what Zaratas saw in imaginative vision: *the descent of the soul into incarnation.* Zaratas was the Persian-born initiate who was known to the Greeks as Zoroaster. He imparted to the Babylonians his clairvoyant perception of the spiritual beings underlying the zodiacal constellations.

---

1   Steiner, *Astronomy and Astrology*, 54. See also CW Nr. 15.

The Geocentric Chart

Through imaginative consciousness, the Babylonian astronomer-priests were able to witness the astonishing spiritual reality of the descent of the soul from the cosmos. This begins after the conclusion of the soul's ascent following physical death, when the soul journeys upward through the planetary spheres and eventually reaches its zenith among the zodiacal beings who encircle creation. This conclusion is known as "cosmic midnight."

While within the realm of the fixed stars, we come to understand that we must *reincarnate* in order to carry out the spiritual resolves that we have gathered during our ascent through the spheres. Here, we feel ourselves to be spread out around the whole of the zodiac, where we gather the necessary forces for the creation of our next physical body. Steiner referred to these forces as the "spirit seed." Indeed, we carry this seed with us as we descend through the planetary spheres upon our approach back to Earth.

The period in the zodiacal realm is of extraordinary significance, astrologically speaking, *for it is where the planetary arrangement of the next natal chart is prepared for each of us.* It is *essential* that we understand that the conditions created within these charts are the ideal ones for the karmic work that lies before us.

When we are ready to make our way back to incarnation, we embark upon our descent through the planetary spheres, a journey that can be experienced imaginatively as Jacob's Ladder. Upon leaving the realm of the fixed stars, we first enter the Saturn sphere, followed by those of Jupiter, Mars, the Sun, Venus, Mercury, and the Moon. Dionysius the Areopagite in the first century, Dante Alighieri in the early fourteenth century, and Rudolf Steiner (among others) have recognized an identical ordering of the planetary spheres, in which the Venus sphere adjoins that of the Sun. This, of course, is at odds with the current astronomical reality of Mercury's closer proximity to the Sun.[2]

The following is a brief description of the stages of the soul's descent, which has been elaborated by Steiner, Powell, and others. As the soul approaches Earth from the zodiacal realm and the "spiritual feet" find each successive rung of Jacob's Ladder, the astral body is built up from the seven planetary realms:

In the sphere of *Saturn* (marked by the orbit of Saturn), Mary, having faithfully guarded the Book into which our True Name is inscribed, bestows upon us the spiritual mission of our coming incarnation — which, once we arrive upon the Earth, will speak to us through our intuition. The Seraphim are the source of our moral impulses, and it is here that we behold "an overview" of the life to come.

In the sphere of *Jupiter* (marked by the orbit of Jupiter), we are permeated by a feeling of joyousness as gravity takes us closer to the Earth. The Cherubim within this sphere bestow upon us the seed impulse of higher thinking and conscience. We thereby receive the wisdom necessary to carry out our spiritual resolves.

In the sphere of *Mars* (marked by the orbit of Mars), we are given a forceful, active grasp of earthly tasks, as well as the courage needed to meet what awaits us on Earth. The Thrones bestow upon us strength of will and the faculty of speech.

In the sphere of the *Sun* (marked by the orbit of the Sun), goodness shines from our inner throne and we gain a new sense of the eternal Self that endures across lifetimes. The Kyriotetes, Dynamis, and Exusiai confer upon us our divine individuality, our source of freedom upon the Earth.

Passage through the *Venus* sphere (marked by the orbit of Mercury)[3] adds loving acceptance of the particular cross each of us is destined to bear, as well as certain knowledge of the karmic group within which our individual destiny lies. The Archai reveal to us our destiny as it relates to matters of the heart. While in the sphere of Venus, we encounter the individualities who will become our parents.

The Archangels of the *Mercury* sphere (marked by the orbit of Venus) bestow upon us the proper measure of mental acuity, health, healing ability, and concern for others. The Archangels reveal to us our karma as it relates to matters of illness and health. It is here that we learn of the folk among whom we will be born, and of the language that will be spoken there.

---

2   This issue will be discussed further within Part III, Chapter 4.
3   The orbit of Mercury is indeed the boundary of the sphere of Venus, and the boundary of the sphere of Mercury is the orbit of Venus. We will endeavor add clarity to the complex subject of the transposition of Mercury and Venus in Part III, Chapter 4.

Our return to the sphere of the *Moon* (marked by the Moon's orbit) means that a new life on Earth is near. At the proper time, the fertilization of the mother's egg takes place, thus laying the biological groundwork for the life to come. But the conception has a spiritual aspect as well, which can take place as much as a few days after the biological conception. This is when the spirit seed that we have carried with us from the cosmos unites with the fertilized egg. From this moment onward, the formation of the etheric body begins, into which the incarnating soul's karma becomes woven.[4] While in the Moon sphere, we are reunited with our guardian Angel, who has waited perhaps centuries for this moment! In her arms we can imagine an impossibly large bundle that is filled with karmic tasks for the life to come. When we take this from her, stumbling a bit under its weight, we nevertheless know that we alone can take full responsibility for its contents. And when the cosmic "gears" align with the starry script determined at cosmic midnight, we take our first breath.

The Babylonian priests beheld "the descent of the stork"[5] at the moment of each conception. Herein lies the true significance of the beloved symbol that announces a coming birth! They knew, too, that each soul approaching the Earth *did so for a reason*, each to fulfill its own destiny task. The nature of this mission was discerned through the study of the geocentric horoscopes that they cast.[6]

To the Babylonians, these horoscopes were "maps of the soul," by which the mystery of personal destiny could be known. Without an awareness that there is purpose and intention for each incarnation, this "map" is reduced to *a mere arrangement of abstract planetary forces* that either aid or hinder our quest for what we want. In reality, the geocentric chart—the way the Angels have "set the table" for our earthly life—reveals the challenges that will be best suited to restoring some degree of karmic balance. And because the sphere of the Moon is where the karma of our moral failings is "stored," this chart not only bears an attachment to our past, it also signifies gazing into the soul through *lunar consciousness*.

To begin our study of the astral signature known as the geocentric chart, we must imagine the subject of the chart—in reality a swaddling babe—as an adult who is gazing upon the starry heavens. (For simplicity's sake, we'll call this individual Rudolf.) Rudolf, who is standing upon the globe at his place of birth, is at the very center of the chart, bridging heaven and Earth. Now, no matter where any of us is upon the Earth—and Rudolf is no exception—the stars and planets rise somewhere in the vicinity of "due east," culminate, and then set somewhere in the vicinity of "due west." This happens every day (like clockwork!) and is known as the *diurnal movement* of the heavenly bodies. Diurnal movement is the result of the Earth's rotation on its axis.

When Rudolf gazes upon the stars of the zodiac from the northern hemisphere, he faces south; thus, east it to his left, and west to his right.

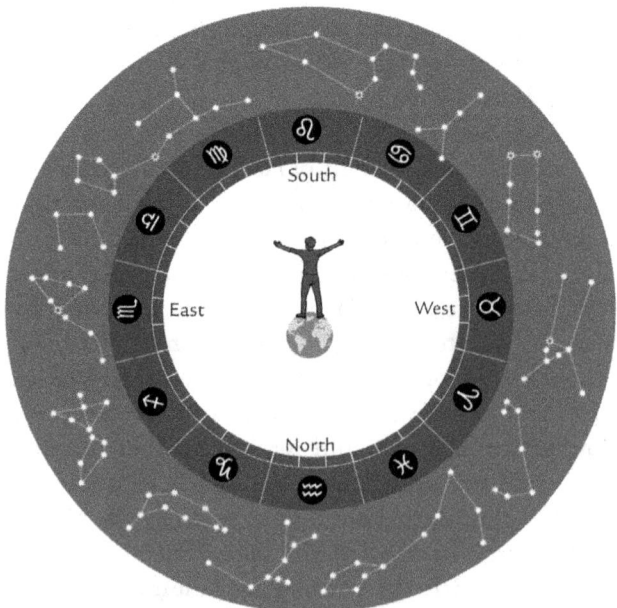

When gazing at the zodiacal stars from the southern hemisphere, however, we must imagine Rudolf facing north; thus east is to his right, and west to his left.

---

4 Powell, *Hermetic Astrology*, vol. 2, 106.
5 Powell and Dann, *The Astrological Revolution*, 10.
6 Powell, *Hermetic Astrology*, vol. 1, 115.

The Geocentric Chart

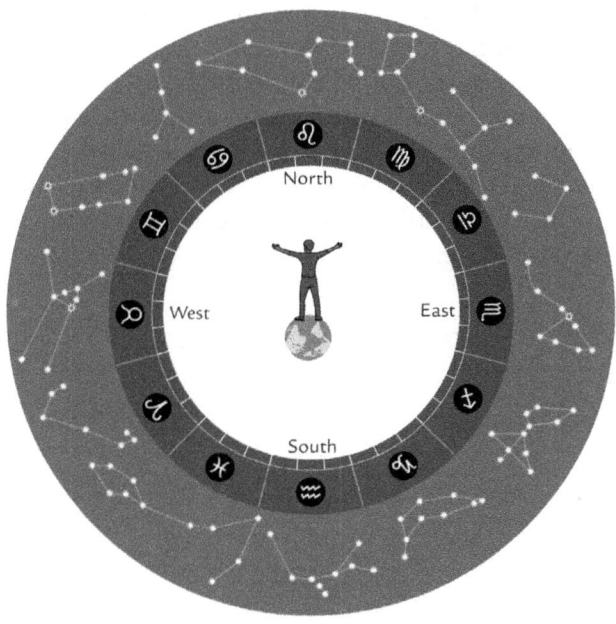

In our illustrations, we notice a horizontal axis running precisely east-west. This orientation of the four direction is based upon the characteristics of the Earth itself—for it is the case that the equator (and any other line of latitude) runs precisely east-west. However, this is *never* what we see in a birth chart.[7]

Astrological charts feature a different horizontal axis—one that represents something else entirely. In the birth chart, the horizontal axis joins the two particular zodiacal degrees that are rising and setting at the time of the birth. These are known as the Ascendant and the Descendant; in both of our illustrations, the Ascendant is at 15° Scorpio, the Descendant at 15° Taurus. Therefore, the axis between the Ascendant and the Descendant does not necessarily indicate east and west at all—although this does happen occasionally. (The reason for the discrepancy between the east-west axis and that of the Ascendant-Descendant axis will be discussed shortly.)

The Ascendant-Descendant axis divides the birth chart into upper and lower sections. Additionally, we might notice a *vertical* axis that divides the chart into left and right, or—in the parlance of the astrologer, an "eastern" and "western" half. Thus the geocentric chart is divided into four quadrants, or *chambers*.

Viewed in the usual way, the geocentric astrological chart reveals an individual's opportunities and challenges. Most of us are accustomed to approaching our birth chart for confirmation of *who we are*—and if the chart fails to provide this, our suspicions about the value of astrology are validated. This is often the basis of the swift rejection of the sidereal zodiac—for it may stand against our conviction that our tropical birth chart describes us perfectly. Yet, there is a difference between personal convictions and *cosmic truth*. Such truth often asks us to re-imagine our tasks, our mission, and perhaps even our own being.

Each horoscope grants us a glimpse into ineffable realms of wonder, which, as expressed by Wordsworth,[8] trail behind each incarnating soul in clouds of glory. And despite the (sometimes dire) nature of traditional interpretations, cosmic benevolence is the root of all horoscopic signatures. Thus do we find cosmic gifts and cosmic impediments inextricably linked.

In astrosophy, we are less interested in Rudolf's *inclinations* than we are in unveiling the nature of the angelic guidance that seeks expression through his chart. The birth chart does not compel us to live in accordance with it; as human beings, we are free to behave as we please. Such freedom allows us to accept or reject the trials and talents inscribed by higher beings. Yet, the lofty resolve that we attain during our heavenly journey toward birth lives within each planetary placement and aspect in the chart. Although most of us don't remember anything about our time in the land of spirit, our conscience retains this memory, which hovers around us like a firefly—briefly flashing light upon fragments born of this timeless sojourn in the heavens.

The geocentric chart, then, is a map *of and for* the soul in which the zodiac, planets, and houses are finely calibrated to present to the individual the proper karmic challenges in proper measure. Although we may have a tendency to resist these tasks with every fiber of our being—as most of us would prefer to give suffering a wide berth—such apparent dilemmas can be witnessed as exit points from the

---

7 The four directions are offered here only in hopes of assisting us in our spatial orientation.
8 William Wordsworth, "Ode: Intimations of Immortality from Recollections of Early Childhood."

eternal wheel of repetition. Steiner assures us that addressing these challenges is our *only* path to true freedom.

It is important to differentiate between the freedom spoken of by Steiner and *what we have come to know as freedom*. To Steiner, "freedom" implied collaboration with the spiritual evolution of humanity, which can be achieved only if we take on the karmic tasks proper to us; in contrast, the modern conception of freedom is more along the lines of *being able to do as we please*. The latter approach will necessarily result in *less* freedom — because the karmic chains that bind us to the Earth will thereby become ever longer and heavier. In other words, living contrary to karmic law will result in greater limitations in the future.

THE HELIOCENTRIC AND TYCHONIC CHARTS

THE GROUND-SHIFTING PROOF that the Sun is the immovable body around which the other planets revolve is attributable to Copernicus (1473-1543). As Copernicus himself suggested, however,[1] there is evidence that this was considered long before the modern scientific age. For example, Archimedes (in the third century BC) wrote that Aristarchus of Samos, a Greek astronomer, spoke of the Sun as immovable. There is also compelling evidence that this was a reality for the Egyptians. In the *Corpus Hermeticum*, the following statement can be found:

> The Sun is stationed in the midst of the solar system and wears the cosmos as a wreath around him. And so he lets the cosmos go on its course, not leaving it far separated from himself, but, to speak truly, keeping it joined to himself; for like a skilled driver, he has made fast and bound to himself the chariot of the cosmos, lest it should rush away in disorder.[2]

The Copernican (or heliocentric) conception of our solar system reflects the entirely real *physical laws* outlined by Kepler in the early seventeenth century. This is consistent with what most of us were taught in school. But did not these lessons carried a certain *dryness*, in which the material reality easily suffocated any feelings of awe that might have otherwise arisen in us during our childhood years? What a shame! Might we not have simultaneously learned that it was a longing to identify the Star of the Magi that lived behind Kepler's study of astronomy? Unfortunately—and inadvertently—Kepler's laws of planetary motion were the agent that led to the *petrification* of the Copernican heliocentric system. In truth, beneath the "stones" lies the work of the three hierarchies of Angels in the Sun sphere—the Exusiai, the Dynamis, and the Kyriotetes:

> In the laws of Newton and, in particular, through the development of *Newton's Laws of Motion* and *Newton's Universal Law of Gravitation*, there can be found a more general explanation of the motions of the planets. In both the works of Kepler and those of Newton, we meet the limitations that have bound astronomy to the mundane world while forsaking higher truths.
>
> [Robert] Powell's penetration of Kepler's laws of planetary motion exemplifies the fruits gained through hermetic (solar) thinking. He has experienced that there are beings behind these laws, confirming Steiner's indications... Powell sees the working of the Spirits of Form (the Exusiai) in the first law; these are the spiritual beings who maintain the elliptical *form* of the planetary orbits. In the second law he sees the Spirits of Movement (the Dynamis), the spiritual beings that regulate the *dynamics* of planetary movement. And in the third law he sees the Spirits of Wisdom (the Kyriotetes), the spiritual beings that bring *harmony* to the movement and the distances between planets in their movements.[3]

If we look to the years between the advances of Copernicus (sixteenth century) and those of Kepler (early seventeenth), we find that there was a wrestling match of sorts over the course of human evolution. In one corner was Kepler; in the other, his great teacher from Copenhagen, Tycho Brahe. Brahe died in 1604 with the following words on his lips: "Let me not seem to have lived in vain." *He was speaking to Johannes Kepler.* What did he mean?

---

[1] Nicholas Copernicus, *De revolutionibus orbium coelestium* I, 10, trsl. E. Rosen, [*On the Revolutions*, Cracow-London, 1978, 22] as cited in *Hermetic Astrology*, vol. 1, 35.

[2] "Asclepius to King Ammon," *Corpus Hermeticum* XVI, 7, trsl. W. Scott, [*Hermetica*, Oxford, 1924; repr. Boulder (CO), 1982, 267] as cited in *Hermetic Astrology*, vol. 1, 35.

[3] Claudia McLaren Lainson, *The Circle of Twelve and the Legacy of Valentin Tomberg* (Boulder, CO: WindRoseAcademyPress, 3rd edition, 2021), 199.

Before the publication of Kepler's laws (1609–1619), the Copernican worldview had not yet taken hold. Brahe, in his last words, entreated Kepler to advance an entirely different perception of the heliocentric solar system. This system was essentially identical to the *Egyptian* system: that is, with the Sun at center of the solar system — "in the midst." Though not yet in wide usage, it is now known as the *Tychonic system*.

Egyptian initiates were able to achieve *solar consciousness*, whereby the spiritual and moral nature of the Sun was felt. Through their spiritual practice, they could *feel* the planets — Mercury, Venus, Mars, Jupiter, and Saturn — revolving around the Sun.[4] Simultaneously, they experienced the Sun's yearly revolution around the Earth in a profound way as they watched it move through the thirty-six ten-degree arcs of space (three arcs in each zodiacal sign) known as the *decans*. This was central to Egyptian astronomy. Furthermore, each decan was assigned a planetary ruler,[5] as illustrated below.

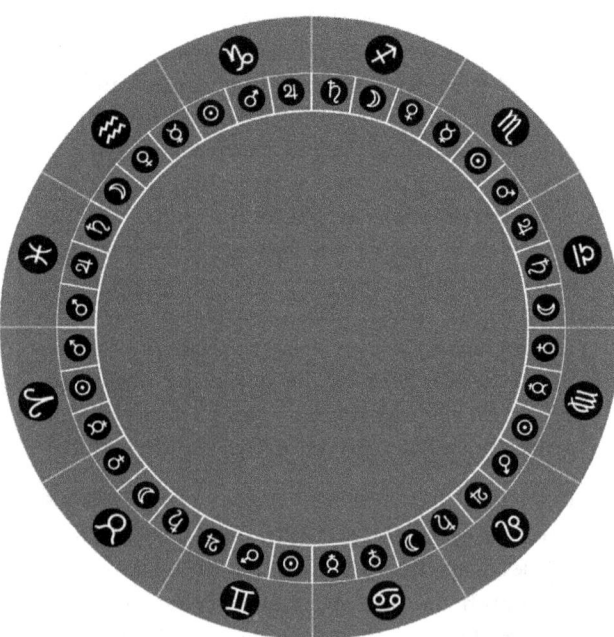

The planetary rulers of the decans

Though difficult to grasp at first, the Tychonic chart is extraordinarily important. For we can see that, within the Egyptian/Tychonic system, the geocentric conception — experienced through the Egyptian priests' observation of the Sun's movement around the Earth — *existed alongside* the heliocentric movement that they beheld in spirit, through their initiation. Though the Tychonic chart reveals *more* than the simple heliocentric chart, it helps to keep in mind that *the heliocentric chart can be found within the Tychonic chart*. In fact, a heliocentric chart becomes Tychonic through the simple addition of the geocentric positions of the Sun and Moon. Additionally, both charts feature the zodiacal degree of the Earth *from the perspective of the Sun*. The Earth — from the Sun's perspective — is always exactly 180° from the zodiacal position of the Sun *from the perspective of the Earth*. We can think of the zodiacal sign of the Earth as our individual "Earth sign"; as such, it indicates the character of our work upon the Earth.

In the heliocentric system, all planets orbit around the Sun; however, within the Egyptian experience of the universe, Mercury, Venus, Mars, Jupiter, and Saturn revolve around the *Sun* — while the Moon and Sun revolve around the *Earth*. Let us take a moment to study the illustrations below, which characterize both the Copernican (heliocentric) and the Tychonic (Egyptian, or hermetic) systems.

Of primary importance within the Tychonic system is the perception that *the Earth is fixed* — whereas in the Copernican, it is the Sun that is immovable. This is the difference. The Tychonic system maintains the preeminence on Earth of the tenth hierarchy — humanity — and its role in the spiritual evolution of the cosmos.

Both systems use the heliocentric positions of Mercury, Venus, Mars, Jupiter, and Saturn (today we can add to this list Uranus, Neptune, and Pluto). Such is the *physical* reality. But the Tychonic alone accounts for the *spiritual* reality of the Sun's revolution around the Earth. The Tychonic system simultaneously upholds both the geocentric *and* heliocentric realities of the cosmos. It might therefore be regarded as a "geo-heliocentric" system.

An analogy lives between the human heart (the microcosm), the Sun (the macrocosm), and

---

4 Powell, *Hermetic Astrology*, vol. 1, 38.
5 The decans are a subject unto themselves — one that is necessarily beyond the scope of this work. The Sun's passage through the 36 decans offers us an opportunity to explore the astrological-spiritual practice of the *Eightfold Path* — exercises directed at the purification of the seven lotus flowers. For those who wish to know more, I highly recommend Randall Scott's *The Christos Sun Meditations: Following the Eightfold Path Through the Decans of the Zodiac* (San Rafael, CA: LogoSophia, 2009).

The Heliocentric and Tychonic Charts

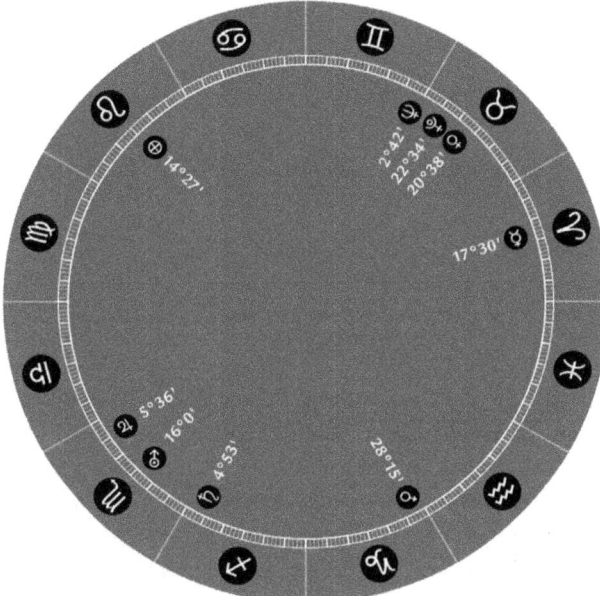

The heliocentric birth chart of Valentin Tomberg

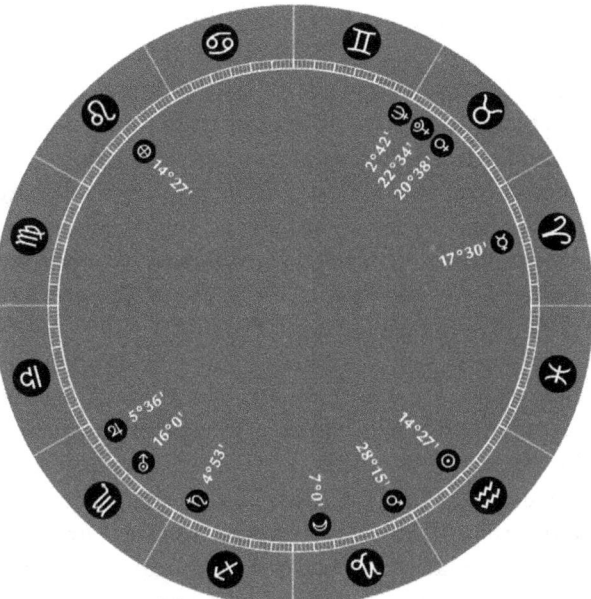

The Tychonic birth chart of Valentin Tomberg adds to the heliocentric chart the geocentric positions of the Sun and Moon

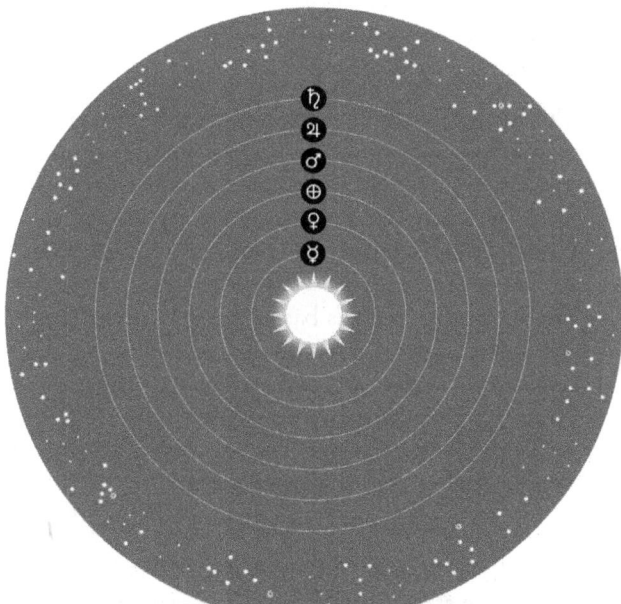

The heliocentric (Copernican) system

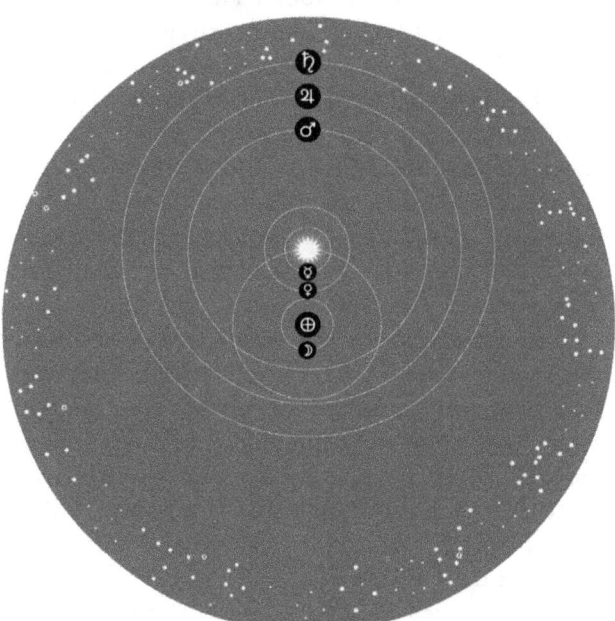

The Tychonic (hermetic) system

the Central Sun (the greater macrocosm). Just as human being is dependent upon the function of the heart for life, so does the Earth depend upon the heart of the solar system—the Sun—for *its* life; so too is the heart of the galaxy, the Central Sun, the "heart" of the system of stars of which our Sun is a part. The Central Sun is not only the "star nursery" for the Milky Way—whereby older stars are pushed outward in a beautiful spiral pattern, as new stars are born from this nursery. *It also signifies where spirit is transformed into matter.* The heart of our galaxy is the source of the eternal, divine spark of each one of us (referred to by Steiner as the "I" of the human being). It is the source of Christ, whose "I" bears the spark of *every* human "I."

This analogy supports the deep significance of the heliocentric and Tychonic charts. Therefore, the *heliocentric* orientation of the planets reveals to astrosophers the eternal spiritual aspect of the individual: the "map of the spirit" that exists high above the geocentric realm of soul and personality. Because we accept the heliocentric placements as an expression of the sovereignty of the Sun—and this is the *source* of the eternal spirit of each individual (the "I")—the heliocentric zodiacal placements cast the spirit's-eye-view upon our earthly troubles. Indeed, these placements serve as "beacons" that call us toward the future. However, it is only through the heliocentric chart's comparison to the geocentric chart that it can be tethered to the Earth at all—for it lacks the terrestrial coordinates (axes and houses) associated with the geocentric chart.

We can look at the heliocentric and the geocentric together and learn a great deal. While the geocentric chart points to the past—through *past* karma—the heliocentric and Tychonic charts point to the *future*—through future karma. The comparison can show you the way out of a "geocentric rut." For example, if Mars is in Taurus in your geocentric chart, but in Aries in the heliocentric and Tychonic chart, we might say that the practical concerns that normally guide the execution of your deeds must not override the ideal that set the deed in motion in the first place.

When aspiring to the ideals of the heliocentric and Tychonic charts, our efforts may not bear fruit until a *future* incarnation. We are often aware that these lofty spiritual intentions cannot possibly come to pass in the current lifetime. Instead, the heliocentric and Tychonic indications are seeds that can be planted and nourished for a future harvest.

For a slower-moving planet, there is little difference between its zodiacal longitude in the geocentric and heliocentric charts. Moreover, the slower the planet, the more likely it is to be in the same sign in both charts. Heliocentric Mercury and Venus, however, can be a full 180° from where they are in the geocentric chart. (This can only happen when they're in *inferior* conjunction with the Sun.) In the following table, you will find the maximum possible disparity between the geocentric and heliocentric positions of each planet.

Mercury	180°
Venus	180°
Mars	47°
Jupiter	12°
Saturn	6°
Uranus	3°
Neptune	2°
Pluto	2°

The Tychonic chart is remarkable in another way. It provides a unique perspective of the human being in the context of the cosmos by affirming *the correspondence between the seven classical planets and the chakra (or lotus flower) system of the human being*. The hermetic man is the archetypal human being, who can be imagined as filling the space of the solar system. To complete the imagination of hermetic man, we think of the seven classical planets aligned linearly so that they create a macrocosmic representation of the human chakra system.[6]

Robert Powell wrote:

> The hermetic chart—the planetary positions at birth drawn up according to the Egyptian system—portrays the macrocosmic relationship between the planets, showing how the cosmic forces from the planets are related to the seven lotus flowers of the microcosm. The hermetic chart is based directly upon the hermetic law of correspondence—*as above, so below*—where the planetary relationships above (in the macrocosm) show simultaneously the interrelationships between the lotus flowers below (in the microcosm).[7]

Brahe's last words brought to light his hope of ultimately stemming the materialistic tide; but in any case, the strictly heliocentric perspective—the one we were all taught in school—won out. As the Copernican system favored by Kepler became fully rooted in scientific dogma, the spiritual truth behind Brahe's Egyptian perspective lay quietly behind a barrier of the certainty of astronomical measurements and formulae. Nearly four centuries later, the *Hermetic Astrology* volumes of Robert Powell have achieved what Brahe could not: the resurrection of the Egyptian cosmic conception.

---

6 Powell, *Hermetic Astrology*, vol. 1, 139.
7 Ibid., 140.

The Heliocentric and Tychonic Charts

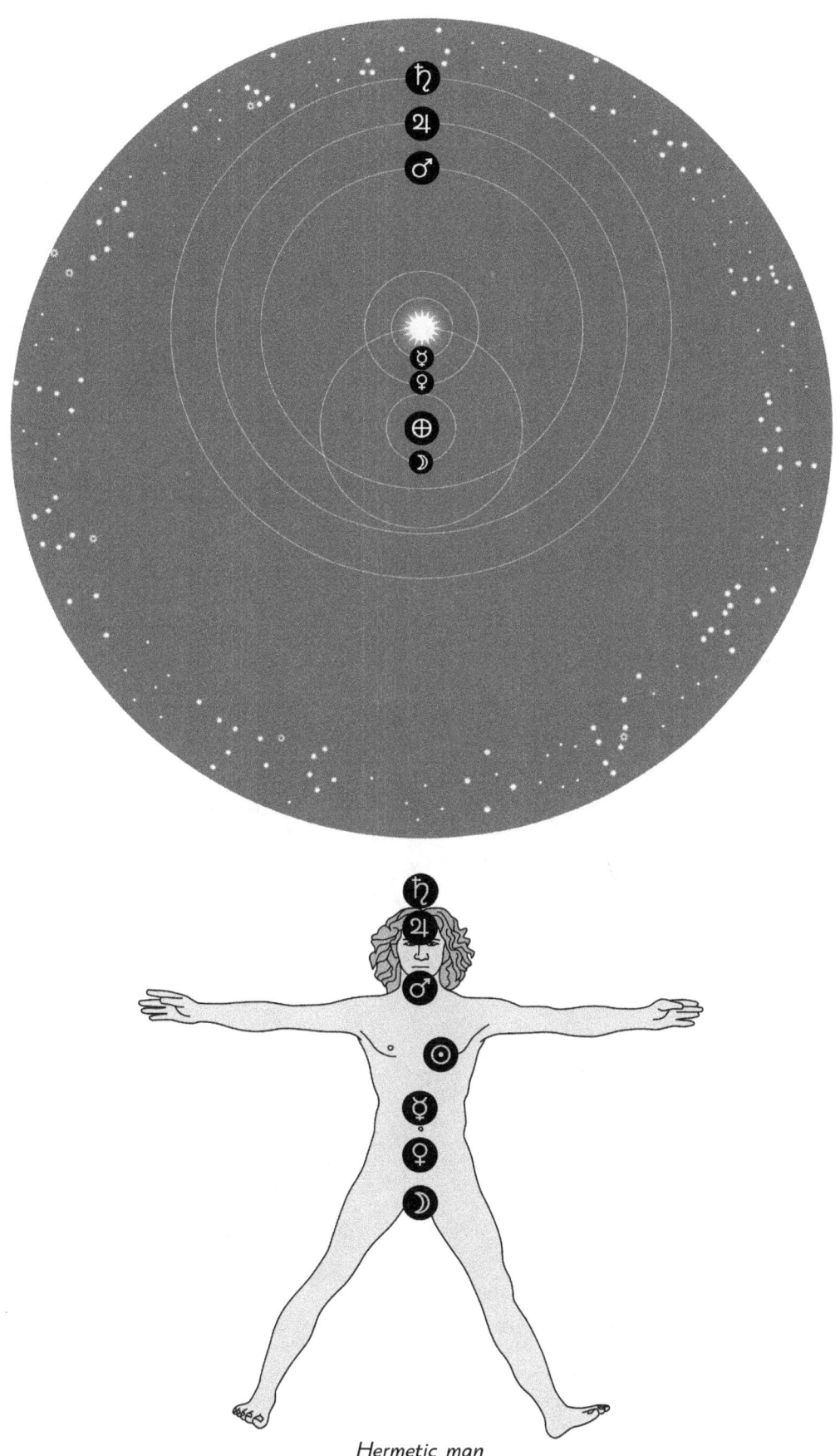

Hermetic man

ASTROLOGICAL BIOGRAPHY

Astrological biography, though its study is complex and requires a certain level of expertise, is an integral part of hermetic astrology. While it is necessarily beyond the scope of this work to go into a great deal of detail, an overview is absolutely in order: For just as destiny is carried over by the stars between incarnations, *the planetary forces of the embryonic period unfold in the life to come.*

Astrological biography begins with *the hermetic rule*. The earliest evidence of the hermetic rule was found in writing fragments from the second century BC. An Egyptian priest, Petosiris, scribed astrological "instructions" for his king, Nechepso—and yet, because Petosiris was regarded as a merely a *mediator* of the wisdom of Hermes, these instructions continue to be known as the hermetic rule.[8]

This rule allows us to determine the time of conception—the moment when the etheric body joins the fertilized egg—by looking to the positions of the Moon and the Ascendant at birth. I will rephrase the hermetic rule as follows:

The Moon at conception is aligned with the Ascendant-Descendant axis at birth. Moreover, the Moon at birth is aligned with the Ascendant-Descendant axis at conception.

That these initiates were aware of the spiritual importance of the moment of conception is one thing, but the fact that they were able to characterize the precise moment in time when it occurred is quite astonishing.

Through the work of Willi Sucher (1902–1985), a new application of the hermetic rule emerged in the 1930s. Sucher discovered that the movements of the planets during the gestational period has a marked and orderly influence on the life to come. These movements include the passage of the planets across the main axes of the conception chart, as well as aspects formed between planets.

Parallel to the development of the embryo in the womb there occurs the formation of the etheric body within the sphere of the Moon (i.e.,

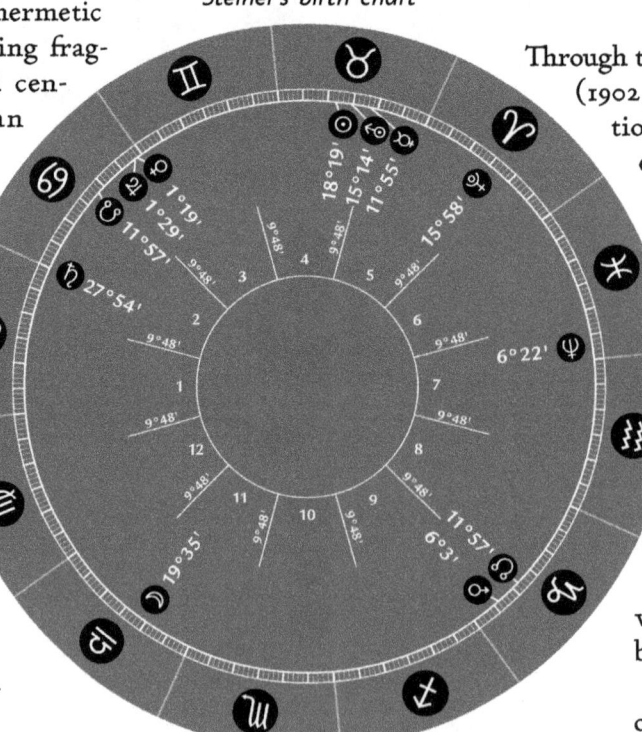

Steiner's birth chart

Steiner's conception chart, as calculated by Astrofire: *the Ascendant (24°48' Leo) assumes the Moon's position in the birth chart, while the Moon (19°35' Libra) assumes the degree of the Ascendant in the birth chart*

---

8 Ibid., 302.

all that surrounds the Earth up to the boundary of the Moon's orbit). The average gestational period of the human being is 273 days. The time required for the Moon to travel 360° around the sidereal zodiac is exactly one tenth of that—just over 27 days. Hardly another cosmic coincidence!

Therefore, between conception and birth, there occur (on average) *ten sidereal revolutions of the Moon*. What Sucher discovered through his biographical research was that there was an obvious correspondence between the first gestational Moon revolution and the first seven years of life, between the second revolution and the second seven years of life, and so on. Furthermore, the unfolding of the seven-year periods of life is prefigured by the movement of all the planets within each of the ten lunar periods of embryonic development. For example, one of the major indicators of change in a person's life is the advent of the crossing of the prenatal Ascendant by the prenatal Sun; the consistency of its relevance is extraordinary.

Let's take a brief look at the Nathan Jesus[9] through the lens of astrological biography. The seven archetypal healing miracles took place between 28/Dec/29 and 26/Jul/32. The corresponding embryonic period, in which the etheric imprint of these miracles was forming, finds Mercury (the divine messenger and healer) moving across *Regulus*, the cosmic heart of the Lion. Never, during this portion of the prenatal period, was Mercury even two degrees away from *Regulus*. I would argue that this suggests that the life-giving forces streaming through the heart of the Lion—compassion, warmth, and courage—allowed these miracles to manifest by way of the Lion of Judah.

To those whose interest extends to astrological chart interpretation, you will need access to an app or program (for example, astro.com) that calculates sidereal astrological charts. Also essential is a sidereal ephemeris, a daily account of the sidereal zodiacal longitudes of our planets. Peter Treadgold's remarkable *Astrofire* computer program, which produces the data seen in *Star Wisdom* also identifies planetary aspects.[10] However, this program is already nearly thirty years old—and an update has not been possible. Fortunately, a new program (accessible through an internet browser) is now under development. Blessings on this undertaking!

The casting of the horoscope brings to expression a psychological mood, which can be formulated as follows: "I have arrived from the cosmos. I look back to the moment of birth, when I separated from the cosmos, when I was born from the cosmic world upon the Earth. I look back to the planetary configuration at the moment of birth to behold my unique relationship with the cosmos as it comes to expression in the relationship between the cosmos and the Earth at that moment, to learn from this relationship about myself and my task upon the Earth."[11]

THE CHARTS OF CHILDREN

Children should have the freedom to experience the joyful unfolding of their lives without the interference of a chart interpretation.

Those of us with the ability to produce an astrological chart need to be *very careful* when it comes to our little ones. Many parents instinctively "do not want to know" what a chart might hold, and I believe that this is an entirely proper gesture of protection, an intuitive appreciation of the importance of freedom in childhood. It is not difficult to imagine how a feature of a child's chart could become a curse, set in stone: *He's always been like that. I knew she'd never be able to do that.* To an impressionable child, these thoughts—even if they remain unspoken—can be damaging in the extreme.

---

9 Though there was only one Jesus Christ who died upon the cross, Rudolf Steiner distinguished between the Jesus of the gospel of Luke (descended from David through Nathan) and that of the gospel of Matthew (descended from David through Solomon). After Steiner's time, a corroboration appeared in the Dead Sea Scrolls. These scrolls revealed that the Essenes at Qumran were clearly expecting *two* Messiahs: one royal and one priestly. A thorough accounting of the two families can be found in Steiner's *The Fifth Gospel* as well as in Powell's *Chronicle of the Living Christ*.
10 Unique to *Astrofire* is its ability to calculate the time of conception by way of the hermetic rule. Additionally, *Astrofire* contains a catalog of cosmic data for Christ's time on Earth.
11 Powell, *Hermetic Astrology* vol. 1, 102.

There are times, however, when we must make decisions on behalf of a child—in which case, knowledge of the birth chart can help shepherd our thought process toward a moral conclusion. We might also wonder what we can do for a child who is struggling; the birth chart can be a powerful source of guidance—provided that we are familiar with the spiritual dimensions of the chart. What does the chart seem to be asking of the child? It goes without saying that providing these insights presupposes both a respect for the individuality that each child is becoming *as well as* for the individual freedom that is shared by all of us. The most important consideration to those who have been asked for an interpretation of a child's chart will be our assessment of the moral uprightness of the person who has made that request. May caution be our guide!

③
THE ASCENDANT-DESCENDANT AXIS

WHEN WE GAZE at the zodiac from the northern hemisphere, we face south. The starry band of zodiacal constellations arcs across the sky (counterclockwise) between the Ascendant and the Descendant, reaching its maximum height directly between the two.[1]

To interpret an astrological chart, we'll return to our imagination of Rudolf at the center of the zodiacal wheel, standing upon the Earth at the location of his birth. All that is visible to him (glorious sunshine, or stars!) is above the horizon; all that is obscured is below it. We then imagine that Rudolf is facing *away* from us, looking in the same direction that we are looking. When in the northern hemisphere, his *left* arm points roughly east, his right arm roughly west.[2] In reality, of course, the size of the Earth in relation to the zodiacal circle is infinitesimal!

When in the southern hemisphere, the *right* arm points roughly east.

As we discussed earlier, the axis that runs horizontally through

The view of the cosmos from the northern hemisphere

The view of the cosmos from the southern hemisphere

the middle of the chart—the *horizon*—is known as the Ascendant-Descendant axis. The Ascendant denotes the particular zodiacal degree that is rising above the horizon as the infant takes its first breath: *It marks the beginning of an individual's life on Earth and is particular to the location of the birth.* The Descendant indicates the zodiacal degree that is setting—about to move below the horizon—at this same moment in time. Though we would like to think of this axis as running east-west, this happens only rarely (e.g., at the spring and autumn equinoxes).

Distinguishing between the Ascendant-Descendant axis and what we know as the true east-west axis is *very important*. The foundation of the Ascendant-Descendant axis is the ecliptic. The foundation of the east-west axis, on the other hand, is the Earth itself. East-west essentially means "perpendicular to the poles of the Earth," in the same way that every line of latitude—including the equator—runs precisely east-west.

---

1 Gazing at the zodiac from the southern hemisphere requires us to look northward; from here, the zodiacal constellations advance in a clockwise direction.
2 From the southern hemisphere, east is somewhere to our right, and west somewhere to our left.

The astrological chart (which, of course, appears flat on paper) actually represents *three* dimensions of space. Although the Ascendant-Descendant axis is expressed as a line, it is in reality a great circle tipped on its side.

Let's imagine that the Sun is aligned with the Ascendant — which, in the illustrations above, is located at 15° Virgo; this means that at the moment of birth, the Sun is making its way above the horizon. We behold, in awe, its ability to set the sky on fire as daylight begins. Life begins to stir! We feel its reach and its warmth, its mercy, its love and forgiveness — and its gift of a new day. We can feel it gain strength throughout the morning as it approaches its "throne" at the top of its path, from which it commands all that it sees. We notice also when the Sun steps down from this throne — when it begins to cede its power to the mysteries of the coming night. This is the dynamic of *diurnal* movement: apparent motion that results from the rotation of the Earth on its axis. It's not only the Sun that appears to circle the Earth each day; all the stars and planets do the same.

Referring to the illustrations above, what do we notice about diurnal movement? In the northern hemisphere, the Sun and other heavenly bodies move *clockwise* throughout the day against the background of the zodiac, which proceeds *anticlockwise*. In the southern hemisphere, diurnal movement is *anticlockwise*, while the zodiac proceeds *clockwise*. Indeed, diurnal motion is contrary to zodiacal direction! True in the northern and southern hemispheres alike, this is more than an abstract observation; it is altogether faithful to cosmography.[3]

Let's review! As we gaze at the zodiac from the northern hemisphere, the zodiacal constellations proceed anticlockwise. From this same vantage, all of the planetary orbits are anticlockwise as well. The Earth's daily rotation on its axis, however, creates the *experience* of watching these same planets move clockwise throughout the course of the day. Heavenly movement and earthly experience are *contrary* to one another.

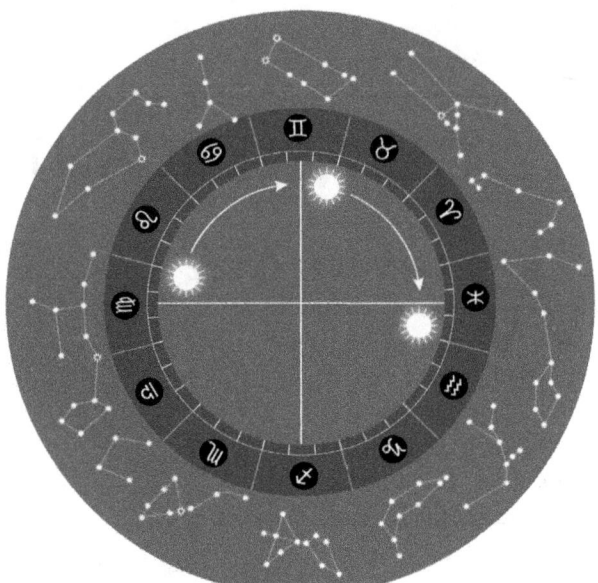

The diurnal movement of the Sun from the northern perspective

When gazed upon from the southern hemisphere — which is a bit like looking at the face of a transparent clock from the rear — the zodiacal constellations proceed clockwise, as do the orbits of the planets. From the southern vantage, the Earth's daily rotation on its axis creates the experience of watching these same planets move anticlockwise throughout the course of the day. Once again, heavenly movement and earthly experience remain *contrary* to one another.

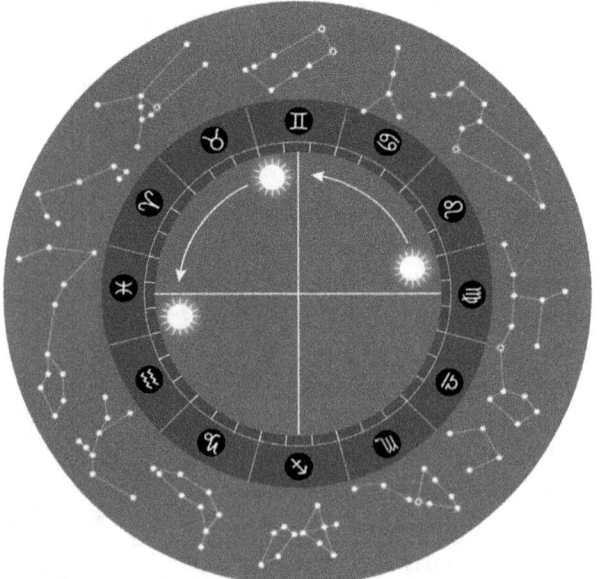

The diurnal movement of the Sun from the southern perspective

---

3 *Cosmography* is the science of the universe that describes both heaven and Earth.

This *resistance* (or, *creative tension*) is descriptive of — and fundamental to — our experience as dual citizens of the cosmos and of the Earth (our *night* and *day* consciousness). When we were at one with the spiritual world, no such resistance existed. There was no one to experience the cosmos from the Earth! With the Fall of mankind came *dissonance* with the spiritual world.

Birth charts are always cast (to my knowledge) with the Ascendant on the left side of the chart. This captures the perspective of those of us in the northern hemisphere. As annoying as this must be to our southern brothers and sisters, it must be emphasized that in terms of chart interpretation, it loses none of its validity![4]

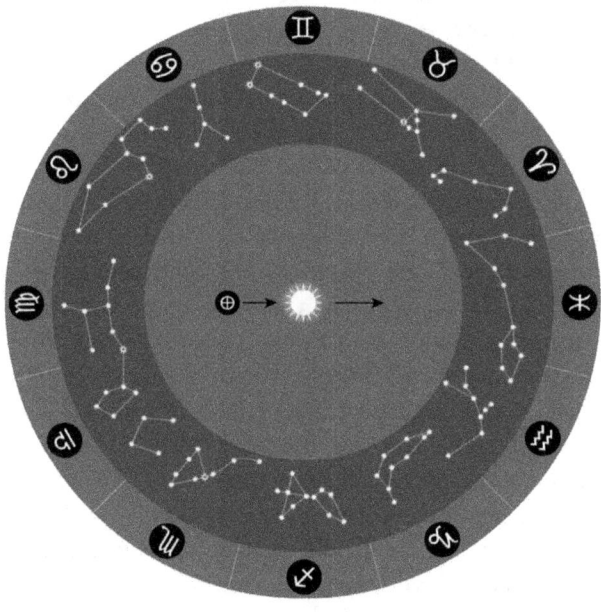

A Pisces Sun

The planets that occupy the top half of the birth chart *always* represent those that were above the native at the moment of birth. If the birth takes place in the daytime, the Sun will be among those in the upper half. If the birth takes place at night, the Sun will be below the horizontal Ascendant-Descendant axis. To establish the "Sun sign," we draw an arrow from the Earth, through the Sun, and out to the zodiacal circle. If the arrow meets the stars of Pisces, the "Sun sign" of the individual is Pisces. This suggests that the "I" of this individual can best find expression through the qualities of Pisces: magnanimity, a sense of the interconnectedness of all life, and awakening to the forces of the underworld and to the Mother who dwells within the center of the Earth. In this case, the Sun *mediates* the forces of Pisces on behalf of the individual. We can imagine the stars of the twelve zodiacal signs imprinted upon twelve mantles. The "Pisces mantle" is ideally worn by every individual born when the Sun was before the stars of sidereal Pisces.

Using the analogy of the Sun's diurnal journey to take a preliminary look at a chart, we could say that it is our proper destiny that the planets in the upper half of the chart work in a more visible way in our life — our outward identity — while planets in the lower portion work more behind the scenes and indicate how we judge ourselves or others.

If most of the planets in a chart are in the upper section, a karmic need to be out in the world in a noticeable way is suggested; this is where we'll need to go to "recharge." When *all* planets are above the horizon, we're usually talking about an individual who is difficult to keep up with. If you are by nature an extroverted go-getter, this arrangement will suit you very well — it will feel like the most natural thing in the world. However, if you ordinarily drift toward solitude, it could spell a lifetime of effort. (The need to be in the world is sometimes affected by a planet below the Ascendant-Descendant axis; this depends on its zodiacal degree, and whether or not it forms an aspect with a planet in the upper section.)

When most of the planets are below the Ascendant-Descendant axis, we usually tend the inner life in favor of the "outer"; we need quiet and solitude to regroup. This will seem easy to natural introverts, but more difficult for those of us who long to be "out where things are happening." Sometimes it is the case that a planet strongly placed in the upper section can serve to "draw" the otherwise introverted individual into view. Either way, the chart shows us what we might work toward, regardless of the difficulty in doing so.

Establishing the Ascendant requires knowing the exact time and location of the birth;

---

4 This will be explained shortly.

without this information, much will remain obscured. When the time of birth is not known, we are left with the zodiacal positions of the planets and the aspects that are formed between them—but no way of knowing the domains of life (represented by the houses) in which the zodiacal indications are meant to find their way through the human "I." In such case, we are invariably left wanting to know more. I guarantee you (100%!) that before long you'll want to know the birth time of *every single person* you meet! Some will guard this information with their lives—perhaps because they intuit its importance.

The zodiacal degree of the Ascendant is, in fact, one of the most important markers of the chart. (The Ascendant becomes even more relevant after the age of sixty-three.)[5] *It reveals what we behold with devotion.* It thereby also illuminates the essence of our individual personality as well as the zodiacal worldview through which we see the everyday world around us. Robert Powell describes it this way:

> [The] Ascendant shows the human being's orientation within the sphere of the zodiac during the building up of the archetype of the physical body... out of the forces of the twelve signs of the zodiac. The circle of the zodiac is revealed in the human being in the spherical form of the head. And just as the orientation of the head is determined by the direction in which the eyes look, so the Ascendant axis coincides with the "direction" in which the human being "looks" whilst indwelling the sphere of the zodiac [in which the human being is a pure spirit], beyond the planetary spheres, in the life after death.[6]

For this reason, Robert Powell refers to the Ascendant-Descendant axis as *the axis of contemplation of the human being.*

When a planet is found within five degrees of the Ascendant, we have an instinctive understanding of the qualities of that planet; we could say that the planet provides a lens through which we *unavoidably* behold the world. When the planet is above the Ascendant, we can add to this the image of a horse just out of the gate, bursting onto the scene, for all to see; when below the horizon, the planet works in manner that is less visible to the outside world. Any planet very near the Ascendant—above it, below it, or directly on it—will naturally exert a strong influence on the free individuality.

Once the Ascendant is determined, so too is the Descendant; they are always 180° apart, and therefore opposite in nature. Through the Descendant we can see the "other"—this can include what we look for and need in another, and perhaps what we reject in ourselves. Any planet within five degrees of the Descendant might reveal the qualities we seek out in others. The Descendent is a key point of the chart because it always represents a great teacher to us, both by sign and degree. In my experience, the positive qualities associated with the zodiacal sign of the Descendant are essential to the expression of the noble spiritual intentions that live within our rising sign. However, it can also be said that the fallen nature of the sign of the Descendant stands as a grave warning—for it can lead us far from the blessings of the sign of the Ascendant. The same dynamic can be observed between any pair of opposites within the zodiac.

Meanwhile, the time has come to add another layer to our delicious cake.

---

5   Sixty-three is the age at which we complete the nine seven-year periods that correspond to the planetary spheres. We then enter the "zodiacal years." The Ascendant is seen as the "line of vision" of the human being; it corresponds directly to our *zodiacal* orientation—i.e., before our descent through the planetary spheres from the realm of the Midnight Sun.
6   Powell, *Hermetic Astrology*, vol. 2, 238.

④
THE VERTICAL AXIS

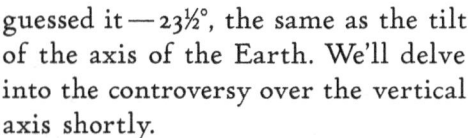

WHERE THERE IS A horizontal axis, can a vertical one be far behind? Just as there is an upper and a lower section of the astrological chart, so, too, can we identify an "eastern" (left) and a "western" (right) side. These indicate the individual's *subjective* nature (the eastern side—that which has a direct bearing on the subject), and *objective* nature (the western side—which is expressed through contacts with others). Neither surpasses the other in importance, for we must all, over time, cultivate both! The goals of those with a dominance of eastern planets at birth tend to be personal and focused on the self, while those with more planets in the west appear to be of a more altruistic nature (whereby success and happiness depend heavily on relationships with others). If it happens that we identify strongly with service to others but have all of our planets in the eastern side of the chart, we would be well advised to pay more attention to our own needs and growth. Similarly, those of us who work tirelessly on our own behalf, and find the eastern side of the chart empty, would benefit from finding more ways to listen to and help others.

Although the vertical axis is represented by a line in the astrological chart, it is in reality another great circle on its side. Here we begin to enter a realm fraught with controversy! For there are two possible vertical axes in the birth chart. The foundation of the controversy is what is known as the "obliquity of the ecliptic." (Pass the Advil!) In plain language, this means that the tilt of the Earth on its axis has rendered the great circle of the ecliptic off-kilter with that of the equator; they can best be imagined as two concentric rings that touch in only two places. The greatest distance between them is—you guessed it—23½°, the same as the tilt of the axis of the Earth. We'll delve into the controversy over the vertical axis shortly.

To understand the importance of the vertical axis, we can hold an imagination of Rudolf, our representative, standing upright atop the globe, arms outstretched.

Forces stream forth from the zodiac above, descending though Rudolf from crown to root. The high point of the chart (what is above us at our birth) signifies the point at which *the stars speak to us*. We draw nearer to that point—through our uprightness—in order to better hear what is being spoken. The point above us at our birth thus indicates a powerful life-long connection to the spiritual world, through which we might realize God's will on Earth. Uprightness, after all, is the first initiative of the growing child; when we are upright, we are ready to act, to make a mark in the world. We set about getting things done—and, certainly, these deeds can also be of a *spiritual* nature.

The high point of the chart reveals to us the character of the initiatives that will be most fruitful in a given lifetime. Put another way, it illuminates our spiritual destiny—the unique zodiacal degree from which spiritual forces are best able to guide the human "I." If in Capricorn, Rudolf will need to pursue endeavors with a great deal of structure and discipline (Capricorn, ruled by Saturn, is master of these characteristics). Firmness must be sought, and efforts of a much more fluid and indefinite nature are less likely to be rewarded.

We can think of this high point as a mountaintop of sorts, whose characteristics are revealed by zodiacal sign and degree. It's reasonable to assume that any planet positioned on or very near this peak has been granted a great deal of power, and that this endowment may be expressed as *authority*. Worth noting, however, is that although the common understanding of this term signifies power over others, true authority does not depend upon coercion; instead, it implies stepping into a role that is protected by our guardian Angel until such time that we are ready to fill it. True authority inspires others. The nature of this authority can be revealed by the uppermost sign and the nature of any planet found within a few degrees of it.

But this peak is also the "can't hide" point of the zodiac! For this reason, it can signal exposure, *humiliation*, or losing face. The gift of a planet on high is offered in response to moral uprightness; and when this virtue is absent, there is the very real potential for a "fall." Even if Jupiter, the beloved benefic, is there, we would still need to continually "earn the right" to remain on the mountaintop. Egotism would otherwise cast us down from it.

One hundred eighty degrees away is the low point of the chart. We can think of it as "the ground of our being," an indication of the inner individual — qualities (thought they might be invisible to others) that need no external validation. The zodiacal sign of this point thereby gives us clues as to the nature of where we might look for inner strength, though we will be asked to bring down to our feet — from *above* to *below* — the qualities of the zodiacal sign above at the holy high place of the chart. Any planet placed near the low point of the chart indicates a spiritual commission to strive to bring into manifestation the virtues of that planet. A planet at the bottom of the chart can engender early karmic wrestles that serve as a nursery for the development of emotional strength. Such strength allows us to find the "treasure" that is buried in the ground below us.

First and foremost to our study is remembering that the Ascendant-Descendant axis — the horizontal axis in every birth chart — identifies *zodiacal-ecliptic* coordinates, not *east* and *west*. Because of this, logic and reason might lead us to conclude that the *proper* vertical axis that corresponds to the Ascendant-Descendant axis is one that is also identified by zodiacal-ecliptic coordinates. This truly vertical axis, which precisely bisects the horizontal, thereby establishes the zodiacal degrees of the firmament that are *directly above* and *directly below* Rudolf. To the extent that they have been identified at all, these two points have been referred to as the north and south ecliptic poles. Fortunately for us all, Brian Gray introduced new terms for these coordinates; he pioneered the use of the terms *ecliptic zenith* (EZ) and the *ecliptic nadir* (EN), better conveying the *spiritual* dimensions of the *true* top and bottom of the chart — to which we can instinctively assign a great deal of importance. Have initiates across the centuries climbed the mountaintop for inspiration, or have they not? *The EZ is "the holy high place" of the chart.*

Because the EN and EZ are always 90° from the Ascendant and Descendant, the Ascendant-Descendant axis and the EZ-EN axis are guaranteed (100%!) to form a perfect cross in space. The beauty and harmony of this system is obvious; the establishment of the perpendicular axis gives rise to quadrants and houses of equal length, no matter where on Earth the birth occurs. The resulting houses thus mirror the equal-length signs of the original Babylonian zodiac: *As above, so below*. Using the EZ-EN axis creates a chart that is easily accessible: all of us have an instinctive relationship to a cross, for it represents our internal struggle for balance and wholeness.

The other way to identify the "vertical" axis is by way of what is known as the MC-IC axis, which connects the *Medium Coeli* (also referred to as the "Midheaven") at or near the top of the chart, and the *Imum Coeli* at or near the bottom. It might be said that the use of this axis with that of the Ascendant-Descendant constitutes an unlawful mixing of two completely different systems — for, as we know, the Ascendant-Descendant represents a coordinate system based upon the *ecliptic*, while the MC-IC represents one based upon the *equator*.

Although the MC-IC axis always runs precisely south-north[1] — like the lines of longitude on the Earth — it is almost never precisely vertical in the astrological chart. Therefore, the MC rarely indicates the highest point of the ecliptic (as the EZ does), but, instead, where the Sun

---

1   In the case of a chart for the southern hemisphere, the MC points north and the IC, south!

The Vertical Axis

reaches its zenith in the middle of the day. *The MC is the "high noon" of the chart.* For locations near the equator, the difference between the EZ and the MC is negligible—but an individual born in Alaska can have an MC that is more than 40° from the EZ! (If this seems nuts to you, you are not alone.) How can an axis that is so seldom vertical be our vertical axis? Its distortion at latitudes far from the equator renders the horizontal and vertical axes so far from perpendicular that the "cross" of the chart—its very structure—is no longer able to support itself. Thus, the MC-IC axis *cannot* represent the zenith and the nadir of the chart!

Where would you go to seek communion with the stars: "high noon" (the MC), or the "high holy place" (the EZ)? Can there be two high points in the chart? Because these questions, in my view, answer themselves, we are left with two choices: to chuck the MC and IC altogether, or to simply use the MC and IC as two "other" features in the chart—as those whose research has upheld the significance of the MC might prefer to do.

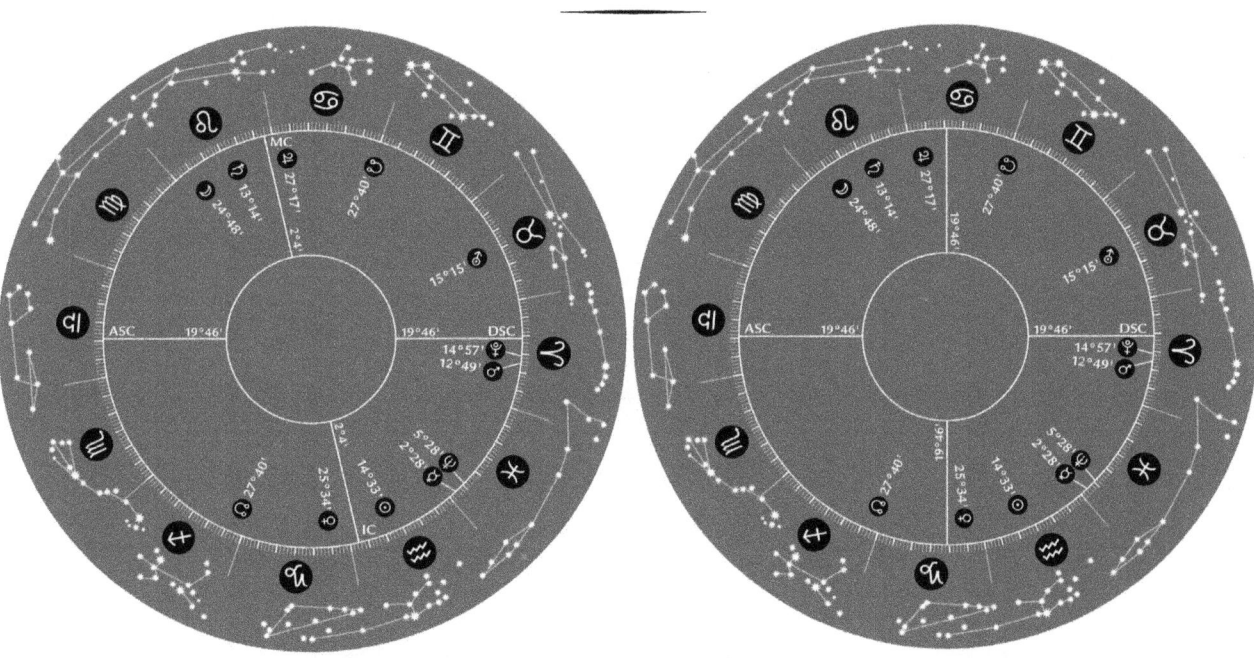

The vertical axis established by the MC and the IC in Steiner's birth chart

The vertical axis established by the EZ and the EN in Steiner's birth chart

Let's use the birth chart of Rudolf Steiner as a basis for comparison between the MC and the EZ.

The MC-IC axis in Steiner's birth chart runs through 2°3' Leo and 2°3' Aquarius.

With Leo at the Midheaven, we could argue that the courageous and bold nature of the Lion was made manifest in Steiner's efforts to bring his spiritual teachings to the world, as was the warm and compassionate interest he had for others. (And yet, this could just as easily be explained by the presence of his Moon and Saturn in Leo.) At the IC is Aquarius, which we could describe as the zodiacal sign of *spiritual science*. Its associated faculty of meditative strength guided his life's work.

What story is told by the EZ? The EZ and EN in Steiner's chart, 90° from both the Ascendant (19°46' Libra) and the Descendant (19°46' Aries), can be found at 19°46' Cancer and 19°46' Capricorn.

With his EZ in the sign of the Crab, we are drawn into a meditation upon the Cancer glyph, within which two spirals nearly touch at its center. In this void we find the chasm between the material and spiritual worlds. This is precisely the abyss that Steiner's initiatives sought to bridge through spiritual science itself. And what of the EN in Capricorn, the sign of *spiritual continuity*? Steiner's teachings on the evolutionary sequence of "planetary conditions" of the Earth presented the "seven days of creation" in a manner that was suitable for the people of his time and place.

Both methods of division of the chart into an eastern and western half have been supported by copious research. Although I used the MC-IC axis extensively in the past, my own intuition repeatedly set me on a return path to the perpendicular axis that is elegantly established by the ecliptic. However, I can advance no claim to certainty in the matter. This is a mystery that must be approached individually and with absolute humility, whereby intellectual speculation might cede to an intuitive sense of the truth. Contrasting the sign and degree of the MC and the EZ in each chart you cast will allow you to draw your own conclusions on the matter.

5

THE QUADRANTS

THE SIGNIFICANCE OF THE FOUR angles must be great, as they refer to the archetype of the four directions of space, the four holy animals (whose representatives can be found in the Sphinx itself), and the four Archangels (Michael, Raphael, Uriel, and Gabriel).

The horizontal (Ascendant-Descendant) axis and the vertical axis divide the chart into four quadrants. The cross thus formed indicates the four points of the chart were thought of by Manilius[1] as the structure upon which the phenomenal universe hung[2]; in the microcosm, we can think of them as the structure that upholds the chariot of our being. They are also referred to as the *angles* of the chart. Under the auspices of the cosmic cross formed by the axis that is precisely vertical—the EZ-EN—we will consequently maintain that the four quadrants are always of equal size: 90°.

Thus, the circle is divided into four quadrants. The ratio 4:1 was identified by Steiner as the archetypal, or perfect, rhythm. Our own rhythmic systems work within this ratio, for the heart beats four times on average for every breath we take. The heart itself has four chambers. We can further marvel at the fact that the average number of breaths taken in a day—25,920—is equal to the number of years required for the vernal point to precess through the 360 degrees of the zodiac. We can hold the four quadrants in imagination as the heartbeats within the "breath" of the whole chart, or as "chambers within the heart of our being."

Astronomica, written by Manilius less than a century after the life of Christ, presents an analogy between the quadrants represented by the chart and the stages of life: the quadrant that begins at the Ascendant relates to the childhood; the one that ends at the Descendant, to youth; the one that begins at the Descendant, to maturity; and the one that ends at the Ascendant, old age. The quadrants, as we can see, advance in a clockwise direction, mirroring the diurnal movement of the planets and stars. In *Astronomica*, the terms used to describe the point that separates the first and second quadrants include "zenith of high heaven" and "citadel of the sky."[3]

Within the 2011 edition of *The Clockwise House System*,[4] Wain Farrants offers a new way of looking at the quadrants that has its origin in comments Steiner made about the four Michelangelo figures in the Medici Chapel in Florence (see illustrations on next page).

Steiner said:

> Let us start with the figure of "Night." Suppose one immerses oneself in everything one sees, in every gesture.... If, having studied every gesture, every movement of the limbs, one asks oneself how an artist would have to portray the human figure if he wished to convey the greatest possible activity of the etheric body in sleep, then he would have to do it out of his artistic instincts exactly as Michelangelo did in his figure. The figure of "Night" corresponds with the posture of the etheric body. I am not suggesting that Michelangelo was conscious of this. He simply did it.
>
> Now let us look at the figure of "Day." This is no barren allegory. Picture the lower members of the human being more passive, and the ego predominantly active. We have this expressed in the figure of "Day."
>
> If we were now to express in the posture the action of the astral body working freely when the other members are reduced to inactivity, then we should find this in the so-called allegory of "Dawn."

---

1 Manilius was Roman poet and astrologer of the first century after Christ, best known for *Astronomica*, a five-part work about celestial phenomena.
2 Joel Matthew Park, "The Tree of Life: Returning to the Origin of the Houses, Part II," *Star Wisdom*, vol. 3 (Hudson, NY: Lindisfarne Books, 2021), 141.
3 See Powell's *History of the Houses* (Epping, NH: ACS Publications) 12.
4 This edition was edited by Robert Powell.

"Night"—etheric   "Day"—"I"

"Dusk"—physical   "Dawn"—astral

And if we sought to express the conditions where the physical body is not altogether falling to pieces, but becomes limp as a result of the withdrawal of the ego and astral body, this is wonderfully portrayed in the figure of "Dusk."[5]

Assigning dawn, day, dusk, and night to the astrological chart can only be done in one way—that of following the Sun.

Steiner spoke of the four-fold human being, consisting of the physical, etheric, astral, and Ego, or "I." Through the physical body we experience all that we take in through the senses. We can place *sensory perception* in the "Dusk" quadrant on the lower right.

The next level in the four-fold composition of the human being is the etheric sheath, without which the physical body is lifeless. Time and time again, Steiner identified the etheric as the milieu of true, intuitive thinking. We can place *thinking* alongside the etheric in the lower left quadrant, "Night."

We experience consciousness through our astral bodies. Within the astral layer of the human being lies the feeling life, as well as thinking that is logical and linear. When we become conscious of this layer, it can be transformed by the "I." When we lack this consciousness, our emotions are changeable, visible, and uncontrolled—all over the place, like air. We

---

5 Rudolf Steiner, *Life between Death and Rebirth* (New York: Anthroposophic Press, 1968), 103-4. See also CW Nr. 140.

The Quadrants

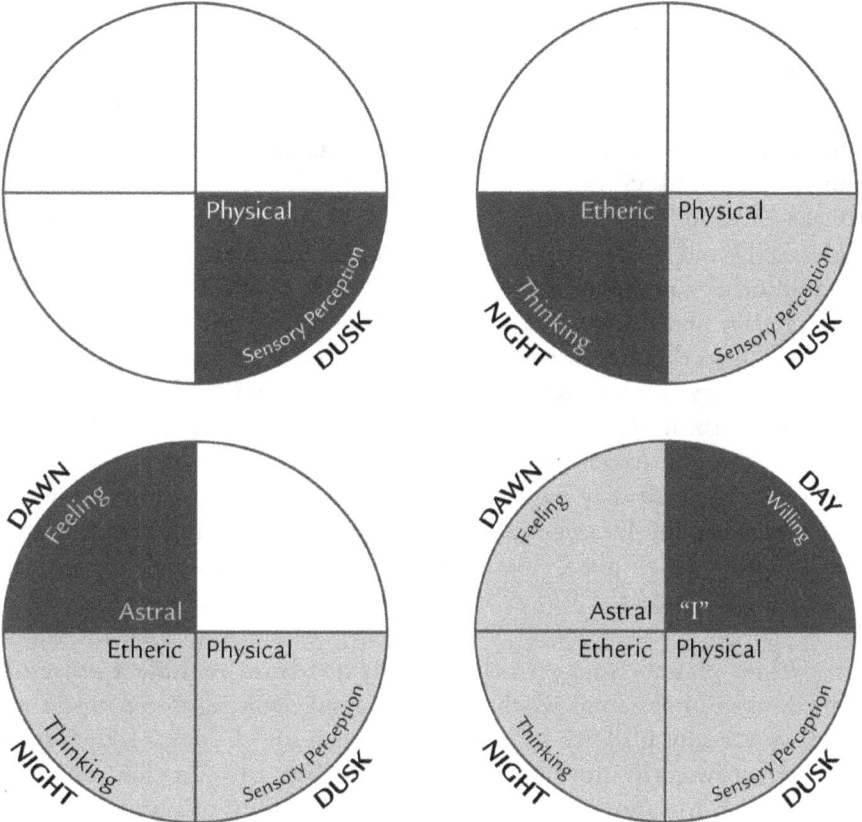

can thus connect *feeling* to the astral quadrant—"Dawn"—on the upper left, keeping in mind that, through the higher nature of the individual, consciousness and control of feelings can be achieved.

Similarly, the Ego, or "I," as pure spirit, clearly bears a connection to the willing aspect of soul; for we can be guided to a higher purpose by morality, which is born of the spirit. Thus we can place *willing* in the "Day" quadrant, the one associated with the Ego.

This is terribly interesting on several levels. Firstly, the quadrants proceed (from lower to higher members) in a clockwise direction, supporting simultaneously the clockwise direction of the houses, which will be discussed in Chapter 6. Secondly, we can observe that the area below the horizon—the "night" side of the chart—is the domain of the physical and the etheric quadrants, reflecting the fact that our physical and etheric bodies are left behind by the astral and the "I" while we sleep. Also relevant is the numbering of the quadrants. We begin our count with the quadrant that proceeds upwards from the Ascendant—the astral (or, feeling) quadrant—and end it with the one below the Ascendant—the etheric (or, thinking) quadrant.

The importance of the boundaries of the quadrants can be looked at another way, as each represents a buffer between the two quadrants it divides. The Ascendant runs between the etheric (thinking/water) and the astral (feeling/air) quadrants, thus offering a contemplative calm that allows us to maintain presence of mind in the face of roiling waves and thrashing winds. Focus on the virtue of the Ascendant thus prevents any adverse collaboration of water and wind that could otherwise create storms within the soul. The EZ separates the astral (feeling/air) from the Ego (spirit/fire). Wind can cause a fire to burn out of control, voraciously consuming everything in its path. Focus on the virtue of the EZ provides a bulwark between raging fire and untethered winds, lest our feelings fan the flames of our egotism. Humility alone—the law of spiritual health—can put out this fire.

The Descendant separates the Ego (spirit/fire) from the sensory (physical/earth). Only an arid wasteland remains after a cataclysmic fire spreads across a dry landscape. The virtue of the Descendant and our regard for others is the antidote for this destructive attitude within ourselves; it reminds us that, through the blessings of our associations with others, the garden of our soul remains lush and vibrant. Lastly, the EN prevents the improper commingling of earth (sensory/physical) and water (thinking/etheric), which would otherwise have the power to undermine our stability and drown us in psychic confusion. Attention to the virtue inherent in the EN provides stability in the presence of what is quicksand to the soul.

Within this imagination, the Ascendant could be known as the nexus of *presence of mind*; the EZ, as the nexus of *humility*; the Descendant, as the nexus of *forgiveness* (on which good relationships with others depends); and the EN as the nexus of *stability*.

Any quadrant *without* planets suggests that this will not be a key area of spiritual work for us — either because we already identify strongly with its qualities, or because the development of these qualities is a task for another lifetime. No planets? Move along and focus your attention on the others, particularly if one of them is packed.

Four or more planets in a quadrant suggest that we must endeavor to further develop the qualities of the associated aspect of the human being. *If there is a busy* physical *quadrant*, grounding and firmness will be required to meet the challenges of life. The commission inherent to this arrangement is to bring talents down to Earth, to the sense realm — in order that they may be relatable to others. We must wrestle our work into manifestation without falling prey to rigidity.

If there is a large grouping of planets in the etheric *quadrant*, we will need to call upon our intuitive thinking capacity to have an impact on the world. A healthy etheric body, much like the Venus chakra, weaves together body and soul. When we cultivate harmony in the etheric through practices such as eurythmy, we experience peace and well-being. This is not to be confused with *inactivity*; resilience, too, might be cultivated, without which the quality of adaptability can render us wishy-washy and adrift in the sea of groupthink.

When the astral *quadrant is host to four or more planets*, we are being asked to develop equanimity of soul as well as clear, logical thinking. The astral aspect leads us ceaselessly to the periphery, where we encounter cosmic thought. Blessings of this quadrant include a sense of scope (imagine an eagle looking down upon a vast landscape) and clarity. A lack of Ego strength governing the feeling life — which can sometimes manifest as an inability to stay with anything for long — can limit our capacity to bring our talents to bear in the world.

Lastly, *when the quadrant of* the "I" *is brimming over*, we are encouraged to light our torch, and to strive to *keep it lit*. This arrangement asks that we stand up before the world for what is right; we weaken the "I" when we allow ourselves to be led by circumstances rather than by the strength of our divine natures. Implicit in this quadrant is the warning against pride and egotism — a "fire" that will be swiftly put out by the spiritual world!

6

THE HOUSES

THE HOUSES OF ASTROLOGY ARE "domains" of space that represent different aspects of human experience and endeavor. The "original" house system was directly tied to the signs of the zodiac.[1] "House divisions," as they are called, likely came to life in Hellenistic Egypt, after Alexander,[2] as there is no evidence of them in Babylon. Although the houses express a *terrestrial consciousness* of life on Earth, they are crucial to chart interpretation because they describe the twelve domains of life upon the Earth, through which our spiritual development unfolds. The traditional descriptions of these realms of human experience are, in large part, consistent, as is their number: twelve. The simplicity, order, and beauty of this number, as an earthly reflection of the zodiac, is obvious.

There are twelve ways to interpret the zodiacal placement of a given planet; without house divisions, we're blindfolded — we have no way of knowing (beyond our intuition) which house-path will best serve the person we're trying to help. Knowing the house cusps with certainty offer a way "into" a chart that is not open to us when the Ascendant is not known — and can thereby show us the way to *healing*.

We can come to an understanding of the importance of the house placements another way. Although *zodiacal* placements are determined solely by orbital speed, *house* placements are the result of the Earth's rotation on its axis. The planets take days, months, or years to make their way through one zodiacal sign, but all of the planets and fixed stars move through all twelve houses every day. *Every single house placement is possible on any given day.* If we add the Ascendant and the North Node to the planetary mix, there are nearly a trillion possible ways to arrange the planets in the houses. Never mind the *zodiacal* placements! Can we doubt the miraculous quality of a birth chart? *Each and every chart* is a "magna carta."

Let it be known that there exist many different house systems, most of which use the MC-IC axis as a quadrant boundary. Some of these systems divide quadrants in houses of equal size, while others do not. Most claim that the houses proceed in the same direction as the zodiacal signs (anticlockwise in the north, clockwise in the south). While most astrologers regard the Ascendant as the *beginning* of the 1st house, others — notably Brian Gray, Joel Park, and Claudia Lainson[3] [4] [5] [6]— place it in the *middle* of the 1st house. We'll dive into this shortly.

Foundational to most house systems is the establishment of the four quadrants. In the Egyptian hermetic system, these were equal in length; and, as a reflection of the diurnal movement of the planets and stars, they proceeded in a clockwise order. The Ascendant was not calculated — it was *observed*. For instance, if Gemini was seen to be rising at the time of birth, then Gemini was the Ascendant. The point directly overhead — the "temple" of the sky — was intuitively understood as one of great significance and power.

Once the MC could be calculated with precision, the MC-IC axis — the axis that runs *true* south-north — replaced the perpendicular axis of old. Though a million miles from perfect, the most commonly used system that accomplishes

---

1 Brian Gray, "Anthroposophic Foundations for a Renewal of Astrology," *Journal for Star Wisdom* (Gt Barrington, MA: SteinerBooks/Anthroposophic Press, 2012), 120.
2 Powell, *Hermetic Astrology*, vol. 1, 2 and 102.
3 Gray, "Anthroposophic Foundations for a Renewal of Astrology," 98-130.
4 Joel Matthew Park, "Saturn in Cancer: Retuning to the Origin of the Houses, Part I," *Star Wisdom*, vol. 2 (Hudson NY: Lindisfarne Books, 2020), 55-62.
5 Joel Matthew Park, "The Tree of Life: Returning to the Origin of the Houses, Part II," *Star Wisdom*, vol. 3 (2021), 141-52.
6 Joel Matthew Park, "The Archetypal Language: Returning to the Origin of the Houses, Part III," *Star Wisdom*, vol. 4 (2022), 95-110.

this is the "Placidus" (named after an Italian monk of the seventeenth century).

When we apply the Placidus system to our clockwise house system, we find that the MC always marks the cusp that separates the 3rd and 4th houses, while the IC marks the 9th/10th house cusp. The Placidus system—and every other approach that uses the MC as a house cusp—almost always results in quadrants and houses that differ in size, sometimes by quite a lot. This difference is exaggerated by distance from the equator as well as by season. (The size of the houses equalizes somewhat around the time of the equinoxes.) Placidus house cusps are determined by the zodiacal distance the Sun appears to travel in two hours—as a result of the Earth's rotation (12 houses x 2 hours = 24 hours). Placidus houses thus represent *temporal* (i.e., not spatial) divisions. If Rudolf is born in northern Canada on the first day of winter, the house sizes will vary wildly.

I have never encountered *anyone* who is fully behind the system of Placidus, yet it is ubiquitous just the same. Many newer systems have attempted to improve upon it by way of mathematical jiu-jitsu (thereby reducing the incongruity of the houses), but they bring to mind Cinderella's stepsisters trying everything they can to fit their feet into the glass slipper!

More recently, many astrosophers have returned to the harmony and beauty of the equal-house system. Its use results not only in four equal quadrants, but also in twelve equal houses that mirror the twelve signs of the original sidereal zodiac of the Babylonians.

We find that planets sometimes switch houses when we apply a different house system to a chart. Those of you who have no experience in chart interpretation are *ideally suited* to the task of comparing the validity of these systems—and any others you choose to explore. This will require a basic knowledge of the meaning of planets in each house, which will be elaborated shortly. I encourage you to apply (at the very least) the equal-house and Placidus systems to every chart you see. In this way you'll be able to evaluate the relative accuracy of the EZ and MC, and of the differing house divisions that they establish. Because of its simplicity and its foundation in the 30° signs of the original zodiac, I believe that the equal house system represents a better point of departure than the others. Additionally, it is my opinion that the application of the equal-house system presents a clearer path to the spiritual truths that seek our understanding through the astrological chart.

THE DIRECTION OF THE HOUSES

Should the houses proceed as the zodiac does, in an anti-clockwise direction? Nearly everyone thinks so. And yet, when we consider the Ascendant, we know that it refers to a point from which planets rise. This is its very meaning!

The diurnal movement of the Sun and the other planets is experienced on Earth as *clockwise*.[7]

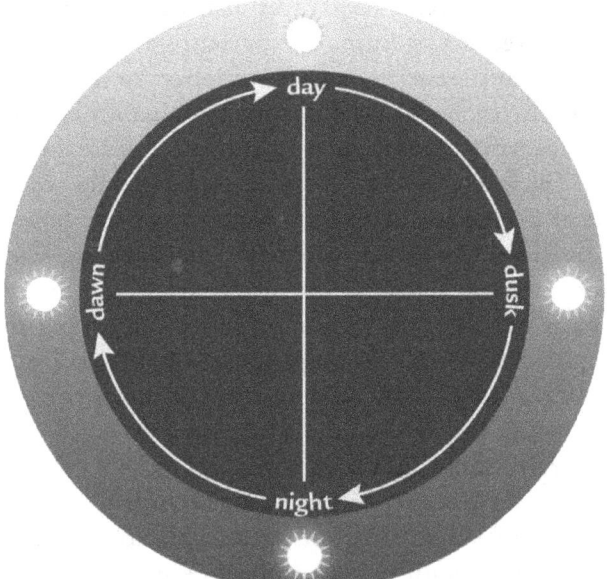

When the Sun is at the point just below the Ascendant, we can imagine that it is about to "arise" and make its presence known. The morning begins as the Sun crosses clockwise over the Ascendant. Again, this is what we see (with our own eyes) and feel (in our hearts) every day. In the east, the Sun "comes to life" as it rises above the Ascendant—just when most of us wake up as day begins. Why, indeed, would the 1st house, which relates to character, personality, and initiative, be assigned to the darkness of

---

[7] In the southern hemisphere, the diurnal movement of the Sun and planets is *anticlockwise*. A discussion of the relevance of the clockwise system to both hemispheres will be explored shortly.

the region below the Ascendant? Jacques Dorsan put it this way:

> The Sun rises, passes through the meridian, descends, and sets. In dividing each quadrant into three, to obtain twelve houses, why, for goodness sake, do we modern astrologers reverse the order of rotation?[8]

We might also take into consideration the following remarkable statement from Valentin Tomberg:

> The Christ inspiration flows from east to west around the whole Earth, bringing about consciousness of universal brotherhood.[9]

Like the daytime journey of the Sun itself, the Christ inspiration continually moves from east to west, no matter where we are on the Earth. It follows the diurnal movement of the Sun. The (northern) clockwise *experience* of the diurnal movement (east to west) of the starry heavens—and of the Christ inspiration—supports the use of what is known as the "clockwise house system." As is typical of most house systems, the clockwise house system divides the heavens around the Earth into twelve domains that represent twelve spheres of human activity through which we might achieve our spiritual development. Thus do the houses "mirror" the signs of the zodiac.

In the clockwise house system, there is a dynamic of resistance—which might be envisioned as gears moving in opposite directions—between the *actual movement* of the planets and the zodiac (on the one hand) and the *geocentric experience* of these movements over the course of the day (on the other). Thereby does this system uniquely reflect the tension between our earthly and spiritual selves. Furthermore, the anticlockwise/clockwise relationship between the zodiac and the houses mirrors the macrocosmic reality of the precession of the equinoxes: for Sophia, in all her wisdom, decreed that the cultural ages upon the Earth would proceed in *reverse* zodiacal order.

The clockwise system is supported by Steiner's representation in color of the eurythmy forms for the zodiac signs, in which the zodiacal signs proceed *clockwise*. Aries is on the left, straddling the "horizon," opposite Libra, which on the far right.

Owing to the correspondence (by way of analogy) between the zodiacal signs and the astrological houses, Joel Park wrote:

> Although he never *explicitly* named it as such, *implicitly* Rudolf Steiner seemed to use a clockwise house system throughout his career as a spiritual researcher. It is this, as far as the author can tell, *only* this, that makes sense of his statement that the Twelve Moods of the zodiac express the movement of the planets through the twelve signs of the zodiac *in the course of a day*—as none of them, even the rapidly moving Moon, moves through all twelve signs in one day.[10] However, all of the planets and fixed stars, on a daily basis, move in a clockwise direction through all of the twelve houses or "temples" of the firmament from the geocentric perspective.[11]

Nevertheless, the clockwise house system is another "skunk at the debutantes' ball." Just as

---

8 Jacques Dorsan, *The Clockwise House System* (Gt Barrington, MA: Lindisfarne Books, 2011), 38.
9 Tomberg, *Christ and Sophia*, 48.
10 This observation contrasts the gradual *orbital* movement of the planets through the zodiacal signs over the course of long periods of time to the *diurnal* movement of the planets through all twelve houses each day that results from the rotation of the Earth on its axis.
11 Joel Matthew Park, "Saturn in Cancer: Returning to the Origin of the Houses, Part I," 61.

the fundamental truth of the sidereal zodiac was shrouded for centuries by the illusion of the tropical zodiac, so too has the original house system — the clockwise system — been entombed beneath the mighty tower of its opponent. In my estimation, the anticlockwise house system represents a grave departure from the fundamental reality of true astrology.

Park wrote further:

> [At his death] Christ descended into the subearthly spheres, navigating his way back to the Mother in the depths. At this moment, he *pulled along with him* the entirety of the cosmos, so to speak, distilled into the seed of the Tree of Life, his etheric body. He planted the seed in the heart of Shambhala, the lost Paradise. Then, at the moment of his Resurrection, we could say that what he had implanted — the image and distillation of the entire cosmos — was "pulled inside out." What was above went below: *What was counterclockwise turned clockwise....*
>
> [In] the horoscope of Christ's Resurrection we see the east-west axis is like a pivot around which the entire form of the outer cosmos inverts.... But Aries corresponds to the 1st house (as it does in *every single horoscope*), and just above is the 2nd house, corresponding to Taurus.... Whereas the sign of Capricorn is above, and the 10th house (corresponding to Capricorn) is below; the sign of Cancer is below, and the 4th house (corresponding to Cancer) is above.[12]

In other words, the zodiacal wheel proceeds *anticlockwise*, while the houses unfold *clockwise*. Park continues:

> And so, we see the true significance of the houses; they reveal to us the workings of the inner Earth in a deceptively simple way. The clockwise motion of the planets throughout the course of the day in relationship to east or west, above and below, is an indicator or significator of the positions of the "inner planets" in the heart of the Earth — the realm of the Mother....
>
> The experience of the houses takes us not out into the starry heavens, but deep into the heart of the Earth — the twelve houses, or temples, of the Mother.[13]

Each house has two cusps — a beginning and an end — and the signs of both cusps (as well as their rulers) offer further enlightenment as to the manner in which the individual can best meet the affairs of that house. Furthermore, it is obvious that each cusp is shared by the houses that it separates. To determine which cusp is more consequential to any given house, we need only look to the diurnal movement of the Sun — whereby we might deduce that the cusp that the Sun crosses to *enter* a house is the primary one, while the cusp by which it makes its exit is the less important of the two. In other words, the cusp shared by the 12th and 1st houses is more significant to the 1st house than it is to the 12th. However, there exists disagreement about where these cusps should rightly be placed.

As the Ascendant marks the point at which heavenly bodies rise into view — *as well as* the rising degree at the beginning of life itself — it is generally argued that the Ascendant established the 1st house cusp. And yet, Brian Gray and Joel Park have made profound philosophical and theological arguments for the placement of the Ascendant in the *center* of the 1st house. How might this be understood?

Birdsong begins before sunrise; life stirs with the anticipation of the coming glory and warmth of the Sun. Might the method of analogy[14] lead us to the conclusion that when the birds begin to sing, the Sun has *already* entered the temple of the 1st house? In this case, 12th/1st house cusp would be placed below the horizon.[15]

We can also look to Steiner to garner support for this cusp system. When we ponder Steiner's eurythmy color wheel, we notice that Aries and Libra *straddle* the horizon on the left and the right. Thus the zodiacal stars designated by Steiner as "constellations of light" (Aries, Taurus, Gemini, Cancer, Leo, Virgo, and Libra) are

---

12 Joel Matthew Park, "The Tree of Life: Returning to the Origin of the Houses, Part II," 145.
13 Ibid., 150–52.
14 The method of analogy — which is fundamental to hermeticism — was introduced in "The Sun" on pages 45–46.
15 Within this house system, the boundaries of the four quadrants would remain at the Asc, the EZ, the Dsc, and the EN — but would thereby appear to "float" in the middle of the 1st, 4th, 7th, and 10th houses.

all above the horizon, while the "constellations of darkness" (Scorpio, Sagittarius, Capricorn, Aquarius, and Pisces) are below it.

Another contemplation for this placement of the cusps lies in Steiner's teachings on the zodiacal and cultural ages. It takes time for a new zodiacal age to be absorbed into the culture — for we know that a new *zodiacal* age begins long before the associated *cultural* age does. Might we make a comparison by imagining the 12th/1st house cusp as the start of the zodiacal age, and the Ascendent as the moment when we awaken to its impulses?

You can readily compare these differing concepts of cusp placement by paying close attention to any planet you encounter within 30° of the Ascendant. A planet just below the Ascendant, for example, will be in the 12th house in the "Ascendant-as-cusp" system, but in the 1st house when the Ascendant falls in the middle of the 1st house.

The sign and ruler at the start of any house is the weightier of the two. We consider this automatically when we look to the 1st, 4th, 7th, and 10th houses, the four *angular* or *cardinal* houses of the chart. Although a detailed study of this facet of chart interpretation is beyond the scope of this book, it can readily be discerned that the house that begins with an Aries cusp (to take an example) will designate in which domain its ruler (Mars) will call you to summon initiative.

Our attention is immediately drawn to any house cusp that occurs in the zodiacal constellation of the sign to which it is analogous (i.e., an Aries 1st house cusp, a Taurus 2nd house cusp, and so on). We can intuit this phenomenon as a powerful one, because the sign and the house are "in accord." This does not usually occur; although, when it does, it never affects just one house, but also the *opposite* house (e.g., when Aries is on the 1st house cusp, Libra is on the 7th). This opposing pair will have special relevance to the individual.

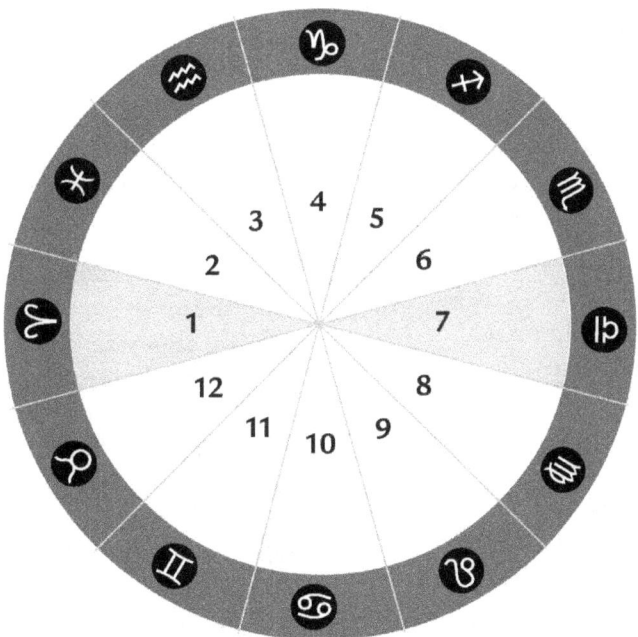

THE MEANING OF THE HOUSES

The finest account that I know of regarding the *traditional* meaning of the houses can be found in Jacques Dorsan's delightful, bold, and informative book — *The Clockwise House System*. The sheer volume of his research is astonishing. Indeed, Dorsan practiced astrology around the world for more than five decades; he began as a tropicalist who arranged the houses in the same direction as the zodiac (anticlockwise) — and became a siderealist (God bless him!) who wrote extensively about the logic, beauty, and efficacy of the clockwise house system. Many of the remarks below are inspired by that work. In general, it can be said that *the greater our spiritual development, the weaker will be our bonds to the traditional meaning of the houses.*

The traditional framework for the astrological houses provides the initial brushstrokes for our canvas. When, by way of analogy, we add to this work an exploration of the zodiacal archetypes underlying the twelve houses, forms take shape upon the canvas, colors deepen, and we embark, together, upon a path of spiritual development. Deeper layers of the meaning of the houses can then be revealed. Joel Park suggests that the archetypal language of the houses can be found through the work of Valentin Tomberg. He writes:

> According to Robert Powell's intuitive research, seven of the Arcana are related to the classical planets; twelve of them are related to the signs of the zodiac; and three are related to the outer planets (including Pluto)....
>
> [The] following system of comparison has presented itself to him:
>
> The Magician (or Juggler) — *The Sun*
> The High Priestess — *Saturn*
> The Empress — *The Moon*
> The Emperor — *Jupiter*
> The Pope — *Mercury*
> The Lover — *Venus*
> The Chariot — *Mars*
> Justice — *Libra*
> The Hermit — *Sagittarius*
> The Wheel of Fortune — *Leo*
> Force — *Virgo*
> The Hanged Man — *Pisces*
> Death — *Scorpio*
> Temperance — *Aquarius*
> The Devil — *Pluto*
> Tower of Destruction — *Uranus*
> The Star — *Capricorn*
> The Moon — *Cancer*
> The Sun — *Gemini*
> The Judgment — *Taurus*
> The Fool — *Aries*
> The World — *Neptune*
>
> Based on this, we would no longer refer to the first house as being analogous to Aries; we would simply call this the house of The Fool....
>
> [Thus] the twelve temples begin to take on much more life, as they are now not only indicators of mundane fortune in different realms like health, family, career, etc., but are *entire archetypal worlds with manifold, multivocal qualities.*[16]

I can feel the axis of the Earth shifting again. When placed with the Ascendant at 15° Aries, does the Sun suggest that "the Magician within" can be actualized through the divine fire of love that is the teaching of The Fool? Alternatively, could it be that the "Fool" in each of us finds its highest expression through the teachings and virtue of the sign of the Ascendant?

The house of the Ascendant—that representing the individual and the beginnings of life—can easily be understood as the house of the Fool; for who among us cannot claim this distinction? And does it not make sense that the house of The Moon (the 4th) should be at the top of the chart, which can be imagined as the crown of the human skull; for when our intellectuality has been materialized, it reaches no further than this bony barrier. And does it not also make sense that Justice (the 7th house) must guide our relationships with our fellows; for when the inner pillars of severity and mercy are not in balance, our connection to others—our "horizontal axis"—is rendered askew. And where else could we place the Arcanum of the Mother—The Star—but at the bottom of the chart, "beneath our feet"?

This introduction to the hermetic approach to the houses—based upon the letter-Arcana of the Tarot—will enable you, dear reader, to go imaginatively into Tomberg's *Meditations*. Embrace them with all your heart and soul, and—little by little—you will come to know them as dear friends who gather around you whenever you need them. Blessings on your journey, and let us pray with Tomberg in "The Hanged Man": May our communities become those of people who *learn from everyone instead of teaching everyone!*[17]

1ST HOUSE (analogous to Aries, ruled by Mars):

Temperament, personality, health and vitality, character, willingness to lead. Who are we? General conditions of existence, especially during childhood. How we see the world. The physical body. Making a strong entrance. Bursting with life. Self-worth.

Imagine this as the temple of the Fool—the

---

16 Joel Matthew Park, "The Archetypal Language: Returning to the Origin of the Houses, Part III," 105-6. [My italics: JH.]
17 Tomberg, *Meditations on the Tarot*, 315.

place where our persona, our individual personhood, dares to become a self-realized individuality. This necessitates that we refuse to bow to limitations imposed by others, but instead find the willingness to act independently of their opinions and acclaim. We are thereby released from all manner of "towers" that have been built—either by early conditioning or by our susceptibility to follow accepted norms. With the Aries power of Martian courage, our selfhood is given every opportunity to soar in devotional pursuit of what our higher Self seeks to realize. Thus do we become leaders into frontiers of wonder as this Self guides us ever forward. The temple of the Fool asks: *Who are we? To what do we devote ourselves with the fire of love?*

2ND HOUSE (analogous to Taurus, ruled by Venus):

Financial fortune in general. How we earn money through personal labors, and the ease of doing so. *What we value.* Banking and finance. Financial status as viewed from the outside. Desire to acquire. Attachment to, or lack of, to material goods. Love of nature. Cultivation. Propensity to build.

Imagine this as the temple of the Judgment—the trumpet blast of inspiration that heralds the rational pursuit of spiritual resources above the temporal pursuit of material gain. When we turn away from the Angels' invitation, we gauge our success according to what we have amassed. It is possible for money to act as a fraternal bond that unites us with our brothers and sisters, whereby no one benefits at the expense of another. In the absence of such a moral tether, however, a kind of economic slavery can result. The temple of the Judgment asks: *What do we value? What can resurrect us from the tomb of materialism?*

3RD HOUSE (analogous to Gemini, ruled by Mercury):

Ambition, striving for success. The desire for movement. Chosen profession and professional vocation. Intelligence, concrete intellect, communications (writing and speaking). Assistance (or lack of it) from those who are close. Deliberately chosen activities. People we see every day, including professional associates. Siblings. Short trips.

Imagine this as the temple of the Sun—the "star" that guides us to our appointed destiny. Following this star requires an intelligence that spans both the vertical of spiritual revelation as well as the horizontal of faithful effort. Our minds are elevated when we direct our consciousness to both the world above and the one below. In the absence of this balance, we may find ourselves flitting from one thing to the next without satisfaction. Herodian temptations often lure us onto paths that we cannot claim as our own. On the other hand, when we follow our star—and no one else's—we find the peace that accompanies alignment with our highest hope. The temple of the Sun asks: *What is the star that we follow? How can we help others to follow theirs?*

4TH HOUSE (analogous to Cancer, ruled by the Moon):

Professional authority. Social position, reputation, and the struggle to maintain it. The need to save face. Career, honors, stature in the world. Prestige and popularity. How we wear our mantle. What you are appointed to do: destiny over which we have no control, good or ill. Maternal hereditary stream, the mother. Being a mother. The family life as visible from the outside.

Imagine this as the temple of the Moon—the one directly above our heads—where matter encounters spirit. Do we guide our human intelligence toward the wisdom of the cosmos, or do we confine it to the limits of our skulls? For if we if we rely solely upon intelligence, we eclipse the creative light that emanates from above, thereby consigning ourselves to stagnate in an "enclosure" of our own making. When we put our faith in matter alone—thus reducing all to weight, measure, and number—the *mobility* at the heart of life no longer holds our interest; we focus only on end results. The temple of the Moon asks: *How do we selflessly participate in the becoming of what is to be? How do we bring the subconscious to consciousness?*

5TH HOUSE (analogous to Leo, ruled by the Sun):

Sentimental relationships, including those with children; instinctive affections. Engaging in that which gives you pleasure. Leisure activities. Vitality. Taking risks; speculative gains (and losses) through chance rather than personal effort. Love of drama and/or the dramatic. Creative endeavors: artistic, literary, or scientific. Early education. This house affords great freedom in our endeavors.

Imagine the temple of the Wheel of Fortune, wherein we find the door[18] that stands between the disgrace of humanity—our condition since the Fall—and its salvation, where might find the seed of all possibilities for future evolution. Within this temple, we are free to stand on either side of this door. On one side, we find the freedom that expresses itself though amusements and sentiment; in this case we are like passengers of the wheel of life, which is then experienced as no more than a series of repetitions: our karma. On the other side, we find *true* freedom—i.e., the free choosing of the resolution of our karma—no matter how little of it can be accomplished in one lifetime. (Such a karmic "assignment" is sometimes referred to as our "dharma": living in harmony with the cosmic order.) Within this domain of hope, where we feel the full measure of our own failings, we harbor compassion for the sins of others. The temple of the Wheel of Fortune asks: *How do we hold open the door between the world of the serpent and that of the Father in heaven?*

6TH HOUSE (analogous to Virgo, ruled by Mercury):

Duties and responsibilities; imposed tasks executed outside of our own initiative. Deeds of service and necessity. Work and conditions of professional life. Worries and wounds inflicted on pride through professional life. Employees and our relationship to them. The capacity to serve. Ill health; diet and nutrition. The marriage partner or best friend. Harvest, savings—all things accumulated. Routine tasks.

Imagine this as the temple of Force—the quality of spontaneous obedience to God that is known also as purity: *Blessed are the pure in heart, for they shall see God.* This is the realm of implicit religion (or virgin nature), in which God reigns through our hunger and thirst for righteousness. "Implicit religion" is characterized by the willingness to reflect the presence of God through contemplation that is serene as well as clear. Alternatively, we might allow ourselves to be swept away by an electrifying flood—agitated, adrift, helpless. While its adversary proffers gold, jewels, and pearls, virgin nature leads us to the Sun, Moon, and stars. It serves the miraculous and supports *health*. It rejoices in the great cosmic ritual of life! The ten commandments (our path of return to virgin nature) signify the *hygiene* of spiritual life. Tomberg's presentation of the commandments makes it clear that *all ten* can be applied to each individual:

> Surrender to the living God ("thou shalt have no other gods before me")
> Non-substitution of products of the human mind, or those of Nature, for the reality of the living God ("thou shalt not make for thyself a graven image, or any likeness")
> Activity in the name of God without making use of his name in order to adorn oneself with it ("thou shalt not take the name of the Lord thy God in vain")
> Practice of meditation ("remember the sabbath day, to keep it holy")
> Continuity of effort and experience ("honor thy father and thy mother")
> Constructive attitude ("thou shalt not kill")
> Faithfulness to the alliance ("thou shalt not commit adultery")
> Renunciation of the desire to accept merit which is neither the fruit of one's work nor the gift of grace ("thou shalt not steal")
> Renunciation of an accusatory role toward others ("thou shalt not bear false witness against thy neighbor")
> Respectful consideration for the private and personal life of others ("thou shalt not covet thy neighbor's house.[19]

The temple of Force asks: *To what or to whom do we offer ourselves in service?*

7TH HOUSE (analogous to Libra, ruled by Venus):

Relationships with others. Listening to others. Alliances, groups. Where we encounter opposition and controversy. Rivals and competitors. The marriage. Diplomacy; getting along with others. Adversaries and competitors that make themselves known to you. Legal agreements, contracts. Theft, lawsuits. How important alliances are in our life. Opposite the Ascendant, the Descendant is also known as the "point of death."

---

18 Claudia McLaren Lainson refers to this as the sabbath door in "The Sabbath Door: The Truth Shall Set Us Free," *Journal for Star Wisdom*, (Gt Barrington, MA: Lindisfarne Books, 2017), 81-105.
19 Tomberg, *Meditations on the Tarot*, 296-97.

Imagine this as the temple of Justice — where dwells the spiritual being who reacts to each and every injustice for the purpose of restoring order. Justice implies peace and harmony, a setting to rights. Of course, human systems of justice are merely pale reflections of the cosmic order; they may uphold little semblance of fairness. As the earnest among us strive for justice, we acknowledge the equal role that mercy and severity must play — for to achieve this equilibrium, these principles must each be brought to bear. While crime followed by punishment might appear to suffice, *forgiveness* opens a window to the spiritual world, a window through which grace might descend. Disharmony in the soul finds remedy in looking to conscience over personal preferences and positions. The temple of Justice asks: *Do we weigh decisions justly? Are we maintaining balance of soul?*

8TH HOUSE (analogous to Scorpio, ruled by Mars and Pluto):

Interest in the occult, at the expense of the trivialities of life. Seeing behind the veil. Profound changes, self-transformation, regeneration. Death and attitude toward it. Sexual instincts. Sources of money and financial obligations that originate with others, including inheritances and legacies. Psychic inheritance. Dreams. Interest in all things "dead": archaeology, antiques, etc.

Imagine this as the temple of Death — the portal to resurrection, or the veil that obscures all that exists beyond the world of the physical senses. Within this temple — wherein all manner of transformations might take place — we approach the threshold and gaze over the dark abyss before us. To cross any threshold, we must acknowledge a "death" — be it of our physical body, an ideal, an expectation, or a frame of mind; this is akin to taking away the stone in front of our tomb, whereby the light of consciousness might enter. Do we fear death? Its purpose from the time of the Fall — i.e., since our separation from the Garden of Paradise — has been to render the spiritual world *unforgettable*. The temple of Death asks: *To what extent are we prodigal sons and daughters whose wandering has driven us ever more remote from the Father?*

9TH HOUSE (analogous to Sagittarius, ruled by Jupiter):

Superior abstract intellect. Higher worlds of thought. Religious and philosophical feeling. The house of doubt. Social works. Interest in (and travel to) faraway places. Scholarly works. Scientific research. Ideals. Higher education and intellectual achievements. Long journeys. The house of the father and the relationship to him. The spiritual master or guru. Spiritual experiences. Belief systems. Experiences through exploration.

Imagine this as the temple of the Hermit — the one who walks alone, needing no affirmation from others, blessed with the certainty of truth.[20] His certainty is three-fold, for the hermit walks with his lamp, his mantle, and his staff. These allow him to experience what we have lost through our pursuit of freedom (which was our proper destiny): imaginations streaming from the thoughts of world creation, inspirations from the harmony of the spheres, and intuitions bearing remembrance of our lost unity with the spirit. Reaching beyond the limits of human cognition, we may take the hard way of the Hermit — to where we can discover the wisdom born of the communion between two opposing concepts (e.g., faith and science). This way demands absolute impartiality. The temple of the Hermit asks: *Do we seek the whole truth?*

10TH HOUSE (analogous to Capricorn, ruled by Saturn):

Heritage and its effect upon us. Destiny and impediments imposed by birth. Ancestors and their collective will. The hidden, intimate side of us and our family life. Hidden treasures. Our shelter and refuge. Conditions of life within the birth family, and attachment (or lack of it) to them. The residence, and real estate in general. Conditions of old age and the end of life.

Imagine this as the temple of the Star — wherein we encounter the spiritual current that acted upon a crying infant in 1770 so that he might become Beethoven. This current is the light-force that directs evolution toward the future, where Christ awaits us all. It links generations through continuity and hope — for what is rooted in the past will bear fruit in the future, although our deeds might not fructify for some time. Christ is the door (the entrance and the exit) of every closed circle — those in

---

20 Lainson, *The Hermit, the Minotaur, and the Shadow of Evil*, 3.

which the human spirit is captive; he reveals the path of spiritual evolution, which assumes the form of a spiral. The Star asks for continuity of effort; it proclaims our duty toward the flow of uninterrupted tradition—and invites us to kneel before it! The temple of the Star asks: *Do we feel ourselves between the divine origin and the divine aim of the world?*

11TH HOUSE (analogous to Aquarius, ruled by Saturn and Uranus):

Connectedness to community and friends; gifts from/to them. Here, the importance of community is stressed over the need for recognition of personal authority and leadership. Educators, clients, pupils. Long-term projects, hopes and dreams that we hold dear, plans for the future. The fulfillment of wishes resulting from our efforts. Predisposition to receive influence streaming from the future. Intimate friendships. Assistance to/from those close to us. Charity.

Imagine this as the temple of Temperance, the spiritual exercise by which we find the source, current, and direction of inner life—and then strive to live in conformity with it. Temperance describes the just measure of the relationship (or circulation) between our eternal divine image and our temporal selves: *What we are.* Temperance draws us to the role of the guardian Angel, the paragon of pure maternal love who awaits our supplication. Whereas Angels move between above and below, interceding on our behalf before the divine world, the temple of Temperance also leads us outward toward the communities with which we might share *inspiration*. Those of us who approach these circles with the attitude of knowing *nothing* (but who simultaneously hold in our hearts the desire to know *everything*) can learn to "think together" with the choir of this community, even if that choir sings anonymously from spiritual realms. The temple of Temperance asks: *Do we think "on our knees," with absolute humility?*

12TH HOUSE (analogous to Pisces, ruled by Jupiter and Neptune):

The secret, hidden life. Delving into the subconscious; mysticism and esotericism. Where demons are revealed. Vices and bad habits. Experience of the occult. Obscurity. Preference for solitude, and for things done in isolation or confinement. Refuge and privacy. Satisfaction and success through research. Caring for those in need. Penchant for research of all kinds. Losses, sorrows caused by others. Hardships. Hidden enemies and their treachery. Flying under the radar. Worries, concerns, despair, self-destructive behavior—which can be courageously overcome through the influence of the spiritual life. Loss of freedom. Limitations and deprivation. The necessity that material attachments give way to concerns of the spirit. Forgiveness.

Imagine this as the temple of the Hanged Man—the one who seeks the spirit as fish seek the sea. On what basis would we choose to be suspended and immobilized like the subject of the card? We do so on the basis of *faith*—the result of the conviction that we bear when we have seen what cannot be seen; and having seen it, we sacrifice in order to *obey*. As if situated between the Pisces fish (one swimming horizontally, the other vertically), the Hanged Man is suspended between Earth and heaven, where dwells our spiritual life. He is a man of spirit as well as a man of righteousness, whose solitude allows him to breathe spiritual "air." This is the "zero point," where we maintain balance between our lives upon the *Earth* and our hunger and thirst for *spirit*. Christ revealed this state as he walked across the Sea of Galilee to the boat carrying his disciples. The Hanged Man knows that, until the end of time, Christ will be walking toward that boat. The temple of the Hanged Man asks: *Are we representatives of humanity toward God, and of God toward humanity?*

THE PLANETS IN THE HOUSES

WE KNOW THAT THE INFLUences of the zodiac derive from the lofty heights that surround the Godhead. They exist far above the level of human personality. The zodiacal sign of a planet bears its "spiritual seed," while its house reveals the best direction for our efforts toward the positive expression of the "zodiacal impulse."

And yet, when we engage in the practical method of analogy — which advances knowledge drawn from the relationship of all things and all beings — we can arrive at the conclusion that each house *bears a relationship* to one of the twelve signs of the zodiac: the 1st house to the first sign, the 2nd house to the second sign, and so on.

If we regard a planet's zodiacal sign as "spiritual instruction," the house placement of the planet provides us with a sort of "user's manual." It shows us the best and most efficient way to reach the spiritual ideal that dwells within the zodiacal sign. The wisdom behind house placements — when heeded — can protect us from distraction and pain.

Let's take the example of those of us born with the Sun and Mars in Aries. A placement in the 1st house (which, by way of the method of analogy, suggests a relationship with Aries, the first sign) mirrors the zodiacal influence; we might thus intuit in this configuration a *magnification* of the impulses of Aries, thereby removing any nuances that might be imposed by a different house. Although we remain in perfect freedom to do otherwise, those of us born under this astral signature are being asked to devote ourselves to the fulfillment of our unique individuality *irrespective of the approval of others.* Whether or not this is accomplished in a visible way is left to the individual. If, instead, we find these planets in the 7th house, we are *still* being asked to energetically pursue our individual personhood, but we must do so in a way that will not damage (and perhaps even takes into account!) associations with others. This is because the success of our self-realization will *depend upon* these associations. A final example: when the Sun and Aries are in the 12th house (that of confinement and solitude), our initiatives might ideally bear a "behind the scenes" quality — or, alternatively, might in some way help those who are isolated from the greater society.

While the *zodiacal* placements of the transcendentals work largely on a collective scale,[1] the *house* placements of the transcendentals are highly personal. We look to the house of Uranus to see where we may find the unexpected upsets in our life — and the vicissitudes of fate that keep our pride in check. We look to Neptune's house to learn in which domain of life we might experience dissolution or deception that can require us to remake ourselves again and again. Lastly, Pluto's house shows us where we may find the earth rumbling beneath our feet — the "volcano" that might be poised to blow at any minute. None of this sounds easy, because it isn't. And yet, it is through the unique trials of Uranus, Neptune, and Pluto that we draw nearer to the highest spiritual faculties. The house placements of the transcendentals draw attention to the kinds of activity through which we are most likely to experience imaginative visions (Uranus), inspirations (Neptune), and bone-deep intuitions (Pluto).

Many of the remarks below, regarding the planets in the houses, were inspired by *The Clockwise House System* by Dorsan. Others emerged from personal experience. I encourage you to scribble in the margins over time, adding your own observations as you make them. Reading about these placements is one thing, but encountering them in those you know is quite another!

When we try to synthesize the meanings of the various features of an astrological chart, let

---

[1] Unless the transcendentals are aspected by other major factors in the chart, their zodiacal sign tends to be felt as "shared" by those of roughly the same age. This is attributable in part to their long stay in each sign (Uranus, 7 years; Neptune, 14; Pluto, 21).

us not forget that its most important element dwells at its center. *For the center is where we find the unique individual around whom the planets are arranged.* We must hold in consciousness the *free will* of this individual—who might accept or reject the guidance offered through the astrological chart. He might strive to improve upon inherent weaknesses, or prefer to leave them as they are for the time being. He might defy the indications of the astrological chart in every way. These conversations take place within the sanctuary that exists between an individual and his "I." Tomberg wrote:

> [Prisoners] of the deterministic house of bondage look to stellar influences (say, in the birth horoscope) as the causal agents of our destinies. For them the stars also are gods before whom they bow down.[2]
>
> It is the "eighth planet" (or, the unknown factor) upon which so much depends in the interpretation of a traditional astrological horoscope, with seven [classical] planets...
>
> [There] is always an X-factor, upon the *use* of which astrological... data depends. It is the factor of *free will* which underlies the traditional astrological rule: *Astra inclinant, non necessitant* ("the stars incline, they do not compel").[3]

May we bow in humility before the free will of the individual!

THE CLASSICAL PLANETS

 SATURN

The house placement of Saturn enlightens us as to the nature of the spiritual mission of the individual, which will be sculpted by the activities under the influence of the house. It has been noted by Claudia Lainson that those who have Saturn situated in the eastern half of their chart tend to have some degree of freedom in the form that their mission will take, while those with Saturn in the western half are more or less "informed" what the mission will be. I have found this to be consistently the case. The house of Saturn is one that will require endurance on our part—for it will strew our path with frustrations, even locking us down from time to time. However, this house reveals to us where we might find great treasure, provided we *persevere*. When the higher nature of Saturn is not met, we can become cynical and severe.

When Saturn is in the 1st house, we'd best avoid pursuits that could be characterized as "flighty" or undisciplined. Though a natural reserve (even wariness) might keep us from activities that are frivolous, we must guard against abandoning fun altogether, lest we become fraught with worry. This can be a "glass half empty" placement, whereby we can be hard on ourselves as well as on others. Saturn in the 1st house typically brings a great deal of determination, along with an excellent memory. Responsibilities often come early in life; in any case, it is important not to avoid those that are laid at our feet. Because of Saturn's connection to the spiritual mission, Saturn in the 1st house suggests that this mission will depend upon the development of our individuality; other commitments must not distract from this task. We must be willing to pursue what we know we must *do*—even if this means doing so with neither the assistance nor the admiration of others.

When Saturn is in the 2nd house, professions with a secure paycheck are favored. We will often need to work very hard indeed, and success might demand that we not be careless with our time or our money. But the 2nd house also enlightens us as to *what we value*, so there will likely be some circumstances, from time to time, that will *force* us to re-evaluate what is most important to us, even if we are led away from what we were taught. What a blessing this can be! The mission might involve working with the land in some way, as well as in building, construction, or real estate. An aptitude for finance can play a part as well. A keen sense of value—the true worth of commodities, time, and knowledge—is often in evidence; hence, frugality typically prevails.

---

2 Tomberg, *Proclamation on Sinai*, 16.
3 Tomberg, *Meditations on the Tarot*, 196.

When Saturn is in the 3rd house, we often find a tendency (alongside a terrific sense of humor) to think methodically and seriously. For those whose nature is to flit from one subject to the next, this placement will provide ample opportunity for growth—for it demands that we be committed to following but one "star": the one that bears our Name. Saturn in the 3rd house asks us to be hermeticists who seek understanding of the world *below* in what dwells *above*. We will need to guard against the sarcasm that Saturn can bring to the mind, lest we convey too much cynicism. This placement typically suits us for tasks that require a great deal of concentration and perseverance. The thirst for education tends to increase with age. As the 3rd is the house of ambition, the presence of Saturn's determination can amplify this to an extraordinary degree.

When Saturn is in the 4th house, there might be a strong desire to be on top of our game, and to stay there. When the lower impulses of Saturn are heeded, this can mutate into a desire to *dominate*. This placement invites us to take on responsibilities willingly and approach them with care and seriousness. Those of us born under this configuration tend to command respect—but this is also the house in which we find that a lack of uprightness can easily lead to a fall from grace (or from power). To guard against this, we need to avoid seeking personal recognition *for its own sake*—so that we can remain upright vessels for truth and integrity. Our mission will be difficult to achieve without visibility in the world (whether welcome or not). Transparency with regard to our moral standing is therefore paramount! This implies the inevitable scrutiny of others, for which we must prepare ourselves. Saturn in the 4th house serves as a warning against the hardening effect of *materialism*.

Saturn in the 5th house, which is analogous to Leo, suggests finding self-expression through educational and creative pursuits. Any planet in this house is conferred a certain amount of *warmth*, and Saturn is no exception; ideally the 5th house draws from us a deep compassion for human failings. The 5th is also the house of sentimental attachments—therefore, these might be colored by Saturn's natural seriousness and reticence. There might be a dislike of being "carried away" by anything—instead, we can often observe a preference for activities that require concentration, memory, and strategy. Although the 5th house is known as the one in which we are most likely to take risks, Saturn brings caution to this equation. There can be a special devotion to children—therefore the mission might involve their education and care.

When Saturn is in the 6th house, there tends to be less free will in the exercise of our mission: We may find that *it* will choose *us*. This tends not to be a "fly alone" placement; therefore we might direct our efforts toward service to others (in any of its myriad forms). However, we must first be certain of the value of what we serve. In the 6th house we learn of the power of kindness and purity, and it is through these qualities that we might best find our strength of purpose. Those of us born under this configuration will likely be sought out for our reliability and precision in dealing with difficult tasks. An interest in the health of the Earth and of our fellow human beings is a frequent focus—through which an attunement to their needs can be achieved.

When Saturn is in the 7th house—that of partnerships of all kinds, including marriage—our success will be affected by our ability to attend to the health of those associations. Such success depends upon whether we seek counsel from our *personal inclinations* or from our *conscience* (which depends upon objectivity). Saturn's accidental exaltation in the 7th house reminds us of the power of Saturn when put in service of resolving conflicts; of course, the artful exercise of diplomacy can also attract assistance. Stability in relationships is ideally a source of security and warmth. The mission might involve anything to do with partnerships: counseling, the law, etc. Whether or not we have anything to do with the practice of law (which is not uncommon), we would do well to devote adequate time to any contract that comes our way—so as not to find ourselves legally bound to something we'd prefer to be free of.

When Saturn is in the house of the occult, the 8th house, we are drawn beyond the limits of the sense world—i.e., to what lives behind the veil of ordinary perception, including the secrets of death and rebirth, of trial and transformation. Because the 8th house has an "otherworldly" quality, those of us born under this placement might also seem to have this attribute—although the mission might lead others to knowledge of spiritual realms. Saturn in the 8th house entreats us to "listen in silence," whereby the "fire" of the spontaneous activity of the spirit might be reflected by the "water" of this silence. Our dreams are a valuable source of supersensible perceptions. The material world is sometimes of less interest to us than what lives outside it, which may be just as well—for our earnings might be somewhat beyond our control. The spouse usually has a strong impact on finances, for good or ill.

Saturn in the 9th house asks us to hold fast to our ideals with deep conviction. When Saturn is in the 9th house, the mind tends to be deep and somewhat austere, and opinions are often made only after long periods of consideration. This simultaneously presents the possibility of becoming overly attached to one point of view, at the expense of the *whole truth*. This placement favors the study of subjects like philosophy—anything abstract that demands much of the intellect. Saturn in the 9th house usually conveys a need to explore, even if only through mental activity; pursuits that span cultural or national boundaries are favored. Those born under this placement often learn through the rigorous questioning of hypotheses. However, when questioning turns to doubt, we can be drawn toward a fatalistic outlook that makes miracles seem impossible.

When in the 10th house, Saturn assumes accidental rulership through its relationship to Capricorn.[4] This is the house of heritage of all kinds, most notably familial and spiritual. Here, Saturn can indicate a childhood full of heavy responsibilities, which can lead us to explore all the various ways in which our free will might be exercised. Saturn in the 10th house asks that we strive to understand the role of tradition in human evolution; as we gaze into the future with hope and courage, we must acknowledge the roots that hold firmly to the past. Those of us born under this configuration tend to look ahead in order to prepare for all manner of contingencies. (Some even plan contingencies to *these* contingencies!) The 10th is also the house of real estate,[5] so this avenue is often a favorable one to pursue.

When Saturn is in the 11th house, we might find that we benefit from mixing with those people of a serious turn of mind. The invitation inherent in this placement is to attend to a connection with our community—both establishing and maintaining its health with heartfelt interest. Although this can require much effort, the mission will be more difficult to accomplish if we lack this connection. Ambitions can be thwarted by overextension; Saturn asks that we focus, and that we not stray too far from the task before us. We need to stay with it for the long haul! Those of us born under this placement are called to do all in our power to behave admirably and reliably. Although friendships are of paramount importance, we must take special care to avoid those who might not have our best interests at heart—for they can do us much harm. Humanitarian causes might spark great interest. *The 11th house asks that we listen for the breath of the spirit that bears whispers of what is striving to manifest from the future.*

Hermits delight when Saturn is in the 12th house! The mission might be pursued in solitude (whether by choice or not), where much can be accomplished through sustained, isolated work. We value privacy highly. This is the ideal placement for research of all kinds, which is conducted with the excitement of a treasure hunter. Mysticism is commonly of great interest—perhaps because the 12th is the house of encounters with beings that dwell beyond the limits of our sense perception. As a state of withdrawal from the world can be very appealing to us, we can attach to this configuration the warning against *too much* solitude, which is so often self-imposed. We might in that case aspire to a rhythm whereby we "come up for air" from time to time. As the 12th is also the house of *treachery*, we do well to minimize this potential pitfall by adhering strictly to the law and to our moral values.

---

4   If a planet rules, for example, the tenth sign of the zodiac, it is said to be the *accidental ruler* of the 10th house. Therefore Saturn is the accidental ruler of the 10th house by way of that house's analogy to the tenth sign, Capricorn.
5   On the zodiacal wheel, the 10th house is at the bottom of the chart, and can thus be thought of as "the ground of our being."

♃ JUPITER

The house of Jupiter suggests the domain of human activity in which we are likely to find support and assistance—whether or not it has been earned. The extent of this support depends upon our own moral integrity and the earnestness of our search for wisdom; it is compromised by overindulgence and overextension—two of the negative Jovian influences that stem from a third: false optimism. Jupiter's house position often indicates the area of life in which our judgment is sound; as the traditional bearer of good luck, Jupiter conveys opportunities for success—and we can make the most of these "breaks" through the practice of this judgment. It is very important that we not take for granted the benevolence that is interwoven with Jupiter's gifts. Indeed, we could go so far as to say that doing so invites downfall.

When Jupiter is in the 1st house, the path to wisdom necessarily requires an effort toward self-realization and independence. We are meant to be *ambassadors* of any planet in this house—and we can represent Jupiter by exhibiting sound, moral judgment and a cheerful outlook. Jupiter in the 1st house suggests that we are self-supporting by way of our natural confidence; this, in turn, implies the potential for leadership. Optimism and benevolence tend to be key parts of the personality; additionally, the characteristic cheerfulness and good sense attributable to Jupiter draw support from others, making this placement one of the best configurations for happiness. The general good fortune that so often accompanies this configuration must not be unappreciated or squandered, lest we find ourselves its orphan. *When Jupiter is in a difficult aspect, there can be an inclination toward self-indulgence.* Like all 1st house placements, this is a subjective Jupiter. When so placed, it allows us to disregard what is deemed "acceptable" to others—so that we can devote ourselves fully to our quest.

Nothing signals the possibility of earning power like Jupiter in the 2nd house—but because of Jupiter's natural generosity, our funds often find their way to charitable donations or to other forms of largesse. Financial support from sources other than earning are often apparent. Work involving finance and investment is favored, in part because of a knack for taking advantage of prevailing opportunities. When the good fortune of Jupiter is offset by poor financial judgment or a challenging aspect from another planet, funds that are counted upon can remain elusive. An overly materialistic outlook can leave the door ajar for economic tyranny, whereby we judge others' worth (and our own) by what they have been able to acquire.

When Jupiter is in the 3rd house, it shines its wisdom upon the intellect, bringing breadth to the mind. This typically confers the ability to grasp the big picture, which can give us an unfailing knack for knowing what to do in any situation. The sense of moral values tends to be strong, due to an understanding of the natural hierarchy of authority. Those of us born under this configuration benefit from an optimistic and enthusiastic outlook. Education of all kinds can serve us well, and professions involving communications are a natural fit. Professional and social success will follow the chase of our ambitions. In other words, we would do well to avoid professions that are not of abiding interest to us. Jupiter in the 3rd house radiates the wisdom of our proper destiny-path; we must therefore be careful that Jupiter's exuberance doesn't take us too far out of our way.

Because the 4th house is a general indicator of destiny, Jupiter here suggests that the table has been laid such that most of it will be favorable—as long as we don't take for granted our good fortune. Consistent with the blessings of Jupiter in the 4th house is the planet's exaltation in Cancer, the sign to which the 4th house finds a relationship. Professional authority and social stature are common. It is almost as if those of us with Jupiter in the 4th house are being pushed toward success, regardless of our efforts to achieve it! And while honors and acclaim are often within reach, we need to keep in mind that the position of the 4th house (at the top of the chart) means that it is at the same time the house from which we have the farthest to fall. Jupiter positioned so near the EZ confers a sense of justice, along with an optimistic and honest nature. However, this placement also serves as a warning against cerebral intellectuality, which can engender an inability to reflect the great thoughts of the cosmos—in favor of the "enclosed" thinking of the human intellect alone.

Jupiter in the 5th house confers vitality and *joie de vivre*—and part of the work associated with this placement is cultivating and nurturing the ability to truly enjoy life. Jupiter here enhances good fortune in the realm of sentimental relationships of all kinds, including those with children. The 5th is the house that shows us how we freely enjoy ourselves—and thus it follows that Jupiter (which bears the forces of expansion) will make enjoyment of life a focus for those born under this placement. Jupiter in the 5th house bestows gusto; having said that, too much gusto can lead us down the path of "living it up." A pleasure-seeking orientation that lacks a sense of personal responsibility can pull us far afield of our karmic work. There is often a love of being out and about, and our cheerful approach to the world can make us sought-after companions. Taking risks might come naturally (more often than not with good results); but if it happens that we are averse to this, we might benefit from taking a chance now and again. This placement favors anything to do with children and education. Creative endeavors are supported.

When Jupiter is in the 6th house, we might turn our attention to the following passage from Psalms: *Truth shall spring out of the Earth*; here the wisdom of nature calls for human understanding. As this is the house that illuminates us as to the state of our health, this placement suggests a certain degree of protection from sickness. (This blessing is simultaneously accompanied by a stern warning against culinary and bacchanalian excess.) Jupiter in the 6th house confers a sympathy for all in search of help. Because this house illuminates the nature of our work and other imposed tasks, Jupiter's presence in it might confer success in this domain, along with a pleasant work environment and the ability to develop executive skills. It is important to nurture good professional relationships. A 6th-house Jupiter implies significant support and assistance from the partner.

Jupiter in the 7th house brings a social conscience through the house's association to Libra. Those of us born under this placement are often given protection from the usual pitfalls of the 7th house: the risks of legal troubles, and of difficulties through the actions against us by visible adversaries and competitors. Social contacts are also usually abundant and successful; therefore, this placement favors partnerships of all kinds. We could look at this from another angle and say that healthy associations with others are critical to general success; consequently, going solo is much less likely to be rewarded. This is typically a happy placement for marriage, in which the committed partnership can contribute greatly to career advancement. Egotism, of course, will work against social and marital success. Jupiter's characterization as the "moral judge" of our solar system suggests that its placement in the 7th house demands that conscience and fairness remain at the fulcrum of our "scales."

When Jupiter is in the 8th house, its natural affinity for metaphysical matters turns to the subject of death (and our experience thereafter). Jupiter leads us this threshold and asks us to dare to seek the treasure that exists on the other side—for every transformation allows us to shed our old "skin," and every death holds the promise of new life. Often the life of dreams is vivid and easily recalled; these dreams can be messengers for the world-thoughts of the spirit. On a more mundane level, the 8th is the house of income not earned personally, including inheritance and the income of those to whom we are attached—therefore Jupiter in this house implies the possibility that such sources of income and property can be significant.

The influence of Jupiter in the 9th house is strengthened due to Jupiter's rulership of Sagittarius. Because the planet implies unbounded breadth—in thought as well as in daily life—this placement might confer an interest in the experience of other cultures, languages, and worldviews. There is much to be gained from venturing out of the confines of our daily lives! To some, this results in wanderlust; others engage in international transactions or pursue an education in worldly matters. This placement offers support for higher education—which, in its ideal form, is a search for the truth. Jupiter in the 9th house engenders a proclivity for a higher order of thought. Broad subjects that explore ethics (as do religion and philosophy) tend to hold our interest. Dorsan emphatically states that the 9th is the house of the father.[6]

---

6   In *The Clockwise House System*, Dorsan supports this assertion convincingly and in great detail.

(We might add to this a "father figure" such as a spiritual master.) He therefore suggests that Jupiter in this house results in a grand "inheritance" from this person: of a mind that is broad, tolerant, and sincere. Indeed, in the absence of difficult aspects to Jupiter in the birth chart, we could generalize by saying that the relationship with the father was likely a good and supportive one.

The 10th house signifies the heritage of the birth family; therefore, with Jupiter as an occupant, we likely receive their support. This might include the possibility of their financial assistance, but even if this is not the case, we'll tend to receive frequent encouragement and advocacy, throughout their lives, from the family milieu. Often we will feel happy in its folds, sometimes even resisting circumstances that take us out of its reach: We are typically individuals who like to "return home." We revere continuity, and find that the security of our "roots" assists us in meeting the future with courage; even the career can transpire under the influence of those in the parental family. A pleasant and peaceful domestic existence—if not in evidence—should be sought. Real estate investments and management are favored. Jupiter in the 10th house suggests happiness and success, which increase with age.

Jupiter in the 11th house—that of community, friendship, and connectedness—highlights the importance of cultivating this vital aspect of life, no matter how elusive it might seem. This placement can bring success to long-term goals and cherished hopes and dreams. However, such success will likely depend largely upon the health and the strength of our friendships. Those within our community tend to support us enthusiastically, and to assist us in the successful attainment of our goals—provided that we approach this with the attitude of humility, and the expectation that we can learn everything when we "think together." The 11th house is one of freedom, which is upheld easily by Jupiter's proclivity for exceeding boundaries. Humanitarian impulses find nutrient-rich soil in this placement—therefore, any pursuit in this direction will be smiled upon by the Great Benefic.

Jupiter in the 12th house implies that our stature might need to be achieved entirely under our own steam. Jupiter is in accidental rulership here, due to the relationship between Pisces and the 12th house; this suggests an easy association between the planet of higher thinking that is *moral* and the house of the hidden, spiritual life. This sector of the chart is one that covers many of life's challenges (as well as the spiritual rewards that can stem from them). And so, with Jupiter as an occupant, protection from most adverse effects of these trials might be forthcoming. We will benefit from periodic isolation, and we might even say that an occupation carried out behind the scenes could result in a position of distinction. Enemies may become friends. The material world seems to diminish in importance over time; we might long instead to devote ourselves to the spirit—which we find far more nourishing to the soul. Our solitude allows us to breathe spiritual "air."

MARS

As we descend through the sphere of Mars, we are in the company of the mighty Thrones: the spirits of will. While in this planetary sphere, we gain a sense of the scope of the tasks that await us in the life to come. The Thrones confer courage, get-up-and-go, and the willingness to defend righteousness—therefore, the house of Mars usually tells us the domain of life in which our destiny requires these attributes. We tend to desire and go after whatever is under the sway of the house. As the god of war, Mars is ideally suited for argumentative conflict—which he sometimes seeks out for his own enjoyment! He comes alive when we stand up for what we believe in; he shows us how to draw a line that must not be crossed. Uncontrolled rage is a manifestation of the *lower* forces of Mars, as are impatience and impulsiveness.

Those of us born with Mars in the 1st house are being asked to actively defend our right to act independently—and life may present us with many opportunities to do so. By way of the house's association with Aries (which is ruled by Mars), this placement asks that we be willing to champion and protect what we know is right. If this is *not* our inclination, we'll need to practice standing up for ourselves and for the object of our devotion: *This* is the commission of Mars in the 1st house. Some of those born under its sway enter the world "armed" and ready to tussle, while other warriors find that their work is best carried out behind the scenes. In either case, this placement asks for us to develop leadership skills. Mars is associated with abundance of energy, but we must take care not to waste it senselessly. A tendency for impatience and impulsiveness can compromise the outcome of our objectives. When in the 1st house, Mars is attended by a warning against taking careless physical risks.

Mars in the 2nd house suggests that we may devote much effort to the task of earning a living and acquiring possessions. This is abetted by the initiative, daring, and capability that are characteristic of Mars. Wherever Mars is, he shouts: *I can do that!* And although Mars in the 2nd house can support good earning capacity, a tolerance for incurring debt can make saving difficult, as can our tendency to spend our recently acquired earnings at our earliest convenience. Extravagance, risk-taking, and undue generosity will likewise not favor the bank account. Any resulting difficulties are caused in part to Mars's accidental exile in the 2nd house (due to its association with Taurus). It is therefore advisable to exercise financial caution. Alternatively, we might imagine our warrior in the 2nd house emerging from the stony tomb of materialism in order to seek counsel with the spiritual world, whence the Father calls: *Remember me.*

When Mars is in the 3rd house, our communications can convey argumentativeness or even aggression when we lack caution. The minds of those of us born under this placement are so quick that it can be difficult for us to wait for others to "catch up." This placement suggests plenty of intellectual activity and deeds that engage our resourcefulness. Because Mars loves a good fight, there can also exist a tendency to seek out arguments. (Indeed, many among us do our best thinking while engaged in them!) Mars in the 3rd house usually confers a great deal of ambition as well as the ability to put plans into speedy action — qualities conveyed by the glyph itself. Personal ambition, however, might be at odds with our spiritual path. Our self-mastery will determine if we're able to see the difference.

Mars is in the 4th house is in accidental fall (due to its exaltation in the tenth sign, Capricorn) — therefore, those among us born under this placement might guard against going beyond the limits of our vitality. The Mars inclination to get things done (and to then check them off our "list") supports the acquisition of earthly honors; however, we might ask ourselves in what ways we assign more importance to the end result — the "harvest" — over and above the processes that yielded that result. While the 4th house signifies the career and social standing (or the struggle for success), it also suggests that these efforts may require bold action from time to time. Criticism can arise through jealousy and rivalry, which thus has the ability to impede our path to success. The 4th is also the house of disgrace; therefore, those of us born with Mars here are reminded that moral and legal conduct are the surest way to avoid it. This placement confers courage and audacity in the face of destiny. It can signify early difficulties with the mother that can persist for a very long time.

Mars in the 5th house warns against depleting our vitality in pursuit of enjoyment. Freedom is a signature of this house; Mars within its cusps therefore signifies that a great deal of energy will likely be given over to such activities (including romantic relationships). A certain impulsiveness might be noted in matters of the heart — a domain in which caution is normally advised. The 5th is the house of risk, and Mars's presence in it implies a comfort in taking on a fair amount of it — particularly in the professional life and through investing. Needless to say, results may not always live up to our level of daring. Those of us born under this placement tend to adopt a frank and direct "take it or leave it" attitude. We work hard, play hard, and admire courage in others. A particular love of children can often be observed. Those of us with Mars in the 5th house run the risk of defining freedom as the ability to please ourselves. Alternatively, we can listen for the knock of our karma — which longs to become conscious within us — and, in anticipation (or, response), elevate our souls through our endeavor to resolve it as best we can.

Because the 6th house is that of imposed tasks and responsibilities — including those related to the profession—much effort will likely be put toward their accomplishment. Matters that might attract include health, nutrition, and the Earth itself. Those born under this placement tend to harbor a strong desire to climb the ladder of success. Because conflict is never far away from Mars, however, there can be difficulties with colleagues; therefore, if we're in a position of authority, we'll need to use it judiciously. Equally important, however, is that we not feel ourselves to be taken advantage of (otherwise, we would do well to consider self-employment). The 6th house also enlightens us as to the spouse; Mars as an occupant suggests that the partner will be full of energy—someone who likes to take charge. As Mars in particular does not welcome being told what to do, this can be a significant source of conflict. Because of the association between Virgo and the 6th house, Mars, our mighty warrior (known for his strength and bold action) encounters a force greater than his own, and must denounce rivalry.

Mars in the 7th house suggests the possibility of tussles among associates and partners; such encounters might be characterized by aggression or even authoritarianism. Still, the attainment of our goals is likely to depend upon these relationships—and these will not thrive in the absence of diplomacy! This may be hard-won. Although to us, our cosmic warrior might not appear to be seeking harmony, this is precisely what the Archangel Michael (Mars) does, as the one who holds the scales—for the justice he renders is in service of cosmic harmony. Michael encourages us to renounce the tendency to take things personally, in favor of *forgiveness*. Those of us without a natural inclination to associate with others will need to cultivate one; indeed, attaining such an ability will be a focus of our karmic work. Due to the correspondence of the 7th house to the law (by way of Libra), Mars's presence here suggests that care needs to be taken in all matters that involve contracts—especially those on behalf of partnerships. This placement typically confers a longing to be attached—although this offers no protection against arguments.

When in the 8th house, Mars stands as a warning against squandering our energy. If there exists an inherent attraction to what might be termed "the underbelly" of humanity, we must proceed with extreme caution, lest we find ourselves enchained there, remote from spiritual assistance. Instead, this placement invites us to direct our energies toward the investigation of hidden realms—whereby we might find satisfaction in exploring various aspects of the "unseen world" and its dynamics. This includes the investigation of the psychology of the human soul, as well as the mysteries of death and of the existence in spiritual worlds between earthly lifetimes. In addition to being the domain of the study of the occult, the 8th house also involves income and assets that originate outside of personal effort (e.g., inheritances). Mars in this house might portend struggles over these assets—but if we are required to defend what is rightfully ours, we will find the courage to do so.

When in the 9th house, Mars often confers the qualities of the pioneer and the adventurer. Those of us born under this configuration might have a passion for travel to faraway places and the energy to get us to wherever we want to go. Because the 9th is the house of ideals, Mars's presence in it signifies the tendency to "go all in" for a chosen cause, which can therefore bear a warning against becoming fanatic about a single perspective. We might then remember that without impartiality, the whole truth *cannot* be known. Mars in the 9th house suggest a willingness to defend our ideals. Skepticism, rather than religious feeling, can drive philosophical thinking. Mars (the planet of conflict and competition) can signify difficulties—and possibly rivalry—with the father, for the 9th is his domain. This is an excellent placement for higher education, in that it often portends much success in academics. It carries a stern warning against harmful speech born of our unrestrained emotions.

Because the 10th house bears a relationship to the final years of life, Mars within its boundaries suggests vitality throughout this period. This energy can be used to great advantage at a time when others around us are slowing down; it is best applied to work or other serious pursuits. Additionally, because Mars is in accidental exaltation in the 10th house (since Capricorn is the 10th sign), its presence here implies that significant achievements can occur later in life—regardless of when these endeavors began. The 10th house is also descriptive of the birth family; Mars within its cusps can therefore be suggestive of an atmosphere within that family that was not without conflicts. This placement indicates possible wrestles with our heritage. As difficult as this can be for a child, it can motivate us to seek happiness elsewhere, to great effect. This placement alerts us to the dangers of an overly critical frame of mind (which can easily alienate us from the goodwill of others). Those of us born under this configuration will find that the greatest opportunity for success lies in approaching the future without losing sight of the past.

Mars in the 11th house (that our fondest dreams) indicates that much effort will be expended in realizing long-held aspirations, which might be humanitarian in nature. Those of us born under this configuration might, however, guard against having more projects than it is possible to see through to completion. In other words, a measured approach bears many blessings. As "measured" and "cautious" are sometimes missing from the dictionary used by Mars, intentional reticence offers the additional benefit of acting as a path of spiritual growth. The 11th is also the house of community (and, therefore, an important source of support); we can thus infer that those of us born under this astral signature might receive assistance from those within it, provided that we acknowledge its value as a source of shared inspiration. Mars in the 11th house can also signify rivalry and conflict within the community group; this peril can be offset by choosing friends with great care. There is typically an affinity for other energetic and courageous individuals.

Mars, representative of material reality, can initially feel a bit at sea in the 12th house, that of "spiritual man." When we turn our gaze above, however, we are able to imagine human deeds in service of divine will—for the 12th house asks that we serve both God and humanity. We might therefore imagine this combination as suggestive of exerting effort toward all that is mysterious and hidden beneath the surface of reality. However, it carries a warning: that all subterfuge holds open a portal for adversarial forces. The 12th is the house of hidden enemies; therefore, Mars's presence here—perhaps more than in any other house—demands self-mastery, lest our lower astral nature provoke unwanted behaviors from others. These behaviors, of course, are all the more dangerous when they are *covert*. Research of all kinds suits those of us born under this configuration, as does any work carried out in some form of isolation; however, it asks that we make every effort to break free from unwanted constraints. It might be our inclination to strive to alleviate the suffering of those in need.

SUN

The Sun represents our individuality and our divine nature, which endure eternally, throughout all of our incarnations. In each lifetime the mantle that the Exusiai, Dynamis, and Kyriotetes bestow upon us is a new one. The house placement of the Sun offers us the opportunity to remember—and resurrect—a facet of our higher nature (the "I"). It shows us where we might "burn" without smoke or crackling fire, thus revealing the activity by which we might best wear the mantle that we have been given. In other words, it signifies the domain of life wherein we are most likely to meet our "star." When we choose to ignore the matters of the Sun's house (as we are free to do), *we might feel as if we're walking through life wearing the wrong set of clothes!* However, when our will is aligned with the nature of the house, our confidence grows, as does the esteem that others have for us. It feels right, even if doing so is very difficult.

The Sun find its accidental exaltation in the 1st house (through the relationship between the 1st house and Aries), thereby suggesting individuals in possession of strong personalities supported by a wealth of will-forces. The 1st house supports the development of this individuality, and here the Sun is a bit like a stage entrance: It announces its presence with confidence and energy. When it is above the Ascendant-Descendent axis, we typically love to be out in the world; when it is below this axis, we may prefer some degree of seclusion. A desire to influence others is commonly noted, along with a ready sense of certainty about what needs to be done at any given time. These individuals might be dignified—even noble—and therefore tend to dislike interacting with those who have not earned their respect. The Sun in the house of the Ascendant is typically a blessing for *health* and *vitality*, which are often found in happy and successful individuals who lead with ease. Given that the Sun is the force that holds together the planets of our solar system into a cohesive whole, those of us with a 1st house Sun might serve this role within a family, group, or organization. Therefore, this placement simultaneously serves as a warning against self-centeredness and egotism.

When the Sun is in the 2nd house, the individuality might seek expression through investing, building, or the cultivation of the land. Although this placement often bestows an easy facility for earning money (thanks in part to our typically strong ambitions in this direction), any of these avenues can lead to living beyond our means. The Sun in the 2nd house commonly portends business acumen; however, financial stability might depend upon those in authority (and possibly the father while we are under his influence). There is much to be gained from spending time in nature or in the countryside; those of us born with a 2nd house Sun might require serenity in order to think things through in a rational manner. Although it can be said that we are usually generous with others, the appetite for money or possessions might veer toward excess—or even compulsion. This can engender a profound indifference to the present. It is love alone that can raise us from this "death."

In charts where we find the Sun in the 3rd house, we can usually identify a childhood that included a good education. (This is the house of early schooling.) Dorsan identifies what he calls the gift of synthesis[7] as emblematic of this placement. There may be talent in academics, including the sciences. The Sun in the 3rd house suggests success in any intellectual career, particularly one involving writing or speaking. We might beware, however, the possibility of dissipating our energy, for fleet-footed Mercury (he of energy easily dissipated) is in accidental rulership in this house due to the relationship between the 3rd house and Gemini. The mind benefits from "quieting" from time to time, as neglecting to "power down" can adversely affect health. Sudden changes in course will tend to work against success. Because the 3rd is also the house of ambition, the Sun's appearance here suggests the presence of this strong motivating force. The longing for social recognition and repute in the eyes of others is usually apparent, as is the hope that our success will reflect well upon our family. But we must ask ourselves: *For what are we striving?* Are we following our unique spiritual path, or one that has been mapped by someone else?

When the Sun is in the 4th house, we can often observe a promising rise in life—which might even be accompanied by notoriety, authority, and responsibility. In general, it can be said that the Sun near the top of the chart will cast sunshine upon our destiny, and that those in power tend to further our success. However, the 4th house warns against the pursuit of material goals alone, particularly if they are self-serving. Those of us born under this placement tend to be self-assured, ambitious, and proud—but (as a result), care must be taken to stave off egotism, which can cast us from our high station. Success depends upon being free of the rule of others, as well upon what might be termed "events of destiny"—strokes of both good fortune and ill fortune (i.e., those beyond the reach of our influence). Because this is a high-visibility placement, popularity is invaluable to our aims, whatever they may be. Through its analogy to Cancer, the 4th house is the domain of the mother—therefore the Sun's presence here suggests happy circumstances while we are in her charge.

A 5th house Sun, owing to the Sun's rulership of Leo (the fifth sign), tends to confer vitality and vigor: get-up-and-go. Here the Sun suggests a hearty interest in those pursuits that are chosen in complete freedom—one example being creative endeavors—as well as in matters of education. We long to share what we have learned! As this is also the house of risk, the Sun's presence here suggests many happy outcomes in this regard—indeed, it might also be the case that windfalls appear out of the blue! Those of us born under this configuration are being asked to stand out in some way, which

---

7   Dorsan, *The Clockwise House System*, 79.

may or may not be in accordance with our temperament. (Be that as it may!) We must guard against the tendency toward every variety of excess, which can diminish us in our own eyes and in those of others. Vanity betrays a lack of compassion for others. A special love of children is often apparent.

The individualities of those us born under a 6th house Sun might seek expression within the natural world, which reveals to us that all life proceeds from a holy source. Understanding and serving nature may be our path to the divine. Indeed, each "tiny life" of the birds

> ...sings the great life and makes heard, through its countless variations, the same news which is as old as the world and as new as the day: "Life lives and vibrates in me."[8]

There is a longing to see our efforts reach fruition—and a talent for bringing them to this stage. This placement confers executive ability characterized by our willingness to assume responsibility, hard work, and ingenious problem solving; however, the precision typical of the 6th house can lead to our getting "lost in the weeds." An overriding need to be of service to the world motivates our efforts. Although the desire to be helpful is overarching (and the ease with which we find satisfying work is considerable), we must guard against any situation that leaves us feeling "used." This speaks to one of the challenges of this placement: misreading boundaries. *We are asked to refine our ability to discern the needs that lie hidden in others' hearts.*

When the Sun is in the 7th house (that of the Descendant, where the Sun sets), our relationships with others are our "school," and they hold the key to our success. As diplomacy is mastered, doors will open. It could even be said that those born under this placement might encounter many opportunities to cultivate and exercise such diplomacy! One of the great gifts of the 7th house is that of *scope*—being able to make a ready assessment of the full reach of a situation. There tends to be a knack for seeing—and accepting—things "as they are." At its lowest expression, this outlook might engender such acceptance by way of "falling asleep"—whereby we renounce our role as a holder of the scales altogether. We would be mistaken to think that the peace that we long for is to be found within this slumber. Many of us born with Suns in the 7th house have an instinctive understanding of the importance of averting fatigue and maintaining inner equilibrium. Adequate rest will be good for overall health; another favorable path to economy of energy is through meditation. A caveat attends this configuration: to stay on the right side of authority and the law, and thereby avoid giving anyone grounds for a complaint. This is, after all, the house of open combat—which includes the forum of marriage!

Those among us born with the Sun in the 8th house might regard it as a commission to shine light into the darkness: to seek to gain insight into the hidden dynamics behind the world of the senses. Indeed, sometimes the interest in occult and esoteric forces—those that dwell beyond the veil of everyday reality—is *so* keen that it can be difficult to focus on more quotidian matters! Our work has the potential to maintain its importance long into the future. We often face death with perfect calm, perhaps because we sense its cosmic purpose—to return us to our true home, the spiritual world. *The rhythms of death and rebirth, and of tribulation and transformation, speak to our souls.* The 8th is the house of inheritance and other sources of income outside of our own efforts. On a material level, the death of another person often improves our fortunes—although we must guard against "squandering our blessings." Occupations that involve relics of the past, or even death itself (e.g., threshold work), can attract.

When in the 9th house, the Sun leads us to our higher nature through our single-minded pursuit of the truth. This can be achieved through a combination of intellectual speculation, our immediate (intuitive) experience, and the application of the ancient expression *As above, so below*. Control of thought is essential to this path—for without it, our personal positions and opinions can occlude truth, which is able to reveal itself only when two opposing concepts are considered equally. The 9th is the house of ideals and profound aspirations; the Sun's presence in it might thus steer us toward efforts to

---

8 Tomberg, *Meditations on the Tarot*, 270.

improve society. The explorative impulse of this house—which engenders an interest in the wide world—can result in a profound love of true wanderlust, or (when this is not possible) of mental "travel" through study. This placement is suggestive of superior intellect and an aptitude for higher education, including teaching. (Due to their moral foundation, philosophy and the law are equally attractive.) Because this is the house of the father, the Sun within it signifies that he will be an important figure in our life—and, in the absence of a challenging aspect with another planet, a supportive and benevolent one. The same might be said of a spiritual teacher.

Within the cusps of the 10th house, the Sun metaphorically enters the domain of the later years of life. For this reason, its presence here suggests fulfillment and success in "old age" (possibly after years of striving), reminding us that what is rooted in the past shall bear fruit in the future. The nature of our true ambitions often remains hidden. This illustrates the "long-haul" facet of Capricorn, the tenth sign. The 10th is also the house of heritage, so we often observe a great love for (and pride in) the birth family, which is usually supportive. However, this house reveals two kinds of heredity: *horizontal* (familial) and *vertical* (spiritual). The Sun in the 10th house suggests the possibility of a distinguished career made possible through the assistance of those in authority. We can be attracted to the business that relates to land use, including real estate. Adequate time for introspection and meditation is beneficial. When we're overly caught up in material gain, the Sun here can impart a hint of severity that can be expressed as an unwillingness to forgive.

The 11th house is that of friendship, community, and dearly held hopes and dreams. Due to its association with Aquarius (the eleventh sign), the Sun in the 11th house inclines us toward humanitarian impulses that often serve as the motivation behind our deeds. Plans that take into account all the measures and attitudes necessary for success are most likely be well-received by others. In other words, a realistic outlook, adequate planning, and follow-through will be essential. Those of us with the Sun in the 11th house are encouraged to be independent thinkers and confident in our own compass, although we may need to answer to authority from time to time. Because this placement calls for connectedness, our success will depend on the cultivation and nurturance of relationships; in any case, the nourishment and warmth that we seek is unlikely to be found in solitary ventures. *We live into our individuality when we recognize that our own voice is but one in a heavenly choir of friends.* Those of us born under this placement are uncannily attuned to what's coming toward us from the future; therefore, we might be sought out for our insights into difficult situations.

The Sun in the 12th house is often seen in charts of esotericists, and it can portend success in related fields. The 12th is a house of mystery, and it is here that we encounter "the unknown." What is unknown to us? Two such mysteries are the realm of spirit (to which we must seek to raise our consciousness) and the subconscious mind (which we must strive to raise up from below). This house has a time-honored connection to what might be called "treachery at the hands of hidden enemies," as well as other hindrances that seem to lie in ambush. It is therefore advisable to exercise caution in what we say and write, and (above all) in whom we place our trust. However, this placement simultaneously gives us an uncanny ability to sense perfidy in others, along with a willingness to call it out. The 12th is the house of *seclusion*—therefore activities that rely upon it (or upon secrecy) are favored. We seem to have been made for research, which is undertaken with glee. Although those of us born under this placement are often very adept at moving about while in the spotlight, we secretly long to slink back to our den unnoticed—or anywhere else that is quiet and peaceful, away from the throng.

VENUS

The Angels of Venus are the mighty Archai, whose long cosmic rhythm influences the character of our culture. Thanks to the work of the Archai, we encounter the circumstances whereby we might find our way to our karmic group. Venus, by house position, shows us what we love—and for what we hold a natural affection. As the planet of love, beauty, and harmony, she is known for the many blessings that she bestows upon us. At the same time, however, Venus represents our karmic burdens—the cross we must carry in our lifetime. Therefore, her house placement also indicates where this cross might feel its heaviest. In other words, she can bring happiness and harmony to the matters of the house, *but these blessings depend upon our willingness to accept the righteousness of our personal karmic necessity.* The house of Venus is the domain in which we are most likely to give of ourselves selflessly.

Venus in the 1st house is commonly associated with charm, warmth, and kindness. Those of us born under this placement will often have a refined sense of beauty that in some cases might translate into successful artistic expression. Because the planet of love engenders empathy and warm interest in others, the social life usually brings great satisfaction and success—and conflicts, in general, are thereby minimized. Relationships tend to be happy and gratifying. Those of us born under this placement often attract a good deal of attention (which may or may not be welcome), due in no small part to the natural magnetism and charm that Venus confers. There can exists a tendency toward superficiality in those who lack maturity. Indulgence and a love of ease can also compromise the formidable blessings that Venus bestows through her placement in the 1st house. Although typically oriented toward interacting with others, the love and devotion that are so characteristic of Venus will assist us in finding the path that we must walk independently: the one toward our higher Self.

When Venus is in the 2nd house—that of resources—she might bring blessings in this domain, either through the relative ease of earning (supported by her accidental rulership of this house) or through the lack of worry about it. There can be a love of all aspects of finance, making this a favorable career avenue, attractive in part due to a longing for security. Associations with others often have a positive effect on income. And let's not forget that Venus is the planet of the arts—therefore, any revenue from art- and beauty-related fields is favored, as is anything to do with hospitality—for Venus, as you might imagine, is an excellent hostess. Those of us born under this configuration feel appreciated professionally, and typically enjoy a happy social life among people who are eager to offer their assistance. Carelessness with money should be consciously avoided, but might ultimately lead us to re-evaluate what is most important to us.

When Venus is in the 3rd house, we instinctively turn to all that uplifts the soul. Though Venus is as busy as a bee here, she brings calm to the matters of the house, which include our communications and frequent interactions with others. Those of us born under this placement typically have a flair for self-expression. The mind, which tends to be free of agitation, is balanced and brilliant. Early education (also the domain of the 3rd house) is favored by this placement. The 3rd house inspires an image of "rising to success"; therefore Venus as its occupant makes this result more likely, both professionally and socially. Relationships with siblings tend to be pleasant and helpful when Venus is not in a difficult aspect with another planet. Venus lends support to our finding peace through the faithful following of our "star." Any pleasure-seeking tendencies might pull us out of alignment with our heart's desire.

When in the 4th house, Venus can confer her blessings upon the character of individual destiny. The 4th is the house of visibility and social prominence—so Venus within its cusps often portends success in career as well as social standing. We can also intuit her influence here by considering the effect of her attractiveness (which is by no means confined to appearance) upon the house of popularity. This placement suggests a supportive relationship with the mother, while in her care. Those of us born under this placement often arouse the sympathy of others, and typically have the ability to enjoy whatever circumstances lie before us—thus reducing the likelihood of solitude from the world. The 4th is the house of *destiny over which we have no control.* When we are smiled upon, we might ask ourselves how our good fortune and position might be called into service on behalf of others. Should this placement bring suffering, however, we might endeavor to approach it as a path of purification—*whereby we remain upright beneath the stars.* Venus in the 4th house asks us to reflect the radiance of the Sun where none can be seen.

Venus is delighted to rest within the 5th house—the sector of the chart concerned with love relationships. Tender Venus is drawn toward romance here, and those born under this placement are typically not wanting in companionship. Due to Venus's ability to get along with others, and her natural diplomacy, relationships (including those with our children) tend to be pleasant and free of major conflict. Venus in the 5th house can entice us to have "the time of our lives," whereby the drinking in of experiences and amusements takes precedence over seeking the "higher plan" behind our incarnation and behind evolution itself. The 5th is a house of enormous freedom, in which we can explore the differences between our personal freedom (pursuing what we want) and the freedom that allows us to loosen our earthly bonds (i.e., by taking responsibility for our karma). We must hold dear the vow to approach each "neighbor" with compassionate interest. This placement can confer an aptitude for teaching.

Venus in the 6th house (that of health) may confer protection from illness, although we can be susceptible to overindulgence in the "good life" or to poor health habits in general. Illness, when it is experienced, tends to result in an unforeseen blessing. Because the 6th is also the house of imposed tasks (such as work), circumstances and relationships within the occupation are usually harmonious. Sometimes we are even able to find work doing what we love to do most! This house also illuminates us as to the characteristics of our spouse or partner; when Venus is within its cusps, she suggests that the partner is often a charming individual who is sometimes artistically inclined. It is essential that those of us born with this placement find someone who can be called upon for loving support. Venus in the 6th house suggests that we might turn our attention to the needs of the innocents among us — and to those suffering in the face of illness. We might listen for the health-giving wisdom of the natural world.

When in the 7th house, Venus (who is in accidental rulership in this house) applies her peacemaking skills to the domain of relationships and associations. Success in this realm depends upon our willingness to listen. The planet of *social artistry* in the house of *sociability* provides the ideal ferment for human contacts of all kinds, including marriage (which is within the influence of this house). Any personal inclination to avoid interaction with others will need to be consciously overcome to the best of our ability. The positive influence of Venus in the 7th house depends upon the quality of our relationships; likewise, the nature of the marriage union will have a disproportionate influence on our destiny. Potential adversaries might be disarmed by our charms and by the ease with which we offer our forgiveness. Jealousy can lead to rivalry and thus compromise our conciliatory gifts. Venus in the 7th usually confers a warm interest in others; the absence of this state of soul stems from the impression that others, though living and breathing, have an existence that is "less real" than our own — whereby we are unmoved by their joys and sorrows.

Venus in the house of profound change — the 8th — often has a fortunate influence upon the character of various events, including death itself — the prospect of which usually instills no fear. By way of our trials, those of us born under this placement tend to exhibit calm as we approach the mysteries of death and transformation. This is perhaps due to an understanding that the spiritual realm can be remembered through such events, and that our distance from the Father can be diminished. As this is the house of inheritance, money (as well as gifts in the domain of the occult) can come our way through death — but we might be dependent upon the goodwill of another (possibly the spouse) in order to benefit. All contracts should be crafted with care. Because assets can sometimes vanish down the drain, we are encouraged to watch over our finances carefully and to avoid descending into a life of ephemeral pleasures. If a windfall occurs, we might ask ourselves how its proceeds could benefit others.

Those of us born with Venus in the 9th house often seek the refined, elevated quality that the arts can provide to the soul. Judgment tends to be sound, and there exists an interest in all matters of a moral nature, including religious or philosophical belief systems. *Thus, the 9th is the house of a higher order of thinking.* A jovial and good-natured outlook is common, and we tend to have a keen interest in faraway lands; furthermore, travel can positively influence both romance and professional success. Higher education is favored because we aspire to improve ourselves. This placement is suggestive of a lack of tension between thinking and feeling; however, when the feeling life is instead exaggerated, it warns against reason clouded by sentiment. The 9th house demands impartiality! Venus in the 9th house might walk the hard and narrow way of the Hermit, who seeks the wisdom born of the collision of opposing theses. *We must listen for the truth.* This astral signature often indicates a pleasant and affectionate relationship with the father.

As the 10th house is that of heritage, the presence of Venus within its cusps often means that childhood was a happy time of life, and that relationships within this family might remain warm and supportive well into adulthood. May it be so! Having said this, those of us born under this placement are encouraged to do everything in our power to *preserve* familial good will, which (as we know) can be a delicate matter. Venus here experiences *hope* through the knowledge that the transcendental Self defies determinism of all sorts—just as the universal sap of life (the agent of *growth*) can overcome and transform the limitations of our physical heredity. The homes of those of us with Venus in the 10th house are ideally open to friends and family: intimate and cozy places to gather, while providing calm and quietude. Owing to the connection between our later years and the 10th house, Venus often bestows happiness and fulfillment upon this period of life—as the righteous remain ever full of sap and green,[9] even in old age. However, we must take care that we don't neglect any unfinished business from the past.

There is a certain longing for the artistic when the planet of beauty is in the 11th house. While occupying the domain of community and friendship, Venus tends to confer happiness and popularity in this arena. This, of course, depends upon compassion and empathy toward others, which might also be referred to as "love of neighbor." Furtermore, it requires that we relinquish seeing ourselves at the center of our existence—and that we instead take our seat among our circle of friends. (Loving and helpful friends serve to "lift us up.") Affectionate associations can be foundational to the success of long-term projects that reflect our beloved hopes and dreams. Indeed, they might even be a source of financial assistance toward these ends. With Venus in the 11th house, much depends upon friendships; this is why we must exercise very sound judgment in their selection. This placement asks for *sobriety*, or *temperance*, in general—so that we fall prey to neither an inflated sense of self nor to losing consciousness within the current of the subconscious (intoxication).

Venus in the 12th house—that of obscurity—suggests an appreciation for seclusion that may even lead to a life choice which can provide it. There might be an interest in being part of a group that bears a spiritual orientation. It is not unusual for those of us born under this placement to favor peace and quiet, and to operate outside of the spotlight. Venus so-placed might confer a deep sympathy for the ill and suffering—as well as for those who have been deemed lost causes. Our sensitivity to such suffering (explained in part by Venus's accidental exaltation in this house) can be very high. As a result of this, we can sometimes be lured by the prospect of "escape" from the human condition. (This is why those with a strong 12th house influence are warned against indulging in drugs and excessive alcohol.) Alternatively, when we make sacrifices for those who need our help, we ennoble those we are comforting as well as ourselves—although the success of these gestures will depend upon the proper assessment of what will be *truly* helpful.

☿ MERCURY

Mercury's house position informs us as to the qualities of the intellect. As the planet of interpersonal relationships, Mercury also reveals our tendencies and abilities in relating to others. Just as strong is the association of Mercury with healing; therefore its house points to what will demand our healing intentions: where we must strive to become "pastors of mankind." Because Mercury is fleet-footed, the matters associated with the house position will experience frequent changes—though it simultaneously confers the ability to adapt to them quickly. Mercury's house

---

9 Psalm 92:14.

position reveals to us where we will find the "spiritual air" that our souls need to thrive.

When Mercury is in the 1st house, a sharp mind, easy communication, and adaptability are intricately woven into the personality of the individual. Those of us born under this placement tend to be ingenious thinkers who are quick on our feet; some will choose to identify as healers. Mercury's high wattage brings curiosity and excitement—although it demands proper "grounding" in the Earth, lest it devolve into nervousness. Our high sensitivity to our surroundings and the goings-on within them suggest that disharmony around us can adversely affect our health. This placement typically portends a talent in writing and public speaking, although the latter might take some getting used to. Those of us born under this configuration tend to be avid learners who always want to know more than is being offered; we are usually on-the-go types who can use our natural adaptability to our advantage.

When in the 2nd house, intelligence and quick thinking are fundamental to earning capacity. The mind often turns to opportunities to make money, no matter how much is in the bank! As a result, those of us born under this configuration tend to be successful in this domain—provided that skills in communication are developed to their fullest capacity. Flexibility might be our greatest treasure, because Mercury in the 2nd house often signals frequent changes in earning endeavors. Mercury's swift and constant movement is thereby suggestive of the importance of more than one source of income. The healing professions might attract. The "Mercury earner" is often an intermediary who works well with others; earnings arise through our ability to facilitate healthy relationships among others. As there exists a connection between Mercury and theft and fraud, we must be wary of losing money through trickery, or of engaging in ventures that rely upon it.

Mercury, the accidental ruler of the 3rd house, works easily here, fostering minds that seek information as if it were nectar. As a result, this is a placement that prepares us for scholarship. Adroit expression through both speech and writing can contribute to success in professions that rely upon these skills. A good early education is common. The sharp intellect that is characteristic of Mercury in the 3rd house can be diminished by a tendency to be distracted. When in the 3rd house, Mercury's adaptability is reflected in an agile mind that can easily juggle many subjects at the same time, including science, the arts, writing, and business. However, those of us born under this combination must guard against the reduction in quality that can result from spreading ourselves too thinly. As the 3rd is the house of day-to-day contacts, these tend to be numerous and pleasant overall. Cooperation is important to professional success. The 3rd house reminds us that the information we have gathered must be carried, like a precious gift, to the manger that can be found at the end of each of our "star paths."

Mercury placed at the top of the chart (in the 4th house) illuminates us as to the manner in which we hold our "cup" aloft. Do we worship human intelligence to such an extent that we extend our cup no further than the top of our skulls? Or do we seek the intelligence of the cosmos, which renders us ignorant in comparison? This placement asks: What are we seeking? Occupations that depend upon quick thinking and a wealth of knowledge are favored. (These can include anything to do with science, literature, or trade.) However, our intellectuality can be compromised by distraction as well as by anxiety. Mercury within the cusps of the 4th house suggests a generally happy situation during youth—one that is often characterized by good health and a positive relationship with the mother (barring a planet in a difficult aspect with Mercury). As we navigate our destiny, we might find the need to dodge and weave— although our natural gift of adaptability will be of great use as we do so. Although those of us born under this configuration can reach great heights, we might prefer to work under the leadership of others. Mercury's association with youth leads to many professional interactions with the young.

When Mercury is in the 5th house, blessings are bestowed upon the intellect, and we admire accomplishments that rely upon it for success. (It can also be said that our intellectuality can be compromised by distraction—as well as by anxiety.) We are attracted to cultural pursuits, including drama and music; and a love of literature is often noted. This placement is ideal for any creative endeavor, as it stimulates creative thinking. Education (both as student and as teacher) is also favored. Because this is the house of taking risks, Mercury's position here bodes well for financial speculation, but we'd best keep in mind that Mercury is not suggestive of stability. There is a marked love of children, and our own are likely highly intelligent. This placement asks us to examine *how* we think. For the brain, as an organ, can only *mirror* consciousness; it came into being after the Fall, and is, in Tomberg's words, *the work of the serpent*.[10] Alternatively, there exists a sanctuary between heaven and Earth which guards the sacred "texts" that are "inscribed" there — texts that are knowable to those who strive to think "with the spirit."

When in the 6th house, Mercury protects health. This is an excellent placement because Mercury is in accidental rulership *and* in accidental exaltation here (due to its analogy to the sixth sign, Virgo). Additionally, Mercury in the 6th house supports work in any health-related field. (Many of us born under this placement long to heal the sick.) We tend to be excellent, intelligent employees, in part due to the frequency that our minds turn to work (and other duties). Unless other indications exist in the chart, this is not a signature of self-employment — but it in no way inhibits our chances for success. Additionally, relationships at work should be pleasant. Anxiety can harm general wellness; the digestive system is particularly susceptible. Taking time to relax and enjoy everyday pleasures is therefore beneficial, as are rhythm and consistency. This placement draws the mind to nature, and to the capacity of its life-forces to heal. Mercury in the 6th house asks us to distinguish between thinking with serene clarity (which engenders tolerance, steadfastness, and patience), and thinking with the "electrifying flood" (which yields agitation and aggression). Do we simply wish to *see* things in order to reflect the good, the beautiful, and the true — or do we see with the aim of bending *what* we see to our will in some way?

When Mercury is in the 7th house, our associates, partners, and contacts occupy a good deal of our thoughts. The social life that develops from these relationships will reflect their quality; associations are numerous, but some of these will inevitably be short-lived. Mercury — already very communicative — becomes even more so when in the 7th house. We often hate to be alone, and therefore might engage in copious texts, calls, etc., when we are. The marriage can be marked by ups and downs, as Mercury is indicative of frequent changes of circumstance in this domain. Lawsuits are to be avoided by whatever means possible. Mercury in the house of open enemies can result in arguments and disagreements with associates — not least, in part, due to our own tendency toward argumentativeness and irritability. Also contributory is our lack of reticence when others say things with which we disagree. We might seek to elevate this quality of judgment by being certain that we have taken the full measure of the situation — as Mercury is excellently placed here for the work of the "pastor of mankind."

When Mercury is in the 8th house, we need to develop control of thought in order to guard against negative thinking. Because anxiety can cause a great deal of strain, it is absolutely essential that those of us born under this placement prioritize mental rest. Indeed, *silence* is the practice by which insights might find us; *without it, we might not be able to hear the goodness and beauty of the thoughts of the cosmos*. We could even say that thinking positively must become a conscious practice — for in the 8th house (which is analogous to Scorpio), we encounter thinking "in the depths," which can include very dark thoughts indeed. Our thinking defies superficiality and can be channeled into the successful study and research of anything serious, including the occult. This combination implies that the mind will remain sharp until the end. As the 8th is the house of inheritance, Mercury within its cusps suggests that income beyond our paychecks is possible. In any event, it's advisable to

---

10   Tomberg, *Meditations on the Tarot*, 248-49. Before the Fall, our intelligence was "vertical"; we were conscious of everything *through* God. When Adam and Eve accepted the serpent's temptation for "horizontal" knowledge — knowledge separated from God — human incarnation began. We have since been denizens of the serpent's world. The work of the serpent comprises every lie that seeks to exalt us above God in heaven, whereby we believe *ourselves* to be the source of light that we used to seek in heaven alone.

remember the wisdom of saving for a rainy day.

When in the 9th house, Mercury works through Jupiter—the accidental ruler of this house—to produce among us profound thinkers who are always keen to learn more. This placement is a hallmark of higher learning and advanced degrees (of which there are sometimes more than one). We find success in endeavors that require an elevated expertise. Those among us born under this placement might travel to the ends of the Earth to meet a spiritual father, whose wisdom transcends human cognition by way of his ability to completely separate himself from collective moods, to silence the racket of the collective voice, and to experience certainty of his intuition through a fully developed sense of realism—i.e., to knowing what *is*. The mind is usually broad, and able to discern the merit in opposing positions. Owing to the connection of this house to Jupiter, philosophy, religion, and the law are often subjects of interest. When Mercury is not in a difficult aspect with another planet, the relationship with the father tends to be pleasant. The mind frequently turns to long journeys—and the facility for languages so often noted in those born under this astral signature contributes to their success.

When Mercury is in the 10th house, our thoughts often turn toward home and family, which might be a source of anxiety. Pleasant and peaceful surroundings—especially into our later years—can therefore mitigate our agitation. In the 10th house, Mercury (representative of terrestrial intelligence, or day consciousness) is being asked to unite with the stars (night consciousness), whereby the fatigue born of anxiety is ameliorated by *hope*. Such hope is the life-giving force that descends from the starry realm. (This factor alone is suggestive of the blessing of mental acuity during the final years of life.) Likewise, intellectual pursuits might bear fruit during this time of life. Due to the analogy of this house to Capricorn (an earth sign), occupations involving the Earth in any way—real estate, agriculture, construction, etc.—are favored, as is a career in public service. Because Mercury is always on the move, this placement suggests that there may be many changes in residence, which are not necessarily unwelcome; however, we must not lose sight of the importance of ensuring that a pleasant home is secured for the last years of our life.

Mercury in the 11th house confers imaginative thinking that is somewhat ahead of prevailing winds. It can increase our powers of concentration. In some cases, thoughts come so quickly and from so many different directions that they seem to be shooting out of a fire hose. As the 11th is the house of hopes and dreams, Mercury here enlivens the mind with many long-term projects; but their success might rely upon the goodwill and assistance of friends and community members. As one signature of connectedness, this placement portends many happy relationships; however, the changeable nature of Mercury implies that many of these may not be enduring. Because these alliances are a source of nourishment to our soul, we must take particular care in discerning the qualities that characterize a good friend. Any tendency to gossip must be overcome. Mercury in the 11th house invites us think "with wings," whereby our thoughts reach vertically toward God as our arms seek to gather those around us in love.

Those of us born with Mercury in the 12th house might eventually find ourselves seeking the acquaintance of an esoteric teacher. There exists an aura of mystery around us that can make it difficult for others to discern who we are. Mercury in the 12th house suggests that the mind might be moored in the realm between heaven and Earth—whereby we hold fast to our terrestrial duties and suffering as we seek the spiritual warmth found in heaven. We accept our "restrictions" upon the Earth so that we might be moved "from above." This placement implies some difficulty in expressing ourselves in a conventional way; some of us do so instead through poetry or music. Our minds turn to all that occurs in isolation: meditation, research, and occupations that occur in isolated settings. The 12th house is that of hidden treachery; care must therefore be taken that indiscreet communications do not precipitate such activity in others. Because the 12th house is also a domain characterized by worry, we must consciously engage in uplifting activities and must rest as needed—particularly if we're "out in the world" for extended periods of time. There is a tendency toward undue modesty.

☽ MOON

The Moon sphere is the repository of our moral failings, which form the basis of our karma during our life on Earth; therefore, the Moon in the chart brings karmic *necessity* to our doorstep. If only this "package" had remained at the warehouse for a while longer! The house position of the Moon thus leads us to what we are least inclined to do—but what we know (on some level) that we *must* do! This is perfectly in keeping with the Moon's association with habitual (read: unproductive) behavior. For it precisely these behaviors that have made our karmic burden heavier! Wherever the Moon is, we need to ask ourselves where personal (unconscious) will might be driving what we are doing. The Moon's house is where we experience doubt, and where—because the Moon moves so quickly—we'll feel tossed about in the affairs of the house.

When the Moon is in the 1st house, our worrying nature can influence our personality by way of excessive modesty and a lack of self-assurance. We can even have difficulty appreciating our own worth, despite others' fondness and admiration for us. As the Moon reflects the light of the Sun, so might those of us born under this placement defer to others' ideas regarding who we are and what we should be doing. But this is the basis of the spiritual work that this placement is trying to elicit, as it is a cry for independence, uprightness, and individuality—to such an extent that we don't mind looking foolish, so long as we are set ablaze by an *ideal*. We must find the will to step inside ourselves! *The Moon in the 1st house asks how we might transform a lack of self-confidence into a carefree renunciation of any claim to position or authority.* This placement bestows sensitivity and a powerful imagination that asks us to pay close attention to our intuitive impressions. The tendency of the Moon to "move on" can instill a desire for change that may or may not be in our best interest.

When in the 2nd house, the Moon is in a strong position due to its accidental exaltation. Based upon our knack for financial sensitivity and ingenuity, this astral signature can confer a talent for handling money. However, if we apply the Moon's changeability to the domain of resources, we might also prepare ourselves for some fluctuations in our income stream. These are best met with inner stability and deftness; indeed, this placement encourages us to have our fingers in many pies—so that we might secure varying sources of income. The Moon's association with the public implies that we may garner their trust through financial acumen. The hereditary family might also influence finances considerably. The 2nd is the house of earning; therefore the Moon's presence in it can result in worry over our ability to acquire enough money to achieve "security." In this way, we give matter more power than it should have. For the good work that we do to earn our money—if done in a manner that doesn't encroach on the freedom of others—is of far greater value than our income.

The Moon in the 3rd house strengthens intellect, although we may have a tendency to doubt our abilities in this realm. This placement confers imaginative thinking and an interest in a wide variety of subjects; and yet, as the appearance of the Moon changes every day, so might its influence in the 3rd house affect our ability to stay on course. When in the 3rd house, the Moon can compel us to take off when monotony threatens—a practice that can make satisfaction more elusive. Might not temptations that strive to pull us away from our star path be disguised as boredom? Our early education might be characterized by many changes of direction. As the 3rd house is that of short trips, the Moon's presence in it suggests an interest in (and a benefit from) frequent changes of scenery. Traditional astrology advises that "popularity" should be cultivated with some care. On a higher level, however, we might imagine that this placement asks that we embrace and put into service *the principle of cooperation*.

The Moon in the 4th house brings our organ of cognition (the brain) into proximity with the spiritual world above us, which is the true origin of spiritual revelation. If our focus is on matter alone, we risk the mechanization of our intellect—whereby we calculate, weigh, number, and measure—but we do not understand! The 4th is at once the house of public favor and that of public disgrace; therefore, we must remember that any amount of the latter (when due to a lack of moral uprightness on our part) can have a disproportionate impact on general destiny. This placement usually offers ease with the public—an attribute which, if not present, can be developed to our advantage. Here the Moon suggests professional adaptability, but frequent urges to change positions must be weighed very carefully. The 4th is the house of the mother (and motherhood), implying that the mother-child relationship is a good place to look for insight into our karmic burden. Women (particularly the mother, early on) will have a strong effect on destiny, for better or worse. This placement often engenders a deep inclination to nurture those we feel need our protection.

When the Moon is in the 5th house, we seek to take part in the blossoming of life. Creativity often flows easily, and we tend to leave our imaginative stamp on whatever we are doing. Affairs of the heart can come and go like the phases of the Moon, but will nevertheless be delightful for the most part. We must, however, take special care that our attachment does not exceed the worthiness of the object of our interest. Our affection to our children is lasting and strong, and it is possible that a child will play an unusually prominent role in our karmic puzzle. In this house, the Moon is brought into the domain of the Sun (ruler of Leo, the fifth sign). Therefore, despite the freedom offered through 5th house activities, we must endeavor to bring the personal will underfoot—for it often leads us into greater servitude to our karmic burden. The analogy (through Leo) between this house and the human heart leads us to the spiritual work inherent in it: to ennoble the "I" so that its forces might be rayed out to the periphery, where egotism has no foothold.

The Moon in the 6th house confers worry over health problems, both real and unconfirmed; therefore, it is of the utmost importance to avoid overwork as well as inactivity, and to keep the body in good condition through proper hygiene, healthful routines, nutrition, and exercise. Medicines should be used with care. We might instinctively identify the natural world—the mantle of Mother Earth—as a source of healing. There is a strong inclination to work, to make ourselves useful; but our tendency to doubt our value in this domain can lead to indecision—whereby we risk the loss of opportunities. Because the Moon always suggests fluctuation, this placement might engender frequent changes in the work environment. Changes in occupation must, however, be considered carefully. It is often the case that more satisfaction can be found in working in the context of a well-structured enterprise than in setting off on our own. A path of righteousness—one without the need to conquer *anything*—allows us to live in cooperation with the rhythm of eternity, "the source of all that is miraculous."

While some of us born with the Moon in the 7th house are inclined toward isolation (in which case many challenges lie ahead!), most of us dislike being alone; moreover, we often feel drawn to unions of all kinds. The chosen spouse or partner will be one of the biggest factors in our karma—and therefore, in our quality of life. We might even call our relationship with this person our "university." This placement indicates the likelihood of meeting many people, but the Moon's fluctuating nature suggests that many associations may not be long-lived. Those born under this placement are typically very sensitive to the needs of others and might be prone to doing (or requesting) more "mothering" than is appropriate. Because this is known as the house of open enemies, care must therefore be taken to avoid behavior worthy of reproach. The same advice might be given in order to minimize the chances of *legal conflicts*, of which this placement is suggestive. When our personal will remains submerged in the subconscious, we compromise our ability to judge impartially.

When the Moon is in the 8th house, we tend to direct our attention to the mysteries that occur behind the veil of the senses. This includes (but is not limited to) the psychology of the human soul, the spiritual world, and death itself—of which we can be intrigued and somewhat fearful at the same time. It's as if those of us born under this placement can't resist diving straight into the deep end of the pool, for we sense that *there* is where life's great treasures are waiting to be found. A disinclination to take life for granted often manifests, and this can be accompanied by a knack for assisting others in times of crisis. Financial affairs can be influenced strongly by marriage—for good or for ill.

The Moon's presence in the 8th house implies that we might receive an inheritance or legacy from the mother (or another woman), which might be of a material *or* suprasensible nature. Any tendency to drift toward the underbelly of society must be avoided, unless our intention is to help those who are caught within it. Notoriety can find us after death.

When the Moon is in the 9th house, creativity of thought mingles with the Moon's inherent imaginative capacity. There might be an aptitude for prophesy; hence, those of us born under this placement are encouraged to put more trust in our gut reactions and to heed our dreams. The Moon in "the house of ideals" suggests that new ideals may replace old ones with some frequency. The wandering Moon finds a traveling companion in the 9th house (analogous to Sagittarius); we may therefore find success and recognition far from home. Because of our preference for thorough research, this is a strong placement for higher education. We might have an interest in the law, in philosophy, and in the study (but not necessarily the practice of) religion. We are "seekers" who long for certainty of the whole truth, but we must learn that it cannot be found in the material world alone. When in the 9th house, that of the father, the Moon indicates a strong karmic bond to him—which might involve an inherited spiritual gift.

In the 10th house the Moon works with the house's accidental ruler, Saturn, to draw our focus to the past. There is a deep interest in our heritage and in history, as well as in tradition. Indeed, sometimes we can dwell unproductively on the past. This lack of progress can be expressed as a dependence upon family members or as a reluctance to find our own way outside of this family. The Moon in the 10th house can engender overall worry about the future—which has the power to cripple our ability to enjoy present circumstances, and may mar our proper relationship to the future. The Moon in the 10th house suggests the possibility of many changes in our living situation, even during old age. As we remember that whatever comes our way is given to us by a world full of wisdom, regardless of life's vagaries, satisfaction should increase with age. Furthermore, those of us born under this placement might take into our hearts the conviction that "hope is the experience of divine light." Since we usually feel that a home should be a warm place in which to nurture and feel nurtured, our surroundings and relationships there can deeply affect our mood. As a general matter, we long to be respected—however, the acclaim that we seek might occur late in life.

The Moon in the 11th house leads us to the importance of friendship and community which must be cultivated with care and approached with humility—for it is here that we stand to learn the most! If, by chance, we lack the ability to open our hearts in service of mixing easily with others, we must do all we can to transform this aspect of our personality. Beyond the inherent value of such friendships, we might also find that they are central to the success of our long-term projects (our hopes and dreams). There is usually no shortage of these dreams, for the imagination tends to be vivid. The ongoing changes in the phases of the Moon suggest that changes within the community—often the result of disagreements—will come and go. We must take these as they come, without feeling personally aggrieved. Though working with the public is a laudable goal, this work is best put to the service of our community as a whole, or to a grander humanitarian purpose. Those among us with an 11th house Moon may benefit from reading (every day!) the following verse from Steiner:

> The healthy social life is found
> when in the mirror of each human soul
> the whole community finds its reflection,
> and when in the community
> the virtue of each one is living.[11]

When the Moon is in the house of the subconscious (the 12th), the mind naturally longs to understand everything that could be called mysterious: all that is hidden from "day consciousness." Indeed, there can be a knack for discerning hidden motives in others. It is usually our preference to operate behind the scenes rather than under watchful eyes. The inner life tends to be rich, and our experience of it is enhanced by peaceful surroundings. Our efforts

---

11   Rudolf Steiner, *Verses & Meditations*, transl. George and Mary Adams (Forest Row, UK: Rudolf Steiner Press, 2004), 117.

bear fruit when conducted in solitude or in a place concealed from the public. We may harbor a secret whose revelation we fear. Fears of all kinds can be magnified by the actions of those who seek to do us harm anonymously. Because of the association between the 12th house and Neptune (its accidental ruler), we are rendered more susceptible than most to the ill effects of alcohol and drugs. When the Moon is in the 12th house, we may feel ourselves suspended between the subconscious and conscious realms; through deeper awareness, however, we might elevate ourselves to the realm that exists between heaven and Earth — where dwells our spiritual life. We might be hesitant to share our needs with others.

THE TRANSCENDENTAL PLANETS

 URANUS

The house position of Uranus indicates the origin of imaginative illumination in our lives — the domain in which we are most like to receive brilliant, ingenious thoughts. It shows us where convention is our enemy, and where we benefit when we resist imposed limitations in favor of originality. However, these impulses can also engender *tower-building*: the "construction" of closed, absolute systems of thought that demand and provoke an intervention from above (the lightning bolt). As such closed systems tend to feel our egotism — inclining us, as they do, to "put our names in lights" — the house of Uranus reveals where *humility* must be cultivated. Shocking, sudden upsets and changes might also be anticipated. Because Uranus is a high energy planet, its house of residence indicates where we might be especially prone to agitation and nervousness.

When Uranus is in the 1st house, its originality and outside-the-box nature is an inseparable part of the personality. Those of us blessed with this placement are supremely independent thinkers who — if this is the cost of asserting our individuality — don't mind ruffling a few feathers. Uranus placed here makes the mind imaginative and sensitive to what is reaching toward us from the future. No one could be less interested in what "everyone else" is thinking and doing — and there is a typically disinclination to be influenced by the opinions of others. Above all, we must feel we are free; therefore we resist (and sometimes resent) constraints of all kinds. Uranus can be accompanied by nervousness, so we must strive to maintain equanimity despite the unusual paths on which we may find ourselves.

When in the 2nd house, Uranus's unexpected changes apply to personal finances; we can bounce quickly from rags-to-riches, as well as from riches-to-rags. Those of us born under this placement have a nose for opportunity and a tendency to take chances when others might not; these are undertaken by way of a keen sense of what is on the horizon. Although this sense might lead us to a favorable financial result, gains can be curbed by a reluctance to keep track of daily accounting. A reliable source of income among the unreliable ones will therefore be essential. The independence for which Uranus in known applies here to the realm of earning; those of us born under this configuration may not be able to tolerate work that does not allow some degree of personal freedom. Nonetheless, Uranus in the house of resources confers a great advantage in any job that requires innovation. The potential for sudden changes of fortune begs us to evaluate what aspects of our lives are more valuable than material riches.

When Uranus is in the 3rd house, the sharp intellect that is often in evidence can catapult us to the cutting edge of innovation, particularly that of a scientific or technological nature. It's best to remember, however, that we might run the risk of immersing ourselves in the virtual world made available to us by way of electronic devices. We enjoy interacting with those of the same intellectual caliber. Uranus in the 3rd house is suggestive of exceptional intelligence; many of us will have had an unusual education, and some of us might even be self-taught. As dazzling as the mind is, however, there remains the possibility of alienating others by our outspoken and unusual manner — which doesn't shy from giving others a shock now and again! This can apply to family members as well. We might also remember that truth can be approached from many divergent paths; therefore, caution (which may not come easily) is advised in all of our communications. It is important that the profession be freely chosen, and that it call upon our imagination and unique perspective on life—for this placement absolutely demands faithfulness to our "star."

When in the 4th house, Uranus brings many sudden changes over which we have no control, particularly in the realm of the profession; abrupt changes might characterize the professional environment or the profession itself. The disruptiveness of these vagaries is somewhat mitigated by our ability to pivot quickly, for which this placement is also notable. Uranus in the 4th house typically portends a certain lack of restraint in dealing with those whom we regard as unduly devoted to hierarchy, or as simply stuck in their ways. We can easily intuit the difficulties that might arise through this behavior; in any case, this placement extols the benefits of self-employment. Abstraction (intelligence separated from its divine source) can harm the quality of our thinking. There can be a sudden and possibly enduring break of some kind with the mother.

When Uranus is in the 5th house—the house of creativity (owing to its relationship to Leo)—imaginative brilliance is expressed through creative activity, including the performance arts. The romantic life can proceed in a way that is out of the ordinary, including but not limited to attachments made and broken with the speed of a lightning bolt—calling to mind the old adage: *Act in haste, repent at leisure.* There can be an unusual break or separation from a child. We would be well-advised to give children born under this configuration a good deal of freedom, as they tend to thrive when independent. Uranus in the house of risk suggests a willingness to take chances, including at the game table; there can exist a sixth sense about when an opportunity presents itself. (Because the results will almost certainly vary, however, we should take heed not to get carried away.) Uranus in the 5th house warns against placing our failures at the feet of "luck"—for when we instead claim these misfortunes *as our own*, we gain the freedom that we long for.

Uranus in the 6th house confers independence. This placement might therefore incline us to bristle under the direction of others—and when we're in in charge, we might encounter difficulties with employees. This is not the signature of nine-to-five careers. Uranus can feel "enslaved" by virtually any form of restriction; consequently, it's important for those of us born under this placement to feel true enthusiasm about the nature of our work. When the frank expression for which Uranus is known begins to manifest as lack of diplomacy, it can harm work relationships; we would thus be wise to carefully evaluate which words might be best left unsaid. The planet of the unexpected adds to this house (that of health) a certain nervousness (which—in and of itself—can compromise our well-being). Although health troubles that unduly occupy the imagination might never come to pass, maintaining a steady regime of nutrition, fitness, meditation, and movement is advised. (We may find ourselves drawn to embrace alternative medicine.) The spouse or partner must be accorded the same freedoms that we ourselves enjoy.

The 7th house asks for compromise and diplomacy, but for those of us born with Uranus within its cusps, this might seem like a betrayal to our individuality. Indeed, we can often feel like outsiders! Uranus in the 7th house suggests that such diplomacy might require a great deal of effort, for this placement can disrupt our ability to achieve peaceful relationships among our associates. This is attributable, in part, to the notable independence of Uranus, which is so often at odds with social harmony. Uranus can compel us to reject what everyone else is doing "just because." Uranus's association with the unusual and the unexpected suggests that marriages founded upon more traditional grounds can suffer; therefore, the marriage often bears an unusual quality. We are most likely to find happiness within those relationships that are based upon true friendship, honesty, and a meeting of the minds. Alliances can end as quickly as they began. The quality of forgiveness can increase the likelihood of their longevity.

Uranus in the 8th house suggests that there tends to be a strong attraction to all that lies hidden from the senses. The mind might even turn toward death; this can include the crossing of the threshold between physical life and spiritual life, as well as the study of cultures past or of relics from them. Death is seen as a *return*, a portal to the mystery of transformation, both fascinating and of eternal relevance to humanity. This placement engenders an affinity for out-of-the-way places and for obscurity itself. As the 8th is the house of inheritance and sources of income that are not a result of personal effort, Uranus placed within its cusps usually signifies changes in fortune after marriage ("for richer and for poorer"). These can manifest as unexpected windfalls or inheritances. Uranus in the 8th house might indicate a different sort of inheritance from a parent—such as that of a brilliant mind or of a supersensible ability. This placement suggests that the unexpected deaths of others can have a disproportionate impact on our lives.

Uranus shares with the 9th house a love of freedom; when in this house, Uranus can stretch its legs and go where it pleases. Those of us born under this placement might follow our ideas 'round the world and enjoy the journey very much. The brilliance and objectivity of Uranian thinking can find free expression in the house of mental exploration—but ordinary "book knowledge" will bore many of us who began life under this placement. Of far more interest will be the personal spiritual path (often out of the ordinary) and anything that might improve the human condition. Uranus in the 9th house suggests a receptive and intuitive mind—one that, by its nature, rejects established ideas in favor of those that might better serve the future. Brilliant ideas can come and go in a flash, so we must make every effort to transcribe our thoughts and dreams in a timely manner. The relationship to the father might be marked by a separation or by other unusual circumstances.

Uranus in the 10th house is suggestive of a definitive "setting out" beyond the birth family; typically, then, our years in this home were not characterized by support and harmony. This separation might even be an essential step along the path of inner growth—indeed, it is often the case that life rewards us when we take steps toward finding our *own* way. Because of the Uranian need to refresh our circumstances and a dislike of convention, there may be many changes of residence throughout our lives; overall, these moves are disruptive, and they may threaten to drain our psychic and financial reserves. Many of us born under this placement can look forward to great satisfaction during life's later years—when we might, at last, find in our endeavors the greatest satisfaction that we have known. There can be a preference for living alone. This placement constitutes a warning against "over-pruning"—for our impulse to reform can inadvertently render a dormant rose bush incapable of flowering in the future.

As accidental ruler of the 11th house (the realm of community and connectedness), Uranus is in a strong position here. The glyph itself suggests a moving out toward the periphery: Uranus takes us to the "outer limits." Friendships based upon shared interests will be most likely to last—but the fickle nature of Uranus can nevertheless be quick to rear its head. On the one hand, community as the coming together of different points of view is the ideal milieu for Uranus; our interests typically have great breadth and we're keen to learn from as many sources as possible. On the other hand, the Uranian resistance to constraints of any kind (particularly those of social convention) can manifest as the sudden taking up and breaking off of friendships. We can thus forget the brilliance of shared inspiration. Those of us born under this placement are often drawn to astrology and to the promise of science. Long-range plans might be characterized by brilliance, although their success might depend upon the assistance of friends.

Uranus in the 12th house suggests that the uniquely independent aspect of Uranus can be forced into hiding by circumstances beyond our control. We often find ourselves engaged in activities that occur in settings removed from public view. Those born with this placement would be well-advised to exercise discretion—particularly in our speech, in which we have raised frankness to a form of art. Because the 12th is the house of hidden enemies, the Uranian tendency to poke a stick at every fallacy is best brought to heel. Indeed, any attacks at the hands of such opponents might be aroused by our brilliance, our success, or by their own resistance to change.

On a higher plane, Uranus in the 12th house signifies an attunement to the spirit, despite being bound to the Earth by way of some kind of limitation. The loving self-sacrifice that rests upon obedience to the spiritual life can mitigate any restrictions imposed by the house.

♆ NEPTUNE

The house position of Neptune reveals to us the domain of life in which we have difficulty maintaining our footing. We'll need to accustom ourselves to experiencing ebb and flow in all that the house implies. Advances and gains can wash away overnight, requiring us to start over—and it can feel as if our ego has been carried away with them. Neptune's house shows us where we must strive for full consciousness, for it is here that we will be most prone to delusion. *By way of Neptune's particular method of hindrance, the Angels draw us to the need for spirituality in our lives.* We look to the house of Neptune for insight into our path of inspiration.

Neptune in the house of the Ascendant (the 1st house) often manifests as a strong "inner voice" that should be heeded. We will likely remember countless situations that might have been improved by having done so. General sensitivity to surroundings and to ambient energy is also characteristic, making us particularly prone to negativity in our environment. Artistic or musical ability is not uncommon. Decisions—which can be elusive—are often based upon wishful (rather than practical) thinking, with varied results. Another danger of this placement lies in the tendency to let prevailing winds determine our course; therefore we must strive to become masters of our own individuality and claim our decisions as our own. Neptune close to the Ascendant can weaken willpower.

When Neptune is in the 2nd house, we tend to value what is inspirational to us and then hope that a living can somehow be made accordingly. Those of us born under this placement often find that ingenuity and creativity are critical to our ability to supplement the bank account. Money can seem to disappear without explanation; fraud can pose a threat as well. Earnings can be difficult to maintain, thereby inviting us to determine what we might deem to be of higher value than money. Nevertheless, we must take care to avoid onerous debt.

We might interpret Neptune in the 3rd house as "aspiring to ideals." These ideals are likely to differ from those of most others. Our mental orientation might be the result of a direct communication with the spiritual world. This placement requires that communications bear the quality of clarity in order to avoid misunderstandings, which might be legion. One challenge that Neptune brings to the 3rd house is that of finding an earthly outlet for all of these wonderful ideas; this might manifest as a talent for an unusual form of writing that carries readers away on the wings of their imagination. However, lingering in dreamland for hours on end keeps us far from our star path. Control of thought will assist us to stay on course.

As one of the four cardinal houses,[12] the 4th house gives any planet in it a bit more relevance. Neptune within its cusps is suggestive of a destiny of a chaotic nature. This in no way rules out the possibility of great success professionally and socially. Indeed, success might manifest in ways that are extraordinary, almost impossible to believe. A profession that relies upon selfless ideals is most likely to bring satisfaction. Moral uprightness alone has the power to minimize the possibility of a "fall from grace" in the eyes of the public. The mother can sometimes have a powerful influence, but our attachment to her might be subject to change; she can be idealized to an unrealistic degree.

When Neptune is in the 5th house—that of romantic attachments—we can have trouble reading what lives behind these attachments. Indeed, at the expense of practical reality, there can be a propensity toward illusion and fantasy as well as susceptibility to deception. A spiritual orientation reveals that we might find greater freedom if we alight from the pleasure-seeking merry-go-round. Liaisons can have an unusual character; we might find our greatest pleasure in relationships based upon a shared spiritual interest. As we watch helplessly, our children can sometimes drift away from us—only to return at a later time. This placement brings

---

[12] The others are the 1st, the 7th, and the 10th.

inspiration to all creative endeavors, including the arts, drama, dance, and music. It favors teaching, perhaps in a spiritual capacity.

When in the 6th house, Neptune can burden us with health concerns that are difficult to diagnose; therefore, we must make certain that our habits regarding food, rest, and exercise are sound. There is much to be gained through unconventional approaches to health. Assisting in the care of those with health problems (including animals) might bring satisfaction, as can ministering to the needs of Mother Earth. *Conscious service* is of great significance for those of us born under this placement — for it's possible that we can be taken advantage of more easily than most in this domain of life. Neptune in the 6th house can engender a particular susceptibility to intoxicants and drugs of all kinds, which are therefore best avoided. The spouse — including his or her state of health — can have an outsized bearing on our destiny.

Neptune in the 7th house can indicate challenges with partners or associates who are uncooperative and difficult to pin down. There can exist a tendency to idealize the married state to the point where reality might be difficult to accept. Indeed, this placement can indicate that we expect the impossible of a partner, or that the same is expected of us. Relationships can be mired in confusion. Those of us born under this configuration benefit from alliances based upon a shared spiritual interest. Care must be taken to avoid becoming embroiled in legal difficulties. Additionally, all business relationships should be undertaken with caution. When Neptune is in the 7th house, opponents might "pull the rug out from under us" in a most surprising way. Discretion (seeing things as they are) and forgiveness are our best deterrents for disappointment.

Neptune in the 8th house engenders inquisitiveness regarding the occult. There exists the possibility of a remarkable clairvoyance or clairaudience. Caution must be exercised, however, because once transported to other worlds, we might be difficult to arouse. These gifts may exist with or without the benefit of a moral bearing. Neptune in the 8th house warns of toxicity in all that we ingest. Neptune within the cusps of the 8th house is *not* the astral signature of those who successfully marry to improve their financial security. There might be subterfuge regarding an inheritance or legacy. A fear of death, if it exists, can be alleviated by an understanding of death as a return to our true home: the starry realm.

Neptune draws the soul toward inspired heights — and therefore finds a happy home in the 9th house (that of ideals). Those of us born under this placement seek beauty in all things; the mind often turns toward religion, mysticism, dreams, the arts, and nature. This, of course, might take us far outside the mainstream, but that is usually of no concern to us. As the 9th is the house of the spiritual master, we might seek guidance from such an individual. We must, however, guard against reaching conclusions by way of our feeling life alone. Ideals and spiritual faculties can be inherited from the father, with whom we usually have a very good relationship. Long-distance journeys might be undertaken in order to escape unfavorable circumstances.

When in the house of the *residence* (the 10th house), Neptune often brings instability in this realm. We can be misled by an ideal (but unrealistic) concept of a different location; changes of residence therefore need to be undertaken with great thought and care. Real estate endeavors that seem altogether secure can dissolve before our eyes. Neptune in the 10th house can also be indicative of a family home that is permeated with an interest in spiritual matters; we might take this up on our own and find that the interest expands as we grow older. We can sometimes observe in the birth home an out-of-the-ordinary atmosphere — or, alternatively, a certain lack of security. Questions of parentage can arise. Neptune in the 10th house asks that we regard ourselves as active participants in the evolution of humanity.

Neptune in the 11th house suggests goals and aspirations that are inspirational (and often of a spiritual nature). The fertile imagination characteristic of this placement, however, is not enough to bring our ideals to realization in the material world. Therefore, the likelihood of our success in this regard will depend upon other indications in the chart (such as Mars or Saturn in aspect to Neptune). We seek the spirit through community and enjoy many friendships among others who also long for its nourishment; these include students of the occult, astrologers, and fine artists. We might long to be part of something "bigger" than ourselves; this is often accompanied, however, by the danger of "losing" ourselves within it. Because of Neptune's ability to weave illusions, discretion is of the utmost importance in choosing our friends—lest they reveal themselves as harboring antipathy toward us. Clarity must be the intention of every communication.

In the 12th house, Neptune (its accidental ruler) suggests a need for an environment that is peaceful and quiet; there is often a love and ease of meditation, as well as a facility for research into the occult. There can be extraordinary spiritual gifts that lead to success in related fields. When Neptune is in a difficult aspect with another planet, we can find ourselves in situations in which our personal freedom is constrained through the treachery and betrayal of others. As Neptune and the 12th house intersect through a shared influence of *sacrifice*, we might be "tried and tested" to the limits of our endurance. And yet, authentic faith allows the cry of Job to resonate within our hearts:

> For I know that my Redeemer lives,
> and at last he will stand upon the Earth;
> and after my skin has been thus destroyed,
> then from my flesh I shall see God,
> whom I shall see on my side,
> and my eyes shall behold, and not another.
> My heart faints within me! (Job 19:25-27)

♇ PLUTO

The influence of Pluto (to the Romans, the god of the underworld) manifests as an unstoppable force that seems to emerge from the depths. And just as there is currently no method of diverting the flow of lava, it's best to accept that profound change is imminent—and to plan accordingly. Earthquakes also provide a telling image by way of the rumbling that is beneath our feet, as well as by the release of subearthly forces through fissures in the Earth's crust. Pluto in the birth chart reveals to us where we can expect such earthquakes to occur—and it is through these same quakes that profound transformation is possible. Pluto brings depth, intensity, and ambition in our approach to the matters of its house. Indeed, such ambition can become obsessive. Because of its association with power, the house of Pluto indicates where we are least inclined to lose control—which is often (at the same time) where we feel fear. We can also see within its sphere of influence the power of intuition—the knowing that lives deep within our bones. The zodiacal sign also gives us a sense of the character of this intuition.

Pluto in the 1st house usually indicates a high level of intelligence. The personality tends to take two forms: either as an intensity that bores into the souls of others like a hot poker, or as meeting the world with absolute calm. But don't let the placid demeanor of these latter individuals mislead you into believing that they are of the kumbaya variety. This placement usually signifies a desire to keep our cards close to the chest, particularly regarding our ambitions. Moreover, it gives us a laser-like focus on what we want to achieve, and we will go to great lengths to realize these goals. Obstacles that are strewn across our path will be overcome methodically; consequently, we will likely be forced to learn how to adapt to crises. The will-to-power impulse conferred by Pluto can be magnified in the first house. Alternatively, *in a way that leaves others completely free*, we might apply our formidable forces of will toward the development of our own individuality. Those of us born under this influence tend to fear anything that we perceive as a threat to our self-realization.

When Pluto is in the 2nd house, we can find ourselves in the grips of a "scarcity mentality," whereby we equate money with survival. The desire for security can become an obsession; this can result in an inability to feel secure despite the bounty around us. The desire-to-acquire might occupy a disproportionate amount of time and energy. There might be multiple sources of income; we can spend prodigiously or guard our resources in a miserly fashion. Though this placement suggests the possibility of dramatic financial changes—even, in the words of Jacques Dorsan, on the eve of harvest[13]—we will likely have the ability to weather these storms.

---

13 Dorsan, *The Clockwise House System*, 153.

Challenges to our security will seem to lead us by the hand toward a renewed sense of what is truly most important to us.

When Pluto is in the 3rd house, the intellect is strengthened. We often feel a need to convince others of our positions. Communications are direct and headed straight to the bottom of the proverbial Mariana Trench, to the exclusion of chitchat and "polite" conversation. Our inclination to leave no stone unturned — while ideal for research or depth psychology — is not universally welcome, and is sometimes received as probing and aggressive. Though diplomacy is not typically a priority to those of us born under this placement, an effort to understand others' perspectives is advised. We long to fly under the radar, lest our strategies be made public. Pluto in the 3rd house invites us to direct our consciousness toward the heights as well as the depths, so that the path that the Angels have set before us can be revealed. There might also exist an intuitive sense of the star that we must follow, as well as an attendant fear of anything that has the power to force us off our path. Those of us who lack a spiritual orientation might fear obstacles to personal ambitions.

When in the 4th house, Pluto confers an uncanny ability to see beneath the appearances of others. Pluto's presence in the house of destiny is suggestive of focus upon personal goals, but many crises will likely be strewn in our path; achievement of these goals can be hindered by upheaval and by the imposition of constraints imposed by others. However, we often brandish a *BRING IT ON* approach to these obstacles, and — somehow, as if by magic — we usually manage to remove them from our path. Periods of ground-shifting change, while not always enjoyed, will be weathered with dexterity. Once we achieve our goals, however, we might find that we are no longer in possession of the goodwill of our professional associates. Sometimes destiny demands that we reinvent ourselves professionally. Periods of crisis can include difficulties within the mother-child relationship. In light of the fact that the 4th house signifies achievement and success, it simultaneously warns against measuring success by material metrics alone. Among those of us born with this placement, we can observe a dread (even a *fear*) of the exposure of our weaknesses.

In the 5th house, Pluto supercharges creativity and inventiveness in the intellect. Because this is the house of risk, there will exist a willingness to involve ourselves in financial endeavors characterized by uncertainty; Pluto compels us to take everything "to the edge." For those of us born under this placement, a voracious desire to partake in all that life has to offer can manifest — whereby we may be dragged into a cycle of being driven by our desires. And yet, we will go to great lengths to avoid feeling trapped! Will we search for the door that takes us beyond the serpent's world — or will we remain within it, hanging on for dear life? When Pluto is in the 5th house, it carries with it the danger that matters of romance can be all-consuming, or even tinged with a whiff of taboo. We must guard against sentimental relationships characterized by obsession, whether we are its subject or object. Pluto in the 5th house suggests that our education is unlikely to be free of upsets. Though our relationships with our children (a 5th house matter) can be made difficult by tumultuous circumstances, our devotion to them will remain unquestioned.

Pluto in the house of imposed tasks (the 6th house) indicates a Herculean ability to be productive while engaged in such activities. When this tendency is not held in check, we can become "workaholics," loath to settle for anything short of perfection. In other words, we might aspire to the impossible! It goes without saying that health and vitality could suffer as a result. We can sometimes observe a preference for work that occurs outside the limelight. Power struggles may arise at the workplace; Pluto in the 6th house invites us to contemplate our own need for conquest in this arena. What is it that we wish to serve with all the passion at our disposal? This placement warns of a partner seeking to control our actions in a restrictive manner. It is also suggestive that the spouse we seek might be a person of depth, intensity, and commitment.

When in the 7th house, Pluto confers a talent for "reading" others — which (of course) will not always be welcome. No one enjoys being figured out so easily! We may harbor a hidden fear of rejection. Those of us born under this placement tend to demand depth and intensity in relationships (all-or-nothing); we seek the association of powerful people, whom we tend to attract. When diplomacy is mastered, we might obtain positions of high rank. There can be power struggles between associates, and we may feel the need to continuously defend our own interests. For this we are well-suited! Marriage will create a dramatic change in life circumstances, and we might feel that the union was unavoidable, "in the stars." With Pluto in the 7th house, we are encouraged to gain control over our volcanic reserves of willforces in order that we treat others mercifully rather than as obstacles to be overcome.

Pluto is in accidental rulership in the 8th house, where it pushes us toward mystery, the occult, or an interest in death—any of which can become a fear and an obsession. This realm of investigation need not lead us into a profound darkness (though this is a risk for the unprepared), particularly if a longing for nearness to spiritual light underlies our motive for traversing darkness. However, it accentuates the need for spiritual protection if we are to do so. Ideally, those of us born under this placement are encouraged to pay close attention to our dream life. We are capable of taking charge masterfully in the event of a crisis—an ability that will not be overlooked by others! We can also observe gifted insights into the psychological motivations of others.

In the 9th house, Pluto engenders a passion for faraway places that can become a guiding principle of our lives. This can be driven, in part, by a fear of being "fenced in." We might even initiate a self-imposed exile from the world that has been familiar to us. We can observe a deep faith (which may not be particularly religious at all) and an insatiable quest for the truth. However, our strong convictions are susceptible to the taint of dogmatism. A religious or philosophical about-face can occur following a profound period of doubt. This is a good placement for higher education, research, or the study of esotericism. Pluto in the 9th house can indicate a difficult relationship with the father—or *as a father*—that might be characterized by power struggles. Pluto in the 9th house asks us to turn our attention to the heart—where contemplation and action are united.

When in the 10th house, Pluto can signify a deep attachment to the family or clan, whereby the birth family can continue to have a significant influence over us. In some cases, we fear being severed from our heritage. There can be skeletons in the family closet. Tussles over family possessions (including real estate) are possible. Intuition regarding the properties of the Earth can be in evidence. Changes of residence can occur under strange circumstances, and crises can compromise harmony within the residence. When we find this placement in the charts of those who had explosive childhood environments, we typically observe (simultaneously) a demonstration of victory over these difficult circumstances. The 10th house supports our interest in our ancestry—a form of *continuity*—but warns us against determinism, which can enchain us to it. Can we instead say *yes* to the promise of the future, and feel it carry us forward?

In the 11th house (that of community, friendship, and connectedness in general), Pluto can engender a fear of loneliness, which might be based upon an intuition about the importance of friends to all born under this placement. Pluto in the 11th house is therefore accompanied by the warning that friendships must be tended with care. Furthermore, it suggests that community will be of primary importance in our lives—indeed, it might be the *source* of our spiritual vitality—making it all the more important that we approach it with humility and a resignation of personal control. It's even possible that our survival might be somehow tied up with our community. This configuration can foster devoted humanitarianism or, alternatively, an unscrupulous attitude toward attaining our long-term goals. The death of a friend can affect us deeply, thereby changing the course of our destiny.

In the 12th house, Pluto can give rise to salvos from hidden enemies. We seem to be protected from serious harm, however, and are adept at emerging victorious from any challenges that might arise. Those of us born under this placement often fear the coming to light of our deepest secrets; we therefore typically prefer anonymity to the spotlight. However, Pluto in the 12th house is suggestive that these "secrets" will periodically present themselves *until* we are willing to shine light upon them and acknowledge their content. As long as we leave them in darkness, we chain ourselves to the layers beneath our feet, thereby renouncing an existence *between* heaven and Earth—the dwelling place of spiritual man. This configuration typically confers much reserve; we might therefore find satisfaction in work that is conducted in seclusion, or that occurs in isolation. Pluto in the 12th house may engender an intuition about what lies behind appearances, making this an excellent placement for research, the occult, or psychology. There is often an attunement to human suffering that can weigh on us heavily.

When a house is devoid of planets—known as "empty"—the affairs of that house will typically not be the focus of our karmic work. It is not quite like drawing a "Get Out of Jail Free" card, but it means that the Angels will likely not be calling on you to confront the affairs of that house again and again throughout your lifetime. Nothing in the second house? Earning a living will not be a major issue for you—meaning that *a)* you have all you need, or *b)* you don't mind *not* having it, or *c)* issues of resources tend to be resolved without extraordinary effort. While empty houses represent domains that require less of our attention, they nevertheless describe human domains common to us all! When there exist no planets to enlighten us regarding this sphere of earthly activity, we look to the ruler of the primary cusp (the one with the greater zodiacal degree) for insight into the character of the goings-on in that house.

If, on the other hand, you have three or more planets (called a "stellium") in one house, hang on! You will be summoned—often—not only to question its concerns, but also to come to terms with those matters over which it has influence.

Though astrological charts display only the northern perspective—the Ascendant on the left, the Descendant of the right, the EZ at the top, the EN at the bottom—it is a remarkable fact that their validity is in evidence for all births in the southern hemisphere. If we were to adapt a birth chart for the southern hemisphere, we'd be none the wiser. This is because the houses, in keeping with diurnal movement, would proceed *anti-clockwise*. The key point here is that the zodiacal and house directions remain (as they must) at odds. *Perhaps it would be more accurate (and engender less confusion) if the clockwise house system were renamed the "diurnal house system."*

The interpretation of this southern chart would be *identical* to that of the northern one. The planets and stars still rise in the east and set in the west! All of the planets are in the same signs and houses! The angles and cusps are unchanged! Therefore, the northern clockwise house chart (though understandably vexing to our southern friends) is equally valid for events that occur in the southern hemisphere. For simplicity's sake, we will leave it at that.

8

ELEMENTAL BALANCE IN THE CHART

ONCE YOU KNOW WHICH houses are the focus of the chart, look next at its elemental balance.

Each sign of the zodiac expresses one of the four elements — fire, earth, air, and water — in archetypal form. The geocentric chart is an "astral document" and therefore can't be looked to for insight into the lively subject of temperament, which is reflected in the etheric body. (Although, in my experience, the geocentric chart of the *conception* of an individual does reveal the dominant temperament that will develop in the life to come.)

The ten planets in the birth chart bear a certain distribution among the fire signs, earth signs, air signs, and water signs. Tally them up. The Angels do not bother to put up billboards that say: *You have get-up-and-go! You're a people person! You're an intuitive thinker!* Instead, they do everything in their power to draw our attention to whatever would best serve our development as *spiritual* beings. This is rarely the easiest thing to do.

One who "masters" the elements could be described as an individual of intensity (fire) who is serene (air), mobile (water), and firm (earth).[1]

Sometimes it happens that there is already a balance among the elements in the chart: two or three planets associated with each element. This suggests that the characteristics we can associate with one element should not unduly outweigh those of another. Alternatively, a predominance of planets in one particular element invites us to familiarize ourselves with the spiritual archetype of that element and endeavor to live in accordance with it — whether or not we feel that we are already so inclined.

 FIRE

The fire element bestows initiative, intensity, creativity, and leadership. It inclines us to want to get things done, and pronto! *Fire longs to awaken others.* It bears vision and the gift of inspiration. Aries inspires ideals; Leo inspires loyalty and nobility of spirit; Sagittarius inspires through its quest for meaning.

Fire implies enthusiasm — it awakens us each morning, asking us what we love and what we'll devote ourselves to today. The fire element bestows upon us the ability to assert ourselves when necessary, and to stand up for ourselves and for others before the world. Where would we be without our fiery protectors?

The fire of our prayers unites us to the spiritual world. Fire is decisive and purposeful; its warmth radiates outward, toward others. Using the analogy of a wood fire, we could posit that the ideal fire is one that burns steadily. We need to tend and feed that fire at a steady pace, so that it neither goes out altogether nor burns out of control at the expense of others. Fire's weakness is pride; it sometimes confers a desire to be in control: *Step aside — I'll handle it!*

When *no* planets occupy Aries, Leo, or Sagittarius in the chart, it suggests that work on the fiery aspects of self is not your primary task for this incarnation. There may already exist a strong connection to the spiritual world; it is also not uncommon to see this arrangement in the charts of "firebrands," but this is not necessarily so. In either case, then, Angels are asking us to direct our efforts elsewhere.

If, however, we see many planets in the sentinels of fire in the zodiac, it usually indicates that we need to find avenues of expression for intensity and enthusiasm that have yet to be kindled. Alternatively, for those of us who consider ourselves to be "full of fire" already, this arrangement suggests that we are being

---

1 Tomberg, *Meditations on the Tarot*, 165.

called upon to *better manage* the fiery qualities we already possess. Examples of poor control of the fire influence include impatience, impulsiveness, and a taste for confrontation.

 EARTH

The earth element confers firmness, stability, constancy, and perseverance. The influence of the element of earth sets us *with balance* upon the ground beneath our feet. It leads us toward a feeling for the Mother who dwells within the heart of our planet. Earth is realistic and dependable. Taurus thinks rationally and seeks security; Virgo separates the wheat from the chaff to determine what is useful; Capricorn longs to climb the highest peaks.

When we behave in a practical, measured manner, our deeds express the quality of the earth element. When unbalanced by the other elements, its influence can lead to rigidity and an unwillingness to change — thereby barring our way to the future. Rigidity, as we know, can be thought of as a hastening of the aging process; it blocks our receptivity to the vivifying force of the Mother within Shambhala.

Being "grounded" allows us to withstand storms of all kinds, including trials of the soul. If our roots are deep enough, we will not topple. Through the influence of the earth element, we are steadfast. The earth element imparts rootedness: to the planet, to our earthly tasks, and to the ones we love. It gives us the inclination to prepare and the wherewithal to endure. It supports life.

If a chart lacks planets in Taurus, Virgo, and Capricorn, expression of earth qualities will not be our key focus this time around. When these planets are found in the charts of individuals who already possess an innate abundance of earth forces (faithfulness of heart, precision in thinking, and firmness of will), the suggestion is the same: to turn our attention to the development of the other elements.

A good number of planets in the earth signs can be regarded as an angelic suggestion to put our effort and energy into the development of earth traits, *over and above* the others. This distribution of planets is often bestowed upon those among us whose urge for change overpowers any inclination to reach our taproots toward the Mother below our feet; however, when an earth-heavy chart applies to an individual who has already mastered steadfastness, it might be the case that a certain refinement of earthy characteristics is called for — in order to bypass any tendency toward rigidity, melancholy, or self-absorption.

 AIR

The air element carries an impulse toward *elongation*. Air moves ceaselessly among us, and — by way of the lungs — within us. When unencumbered, air is light and draws upward with joy; it thus signifies levity. Air seeks to communicate. Gemini gathers and disseminates information; Libra's focus is relationships; Aquarius sifts through a universe of knowledge in order to know truth.

Those who identify strongly with the air element are social creatures who like to keep moving — joyously looking for the next thing to capture their attention — in an effort to outsmart "the dreaded state of boredom." Air seeks stimulation. Air is open to the periphery; it stands for *consciousness* and *clarity*. The air element renders us inclusive and interested in all — and able to assess the full scope of a situation.

When we master the element of air, we experience serenity, its highest expression. This requires a certain discipline of soul — for, as light as it is, air can scatter our attention like so many lost kites. We can thereby find ourselves unable (and unwilling) to commit to anything or anyone. Alternatively, living into the social nature of the air element is the antidote for a feeling of apathy — the condition of lacking warm interest in others.

A chart that has *no* planets in Gemini, Libra, or Aquarius suggests that we might devote our efforts toward development of the qualities of the other elements. This typically — but not always — indicates a person who already identifies strongly with air. Whether or not this is so, we're not to tarry here, as our path to growth will likely be found elsewhere.

A chart that is *overflowing* with planets in air signs asks us to attend to the cultivation of "air" qualities in our life. This will be quite a challenge for those who revel in solitude.

Alternatively, individuals with this planetary arrangement who already identify strongly with the air element will need to work harder to resist the dual hazards of becoming avoidant of conflict and "untethered."

WATER

When water adapts to the shape of the space in which it finds itself—a stream bed, a lake, or an ocean—it expresses its adaptability, one of water's great strengths. Water carries an inherent sense of rhythm across time; it can be still, as it is in a deep lake, or raging, like Niagara Falls. It can ebb and flow. Water represents true thinking, which can be characterized as *flowing and intuitive*—in contrast to the gathering and storage of *information*. When water is calm and limpid, it represents harmony and the peace of meditation. Water bears an impulse of belonging. Cancer concentrates on the family; Scorpio seeks attachment within intimate relationships; Pisces seeks unity with an ocean of souls.

One of the highest gifts of the water element is resilience—indeed, living into this element allows us to respond quickly to changes of circumstance. Sometimes, this can come to expression in compromise. It can easily be imagined that—if dysfunctional—this can lead to being taken advantage of by those inclined to impose their will upon us. Additionally, the water element confers sensitivity to the cares of others, as well as to subtle energies that work invisibly in the world.

A chart devoid of planets in Cancer, Scorpio and Pisces suggests that development of water qualities is to be overlooked in favor of those of fire, earth, and air. Although this often signifies that we have come into the world with adequate resilience and a capacity for intuitive thinking, it also suggests that our attention and efforts are needed in the development of the qualities of the other elements.

For those of us whose water signs are filled with planets, we might need to do everything we can to listen for the "knock of intuition" that is struggling to be heard. Attention to the rhythms of the Earth and of human biography are also advised, as is a daily eurythmy practice. If we already relate strongly to water qualities, having four or more planets in these signs suggests that our efforts might be directed toward avoiding the pitfalls common to "water dominance" (e.g., dependence and "giving in" at the expense of our own interests).

The study of the elemental balance in the chart reveals another facet of the dissonance between the tropical and sidereal zodiacs. Because the tropical zodiac is currently ahead of the sidereal by 25°, the subject will be offered an entirely different distribution of the elements within the chart. This, in and of itself, provides the foundation for a comparison between the two systems.

Again, we don't look at elemental balance to receive confirmation about who we are. Instead, we contemplate it in order to understand how we might better respond to the individual karmic challenges that we agreed to undertake *while we were dwelling within the planetary spheres.*

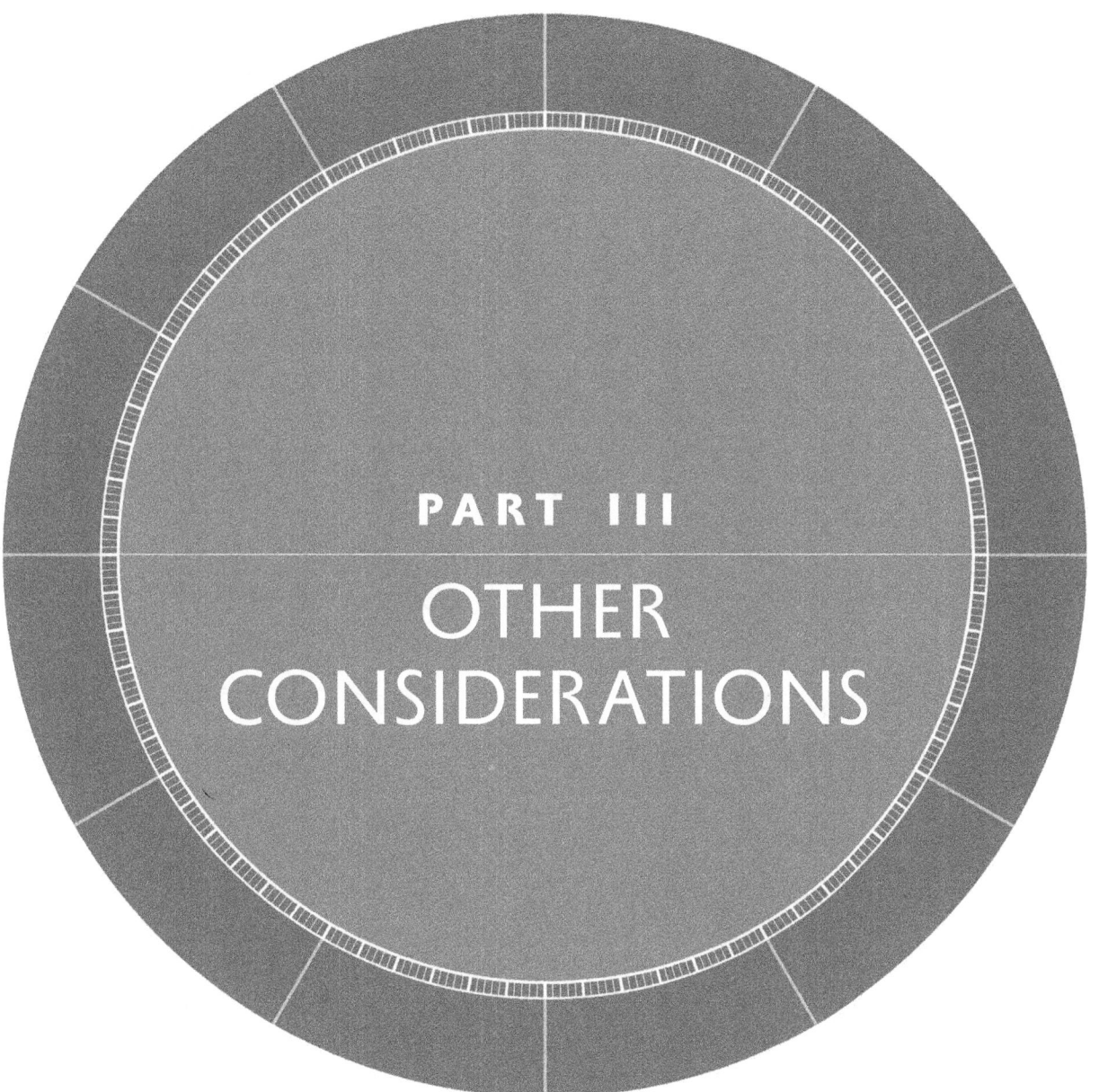

PART III
OTHER CONSIDERATIONS

1
RULERSHIP

THE CONCEPT OF PLANETARY rulership of the zodiacal signs was not known in antiquity; it first appeared in Ptolemy's *Tetrabiblos* (2nd c.). The idea is this: that each planet "rules" one (or two) signs of the zodiac, and that when in that sign, the ruler can most easily come to full, harmonious expression. Originally limited to the visible planets (Sun, Moon, Mercury, Venus, Mars, Jupiter, and Saturn), the transcendentals have been swept into the mix since their discovery in 1781 (Uranus), 1846 (Neptune), and 1930 (Pluto).

Although the rulers could almost be thought of as prerequisite to understanding their associated zodiacal constellations (for they assist us in approaching the mighty resolves of the zodiacal beings), I believe that the term is misleading in that it suggests the planets are exerting influence over the zodiac — and such a concept would turn celestial hierarchy on its head. I'm in no position to upend two millennia of convention, but I believe that when (for example) the Sun is before the stars of Leo (which it rules), we should think of the Sun not as "ruler," but as the planet best able to interpret the spiritual impulses of the Lion. Rulership expresses a *cosmic compatibility*.

The zodiacal sign that a planet rules is known as its "home" or its "domicile." While in this sign, a planet works most easily and harmoniously — i.e., without conflict. I like to think of this domicile as the place within the circle of twelve where the planet can put its feet up on the couch with a delighted exhale and say: "I'm *home*!" A planet in rulership in a birth chart is suggestive that, throughout the associated earthly life, the influence of the ruler will bear an added degree of celestial support. And while Mars in Aries (for example) might contribute to our ability to get our initiatives up and running, it might also demand that we control the inclination to become overly argumentative and impulsive.

It is also the case that a planet is "least at ease" when before the zodiacal sign *opposite* one that it rules. (This is known as being in "exile" or in "detriment.") A planet in exile in a birth chart suggests that the native will need to work harder to bring the planet's qualities to positive expression. Put another way, we could say that the placement provides *resistance* to the native. Within astrosophy, we can regard this as "the fertile soil of spiritual growth."

The celestial wheel shown here depicts the distribution of zodiacal rulers known since Ptolemy.

It would be difficult to conclude that this arrangement lacks purpose and wisdom. If we divide the circle in two where the Sun meets the Moon, we establish one side that begins with the Sun (the "star of the day") and another side that begins with the Moon (the "star of the night"). Interestingly, the axis thus formed — through the Cancer-Leo cusp and the Capricorn-Aquarius cusp — marks the two zodiacal signs thought by the ancients to be the portals for the incarnating (Cancer) and excarnating (Capricorn) souls — the so-called gateways of life and death. The Leo-to-Capricorn side of the rulership wheel begins with the Sun, the "star of the day." From this point of view, the rulers advance (as they do in our solar system) in order of increasing remoteness from the Sun: Mercury, Venus, Mars, Jupiter, Saturn. We observe the same order when we turn to the Cancer-to-Aquarius side of the wheel, which begins with the Moon, the "star of the night."

Additionally, as we study the wheel of rulers, we observe that Venus (Taurus and Libra) and Mars (Scorpio and Aries) form two opposing pairs, as do Mercury (Gemini and Virgo) and Jupiter (Sagittarius and Pisces). The Sun (Leo) and Moon (Cancer) are opposite the two Saturn-ruled signs, Capricorn and Aquarius. These pairings reveal profound symbiotic relationships that exist in the macrocosm: Venus and Mars, which are different in every way (but are inexorably attracted to one another); Mercury and Jupiter, which are representative of human intelligence and cosmic wisdom; and Saturn (cosmic will) with the Sun (moral will) and the Moon (personal will).

What of the transcendental planets? Since their discovery, it is commonly accepted that they each serve as a "secondary ruler" to one of the zodiacal signs. Uranus acts as a secondary ruler of Aquarius; Neptune, of Pisces; and Pluto, of Scorpio. So convinced of this, some astrologers have chucked the classical rulers of Aquarius, Pisces, and Scorpio altogether, upending what has been known for millennia!

It is true that things need to be upended from time to time. A clear connection can certainly be discerned between the natures of the transcendentals and the signs that they are said to rule. At the very least, I would refine the term *secondary* by stating that, because of our unusual relationship to the transcendentals, it should be said that they "rule from afar"—as if from behind a veil. Furthermore, since it is not possible to advance the thesis of secondary rulership with the same certainty that we have for that of primary rulership, caution is called for. Perhaps we were too hasty in making these assignments.

Jacques Dorsan, the great French siderealist, offers us a far richer analysis[1] that advances the wisdom which lives behind the distribution of the rulers described above. Beyond Saturn lies Uranus; beyond Uranus, Neptune; and beyond Neptune, Pluto. If we turn to the Sun's half of the rulership circle, we could apply secondary rulership of Uranus, Neptune, and Pluto in the following way: Uranus/Aquarius, Neptune/Pisces, Pluto/Aries. Turning to the side of the circle that begins with the Moon, Uranus would

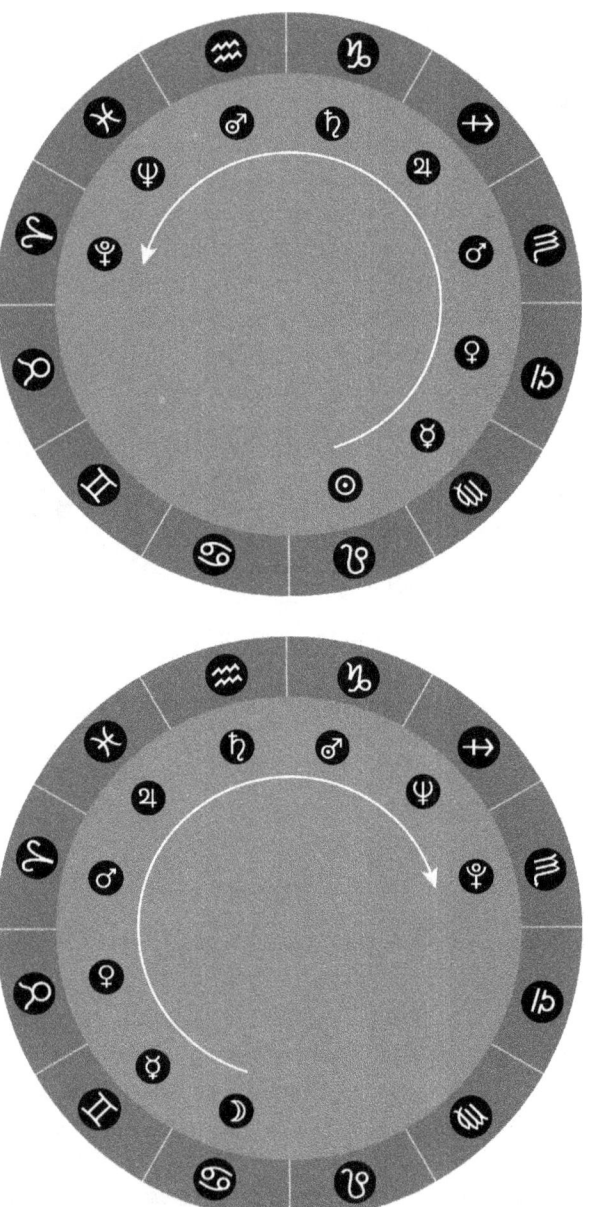

naturally be the secondary ruler of Capricorn, Neptune of Sagittarius, and Pluto of Scorpio. Dorsan is suggesting that the transcendentals exert rulership in a more *visible* way (consistent with outer reality) through Aquarius, Pisces, and Aries—and in a way that is more *hidden*

---

1 Jacques Dorsan, *Retour au Zodiaque des Étoiles: Vous n'êtes pas né sous le signe que vous croyez* [*Return to the Stellar Zodiac: You're Not the Sign You Think You Are*] (Paris: Dervy-Livres, 1986), 51-53.

(consistent with suprasensible reality) through Capricorn, Sagittarius, and Scorpio.

Further research will determine the validity of Dorsan's reasoning. In the meantime, we will continue to accept Uranus, Neptune, and Pluto as the secondary rulers of Aquarius, Pisces, and Scorpio, respectively.

Because of the relationship between the houses and the signs — through the use of analogy — planets are said to be in "accidental rulership" and "accidental exile" when in the *house* that corresponds to the *sign* of rulership or exile. For example, because the Moon rules Cancer (the fourth sign), the Moon in the 4th house achieves accidental rulership, and has therefore a certain affinity with the affairs of the house. Alternatively, the Moon in the opposite house (the 10th) is said to be in accidental exile, where it is considered to be less "at ease."

2

EXALTATION

THE TEACHING OF EXALTATION is one of the oldest principles in astrology; it reveals that there is one place among the circle of fixed stars at which each planet is its most powerful and influential. Like the original sidereal zodiac, exaltation is rooted in ancient Babylon, where inscriptions indicate that its origin *predates* the introduction of the sidereal zodiac (around 500 BC) by more than two centuries.

To the Babylonians, the concept of exaltation was known as *qaqqar nisirti*,[1] or the "place of secret revelation." Because these "places" were identified *before* any zodiacal coordinates came into being, the Babylonian understanding of exaltation must reflect a different consciousness—one that was able to intuit clairvoyantly the "place of secret revelation" of each planet. To understand this consciousness, we must look to the stars. It was only later that the exaltations of the classical planets were assigned specific *degrees* of the zodiac.

Let's jump ahead to the geocentric points of exaltation that are elaborated in the Zoroastrian text known as the *Bundahisn*.[2] They refer to the moment in time that might be imagined as *the beginning of human incarnation*—when human evolution (characterized by toil, suffering, and death) began. We might also think of this as the moment when humanity's consciousness was awakened to the cosmic world. Though this event was accompanied by the "rushing in" of Ahriman—when the previously motionless world was set into motion—the *Bundahisn* indicates that the Sun (and all of the other planets) at the "birth of humanity" are exalted.[3] Perhaps this occurred in order to give us the best possible start!

We might notice the addition of the Moon's Nodes in the exaltation panoply; their exaltations seem to be of Zoroastrian origin (age unknown) and designate a special relationship between the Nodes and the Milky Way—for these points of exaltation occur very close to where the great band of stars of our galaxy intersects the zodiac (currently at 5° Gemini and 5° Sagittarius). In the Zoroastrian astrology of old, the Milky Way was known as the "brilliance of the dragon,"

Sun	19°	Aries
Moon	3°	Taurus
Mercury	15°	Virgo
Venus	27°	Pisces
Mars	28°	Capricorn
Jupiter	15°	Cancer
Saturn	21°	Libra
North Node	3°	Gemini
South Node	3°	Sagittarius

---

1   Robert Powell and David Bowden, *Astrogeographia* (Gt Barrington, MA: Lindisfarne Books, 2012), 31.
2   The *Bundahisn* is the "Pahlavi (Zoroastrian) equivalent of the biblical Genesis, which expounds Zoroastrian ideas on cosmology and cosmogony." Robert, *Hermetic Astrology*, vol. 1, 13.
3   Powell, *Hermetic Astrology*, vol. 1, 13-17.

descriptive of the creature that seemed to encircle the celestial globe.[4]

All of these points of exaltation are "fixed" in the sense that they are accepted by all astrologers and considered to be immutable across time. This raises another problem for tropical astrology! For if the Sun is exalted at 19° Aries, we are presented with two different dates at which this occurs—the 8th of April in the tropical zodiac and the 4th of May[5] in the sidereal. The Sun *can't* be exalted twice in one year!

It must be emphasized that this geocentric horoscope reflects the *spiritual* perception of the beginning of time. In fact, since Mercury can never be more than 28° from the Sun, this horoscope is an impossibility in *scientific* terms. We therefore need to place before our imagination the significance of the planets "enthroned" at exaltation *at the moment of the birth of the world*. This is a spiritual reality that is remembered each time the planets return to their position at this "birth."

Through the lens of modern astronomy, exaltation might be viewed as the peak of a planet's apparent orbit around the Earth. For example, as the Sun reaches the high point of its yearly circuit around the Earth at the summer solstice, we can think of it as "exalted." The other planets trace a similar path, each moving slightly above and below the ecliptic as they circle the Earth. Directly opposite the zodiacal degree of exaltation is the degree of a planet's "fall"—the lowest point of its orbit. The two points at which the orbit crosses the ecliptic are its *ascending* node and its *descending* node. In the case of the Sun, these nodes are referred to as the spring and autumn equinoxes, respectively.

Might we look at the "birth of the world" as recording the moment in time when the Sun was at summer solstice? In this case the vernal point in the horoscope of the world can be determined easily—simply by subtracting 90° from the exaltation point of the Sun, as this is the invariable distance between the degree of the vernal point and that of the summer solstice.[6] This puts the vernal point in this horoscope at 19° Capricorn. Powell wrote:

> [The vernal point] is therefore the point in the zodiac where a new solar impulse, drawn from the sphere of the zodiac, begins to unfold during the course of the year... This gives rise to the zodiacal ages, specified by the vernal point's location in the various signs of the sidereal zodiac, [which is] determined by the precession of the equinoxes.[7]

The last zodiacal age of Capricorn occurred during the Atlantean Epoch (between 21,386 and 19,226 BC). This is immensely important to our study, because it allows us to surmise that the "birth of the world"—when Ahriman "rushed in"—occurred during the zodiacal age of the Goat, in the same way that the age of Aries provided the background for the birth of Jesus. This offers a deeper understanding of the following passage from Matthew's gospel:

> When the Son of Man comes in his glory, and all the Angels with him, then he will sit on his glorious throne. Before him will be gathered all the nations, and he will separate them from one another as a shepherd separates the sheep from the goats, and he will place the sheep at this right hand, but the goats at the left. (Matthew 25:31-3)

Here it is necessary to take a detour into the fundamental hermetic concept of "enthronement." The Egyptians observed the four solar markers of the year—vernal point, summer solstice, autumn point, and winter solstice[8]—with great interest. Indeed, they were integral to their cosmology, for the Sun's passage through these points played a significant role in the mystery tradition of ancient Egypt.[9] Many pyramids (and the Sphinx) face east, so that they greet the rising Sun at both *equinoxes*; whereas numerous temples are oriented so that they face the rising

---

4   Powell and Dann, *The Astrological Revolution*, 104.
5   These dates are relevant for 2022.
6   The four cardinal seasonal points of the Sun's annual apparent journey around the Earth are always 90° apart. The same principle can be applied to the following four points of any planet's orbit: ascending node, exaltation (or "enthronement"), descending node, and fall (or "imprisonment"). By knowing the degree of any one of the four points, the others can be readily determined.
7   Powell, *Hermetic Astrology*, vol. 1, 53.
8   These were explained from the astronomical perspective in the third chapter of Part I.
9   Powell, *Hermetic Astrology*, vol. 1, 11-12.

or setting Sun at one of the *solstices* (Karnak being one example).

The summer solstice in particular represented to the Egyptians a special time at which revelations from the cosmos might reach those among humankind who were receptive to them. The Sun-god at the zodiacal degree of the summer solstice was thus imagined to be "enthroned"—in its full power and intensity. Alternatively, the Sun was considered to be "imprisoned" (and thus weakened) at the winter solstice.

We can expand upon this concept by imagining—from the Egyptian perspective—the annual anticlockwise orbit of the Sun around the Earth[10] as the stages of the reign of a king. At the top of this circle is the degree of the Sun's *enthronement*; at the bottom, the degree of its *imprisonment*. Directly between these points are the spring and autumn equinoxes, which can be imagined as balance points between the other two.

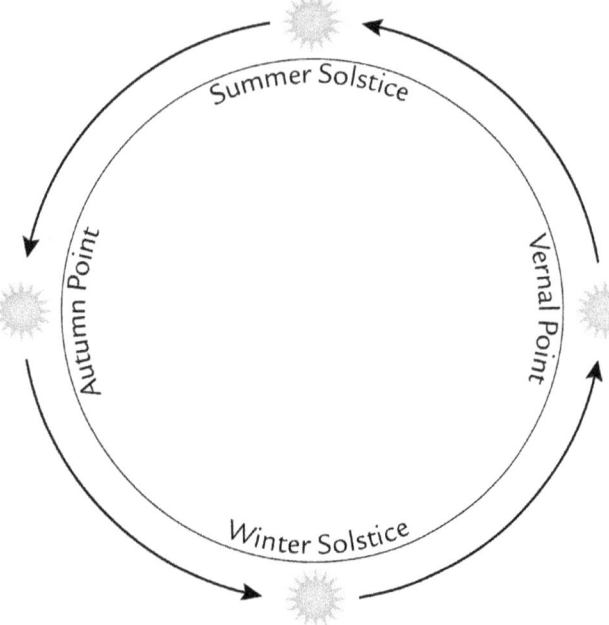

The four solar markers of the year

Let's begin at the spring equinox: the moment that the "king" rises from the relative obscurity of the region below the circle to the visible world above it. This is the "king's" ascending node, or vernal point. From here he begins his ascent toward his "throne" at the top of the circle: the king's summer solstice. Once he takes his seat, he is *enthroned*. From this position, he is best able to radiate love and wisdom toward his kingdom upon the Earth.

When the king steps off his throne following the summer solstice—and embarks upon his downward journey toward the fall equinox—we can feel the decline of his command. Once he crosses the descending node (from above to below) at the autumn point, he leaves behind the "visible" portion of the wheel and enters the darkness of the world below it. The king continues to cede power as he moves downward, until he finds himself *imprisoned* at the winter solstice. When the king is able to break free of his constraints, he begins his ascendency toward the ascending node once again.

Because a planet at exaltation in an astrological chart signifies that the planet is at its "place of secret revelation," it should be seen as both a gift and a spiritual commission that is best not squandered. But just as righteousness is stalked by darkness, so also do planets at exaltation attract the attention of adversarial beings. These beings work to distort each planet's influence into its lowest form; therefore we are called upon to remain vigilant so that their efforts cannot succeed. For example, Jupiter at exaltation can confer natural authority, generosity, perspective, and wisdom. Through the workings of maleficent beings, however, we might succumb to egotism and be strongly tempted to coerce others to achieve our aims.

When 180° from the point of exaltation, a planet is said to be in "fall"; this is the point at which a planet is deemed to be at its weakest. The presence in a birth chart of a planet at its fall can be regarded in two ways: Either the planet's characteristics are not meant to take center stage in the life to come—or, it is the intention of the Angels that we work all the more diligently to bring the planet's positive qualities to expression.

A planet at any degree of its zodiacal sign of geocentric exaltation will confer strength of expression—as will a planet in the house that,

---

10 This is to be distinguished from the diurnal movement of the planets and stars around the Earth that is a result of the Earth's rotation on its axis. Diurnal movement is experienced as clockwise in the northern hemisphere, and anticlockwise in the southern.

by analogy, corresponds to its *sign* of exaltation. For example, the Sun at any degree of Aries (the first sign) *or* the Sun in the first house (analogous to Aries) will be noteworthy. Planets are said to be in "accidental exaltation" and "accidental fall" when they occupy the house analogous to their zodiacal signs of exaltation and fall. We can use the example of Saturn to illustrate this point. Saturn is exalted in Libra (the seventh sign) and is conferred accidental exaltation when in the 7th house. It is therefore in "fall" in Aries (the first sign), and in "accidental fall" when in the 1st house.

Though the invisible axes that connect the planets and Moon's Nodes move backward through the zodiac over time (each at its own rate),[11] the points of *primal*—or *classical*—exaltation of the Sun, Moon, Mercury, Venus, Mars, Jupiter, Saturn, and the Nodes are "fixed." The fixed exaltations might be thought of as commemorations of the birth of the world. Let's endeavor to look at the exaltations through the eyes of the ancient stargazers.

When we contemplate the fixed exaltation of the Sun at 19° Aries, we can imagine the Sun before fiery Aries as the upright individual who—although he is free to act on his own behalf—chooses to devote himself to what he believes in. The Sun's nature is radiant; it reaches outward. There exists no obvious stellar association at this degree of the Ram, which lies just beyond the stars of its horns. If we venture beyond the Ram, however, we notice another factor of possible importance. The exaltation of the Sun is 60° from *Sirius* (at 19° Gemini)—which is sometimes referred to as the star of Isis. This angular separation (known as a sextile) confers harmony. Might it be that a harmonious relationship to Isis (the divine feminine) enhances the power and glory of the Sun (the divine masculine)?[12] Another consideration is the positioning of the exaltation nearly opposite to that of Saturn. These planets are felt to be opposite in nature, which perhaps suggests a power in any opposition between them (Steiner's natal Sun and Saturn were in opposition, though not exalted.) The Sun was at 19° Aries during the nighttime conversation between Jesus and Nicodemus (9/Apr/30).

When we contemplate the fixed exaltation of the Moon at 3° Taurus, we observe the Moon entering the star cluster known as the Pleiades (5° Taurus), whose stars are the seven "sisters" (the daughters of Atlas) who stand in loving community as one. Indeed, the Pleiades bear the mystery of the "secret revelation" of the Moon. When before the stars of the Bull, personal will (Moon) is brought into a sacred communion with divine will (Taurus); the Pleiades thereby ennoble the personal will so that we might act in the best interests of the human community. The Moon was at 3° Taurus a short time before the healing of the paralyzed man.

When we contemplate the fixed exaltation of Mercury at 15° Virgo, we encounter what can be imagined as the womb of the Virgin. Among the stars of Virgo (an earth sign), Mercury maintains its communion with the healing forces of the Earth. Aligned with this degree of the Virgin is *Vindematrix* (15¼° Virgo), the one who eternally cultivates the new wine of divine love. When Mercury is within the folds of the Virgin's mantle, purity of thought is especially accessible to us. Virgo blesses Mercury with the faculty of courtesy, whereby we might avoid communications that wound others. Mercury was near this degree at the Baptism of Jesus.

When we contemplate the fixed exaltation of Venus at 27° Pisces—we do not find alignment with a specific star. Instead, this zodiacal degree leads us to the celestial cord that connects the two Pisces fish, whereby Venus is suspended between heaven and Earth. In this region of the fixed stars, we can imagine Venus swimming with the speed and adaptability of a mermaid as she seeks a connection to all in the human family. Perhaps it is here that Venus is most willing to sacrifice on behalf of humanity—for Venus was very near this degree throughout the Passion of Christ. The exaltation of Venus is sextile (59°) to that of Mars, suggesting that a harmonious interaction between the forces of

---

11 This is known as *precession*.
12 At the time of the age of Taurus, when the Egyptian culture was dominant, the Christ spirit had descended to the level of the Sun. The Egyptians beheld the Christ as Osiris—hence the special connection to Isis through Sirius.

the two planets is foundational to the higher manifestation of both.

When we contemplate the fixed exaltation of Mars at 28° Capricorn, we find Mars in communion with *Deneb Algedi* (28¾° Capricorn), the star that marks the tail of the Goat. In the animal's tail lies the physical representation of concentrated will-forces. These, along with the inherent perseverance of Capricorn's ruler—Saturn—temper the impulsive instincts of Mars. Courage, the Capricorn virtue, enables our warrior to overcome fear in the face of change. When exalted, Mars might incline us to accomplish spiritual deeds upon the Earth. Mars was very near this degree at the healing of the nobleman's son.

When we contemplate the fixed exaltation of Jupiter at 15° Cancer, we are drawn to the region of the fixed stars marking the end of Praesepe, the star cluster otherwise known as the Beehive or the Manger. Why would the Emperor be brought here? Ancient stargazers believed this star cluster to be region of the fixed stars by which souls descend into incarnation in order to gather the nectar of worldly wisdom and experience. Two myths of Zeus, earthly representative of Jupiter, speak of caves. (We can imagine that the Crab's shell forms a sort of cave.) After Zeus was born in a cave inhabited by sacred bees, the bees provided nectar to the newborn; later, Zeus's father (Chronos) confined him to a cave so that he might know his cosmic purpose through inner, contemplative work. During his seclusion, eagles nourished him with the nectar of higher thinking. Jupiter reached 15° Cancer as Anne Catherine Emmerich received the stigmata.

When we contemplate the fixed exaltation of Saturn at 21° Libra, we encounter the star *Zubenelgenubi* (20½° Libra), the constellation's brightest star, in the region of the southern balance pan. Although Saturn is known for sobriety and depth of thought, its influence can also engender severity—born of a renunciation of joy. This region of the fixed stars decrees that for severity to achieve justice, it must invite mercy to be its companion. Libra's ruler, Venus, lightens the heavy responsibilities of Saturn through her assurances that none of us is alone. Saturn was in Libra at the birth of the Blessed Virgin.

When we contemplate the exaltation of the Moon's North Node at 3° Sagittarius,[13] the nodal axis is brought into alignment with the Milky Way; for as we gaze toward this zodiacal degree from the Earth, we orient ourselves toward the Central Sun, the creative force behind all of existence. The mystery borne in this exaltation brings the Nodes—which signify an alliance between the Moon and the Sun (our two luminaries)—into alignment with the great luminary, the Central Sun, whose scope (in the words of Robert Powell) is such as to hold more than one hundred billion suns (not planets!) in their orbits around it, including [our] Sun![14] Noted earlier is the significance of the two zodiacal points at which the Milky Way crosses the ecliptic (at 5° Gemini and 5° Sagittarius). Is it possible that these are the true exaltations of the Nodes? The North Node was at 3° Sagittarius at the conception of the Nathan Mary.

Hermetic astrology distinguishes between *heliocentric* exaltations (which occur which occur when they reach their maximum northerly latitude in their orbit around the *Sun*) and the fixed, *geocentric* exaltations. These heliocentric exaltation points are not static: Each moves backward through the zodiac at a different pace. Recalling that the heliocentric chart is a *map of the spirit*, we can intuit the great spiritual guidance held within the moving exaltations. Below, you will find the current points of heliocentric exaltation (rounded to the nearest degree):

Mercury	24°	Cancer
Venus	22°	Leo
Mars	25°	Cancer
Jupiter	16°	Virgo
Saturn	29°	Virgo
Uranus	19°	Leo
Neptune	17°	Libra
Pluto	26°	Virgo

---

13   The South Node is thus exalted at 3° Gemini.
14   Robert Powell, "The Healing of the Man Born Blind and the Central Sun," *Journal for Star Wisdom* (Gt Barrington, MA: Lindisfarne Books, 2016), 32.

3

RETROGRADE MOVEMENT

WE KNOW THAT ALL OF THE planets in our solar system orbit in the same direction: anticlockwise (from the perspective of the northern hemisphere), or clockwise (from the perspective of the southern hemisphere). What, then, is the meaning of retrograde (or, backward) movement?[1]

To understand retrograde movement better, we need to create two categories of planets: those that are beyond the Sun and those that move between the Sun and the Earth. In the first category are Mars, Jupiter, Saturn, Uranus, Neptune, and Pluto. Though the transcendentals—the three outermost planets—are invisible to us, they behave just as Mars, Jupiter, and Saturn do in this regard. For this category of planet, retrograde motion is an annual affair, occurring once a year, and its duration is inversely proportional to orbital speed: The slower the planet, the longer its retrograde period.

Retrograde motion of this type occurs when the Earth and the planet in question are on the *same* side of the Sun.

We will start by imagining that the Sun is in Leo: From the Earth, we can draw a line through the Sun and onward toward Leo. At the same time, however, from the Sun's perspective, the Earth stands before the stars of Aquarius: We can draw a line from the Sun, through the Earth, and onward to Aquarius. In our example, Pluto is also in Aquarius (from the Earth, we can draw a line through Pluto and onward to Aquarius). The Earth and Pluto are "near" each other, on the same side of the Sun. The best way to understand retrograde movement is to think of a speeding car (Earth) passing a bicycle (Pluto). From inside the car, Pluto appears to *back up*. In our example, we can predict that Pluto will be retrograde in late summer, when the Sun is in Leo. The same thing will happen at roughly the same time the following year.

Considering the second category of planets (those between the Earth and the Sun) requires a change in orientation. We begin by noting that both Mercury and Venus continuously orbit the Sun in an anticlockwise direction.[2]

Pluto appears to move retrograde when on the same side of the Sun as the Earth

From the perspective of the Sun, Mercury and Venus are always moving forward through the zodiac. But if observed from Earth, when either planet is between point *a* and point *b* of its orbit, we observe it moving forward (anti-clockwise, in zodiacal order) before the background of the stars. Between point *b* and point *a*, its zodiacal longitude appears to us to regress (to move clockwise, contrary to zodiacal order).

---

1 The Moon stands apart from this inquiry. As we view it from the Earth, it never appears to move backward.
2 When observing the planets from the *southern* hemisphere, their orbits, like the zodiac, appear to proceed *clockwise*.

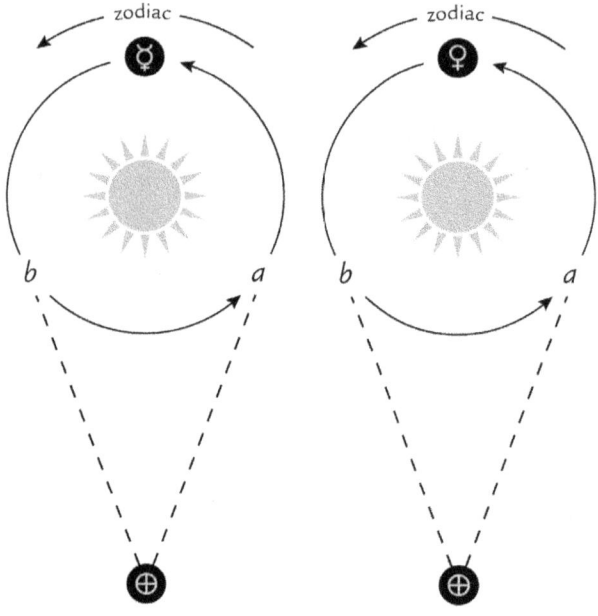

From the southern hemisphere, the retrograde motion of Mercury and Venus can be represented in this way:

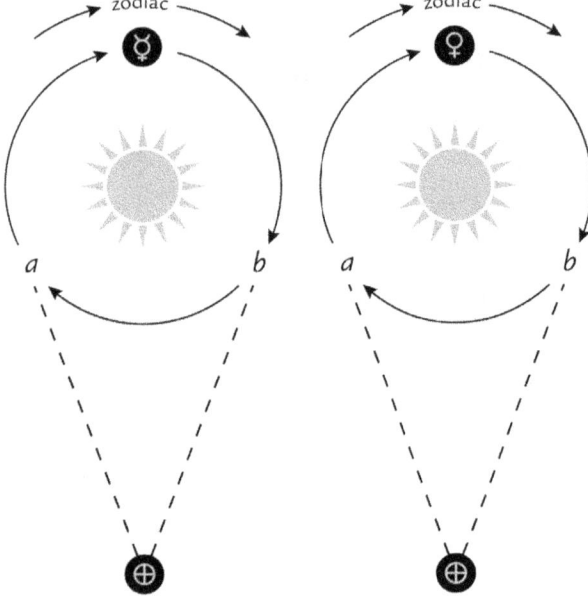

Here, when either planet is between point *a* and point *b* of its orbit, we observe it moving forward (clockwise, in zodiacal order) before the background of the stars. Between point *b* and point *a*, its zodiacal longitude appears to us to regress (to move anticlockwise, contrary to zodiacal order).

Why does any of this matter? Conventional astrology advises us that a retrograde planet causes confusion and trouble — for example, surgery is warned against when Mars is retrograde (there is a correspondence between Mars and sharp objects), and clear communication is difficult when Mercury moves backward. But does a highly trained surgeon so easily become a plaything of circumstance? Are we truly less capable of kind, clear communications when Mercury is retrograde? Through *astrosophy*, a new understanding of retrograde movement is coming into being.

Thinkers like yourselves, who seek *revelation*, will help to bring more clarity to the meaning of retrograde movement. I can only add that, in my own experience, such movement can be a blessing. Indeed, because *when planets back up, they slow down*. And this provides an opportunity for "interiorization" — which may quietly bring to consciousness the spiritual workings of the planets in our lives, so that they may be strengthened within us.

4

THE TRANSPOSITION OF MERCURY AND VENUS

THE TRUTH BEHIND THE TRANSposition of Mercury and Venus, the two planets (other than our Moon) that move between the Sun and the Earth, cannot be understood through ordinary consciousness. The fact that the explanatory writings of Steiner, Vreede,[1] Sucher, and Powell on the subject have left many of us none the wiser leads us to wonder if the mysteries therein must—for the present—remain occult (unrevealed). Steiner mentioned one of the reasons for this phenomenon:

> [The names of Mercury and Venus were] mixed up by later astronomy. What is today called "Mercury" was called in ancient teachings "Venus"; and in all of the old teachings, the planet now referred to as "Venus" was called Mercury. Mark this well: *One does not understand the old writings and teachings if one applies what is said there about Venus and Mercury to what is meant today by the same names.*[2]

Should the esoteric names of these planetary spheres rightly be the heritage of the consciousness soul, in an age wherein occult truths must be unveiled? Perhaps if the "spirits of darkness" had grasped these mysteries earlier, they could have used this knowledge in a destructive manner that might have harmed the proper development of human consciousness. Would prudence suggest that these names remain veiled for a time? We don't know.

Within the *Copernican* worldview there is certainty that Mercury—the planet with the fastest orbit—is closest to the Sun. There is equal certainty that the orbit of Venus circumscribes that of Mercury and is therefore closer to the Earth. This is the *material*, astronomical reality.

The Babylonians beheld, in picture consciousness, the passage toward Earth of the soul through the planetary spheres in the following order: Saturn, Jupiter, Mars, Sun, Venus, Mercury, Moon. This purely geocentric organization—which culminated in the *Ptolemaic* system—presents us with the *spiritual* reality that the sphere of Venus is adjacent to that of the Sun.

Anyone who brings an esoteric perspective to bear on the kind of world conception derived from Copernican tenets will have to admit that, although these ideas can lead to great achievements in the realm of natural science and in outer life, they are incapable of promoting any understanding of the spiritual foundations of the world and the "things of the world." Indeed, there has never been a worse instrument for understanding the spiritual foundations of the world than the ideas of Copernicus—never in the whole of human evolution! The reason for this is that all these Copernican ideas are inspired by Lucifer. Copernicanism is one of the last attacks, one of the last *great* attacks made by Lucifer upon the evolution of humanity.

In earlier, pre-Copernican thought, the external world was indeed *maya*, but much traditional wisdom—much truth concerning the world and the things of the world—still survived. Since the time of Copernicus, however, the individual person has *maya* around him not only in his material perceptions, but also in his very concepts and ideas... In the near future, however, it will be realized that the view of the world of the stars held by Copernicus is much less correct than the earlier Ptolemaic view. Indeed, the view of the world held by the school of Copernicus and Kepler is very convenient,

---

1   Elisabeth Vreede (1879-1943) served as the head of the Mathematical-Astronomical Section of the School of Spiritual Science.
2   Rudolf Steiner, *The Spiritual Hierarchies and the Physical World* (Gt Barrington, MA: SteinerBooks, 2008), 74-75. See also CW Nr. 110.

but as an explanation of the macrocosm, it is *not* the truth.[3]

The modern mind sides with the Copernican-astronomical model as the true one. It presumes, with the hubris characteristic of it, that the Babylonians must have gotten it wrong — i.e., they must have incorrectly *surmised* that Mercury was closer to Earth than Venus because of its greater speed. The Copernican system has isolated us from the heavens, leaving us alone with our calculators, slide rules, and formulae.

Copernicanism, the heliocentric reality, will thus lead us no closer to this truth. Perhaps we can come nearer to it by taking into account Christ's descent from the Sun, by which he became the spirit of the Earth:

> Christ came to Earth through the sacrifice of the Archangel Jesus being. He brought from the highest heaven something of the Central Sun to rest within the being of the Earth herself. Through Christ, the Earth became the focus for the work of spiritual beings throughout the cosmos.[4]

Christ asks that we perceive *through our hearts*. When the heart awakens, it gains the perspective of the "I," the eternal part of us that was born of the Sun. From this vantage, we look downward (from above to below) to the presence of the Christ-spirit indwelling the Earth. We see, then, that the planet Venus is nearer than Mercury to the *new* Sun, the one that is forming within the center of Earth and will be liberated at the conclusion of Earth evolution. The "I" of each of us looks toward this future. This is precisely what is revealed in the Tychonic (hermetic) system.

Tomberg made the remarkable statement that Calvary — to supersensible perception — can be known through Venus, as can the Resurrection through the Sun.[5] The Crucifixion necessarily preceded the Resurrection; likewise, each of us must endure a personal "crucifixion" in order to experience "rebirth." It seems, then, that the Sun and Venus must ultimately become *contiguous*.

One must be a spiritual Olympian to untangle the threads of this transposition. When we look to the heavens, we learn that the mysteries of these planets are intimately connected to one another. As we know, connecting the inferior *or* superior conjunctions of Venus (which corresponds to the 6-petalled lotus flower) results in a near-perfect pentagram — but it is also true that if we track both the inferior *and* superior conjunctions of Mercury in about a year's time (which corresponds to the 10-petalled lotus flower, seen clairvoyantly as one pentagram superimposed upon another), we will be in the presence of a great cosmic hexagram — much like the star of David. And can it be a mere coincidence that the temperature at the center of the Earth — 10,000° Fahrenheit[6] — is the same as that on the surface of the Sun? Could it not be that Venus, now nearer the Earth, is answering the trumpet's call from the future of the Earth-Sun?

---

3   Rudolf Steiner, *Christian Rosenkreutz: The Mystery, Teaching and Mission of a Master* (Forest Row, UK: Sophia Books, 2001), 54-55. See also CW Nr. 130.
4   Lainson, *The Circle of Twelve and the Legacy of Valentin Tomberg*, 209.
5   Tomberg, *Meditations on the Tarot*, 458.
6   Equivalent to 5538° Celsius.

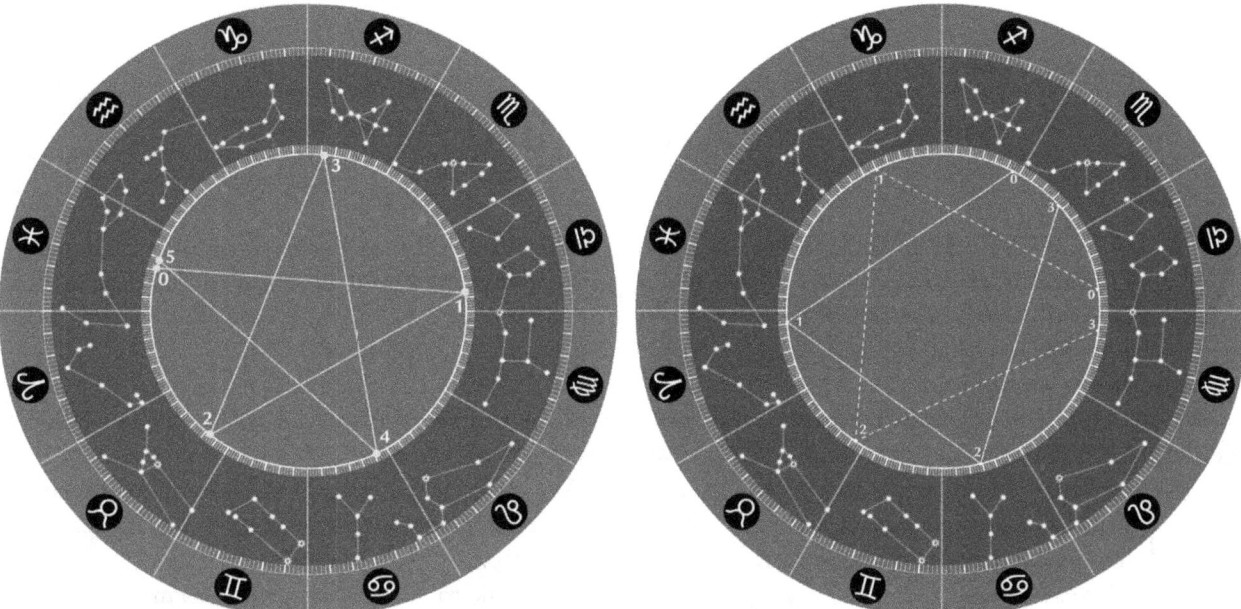

The Venus pentagram formed by superior conjunctions between Mar/2013 and Mar/2021

Superior (solid) and inferior (dotted) conjunctions of Mercury between Dec/2020 and Nov/2021

We live in a time when two "world orders" vie for the attention of humanity: one from the bony skeleton of Typhon's[7] materialism and the other from the rising tide of Hermeticism. *To take in the meaning of the Earth as the center around which revolves the Sun requires a new type of thinking. Such thinking integrates the continuous change that was set in motion by the Mystery of Golgotha.* We once thought the world was flat; we now think the stars are mere rocks and gases. The new frontier of science is the spiritual journey we will take as we seek to overcome Lucifer's illusions.[8]

---

7 Typhon is the Greek name for Ahriman, or Satan.
8 Lainson, *The Circle of Twelve and the Legacy of Valentin Tomberg*, 207-8.

5

LET'S TAKE A BREATH

WE CAN NOW LOOK AT A natal chart and identify which zodiacal degree is rising in the east. This is the Ascendant, which represents the world outlook of the individual.

We next identify the Descendant, the Ecliptic Zenith (EZ), and the Ecliptic Nadir (EN). We assign particular importance to the EZ as the "high holy place" of the chart.

We note which opposing signs and degrees that these axes connect.

The cross formed by these two axes allows us to determine the boundaries of the quadrants and the houses.

We take particular interest in the zodiacal degree and house placements of the Sun and Moon.

We then note the zodiacal degree and house placement of the other eight planets and of the Moon's Nodes.

We notice the zodiacal signs in which many planets are gathered together, as well as which quadrants and houses are occupied by the greatest number of planets.

We observe the elemental balance of a chart as well as the location of the ruler of the primary cusp of each house.

We can assign greater or lesser influence to planetary positions according to exaltation and rulership.

We look to Appendix 3 to determine if there are any planetary correspondences between the birth chart and the life of Christ. We notice if the planets align with the sidereal longitudes of important stars and their constellations.

We are now ready to move on to planetary relationships.

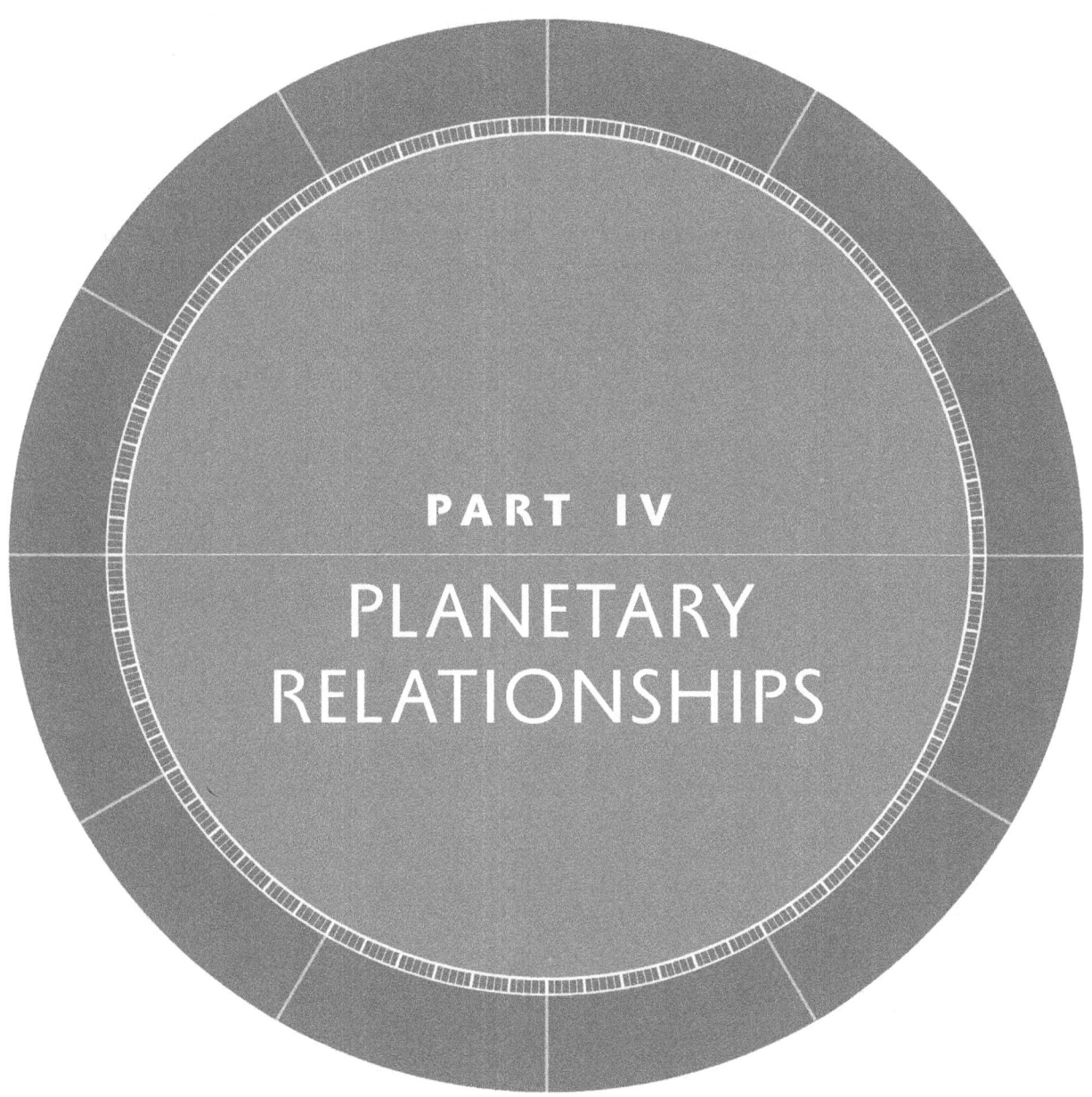

PART IV
PLANETARY RELATIONSHIPS

BEFORE PROCEEDING, I WOULD like to state my viewpoint emphatically: *The most meaningful understanding you will have of a chart is its relationship to the life of Christ.* This is not a statement of devotion to a religion, which I cannot claim to have. Instead, it rests upon the recognition of Christ as the center of the "cross of humanity."

Humanity's cross stretches vertically, *between heaven and Earth*; it also stretches horizontally, *across ages of time*. Christ's spirit created a gateway to the spiritual world *above* for humanity *below*. And through his sacrifices on our behalf,[1] Christ has redirected the whole spiritual history of humanity since our separation from the Father at the Fall. Without the sacrifices of Christ, humanity would never have risen above the animal kingdom! Under his loving guidance, we might be ushered back — atoned, and forgiven — to the spiritual world.

Steiner referred to the Mystery of Golgotha[2] as the "turning point of time" because it served

---

1 For further information on this complex topic, please see the appendices of Tomberg's *Christ and Sophia*.
2 This term encompasses the Passion of Jesus Christ, his descent into hell, and his Resurrection.

as the "hinge" upon which the direction of human evolution turned from our *involution* (into earthly life) to our *evolution* (back to the spiritual world). Our "exhalation" from the spiritual world is thus followed by our "inhalation"—whereby we return to the world from which we came.

After the Mystery of Golgotha, humanity's path back to the unity of divine wholeness was charted. Through the intercession of Christ, we were shown our divine, immortal core. Surely all of the heavenly bodies that bore testament to this life have much to teach us!

Thanks to the work of Robert Powell, we can establish these relationships through the corresponding zodiacal degrees of the planets, as well as through the aspects that they form. (Lists of both are provided in Appendices 2 and 3.) Our depth of understanding of Christ's life is much enhanced by the esoteric wisdom of Steiner and Tomberg, as well as by the detailed accounts of the visions of Anne Catherine Emmerich—whose descriptions allow us feel as if we're walking alongside Jesus.

1

PLANETARY ASPECTS

ASPECTS—OR, "ANGULAR RELAtionships"—between planets constitute a major component of chart interpretation. Each planet bears an angular relationship to all the others; this is determined by drawing two lines (from the two planets in question) to the center of the astrological chart. The angle formed by the two radii is known as their "angular separation." In the case of a geocentric chart, the Earth can be imagined at the center of the wheel; for the heliocentric, it is the Sun that has this honor.[1]

In our example, Venus and Neptune are 90° apart. An astrological chart would add a line connecting the two planets, representative of the aspect formed. The fact that Neptune is exponentially farther from the Earth than Venus is not relevant. Only zodiacal longitude determines angular separation.

Though there exists some disagreement regarding which aspects are significant, the effects of certain aspects have been observed over time with remarkable consistency. There is widespread agreement that conjunctions (0°), squares (90°), and oppositions (180°) act as midwives to our growth and evolution, and that trines (120°) and sextiles (60°) provide support and ease, offering us no resistance whatsoever. Many astrologers also find meaning in a dizzying array of other, minor aspects (some of which require a protractor or calculator to identify). I instinctively reject these broad aspect sets because of their complexity—a characteristic that is so often employed to distract us from the truth! You may draw a different conclusion.

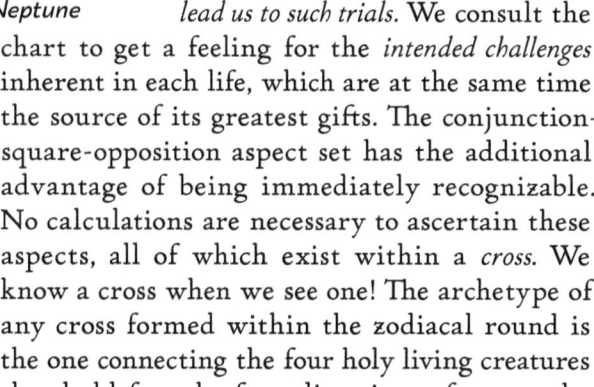

Venus forms a square aspect to Neptune

Compared to most aspect sets, the one commonly used by astrosophers is short: It includes only conjunctions, squares, and oppositions. Higher knowledge is reached through a process of trials, but trines and sextiles—the "happy" aspects—are omitted here *because they do not lead us to such trials*. We consult the chart to get a feeling for the *intended challenges* inherent in each life, which are at the same time the source of its greatest gifts. The conjunction-square-opposition aspect set has the additional advantage of being immediately recognizable. No calculations are necessary to ascertain these aspects, all of which exist within a *cross*. We know a cross when we see one! The archetype of any cross formed within the zodiacal round is the one connecting the four holy living creatures that hold fast the four directions of space: the

---

1 Planetary aspects are identified within both the geocentric and the heliocentric charts in the same way. However, we approach them differently within the Tychonic chart. The Tychonic (or hermetic) chart affirms the correspondence between the planets and the human chakra system—therefore Tychonic aspects take into consideration *the order of the lotus flowers*. For example, because Venus and Mars are on opposite sides of the center (heart) chakra, Venus and Mars in opposition in the Tychonic chart are considered to be working together in a coordinated fashion, as they do in the chakra system. Alternatively, Jupiter and Mars in the Tychonic chart—on the same side of the Sun chakra—are thought to be polarized when in opposition. Those interested in knowing more can find it in Robert Powell's *Hermetic Astrology*, vol. 1.

Bull, the Lion, the Eagle/Scorpion and the Angel.

Another argument, one that relates to geometry, can be made to support this choice. Triangles (and three-dimensional structures composed of them) are the most stable forms. Rael and Rudhyar wrote:

> Triangles are balanced and self-sufficient. In and of itself, [a triangle] is a configuration devoid of tension. It does not indicate any drive toward anything.[2]

Two entirely complete and "self-sufficient" triangles represent the Divine Masculine and the Divine Feminine Holy Trinities:

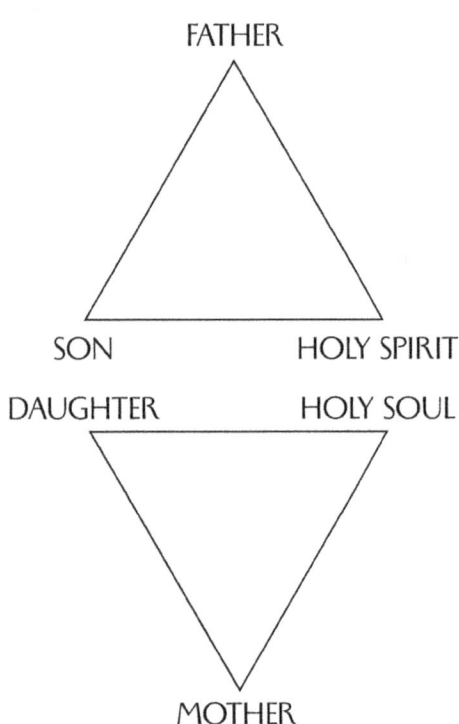

If we were to set about constructing Platonic solids[3] by connecting their edges, we would find that those forms whose sides are triangles—the tetrahedron, octahedron and icosahedron—are self-supporting, while the others, including the cube, collapse. *Trines and sextiles do not ask anything of us, whereas conjunctions, squares, and oppositions do!*

Because exact aspects are rare, it is customary to establish an acceptable orb of deviation, within which the aspect can still confer influence; I use an orb of 5°. This means that two planets can be considered conjunct, square, or opposite even if their angular separation is up to 5° from "exact." For example, if Venus is at 15° Libra, Mars forms a square aspect to Venus when it is between 10° and 20° of Cancer *or* Capricorn. Needless to say, *the closer to exact the aspect is, the more influence it will have*. All tight aspects jump off the chart!

Although a chart "freezes" the cosmos into a certain configuration, it is important to remember that the planets are always on the move. My favorite conceptual framework for planetary

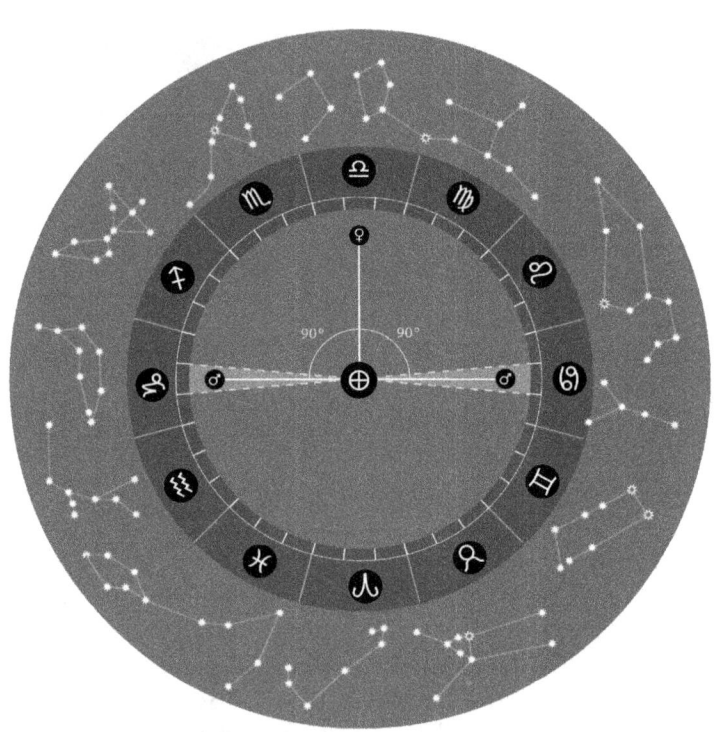

Mars squares Venus when anywhere within the shaded areas

aspects is presented in Rael and Rudhyars's *Astrological Aspects*. It gives a feeling for the movement of the planets in relation to one another, which we can understand better through the analogy to the phases of the Moon. *Any* two planets—not just the Sun and the Moon—can be regarded in terms of their cycle: They come together at a given zodiacal degree ("New Moon"), form

---

2   Leyla Rael and Dane Rudhyar, *Astrological Aspects: A Process Oriented Approach* (Santa Fe, NM: Aurora Press, 1980), 187.
3   Plato identified the only five three-dimensional shapes that have congruent sides and congruent vertices. They are the tetrahedron (four triangles, four vertices), the octahedron (eight triangles, six vertices), the icosahedron (20 triangles, twelve vertices), the cube (six squares, eight vertices), and the dodecahedron (twelve pentagons, 20 vertices). Each was understood to be a reflection of a spiritual archetype: tetrahedron/fire; octahedron/air; icosahedron/water; cube/earth; and dodecahedron/the etheric.

a square as the faster planet "waxes" past the slower ("First Quarter Moon"), face each other in opposition ("Full Moon"), form a square as the faster planets "wanes" and begins to draw nearer the slower ("Last Quarter Moon"), and, finally, form another conjunction *at a different zodiacal degree* (the next "New Moon"). When we look at aspects this way, it's helpful to understand that the faster planet sets the pace.

Another analogy that is helpful in approaching this subject is that of the life cycle of a plant. We can think of a *conjunction* as the seed, the *first square* as the emergence of the leaves, the *opposition* as the plant in full flower, and the *final square* as the moment when the leaves are shed. Each of these phases has very distinct characteristics.

The duration of these cycles (and, by extension, of their phases) differs for each planetary pair. Jupiter and Saturn meet every twenty years. Neptune and Pluto wait five centuries to reunite (this last occurred in 1892). These repeating aspect cycles express a shared rhythm that is unique to each pair. Remember: When the faster planet is at the zodiacal degree that is 90° *ahead of* that of the slower planet, we're looking at the "First Quarter Moon." In the case of the "Last Quarter Moon," the faster planet will be 90° *behind* the zodiacal degree of the slower one.

In addition to the type of aspect that is formed, we look to the nature of the influence of each planetary pair. The symbols for these aspects are universal: ! for the conjunction, # for the square, and " for the opposition.

☌ CONJUNCTIONS

A conjunction—analogous to a New Moon, when the Sun and Moon are aligned—represents the start *and* end of an aspect cycle: Where we find the hidden quality of pure potential, which is entirely subjective; indeed, a conjunction bestows a seed for growth that is meant to be planted in the fertile soil of the soul. Here, the combined expression of the planetary pair must take root. The conjunction is a wellspring that urges us to move ahead, even though we do not know exactly where we are going. As two planets meet, an agreement of sorts occurs: the slower planet provides to the faster a framework for the direction of its future growth. The most important point to make about conjunctions is this: *The energies of the planets involved need to be working toward the same objective in a coordinated manner.*

This is not always easy, even for a very compatible pair like the Sun and Mars, in which Mars's fiery, intense nature easily stands up to the Sun. Though this conjunction is likely to bring an easy sense of "knowing what to do" and "how to get things off the ground," it will prove a great challenge if the subject of this birth chart is by nature melancholic and introverted. Through the lens of astrosophy, we'd look at this as a "cosmic commission" to develop creativity, fire, and initiative. Alternatively, an individual who is naturally choleric would identify easily with the nature of this conjunction—but might find it very hard to control impulsivity, argumentativeness, and the tendency to steamroll others. This aspect, like all others, is present in the birth chart in order to ferment spiritual growth. Affecting the means of such growth are the soul disposition and temperament of the individual, as well as the house placement and zodiacal sign of the conjunction.

Let's take the example of two planets in conjunction that are very different in nature: Saturn and Uranus. Saturn promotes structure, endurance, and focus—while Uranus is apt to fly off at any minute, taking us with it. Saturn requires a certain amount of restriction, while Uranus, with a constant ear out for what is trying to find its way to us from the future, defies it. It is not unusual for those of us born under this conjunction to minimize the qualities of one planet over the other—in the same way that I would want to slink into a corner if I found myself standing next to Gisele Bündchen. But this we must not do!

The "karmic ideal"[4] is that the planets work equally toward the same purpose. Supporting this effort is the fact that most conjunctions occur within the same sign and house. Those born with several conjunctions tend to be self-motivated and driven people with intense focus—a disposition that sometimes comes at the cost of a certain lack of objectivity.

---

4 "Karmic ideal" refers to the spiritual intention behind the aspect. The implication is that consciously taking up this ideal as a path of growth—however difficult it might be—will best serve our efforts to restore karmic balance.

◻ SQUARES

Square aspects are usually experienced as the most difficult to work through; they can leave us feeling *blindsided*. Squares tend to make us especially off-balance, forcing us to change gears. Courage is needed to cope with square aspects, because they demand changes that we are reluctant to make; they "throw down the gauntlet." Will we retreat in fear into familiarity, or step up to the challenge?

Squares happen twice within a cycle. The first occurs after the conjunction, when the faster planet is 90° ahead of the slower one; this aspect can be compared to the "First Quarter Moon." Rael and Rudhyar describe this as a release from "source":

> At First Quarter the Moon is no longer pushed, as it were, by the power released at conjunction, but is geared toward or "drawn on" to the opposition by the "promise" of the Full Moon.[5]

The advent of the first square implies that we must stop relying on the comfort and security of the past (i.e. moving away from the "source")—and instead take active and creative steps to move toward our new goal. In a birth chart, a "waxing" square signifies that circumstances beyond our control will arise that will require us to *act*, lest we careen off course. It represents a crisis point where, in a mode of resolute decisiveness, we must begin to stand on our own two feet. Will our "leaves" be of the old vine or of the new?

The second or "waning" square poses an entirely different challenge. For at this phase of the cycle, the flowering has come and gone; the relationship between the two planets in question will soon lie dormant again in a new "seed." Rael and Rudhyar call this the phase of "revaluing."[6] The change of course that is called for at this moment will lead us back toward the more interior experience of the coming "New Moon." We can make an analogy within the life cycle of the plant to the moment when the leaves drop away; so, too, must we "let go" of our leaves before we return to "source."

Just like the "First Quarter Moon," this square is experienced as a sort of crisis. In this case, though, we are being called to reorient ourselves *inwardly*, in the realm of objective consciousness. Perhaps something we have believed for a long time is best left behind. Or it may be that we need to sever one last tie to our "point of origin."

Squares that involve the transcendentals are especially challenging. This is due to the fact that temptation can pull us further from positive resolution of conflict. And although such squares require even *more* effort to resolve, they present us with the opportunity to accomplish a great deal in doing so. It makes sense, then, that those born without square aspects in their charts tend to be happier with the status quo.

These aspects nearly always occur within two signs of the same quality (cardinal, fixed, or mutable) that are elementally at odds. For example, squares within the cardinal signs will occur between fire and water (Aries and Cancer), water and air (Cancer and Libra), air and earth (Libra and Capricorn), or earth and fire (Capricorn and Aries). Each of these combinations brings together masculine (fire and air) and feminine (earth and water) forces—in other words, they do not always see eye to eye!

⚼ OPPOSITIONS

When we view the opposition in terms of *phase*, we arrive at the halfway mark, analogous to the "Full Moon," at which the Sun and Moon are directly facing each other. This is the point at which the Moon (or the faster planet of the pair) is ideally "reflecting" the wisdom of the slower planet. We can think of the faster planet as having achieved maximum visibility in the world—like a plant in full flower. At this point in the cycle, objectivity and awareness are at their peak; we could call it the "consciousness of summer."

Opposition occurs when two planets are zodiacally as far apart as they can be: They represent an antinomy. However, although the planets are *polarized*, exact oppositions always occur in signs that are *elementally complementary*: fire with air, or water with earth. Here we have something to work with! Fire heats air, allowing it to rise,

---

5   Leyla Rael and Dane Rudhyar, *Astrological Aspects: A Process Oriented Approach*, 44.
6   Ibid., 72.

Planetary Aspects

while air fuels fire; water sustains life upon the earth, while earth gives water direction and allows it to flow. Planets in opposition must stand together *as two pillars of the same structure*. As such, the qualities of one planet must *not* overpower those of the other. Neither can grow in the presence of the "shade" of the other.

This is more difficult than it sounds, for when we relate to or believe in something, it is human nature to reject its opposite. Let us imagine ourselves at the fulcrum of a seesaw, with a planet at either end. A constant state of being awake to both sides is needed to maintain the dynamic balance between the two, through which the opposites can be united and thus *elevated*. Feedback regarding our handling of oppositions tends to come from relationships with others. Where are the planetary influences "locking horns" with one another, rather than finding the middle way? What is required of us to end the tug-of-war and thus bring the two forces into equilibrium?

How, exactly, is equilibrium achieved? In *Meditations on the Tarot*, within the letter-Arcanum "The Hermit," Tomberg warns against a *blending* of the opposing principles. (If we mix yellow and purple, orange and blue, or red and green, the result is always the same: a dull brown.) And yet, when we seek the middle ground by *finding the average* between the two, we are true to neither set of principles! Both methods operate on the horizontal plane alone, in which differentiation is magnified.

Instead, to achieve *synthesis* between opposites—an interaction that honors and elevates both sides—we must endeavor to separate ourselves from our personal positions and ideas, while seeking the objectivity characteristic of an eagle. Wisdom manifests from above, not from left or right. The absence of planetary oppositions in the birth chart can be suggestive of a lack of objectivity and a disinclination to accept advice. Although those of us born without oppositions might be spared from the planetary wrestling match that can occur between planets, each of us is nevertheless born with three zodiacal oppositions that must be brought into harmony: the Ascendant-Descendant axis, the EZ-EN axis, and the axis of the Moon's Nodes.

THE MEANING OF PLANETARY PAIRS IN ASPECT

THIS SECTION MIGHT BETTER bear the title: "One Imagination of the Meaning of Planetary Pairs in Aspect." It is certainly the case that they can be approached by way of many paths, each bearing a rich interpretation. Mythology, for example, reveals a *universal* application of the dynamic between two planets. Knowledge of the chakras (as they apply to the seven classical planets) brings planetary dynamics to a very *personal* level, owing to the chakras' role as mediators between the planetary forces and the human soul. So, too, can we consult the Tarot for the archetypes therein. For, as "prodigal sons and daughters," those among us whose souls hunger and thirst for the inexhaustible flame of the spirit will thereby be filled with the nourishing wisdom that lives within the spiritual archetypes of the planets.[1] Furthermore, when we look to events within and surrounding the life of Christ that occurred under the various planetary pairs,[2] we find their highest expression. Each path—and you may find others—looks to the spiritual world *above* in order to make sense of our tangled temporal lives *below*.

It is the author's hope that the following discourses will serve as a "secure foothold" from which further inquiries might be approached with humility and wonder.

☉ SUN

SUN–MOON

The phases of the Moon—New, First Quarter, Full, and Last Quarter—are the most visible planetary relationships, and, therefore, the most frequently followed. The Sun represents the radiant fire of creative activity. The Moon generates no light of its own; it can only reflect—or sometimes *eclipse*—the light of the Sun. The Moon is the reflective "water" to the Sun's divine "fire," without which we could never bear the Sun's radiance. Aspects between them express the potential for cooperation between wisdom (Sun) and intelligence (Moon). Additionally, the Moon reveals the *personal* (or, arbitrary) will, while the Sun represents *moral* will: that which has been purged of personal concerns, also known as "placing the Moon under our feet." This can occur by way of drawing the Christ Impulse into ourselves.

The antithesis of this ideal lies in the image of the Sun fully eclipsed by the Moon, for it describes the personal will "blotting out" or overtaking the moral impulses of the Sun within the "I" of the human being. Indeed, Steiner indicated that during a solar eclipse, "the unbridled [evil] impulses and instincts of humanity surge out into the cosmos" for the Sun's rays, which normally consume them in its fire, are blocked by the Moon.[3]

The Sun and Moon are conventionally thought of as standing for spirit and soul. This is certainly true, but I believe it is more fruitful to think of them in terms of the potential for spiritual growth that leads us toward the future (Sun karma), and spiritual stagnation that ties us to the past (Moon karma). Aspects between the Sun and Moon will bring this theme to the foreground, suggesting the need to evaluate the desires of the personal will in terms of their moral content. At the New Moon, our will-forces tend to be emphasized in our thought life; we can regard the lack of moonlight as an opportunity to draw inward, whereby we might be more inclined toward the spirit. Alternatively, the Full Moon signifies the ideal opportunity

---

1 These archetypes are richly depicted in *Meditations on the* Tarot. The relevant letter-Arcana are I, II, III, IV, V, VI, VII, XV, XVI, and XXII.
2 These are listed in Appendix 2.
3 Steiner, *Astronomy and Astrology*, 198. See also CW Nr. 213.

for our will to receive the moral impulses of the Sun; these might encourage us to engage in deeds of service. At the First and Last Quarter Moons, it is the feeling life that is emphasized.

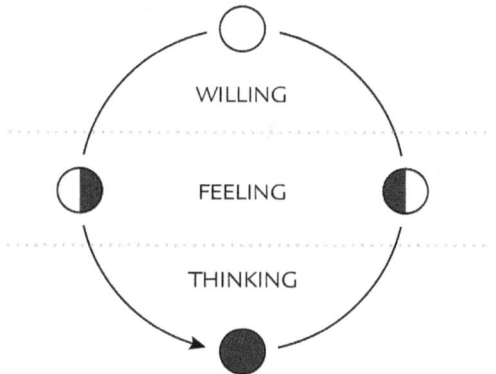

The orbit of the Moon from the northern perspective

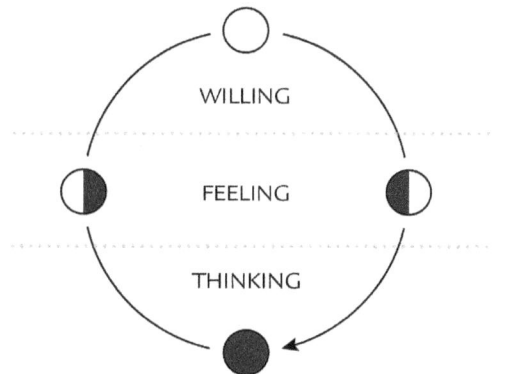

The orbit of the Moon from the southern perspective

There was a New Moon at the conceptions of the Solomon Mary, the Nathan Mary, John the Baptist, and the Nathan Jesus. The Moon was Full at the Crucifixion.

SUN–MERCURY

The sole aspect that the Sun and Mercury can form in the geocentric chart is the conjunction. As we know, it can occur when Mercury is between the Earth and the Sun, as well as when it is between the Sun and the zodiac. An astrological chart will not distinguish between the two, but an ephemeris will; when Mercury moves forward through the zodiac before and after the conjunction, it's a *superior* conjunction (when Mercury is on the far side of the Sun). If it's retrograde before and after the conjunction, it means that we're looking at an *inferior* conjunction (i.e., when Mercury is between Earth and the Sun).

Both conjunctions confer tremendous "wakefulness" that can manifest as extraordinary intelligence or as a gift for articulate speech and writing. When we take into account Tomberg's statement that Wednesday (Mercury-day) can now be thought of as the day of the "pastors of mankind," those born under the Sun-Mercury conjunction must ask themselves how they might fill this role. Are we cultivating light on behalf of others? Do we show concern for what ails them? Mercury, like any planet aligned with the Sun, will have a special bearing on the nature of the "mantle" that we are to strive to wear during the present incarnation.

The difference between the two conjunctions is subtle, and yet important. For those born under the superior conjunction, there tends to be a voracious gathering of information. The mind is so versatile and eager, it can *race*. The impulse of Mercury when beyond the Sun is objectivity; however, it can leave the mind without the necessary discernment to sift through what we have gathered. For those born under the inferior conjunction, the focus of thought is more subjective and inward; we tend to carefully evaluate and sort what we have learned—so that we can come to know true wisdom.

In the cycle of the Sun-Mercury conjunctions, we can intuit the process of spiritual respiration. The inferior conjunction—when Mercury is closest to the Earth—can be imagined as the moment when our prayers are gathered by Mercury to be carried to the Angels. At the superior conjunction, we can experience benediction, or the answers to these prayers. At the healing of the man born blind, Mercury was in inferior conjunction with the Sun.

SUN–VENUS

The Sun and Venus cannot form a square or opposition in the geocentric chart; the only possible aspect between them is the conjunction. When aligned, our true Self is often met through the qualities and endeavors that Venus suggests: listening, social charm, artistry, and the inclination to promote peace and harmony in relationships. Those of us born with this conjunction typically identify strongly with these traits. Venus brings happiness and harmony when negative Venusian traits are avoided:

laziness, insincerity, and envy—in the absence of any real effort to improve our own situation.

Because Friday (Venus-day) can now be considered the day of Calvary, we can regard the Sun-Venus conjunction in a new way. This holds special significance when Venus is aligned with the Sun; we must contemplate the nature of the "personal cross" that must be carried in order that we draw nearer to our "I"—and thus be filled with the cascading current of divine love that is Christ.

We can find much comfort in the fact that that Venus gazes deeply into our souls. From Steiner:

> The Earth is, so to speak, her lover.... [She] lovingly reflects whatever comes from the Earth.... The truth is that human beings on Earth can do nothing in the secrecy of their souls without it being reflected back again by Venus. Venus gazes deeply into the hearts of human beings, for that is what interests her—that is what she will allow to approach her.[4]

How this might be accomplished cannot be known through grasping, for this "door" cannot be opened from our side. Instead, we must ask, seek, knock, and *wait*. The answer will be revealed, through grace, at the proper time. The inferior conjunction of the Sun and Venus can be imagined as "the moment of our asking"; at the superior conjunction, our answer might then be revealed. Venus was in superior conjunction with the Sun as Jesus healed the blind youth named Manahem.

SUN–MARS

Mars brings energy to the endeavors that draw us closer to our "I." Those of us born with Sun-Mars aspects often take our first breath with a sword in one hand—though some prefer to keep it hidden in its scabbard until it's needed! This planetary pair asks for strength, courage, and decisive action, although these actions might also be carried out behind the scenes. There is, of course, a difference between engaging in a righteous "battle" and going out of our way to seek out opponents, which can sometimes be lost on Sun-Mars individuals. We might thus observe either a tendency to *resolve* conflict, or to *create* it. To discern between the two, we can ask ourselves: Will my actions ready me for the threshold that Michael guards, or prove me unready? As hatred and fear cede to love and forgiveness within our hearts, we are better able to serve truth and goodness. The Sun was square Mars at the miraculous draught of fishes.

SUN–JUPITER

The Sun-Jupiter planetary combination engenders receptivity to the thoughts and comfort of the Holy Spirit. This is an expansive pairing that has the potential to confer optimism, generosity, and an anything-is-possible attitude that can be inspirational to others. When we forget the wisdom inherent in the rhythms of expansion and contraction throughout the natural world, these gifts can incline us to take on too much. Many of us born under these aspects live our life as an endless quest for higher knowledge. When brought low, both planets can inspire egotism, over-confidence, and the tendency to expect the impossible from self and others. At its very worst, it inclines us toward tyranny. Its highest expression—the union of morality and wisdom—can be found in the life of the Nathan Jesus, at whose birth the Sun was square Jupiter.

SUN–SATURN

All Sun-Saturn aspects carry the potentiality of higher will; they ask if we are prepared to follow our spiritual destiny. We can imagine them as a meeting of the cosmic Self with cosmic truth. No one of good sense could imagine that they would simultaneously convey lightheartedness and jocularity! Instead, these aspects urge us toward seriousness, discipline, and endurance—all of which may well be needed in order achieve our spiritual goals. Because these qualities are often at odds with the human desire to "let go" and have a jolly time, these aspects can cause inner conflict to the extent that their spiritual dimension is not understood. Moreover, these aspects often place obstacles in our path that can limit our personal freedom; their purpose is to keep us as close as

---

4 Steiner, *Astronomy and Astrology*, 123–24. See also CW Nr. 226.

possible to our proper path. Sun-Saturn aspects often signify that we will be called to shoulder a good deal of responsibility. All aspects to Saturn engage the presence of the Virgin, to whom we can turn when our burdens feel heavy. The Sun was square Saturn as Jesus died upon the cross, and opposite Saturn at the birth of Rudolf Steiner.

SUN–URANUS

This combination highlights the wholly unique nature of the individuality. This theme will arise again and again, whether or not we cherish our existence outside the mainstream; our strong attunement to innovation and to the future can contribute to the distance that may exist between us and family, as well as between us and the culture. The importance of freedom and independence to the individual is usually paramount. When poorly understood, these aspects can seed rebellious tendencies that abhor tradition; when they are embraced, we can become the vessels of revelations from the Holy Spirit that will serve the future without compromising the rich gifts of the past. Increasingly, truth is revealed within communities; but this *cannot* happen when egotism — the tyrant that lures us to set ourselves above our fellows (fallen Uranus) — has crept into their midst. The Sun was conjunct Uranus at the healing of the nobleman's son.

SUN–NEPTUNE

Sun-Neptune aspects confer compassion and the desire to help those in need. Neptune brings a dreamy quality to all it touches, making us receptive to inspirations from the divine world — one example being musical inspiration. (We find Sun-Neptune aspects in the charts of many musicians.) This sensitivity can be dimmed, however, by the abandonment of our consciousness, for Neptune can draw us into the world of illusion, in which we believe feelings stand above the truth and responsibility. Its influence depends on our moral development. Will we listen to the wisdom of Sophia or (instead) to the magnetic siren call of the woman of Babylon, who can quickly disfigure the solar ideal of "benevolence for all." The Sun was conjunct Neptune at the healing of the paralyzed man.

SUN–PLUTO

This combination bestows deep ambition and drive, and those of us born under these aspects can adopt a do-whatever-it-takes attitude that can make us somewhat of an "unstoppable" force. Pluto's particular lure is the promise of power over others; the amoral who are under its sway will pursue it at any cost. Power's adversary is obedience to the will that is higher than our own. The Sun and Pluto in aspect summon an imagination of evil's struggle to overcome goodness; in human beings, this often arises in the form of an encounter with temptation. Those of us born under this aspect tend to exhibit an inherent interest in what "lies beneath" — and it can even seem as if we're *drawn* to the threshold of crisis, knowing on some level that these experiences are needed in order that we may be transformed. These transformations can involve seismic shifts that have the power to topple the unprepared. The Sun was conjunct Pluto during the temptations in the wilderness.

MOON

MOON–MERCURY

Imaginative thinking is implied with this aspect pair. Mercury-Moon aspects bring to mind the image of the healing light of Mercury shining upon all that is occulted by the Moon. In astrosophy, the Moon represents our personal (arbitrary) will, which is driven — alas — by forces that remain largely in the subconscious. Mercury is the alarm clock that strives to arouse us from our waking slumber. Which of the five dark currents of the will — the desire to take, to keep, to advance, and to hold onto at the expense of others, and the desire for personal glory — have we allowed entry into our souls? For it is these currents that distance us from the Father, from the Son and from the Holy Spirit. If, instead, we renounce these lightless forces, we can be filled with radiance from above — whereby our longing to serve others will be the guide of our deeds. This pairing implies that the positive expression of Mercury traits will be critical to the lightening our karmic burden. The Moon was square Mercury at the first conversion of Mary Magdalene, and opposite Mercury at her second conversion.

MOON–VENUS

This combination confers a keen sensitivity to beauty and to all that lifts the soul. One challenge inherent in these aspects is a dynamic between individual will and the requirements of the social sphere (including our karmic group). We can embrace a "neighbor" as an object of affection (rather than as a source of irritation) when we recognize in him one with whom we existed in paradise, and with whom we beheld the dawn of humanity. The higher meaning of these aspects lives in a willingness to direct our personal, arbitrary will toward the carrying of our own cross—rather than toward the satisfaction of our feelings. Moon-Venus aspects are sometimes characterized by a longing to maintain harmony, one that can entail "giving in" without a fight. "Giving in" might also manifest as an unwillingness to fight for our higher destiny, in favor of pleasing others. The Moon was square Venus at the Baptism.

MOON–MARS

When the personal will is allowed to take the reins of our "chariot," we might eventually be found upended in a ditch alongside the road. This is not to say that we should ignore our inclination to be active and involved in life's affairs—for these aspects ask that we take up our swords now and again. But for what do we fight? When self-mastery holds sway, we bow in humility to what is right—and we fight to uphold righteousness, without pride, to the extent that we are capable. Decisiveness (a noted gift of these aspects) engenders righteous deeds—even sacred magic—when guided by the world-thoughts of the spirit. Alternatively, impulsiveness, impatience, and competitiveness are born of the subconscious stirrings of the personal will. The Moon was square Mars at the cleansing of the temple.

MOON–JUPITER

Jupiter confers warmth and generosity upon the Moon, as well as optimism and broadmindedness. Many born with these aspects resist rest, despite the need for it. One notable theme is that of natural, moral authority; these aspects call us to *find* the authority that is properly ours, and to *not* exceed it. This can be a particular challenge for many of us, in whom there might exist a tendency to sell ourselves short; we might then seek authority in others, while at the same time longing for their esteem. The modern conception of esteem, however ("stardom" and the like), can be gravely misleading—for true authority requires that we renounce recognition altogether. When we heed the lower forces of Jupiter, we seek to compel others to do as we would wish. We might even smother them in our protective embrace. Alternatively, we might renounce "personality" in order to strive to become vessels for the wisdom and radiance streaming from above. The Moon was conjunct Jupiter at the turning of water into wine, and square Jupiter at the Transfiguration.

MOON–SATURN

As the Moon reflects the light of the Sun, so too does the High Priestess (Saturn) reflect the fiery radiance of the spirit. She is the "sea of glass" that makes consciousness of divine radiance possible, intimating to us what might be developed when our personal will-forces are stilled. Alternatively, we can be caught in turbulent whirlpools of despair and doubt—which are the result of disturbances within our will. The Moon and Saturn share a nurturing impulse, for the Moon represents motherhood—through *horizontal* heredity—while Saturn nurtures our spiritual development—our *vertical* bloodline. (Indeed, it is *she* who knows our true Name.) Both the Moon and Saturn render us well-disposed to listen in silence. This combination may engender circumstances that can feel restrictive if we remain ignorant of their true purpose. At its highest expression, we encounter in this aspect "a woman clothed with the sun, with the moon under her feet, and on her head a crown of twelve stars."[5] The Moon was conjunct Saturn as a group of Pharisees attempted to cast Jesus down from the brow of a hill.[6]

---

5 See Revelation 12:1.
6 Anne Catherine Emmerich said that Jesus, with the help of angelic beings, passed as if invisible through the midst of the crowd. See Luke 4:29-30 and *The Visions of Anne Catherine Emmerich*, vol. 2, 12-13.

MOON–URANUS

Moon-Uranus aspects bear the possibility of spiritual illumination (or, *clairvoyance*), whereby we might become vehicles for divine truth — provided that our "verticality" is maintained. The earthly corollary for this illumination is intellectual brilliance, or cleverness, which need not necessarily reflect any truth at all — and might also incline us to boredom when our need for constant stimulation is not met. These aspects carry the impulse of the reformer; they confer a strong will, as well as a need for independence and freedom. If we instead heed the call of fallen Uranus, our independence might thrive on egotism — perhaps even manifesting as a desire to "put our name in lights." When the temptation of pride is overcome, we seek our place as one of many within our community, and approach it with humility. The Moon was conjunct Uranus at the birth and death of the Blessed Virgin.

MOON–NEPTUNE

This combination can confer a mighty sensitivity to our environment and to the feelings of others. It often provides fertile soil for visions. However, caution is needed, for through Neptune we encounter the temptation of casting ourselves from the pinnacle of reason and conscience, whereby we seek above all to satisfy our feelings. Under Neptune's influence, we might fall prey to the sphere of mirages — the source of illusions that are deceptively clothed in truth. Moon-Neptune aspects remind us to be prudent, for they can engender both circumstances and relationships from which discernment might serve as our only escape. Shall dazzling joy — i.e., life stripped of obligation and responsibility — be our master, or shall *truth*? The Moon was square Neptune at the summons of Thomas.

MOON–PLUTO

Moon-Pluto aspects bring to our attention the need for consciousness regarding the origin of our will-forces, for the subearthly forces of Pluto — if we allow them to — can take hold within us and render us servants of Ahriman. In those of us born under these aspects, feelings tend to run very deep indeed. This planetary pair confers intensity, drive, and power, and implies that there might be many occasions in life that test our proclivity to bend others to our will. When Pluto brings crises (as it often does), we can regard these as opportunities to kneel in obedience before the will that is higher than our own. Which master do we serve? The one that offers power, or the one that provides the nourishment of divine love? The Moon was conjunct Pluto at the birth of the Solomon Jesus, and square Pluto at the union in the temple.

 MERCURY

MERCURY–VENUS

These aspects ask us to seek harmony between heart and mind — whereby our thoughts and communications are warmed and calmed by love, and our emotions are tempered by logic and reason. Through our capacity to love, aspects between Mercury and Venus open paths to healing. Venus confers the ability to still the busy mind, and it is Mercury's light that can shine into the dark recesses of the soul — revealing to us what might be changed through our humble efforts. Mercury was conjunct Venus during the descent into hell.

MERCURY–MARS

Aspects between Mercury and Mars can agitate the mind, causing argumentativeness. Restraint and patience might then be unable to find a footing. Conclusions (and judgments) can be reached in haste under the influence of this planetary pair, thereby reminding us of the value of mercy. These aspects ask us to forgo aggressive communication in favor of speech that acts as a healing balm to others — for truth can always be spoken with tact and kindness. This requires that we give up "competing" with the goal of showing what we know (speech inspired from below), a trait which our schooling has typically drummed into us. It is only through such renunciation that our minds can be opened to the Michaelic truth that is seeking our notice. These aspects can be associated with an energetic and quick mind, as well as with the possibility of communicating with decisive clarity — which brings power to our words. Mercury and Mars were conjunct at the birth of John the Baptist.

MERCURY–JUPITER

Jupiter increases the (already impressive) optimism, humor, and goodwill of Mercury, giving us the ability to inspire confidence in others. Jupiter opens the mind; its broadening effect on our thinking can be accompanied by a lack of interest in details. The "big picture" nature of Jupiter typically leads to an interest in the wide world beyond our front porch. Those born with these aspects will at some point wrestle for a balance between our attention to detail and our ability to analyze (Mercury), and a broad worldview that serves conceptual synthesis (Jupiter). Our judgment can thereby be affected, for good or ill. Within this relationship lives the potential for thoughts imbued with a moral impulse. It asks that we strengthen our judgment. These aspects confer a love of learning, but we must beware mistaking a large cache of information for wisdom. Mercury was conjunct Jupiter at Pentecost.

MERCURY–SATURN

Saturn strives to influence our thinking with focus, discipline, and *concentration*. It signifies mental discipline, in part due to our ability to avoid mental clutter. Such discipline thereby enables us to master our subject of choice with great depth. While Saturn brings precision to our thought processes, it has the potential to make us blind to what's around us—so we must remember to take our nose off of the grindstone from time to time! There tends to be a respect for established method. This combination summons the image of light that may have been hidden under a bushel; this, in turn, begs the question: *Why do we keep it there?* Because this aspect can incline us to demand a great deal of ourselves and of others, it can also bring pessimism. Thus, we can overlook what is good and beautiful by focusing on criticism alone. This can be overcome through an awareness of the purpose of our mission and the willing acceptance of the personal responsibilities that accompany it. Positivity attracts heavenly and human assistance. Mercury was square Saturn at the birth of the Nathan Mary.

MERCURY–URANUS

Mercury and Uranus are a high-frequency pair that can confer clarity of thought and brilliance—or, alternatively, an anxious and nervous mind that has difficulty settling down. The mind tends to be highly original, and subject to flashes of insight. This pairing can illuminate not only what otherwise would remain in darkness within the soul; it can also elicit new forms of perception that are striving to reach those of us who long to serve the evolution of humanity. However, aspects between Mercury and Uranus challenge us to separate truth from lies. Our frank and honest manner of speech might require that we remember the value of *tact* in nurturing relationships with others. The brilliance of Uranus seeks reflection in human thought, although it can also ensnare us in "electrified" thinking that strives to convince us that stones are bread—whereby we can become useful pawns in service of those who wish to sever our connection to the spiritual world. Mercury was square Uranus at the births of John the Baptist and Anne Catherine Emmerich.

MERCURY–NEPTUNE

Mercury–Neptune aspects can bring inspirations and healing forces from angelic realms. This is a highly intuitive combination that can confer a remarkable sensitivity to what exists beyond the world of the senses. If our connection to reality becomes too tenuous, however, we risk being swept away by a current of illusion and deception. When in aspect, Mercury and Neptune compel us to seek out all that which is uplifting to the soul. They ask that we maintain a warm interest in all that we meet! Alternatively, we can attune ourselves to the cynicism of Ahriman—whereby our souls become increasingly chained to matter, like Andromeda: helpless and doomed, without a lifeline to the spirit. Mercury and Neptune may engender a lack of clarity in our thinking that can be mitigated through quiet contemplation. Mercury was conjunct Neptune at the feeding of the five thousand and at the walking on the water; the two planets were square at the birth of Valentin Tomberg.

MERCURY–PLUTO

Pluto brings to Mercury both insight and depth; together, they seek the truth that exists behind appearances. Typically noteworthy is an aversion to chitchat, and when those of us born with these aspects speak, we tend to go straight to the deep end of the pool. Mercury-Pluto interactions urge us to summon the courage to shine light into all that hides in the dark crevices of our subconscious—wherein we can find impulses that have been set in motion by subterranean currents of will. Minds turned toward the Father of creation can thus be bathed in cosmic light. These aspects confer an intuitive sense of what might be called "the heart of the matter," which might be placed in service of fostering transformation in others, or of wounding them by "lowering the boom" with calculated precision. Mercury was conjunct Pluto at the second conversion of Mary Magdalene.

♀ VENUS

VENUS–MARS

As with all "opposites," Venus and Mars in aspect must find a way to *elevate* each other, rather than allow one of them to be celebrated *at the expense of* the other. They ask that we strive to use our speech in a loving manner, and to perform deeds that have the ability to weave us together. In the event that the conciliatory nature of Venus is challenged by Mars, this might not be easy. At their worst, these aspects can create emotional drives so strong that they render us indifferent to the consequences of our actions. Therefore, Venus-Mars aspects call for self-mastery as well as a love of our "neighbors." Rivalries are to be consciously avoided. This combination might also engender poetic and artistic talent, as well as the wherewithal to give form to these abilities. When expressed in a highly moral manner, Venus and Mars in aspect bear the impulse of the peacemaker. Venus was conjunct Mars at the births of the Nathan Mary and the Nathan Jesus.

VENUS–JUPITER

The two benefics in aspect can be the source of many blessings, including forgiveness, optimism, social consciousness, and harmony within our community. Wise Jupiter can bring steadiness and moral direction to the soul; when this is lacking, the magnification of our emotions can result. Venus-Jupiter aspects have the power to incline us toward *ease*, one of the time-honored lures of Ahriman. This might be avoided by becoming aware of any existing tendency toward idleness and indulgence. This is a fun-loving combination that tends to draw goodwill and support from others; however, this is easily undermined by vanity (which can be considerable). Mighty Jupiter shines the light of wisdom onto the nature of our "personal cross." Venus was square Jupiter at the commissioning of the disciples.

VENUS–SATURN

Saturn tends to push us inward toward quietude, where the soul might feel the weight of its destiny. To the extent that we are unaware of the spiritual purpose that Saturn conveys, this weight can feel quite heavy indeed—like an anvil upon the soul—and may manifest as a sort of cool restraint. We might feel our limitations keenly. The deeper meaning behind this planetary combination lies in the image of Mary at Golgotha: witnessing, despite personal agony, the completion of the mission of her son. These aspects ask that we faithfully witness the unfolding of our *own* mission, and kneel before the creative power of our destiny! When we do so in full consciousness, the Virgin will be our companion. Venus was conjunct Saturn at the Visitation (of the Nathan Mary) to Elizabeth.

VENUS–URANUS

The longing for freedom can be so pronounced in those born under these aspects that compromise can be viewed as a loss of individuality; this is a false conception (born of the "Belt of Lies")[7] that can alienate us from others. However, Venus-Uranus combinations do entreat us to rise above convention so that our hearts can open to revelations from the future. What towers have imprisoned our souls? What flawed conceptions of the past continue to limit our ability to love our neighbors as the great teachers that they are? This pairing suggests thunderbolts to the soul that strive to awaken us to the truths of the spiritual world—which (at the same time) alert us to the disharmony that materialism has created. Venus was conjunct Uranus at the raising of Lazarus.

---

7 See *Meditations on the Tarot*, 281, 634.

VENUS–NEPTUNE

Aspects between Venus and Neptune can open the soul to Sophia, and incline it toward what is inspirational. A dreamy and imaginative pair that often resists clear boundaries, Venus and Neptune sometimes lack oomph regarding "real-world" tasks; they can even lead to escapism. (These two so enjoy remaining in the clouds!) Alternatively, the Venus-Neptune combination can prepare our souls for the instreaming of healing forces, provided that a balance in the feeling life (which might otherwise be known as "listening") has been achieved. These aspects can be expressed as a longing for the unobtainable or as impossible expectations regarding others. Because there exists the willingness to sacrifice, we benefit from striving to develop discernment—which thereby empowers us to make an accurate assessment of when to sacrifice, and when to remain still. Venus was conjunct Neptune during the three temptations in the wilderness.

VENUS–PLUTO

Venus in aspect to Pluto summons an imagination of the one force that can overcome fear and evil in an instant: *love*. While it's true that Pluto's wilting glance is capable of scaring Venus into submission, when we accept our own suffering as the proper condition for our spiritual evolution—and can thus turn our gaze to the suffering of others—*we can hear Pluto speak from the heart of our Father in heaven*. When we're unable to find balance in the feeling life, however, Venus can magnify the jealousy and obsession that are characteristic of the fallen forces of Pluto. Pluto gives Venus a heightened magnetism, as well as an intensity that she normally lacks. We can intuit within the relationship between Venus and Pluto the potential for a deep love for the Father. Venus was opposite Pluto at the Assumption of the Solomon Mary.

♂ MARS

MARS–JUPITER

Mars and Jupiter in aspect present to us the desire to expand and venture forth beyond what most would consider prudent. Everything seems possible! The challenge inherent in this pairing, which represents the "crusader duo" of the solar system, is *self-mastery*—without which its blessings of courage and enthusiasm will serve as little more than an appetite for conquest and a tendency to get into tussles. This is a shame, because Jupiter magnifies the courage of Mars as well as its refusal to back down—thus making it ideal for the protection of deeply held convictions and beliefs. Those of us born under these aspects are typically enthusiastic, attracted to risk—and disinclined to give up. Mars was conjunct Jupiter at the healing of the paralyzed man.

MARS–SATURN

This planetary combination seeks to align our deeds with our spiritual mission, and sometimes this can require a will of iron—for we might find it necessary to protect and defend that mission against all the distractions that seek to draw our attention elsewhere. Though it is true that these aspects highlight the tension between lower desires and higher resolves, this planetary combination also bears the potential for understanding and rectifying this struggle. Saturn strives to focus our will-forces in a manner that can feel restrictive, and therefore frustrating. When the spiritual perspective is lacking, Mars and Saturn can foment resentment for the duties we've been given. Alternatively, as we find we're able to summon all the strength and stamina that we need, it can make our burdens light. Actions that are chosen deliberately—and are also based upon a realistic foundation—are most likely to meet success. Mars was opposite Saturn at the union in the temple.

MARS–URANUS

This somewhat combustible pair—the stick of dynamite that's inches from the lit match—signifies an explosive force that is ideally placed into service of needed reforms. There is often in evidence a high degree of tolerance for dangerous (or otherwise bold) action, and notable impatience. Mars and Uranus engender an "out of the box" sensibility—one that is often accompanied by a feeling of resentment toward any effort to be put back "into the box." These aspects remind us that it is incumbent upon each of us to recognize the deeds that represent our unique part in serving the future; instability in the astral body (Mars) can block our receptivity to the messages from the Holy Spirit (Uranus) that shed light upon these deeds. Revelations from Uranus seek to ennoble our speech. Mars was square Uranus at the turning of water into wine.

MARS–NEPTUNE

Between Mars and Neptune weave forces of inspiration that seek to become deeds upon Earth through human effort. This pairing has the power to make us warriors of the spirit; we can see in it the ability to pursue our ideals and inspirations—but it is also possible for us to prefer the comfort of our dreams, whereby our resolve can be dissipated and lost. It reveals the way that materialism can cast the soul into isolation—and warns us that our desire nature can become enchanted by the glittering finery of the anti-Sophia. The lower forces of Neptune stream from Arhiman's domain, and can therefore trap our emotions in the prison created by our sympathies and antipathies—thus perverting our motivations into expressions of "survival of the fittest." (Robespierre and Napoleon were both born under the conjunction.) Will we answer Sophia's call to brother- and sisterhood, or will we allow our desire nature to cloud our souls with confusion? Mars was conjunct Neptune at the healing of the nobleman's son, and square at the birth of Kaspar Hauser.

MARS–PLUTO

Within this combination lives a formidable force of raw power that can run amok when the personal desire nature is allowed to determine its course. In this case, aggressiveness is lured from the shadows, seeking beings and situations that can be dominated. Because both Mars and Pluto can summon fear within us, these aspects require that we face fear straight on—as Michael did—and consign evil to its chains; for only then will we be able to walk the true path of our destiny upon the Earth. What allows us to summon this courage is the memory of our divine origins, and the love of the Father that is the source of the universe. Much can be accomplished by sheer force of will, although there can exist a tendency to work to the breaking point. Mars was conjunct Pluto at the births of the Solomon Mary and of Rudolf Steiner, and in opposition at the birth of Anne Catherine Emmerich.

 JUPITER

JUPITER–SATURN

When Jupiter and Saturn meet at the same zodiacal degree, it is known as a Great Conjunction. This celestial meeting portends spiritual events of importance, and can even result in widespread social change. The character of that change can be found within the sidereal sign of the conjunction, as well as in the element that the sign expresses—for these conjunctions stay in the signs of one element for an average of over two centuries. Each individual born under this conjunction is asked to participate in the change that is striving to manifest. The spiritual beings of Jupiter and Saturn look toward humanity and wonder how we will respond to the challenges before us. Will we awaken to moral law? Jupiter was conjunct Saturn at the conception of the Solomon Jesus.

JUPITER–URANUS

This freedom-loving pair inspires expansion, innovation, and reform. When we stand in humility before the light of the Holy Spirit, we become open to new worlds of thought. However, this combination also warns of egotism in those who fall prey to imaginations from lower realms. When born under its influence, the outlook tends to look beyond existing limitations, and there exists a willingness (or eagerness) for change. These aspects suggest the possibility of a sudden change in our deeply held beliefs—or, at the very least, the tendency to re-evaluate them from time to time. Caution is the watchword here, for no other planetary combination is so apt to rush headlong into the unknown. Both Jupiter and Uranus can seed *self-absorption* in the soul. This cycle lasts about fourteen years. Jupiter was conjunct Uranus at the birth of Valentin Tomberg; it was square Uranus as Jesus taught regarding the baptism by fire.

JUPITER–NEPTUNE

True altruism lives within this planetary pair! Jupiter and Neptune have a thirteen-year cycle that can be characterized as a test of our faith that may have nothing to do with religion whatsoever. Jupiter-Neptune aspects might provoke circumstances that require us to renew or certainty in this faith. There can exist a tendency to promise more than is possible to fulfill, and our natural generosity can lead us to give more of ourselves than is wise. This is a planetary combination of big dreams and mighty ideals—out of which creative inspiration can flourish! Egotism, however, makes us susceptible to delusion and manipulation. Jupiter was square Neptune at the healing of three blind boys.

JUPITER–PLUTO

When Jupiter's expansive quality interacts with Pluto, we can find raw drive and power that creates the impression that nothing is impossible. (Though this is sometimes obscured by a mild-mannered veneer, as in the case of Bill Gates—who was born under the conjunction.) How will that power be used? Will it *serve* others, or will it *destroy* them? (Jesus endured the Passion under the Jupiter-Pluto opposition.) Jupiter in aspect with Pluto brings before our imaginative vision a community that serves the will of the Father; within this community, wisdom prevails over tyranny. This combination can create deep *religious* conviction. The Jupiter-Pluto cycle is twelve years in length. Jupiter was opposite Pluto at the raising of Lazarus.

 SATURN

SATURN–URANUS

This is a complex combination due to the completely different natures of the two planets. Saturn brings focus that asks us to attend to the foundation of our lives; alternatively, Uranus tends to bestow a freedom-seeking, future-oriented approach to every situation. This can create a sort of tug of war between constancy and change, between attunement to the past and to the future, and between responsibility and freedom. The combination implies constraints and impediments that are strewn in our path and need to be surmounted—but which, as Beethoven (born under a conjunction) found, need not work against us. Why run headlong into the future unprepared, risking the loss of everything that has served as our support? Aspects between Saturn and Uranus imply a spiritual mission that assists in guiding humanity toward a new future. Saturn was square Uranus at the conception of the Solomon Mary.

SATURN–NEPTUNE

Saturn and Neptune create a blend of reality and unreality that can be difficult to resolve—for the life structures (Saturn) that we have carefully created can be washed away (Neptune) with little notice. It's as if we're being pulled *toward* reality (by Saturn) and *away from* it (by Neptune) at the same time. One of Neptune's blessings is its challenge to the dominance of materialistic reality; like waves upon the shore, it repeatedly and rhythmically entreats us to bring a spiritual direction to the soul. The themes of duty and sacrifice are also brought into focus with this planetary combination; it was present at the October Revolution, as well as at the fall of the Berlin Wall in 1989. Often noticeable is an acute sensitivity to the sorrows that weave us together. The cycle's duration is thirty-six years. Saturn was opposite Neptune at the conception of the Nathan Jesus.

SATURN–PLUTO

Severity can threaten to harden our souls through the influence of this planetary pair. Together, Saturn's scythe and Pluto's earthquake can leave us feeling that our security is under siege. We might feel forced into periods of "starting over." (The conjunction overlighted the independence of India and Pakistan in 1947, and of Israel in 1948.) One reaction to this state of affairs is to seek to control everything and everyone around us, without remorse. (The last conjunction occurred as the viral pandemic and its draconian lockdowns began in 2020.) And yet, weaving between Saturn and Pluto is the love of the Mother and the Father, the source of our spiritual life: the *tender* love that assuages all our tears, and the *commanding* love that directs our steps toward what is good for us.[8] When we look to the Father in the heights, we are empowered to achieve our mission on Earth. The length of this cycle (roughly thirty-three years) is the same as that of the etheric Christ.[9] Saturn was opposite Pluto throughout the temptations in the wilderness.

---

8 Tomberg, *Meditations on the Tarot*, 293.
9 Christ is now "reincarnating" in an etheric body, whose rhythm is 33.3 years—the same period of time between his birth and his

♅ URANUS

URANUS–NEPTUNE

The Uranus-Neptune cycle lasts about 170 years. Richard Tarnas's title for his section on this combination is "Awakenings of Spirit and Soul." Aspects can coincide with the emergence of artistic or literary genius. Boundaries can dissolve into the ether. Spiritual ideals can capture a generation, causing shifts in cultural vision and the emergence of new spiritual paths. Two examples offered in this chapter are the spiritual movement led by Saint Francis, and the birth of Thomas Aquinas. The conjunction of Uranus and Neptune in 1821 occurred within a year or two of the births of Walt Whitman, Herman Melville, Dostoyevsky, and Florence Nightingale. Fortunately for us, we find their conjunction in the birth charts of those born in the early 1990s, for much is resting on the shoulders of this generation. Uranus was square Neptune at the conception and birth of the Solomon Mary.

URANUS–PLUTO

Uranus and Pluto meet in conjunction approximately every 140 years. Under the influence of this aspected pair, we experience collective encounters characterized by the combination of rebellion, disruption, and innovation (Uranus) with the overwhelmingly destructive and regenerative capacity of Pluto. Kaboom! When these are present in the birth chart, we often find that we are drawn into the collective impulse of Uranus and Pluto in order that we might contribute to its peaceful and productive expression in the culture.

Richard Tarnas's *Cosmos and Psyche*[10] is a source beyond compare for a long and compelling list of historical manifestations of Uranus-Pluto aspects. (These include the French Revolution and the turbulent 1960s in the West.) In *Cosmic Christianity: The Changing Countenance of Cosmology*,[11] Willi Sucher applies the timeline of this cycle to the unfolding of esoteric Christianity; the advent of Manichaeism, Parzival and the Troubadours, and the Order of the Knights Templar can thereby be viewed as the highest expression of the Uranus-Pluto cycle. Uranus was opposite Pluto at the births of the two Jesus children and Valentin Tomberg.

♆ NEPTUNE

NEPTUNE–PLUTO

Neptune and Pluto find each other at the same zodiacal degree only twice in a millennium. On a collective scale, we can observe massive shifts in ideals. The culture can be transformed by way of the spirit—or else, by way of mass consciousness (which serves the interest of the adversaries of Christ). The last conjunction of Neptune and Pluto occurred around 1891. The year or two surrounding this conjunction saw the births of Yogananda, Nehru, and Chekhov—as well as those of Hitler, Mao Zedong, and Franco.

I would like to express gratitude to the individual who was Peter Treadgold, the computer genius behind *Astrofire*. This unique program allows us to walk with Christ, minute by minute, under the stars as he saw them. It has changed many lives in profound ways.

Let us consider the magnitude of the accomplishment of accurately dating the events in the life of Christ. The associated planetary positions remained obscured until the 1990s, when Robert Powell shared the results of his decades of work on the subject. Through modern computing, the written accounts of the visions of Anne Catherine Emmerich—an unworldly nineteenth century seer—were brought into alignment with astronomical tables for the time of Christ. If the reader wishes to know more of this remarkable accounting, it can be found in Robert Powell's *Chronicle of the Living Christ*. It will simply be said here that if we take into account only Emmerich's voluminous details regarding the Hebrew calendar, the days of the week, and phases of

---

Resurrection. Following Christ's death, his etheric body remained intact and began its ascent toward cosmic heights. Its subsequent descent was completed in 1899, and (by 1933), its integration into the Earth's aura was complete. For more on this subject, see Robert Powell's *The Christ Mystery*.

10   Richard Tarnas, *Cosmos and Psyche* (New York, NY: Penguin, 2006), 141-205.
11   Willi Sucher, *Cosmic Christianity & The Changing Countenance of Cosmology* (Hudson, NY: Anthroposophic Press, 1985), 111-20.

the Moon, the dating is as near to statistical certainty as it is possible to be.

Take a moment to comprehend the consequence of this facet of the work of Dr. Powell. *We. Know. The. Full. Cosmic. Chronology. Of. The. Life. Of. Christ.* Within the chronology lives guidance for humanity, for all time.

Our knowledge of the details of the life of Christ has two sources: the four Gospels, in addition to what Steiner termed the "Fifth Gospel"—which, together, reveal the entirety of Christ's life on Earth. The humble Anne Catherine Emmerich was able to "read" from this "Fifth Gospel," as were Rudolf Steiner, Valentin Tomberg, and others. Claudia Lainson tells us more about the Fifth Gospel:

> The time for lecturing and note-taking will soon be left behind us. And as we learn how to enter this library, we will read in these images the revelation each moment requires us to see. Valentin Tomberg refers to this as the "sanctuary of the everlasting zones," wherein remain the "holy symbols of the cosmic elements." Such symbols are the protecting garments of truth behind which lie words of wisdom. Upon entering this sanctuary, as images appear to us that we can read like a book, we behold wonder after wonder. Thus do we find our way along the many corridors of this great library, nestled as it is in Earth's etheric mantle.
>
> The Book that herein can be read—otherwise known as the Fifth Gospel—is the Life Tableau of Christ. What was recorded by the four evangelists is not complete. In the great Book, however, each moment of his 1290 days upon the Earth has been inscribed. It will continue to radiate its teachings until the very end of the world.[12]

The list provided in Appendix 2 has been extrapolated from the dating established by Robert Powell. It offers the possibility of allowing the details of the events themselves to inform us about the true meaning of the astrological aspects that are associated with them. With this list, we can come to know astrosophy by exploring the powerful connection between a present-day aspect—or one in an astrological chart—to the same aspect within the context of the Christ chronology. Because the planetary aspects recur over time, echoing the harmony of the spheres, we can begin to contemplate the mighty spiritual intentions behind these rhythms.

When we attempt to live into these intentions, we are thus blessed with the sensation of moving *forward*, toward an ideal, in the company of others. *Astrosophy allows us to know karma as an essential, moral force that is an expression of the love that binds the universe.* We can begin to experience destiny as the result of the loving intention of the nine hierarchies of Angels. How we respond to it is our own affair; if we choose, as free beings, to work willingly with the forces of destiny, we will experience growth. We are also free to look the other way.

This approach constitutes a new way of studying astrology. Reverence and wonder must be our companions. Therefore, we must first empty our minds of what we think we already know. May we journey together joyfully, in search of the truth.

---

12 Lainson, *The Hermit, the Minotaur, and the Shadow of Evil*, 23.

3

COSMIC TEMPO
KNOWING THE PLANETS THROUGH RHYTHM

ONE OF THE EASIEST WAYS to deepen our understanding of the planets is through the study of the cosmic rhythms that lie behind our biographies. The etheric body, a *time body*, is particularly attuned to the unfolding of cosmic rhythms. Moreover, we can strengthen this aspect of our being by becoming aware of the role of these rhythms in our lives.

Rhythm speaks to the heart. Tomberg wrote that joy is "the state of harmony of inner rhythm with outer rhythm, of rhythm below with that from above, and, lastly, of the rhythm of created being with divine rhythm."[1]

The whole of life proceeds rhythmically. Each stage of evolution — known in Hindu cosmology as a *manvantara* — is followed by a state of rest, or *pralaya*. We are breathed out of the spiritual world as we are born, and upon our death a great cosmic inbreath signals our return. Through the seasons, we experience the inbreath and outbreath of Nature. The flowering of a plant is followed by its dormancy as a seed. Sequentially, planets pass through zodiacal signs that are masculine (those associated with fire and air) and those that are feminine (those associated with earth and water). The most fundamental of the planetary rhythms is that of the seven-year periods.

THE SEVEN-YEAR PERIODS

The seven-year divisions of earthly life were known in antiquity — possibly several centuries before Christ.[2] Shakespeare immortalized them in *As You Like It*[3] and Rudolf Steiner breathed new life into the character of this unfolding by revealing the planetary influences within it. The planetary sequence that underlies the seven-year periods is a mirroring upon the Earth of the sequence of the planetary spheres beheld by the Babylonians (Moon, Mercury, Venus, Sun, Mars, Jupiter, and Saturn). Because each level of angelic beings holds sway over seven years, the influence of the Sun sphere — host to the Exusiai, Dynamis, and Kyriotetes — lasts twenty-one years. Beyond these seven spheres (from the spiritual perspective) lies the realm of the fixed stars: the domain of the zodiac. Once we "age out" of the planetary spheres at 63, it is the zodiac — and the sign of the Ascendant in particular — that exerts the strongest influence on our lives.

The character of the unfolding of this sequence is a direct result of the experience of the soul's journey through the spheres after death (i.e., after our previous life). Each stage represents a threshold of consciousness that moves us toward independence and self-awareness. As these stages were the subject of so many lectures by Steiner, they will be discussed only briefly here.

Although, for most of us, our years upon the Earth are only a fraction of the time spent in the land of spirit, our sojourn among the stars is largely forgotten by the time a new life on Earth is begun. What we do know about this experience is thanks to initiates across the centuries — who are remarkably consistent in their descriptions — and to those who return from the brink of the threshold with details of their near-death experiences.

Our heavenward ascent of Jacob's Ladder after death comprises a long backward glance upon the life just lived, as well as the determination by our "I" (with the assistance of the hierarchies) of the ideal circumstances for the next life on Earth. This intent is "captured" at cosmic midnight in

---

1 Tomberg, *Meditations on the Tarot*, 630.
2 Powell, *Hermetic Astrology*, vol. 2, 101.
3 William Shakespeare, *As You Like It*, 2.7.139-166. The relevant passage begins with "All the world's a stage."

the intended astrological chart of the birth to come, and as we descend Jacob's Ladder on our earthward journey, the resolves inherent in the birth chart are reaffirmed (level by level) with the angelic beings of each planetary sphere.

From the perspective of materialism, this journey is entirely unquantifiable. The intellect's inability to describe this phenomenon has resulted in a doubling down on the idea that death signals a release into the void, and nothing more. This has led many of us to do everything in our power to keep death behind the barricades — and to "live it up" with abandon until the barricades fail; unfortunately, this lifestyle has the power to *sever* our connection to our divine "I" — as well as to the source of goodness, love, and beauty that radiates from the spiritual world above. The materialistic worldview, in effect, *chains us to the Earth*. It leaves us ignorant of the spiritual journey undergone between lifetimes, and of the relevance of this journey to the life to come. In truth, our years on Earth mirror our last ascent to the stars — i.e., after death — *with cosmic regularity*.

THE MOON YEARS: 0–7

The departed soul's journey through the Moon sphere — also known as *kamaloka*, or Purgatory — consists of a moral review of our life: How did our thoughts, feelings, and deeds affect those around us? It can well be imagined that this review is usually accompanied by feelings of shame, guilt, and even helplessness — for we know that we must wait for the next incarnation to redress our wrongs. Judith von Halle asserts that the *kamaloka* experience, which can otherwise be described as a personal descent into hell, is in no way punitive, but instead represents *a process of redemption*:

> [This] healing process of the soul — which may well not wish its passionate 'convictions' to be easily relinquished, nor want to be disillusioned about the suffering it caused others, nor even to feel this suffering at first hand — can be experienced as very unpleasant, and even deeply and bitterly painful.[4]

If there is an Accounting Office in the Moon sphere, it is adjacent to its cavernous Storage Facility. Once our new karma has been reflected to us, as in a mirror, it is set aside by our guardian Angel until our next approach the Earth — when the proper selection of karmic baggage will be returned to us. Each valise (or steamer trunk!) is stuffed with everything you can imagine — *and everything in it has your name on it*.

Our sojourn in the Moon sphere is reflected in the first seven years of life. The physical development of the infant is centered in the brain, as is evidenced by its proportionally large head. In regard to the psychic (soul) development, we look to the root chakra and its connection to heredity. A child's world during these years is the mother, the father, and the family. From them we either receive the love and support we all crave, or we don't. Whatever the nature of our formative experience, we have absolutely no ability to change our life situation. Karma forges a bond to the past that can't be broken until we are older.

THE MERCURY YEARS: 7–14

Our departed soul goes onward to the sphere of Mercury, where we come to know the spiritual purpose of the illnesses from which we suffered in the past lifetime. The Archangels bless us with these insights, as well as with those connected to the karmic consequences of our illnesses — anything from having caused worry in others to the need for a loved one to fulfill the role of caretaker. As the Archangels, the *cosmic healers*, reveal the spiritual aspect of our illnesses, a profound healing takes place.[5]

Because Mercury oversees our interpersonal relationships, the realm of the Archangels also reveals to us the extent to which we exhibited a warm interest in others. If the life behind us was largely spent preoccupied with our own troubles and joys, we feel a certain loneliness here, while the more selfless souls find companionship and comfort.

The soul's passage through the sphere of Mercury is reflected in the child's physical development between the ages of seven and fourteen, during which the focus of activity is in the

---

4 Judith Von Halle, *Descent into the Depths of the Earth* (Forest Row, UK: Temple Lodge Publishing, 2011), 13.
5 Powell, *Hermetic Astrology*, vol. 2, 114.

lungs—and, by extension, in the entire rhythmic system. (Indeed, it is the growth of the chest that is most prominent during these years.) This is statistically a period of good health—for example, children in this exact age range are given a certain protection against the most common childhood leukemia. It is also a period of growing interaction with peers. By now, the child's world has expanded to include the surrounding community, which is ideally a source of a great deal of guidance and support.

From the perspective of psychic (soul) development between seven and fourteen, however, we turn to the sacral (Venus)[6] chakra, which helps us bring to focus the feeling life of children, who at this point tend to live strongly into their sympathies and antipathies: a bubbling cauldron of feelings that they are yet unable to evaluate or control.[7]

THE VENUS YEARS: 14–21

In the Venus sphere, the domain of the Archai, light is shed on relationships of love and on connections within karmic groups. The Archai see to it that we incarnate at the proper time—so that we are given the opportunity during our life on Earth to meet and interact with those individuals and groups through which we can best work through our karma. Isn't it amazing? The level of strategy going on up there is—quite literally—otherworldly!

The Archai unmask the real nature of our romantic relationships. Were we kind? Committed? Selfless?

> To the extent that love is not completely pure, a purifying of the soul takes place in the Venus sphere so that "true love," which is purely selfless in nature, may prevail in the place of egotistical impulses.... [In] the Venus sphere, through the Time Spirits [Archai], we become bathed in *pure, cosmic love* that heals us of any traces left of egotistical aspects interwoven into our relationships from earthly life.[8]

Our time in the Venus sphere is reflected in the physical human being between the ages of fourteen and twenty-one, during which children are then immersed in the culture that surrounds them. May God protect our teens! The onset of this period, of course, coincides with puberty and the nascent interest in romance. Growth, at this time, is most pronounced in the limbs.

In terms of psychic development in this period, however, we must look instead to the Mercury chakra: Through Mercury's influence, intelligence is awakened, along with a yearning for meaning.

The Angels, Archangels, and Archai—as the spirits closest to the Earth—are those most intimately involved with our day-to-day affairs. Steiner attributed to the Moon, Mercury and Venus the forces of *destiny*. The karma inscribed within their spheres results from our relationships to others. This karma is attached, therefore, to a certain *necessity*—which is commonly experienced as a lack of freedom.

THE SUN YEARS: 21–42

Within the sphere of the Sun, we encounter our true, moral essence: the unique, divine individuality—our "I"—that has hovered, glowing, above us throughout each of our incarnations. We can think of the "I" as *the star above our heads*. Within the sphere of the Sun, only pure goodness exists.

The higher Self is purely moral; and in the light of the Sun spirits (known as the Exusiai, Dynamis, and Kyriotetes), we are able to evaluate the extent to which our incarnation unfolds (or *has* unfolded) in accordance with the great ideals of human and cosmic evolution.[9] The orientation of Sun karma is the future, and it thus consists essentially of the resolve to live more in accord with the higher Self and these future ideals. Sun karma is engendered through our becoming aware of the discrepancy between our higher Self and the actual life lived on Earth.[10]

---

6   This is yet another contemplation for the question of the transposition of Mercury and Venus. For an overview on this issue, discussed in Part III, Chapter 4.
7   William Bryant, *The Veiled Pulse of Time* (Gt Barrington, MA: Lindisfarne Books, 1993), 52.
8   Robert Powell, *Elijah Come Again* (Gt Barrington, MA: Lindisfarne Books, 2009), 166.
9   Ibid.
10 Ibid., 167.

The journey through the sphere of the Sun is reflected in the next incarnation in three consecutive seven-year periods. (These account for the three choirs of Angels working within this realm.) Not until the onset of young adulthood does the "I" begin to incarnate fully. As this happens, goodness and morality can gradually suffuse our feelings, thoughts, and deeds—generally in that order. From Powell:

> [During these years, the] human being "finds" himself, his identity, after passing through the often-turbulent storms of youth. His true identity begins to manifest with the "shining in" of the Sun during this period of life. It is also the time during which tasks of destiny begin to approach the human being.[11]

THE MARS YEARS: 42–49

As we ascend further, we encounter the spheres of Mars, Jupiter, and Saturn, where the Thrones, Cherubim, and Seraphim dwell. Constituting the first hierarchy of Angels, these beings are actually *zodiacal* beings who have descended to our solar system to be of assistance to humankind. We can thus expect our sojourn within these spheres to reflect a very high level of consciousness indeed. Together, the Thrones, the Cherubim, and the Seraphim provide a *wider context* for our Earthly existence.

Within the sphere of Mars, we are able to begin the review of our past incarnations, experiencing each as a "creative deed"—by which we can come to an understanding of the totality of this sequence, and of the success of the last incarnation within it.[12] The resolve to come nearer to it in the future is integral to our Mars karma.

As we enter our Mars years, we are forced to confront the conflicts inherent to this time period: leaving youth behind (a phase of confusion), as well as a yearning to break free and to make a mark on life. To those who have previously shown no inclination toward the spirit, our comfortable lifestyles—like our convictions—may have hardened into concrete straitjackets.[13] With the influence of Mars comes high energy in search of an outlet. Depending on one's self-mastery, the outlet might be anything from a trip to Vegas to a renewed commitment to a spiritual path.

THE JUPITER YEARS: 49–56

The great review of past incarnations gets broader still in the sphere of Jupiter: the domain of the Cherubim. Through Jupiter comes the wisdom of the Holy Spirit. We begin herein to gain insight into the meaning of each incarnation in relation to the purpose of the individuality across time. Moreover, we come to know the higher wisdom that lives behind the sequence of incarnations.

Throughout the Jupiter years, we seek perspective on the life behind us. If we actively strive to bring the light of wisdom to our past deeds and accomplishments, our initiatives are given a fresh burst of energy, and our ability to do good in the world thereby expands. Now that some of the vim and daring of youth has ebbed, we come to rely increasingly on *inner* strength, as well as on the faith and hope derived from spiritual experience. If reserves are low, this can be a difficult period.

THE SATURN YEARS: 56–63

The Saturn sphere presents the final bridge that must be crossed in order to reach the zodiacal realm of the fixed stars. Robert Powell wrote:

> Here there takes place a beholding of the tableau of all earthly incarnations from a moral perspective. We realize, with the help of the Seraphim, how much (or little) of our preceding incarnation on Earth was aligned with the higher moral demands of world existence.[14]

From this perspective, personal wants and opinions fade into nothingness. Even if one's spiritual strivings on Earth have not resulted in being "awake" for these revelations, they remain with us on some level; for example, when we know—deep within our bones—that a life-changing event is about to occur, or that—at a glance—we're beholding the one with whom we'll share our life.

---

11 Powell, *Hermetic Astrology*, vol. 2, 138.
12 Powell, *Elijah Come Again*, 167.
13 Bryant, *The Veiled Pulse of Time*, 73.
14 Powell, *Elijah Come Again*, 168.

The Seraphim confront us with the following questions: To what extent did we recognize our spiritual mission? How effective were we in bringing it to life? The true answers are recorded *as memory* in the Book of Life held by the Blessed Virgin. Now comes the time to end the backward glance to the life just past.

THE ZODIACAL YEARS: 63 AND BEYOND

Once we ascend beyond the sphere of Saturn, we enter the realm of the fixed stars:

> After completing the passage through the ranks of the nine spiritual hierarchies...which is at the same time the journey of the soul through the planetary spheres (Moon, Mercury, Venus, Sun, Mars, Jupiter, Saturn), the human being—as a pure spirit—enters the divine world, the realm of the fixed stars (zodiac).[15]

In the zodiacal realm there occurs a meeting with the Father, although this is remembered only by the great initiates; the rest of us enter what Powell refers to as a kind of "swoon," leaving us unable to maintain consciousness.

During our sojourn among the stars, we resolve to return to another incarnation. This decision is made in complete freedom. We can wonder why, once up there, there would be any inclination at all to return! But Steiner insists that a longing overtakes us—a longing to set right our past errors on Earth. Elisabeth Vreede describes it as a hunger for *gravity*:

> Earthly gravity alone stands only at the foot of the ladder that leads from the cosmic-moral realm.... The human being would be unable to endure life forever in the light of the spiritual world and thus has a hunger for the heaviness of the physical world.... The human being longs for the reassuring solidity that the Earth, with its gravity, provides.[16]

Having made this decision, we approach cosmic midnight—also known as the midnight hour of existence. This is literally the halfway mark, the turning point of our time in the land of spirit, at which we choose the birth horoscope of the coming incarnation and begin our descent through the fixed stars and the planetary spheres. *At the exact moment when the zodiacal positions of the planets surrounding an infant mirror those of the intended birth horoscope, the baby's first breath is taken.* Steiner made the amazing claim that our brains bear the imprint of our individual horoscopes:

> The active forces of the starry world push us into physical incarnation. Clairvoyant perception allows us to see in a person's organization that he or she is indeed the result of the working together of such cosmic forces.... If we photographed a person's brain at the moment of birth and took a picture of the sky directly above his or her birthplace, the two pictures would be alike. The stars in the photograph of the sky would be arranged in the same way as certain parts of the brain in the other picture. Thus, our brain is really a picture of the heavens, and we each have a different picture depending on where and when we were born. This indicates that we are born of the entire universe.[17]

This "picture of the heavens" referred to by Steiner is itself the origin of other cosmic rhythms—those that depend upon (and proceed from) the details found within this heavenly image.

PLANETARY RHYTHMS IN RELATION TO THE BIRTH CHART: RETURNS AND TRANSITS

The rhythms of the movements of the planets become most personal when compared to the birth chart. Much light can be shed upon our biographies through becoming attuned to the wanderings of the planets against the background of the fixed stars:

> *For the Christ Will in the encircling Round*
> *Holds sway in Rhythms of Worlds*
> *Bestowing Grace on the soul.*[18]

---

15 Ibid.
16 Elisabeth Vreede, *Anthroposophy and Astrology* (Gt Barrington, MA: Anthroposophic Press, 2001), 173-74.
17 Rudolf Steiner, *The Spiritual Guidance of the Individual and Humanity* (United States: Anthroposophic Press, 1991), 62. This is one of the few collections of Steiner's lectures that he himself edited after their transcription.
18 From the second verse of the Foundation Stone Meditation, received by Rudolf Steiner on Christmas Day, 1923.

Sophia, bestower of Grace, is the architect of these rhythms. It is her voice that is heard through their manifestation over time. Such rhythms provide predictable challenges and opportunities that serve as a lifeline from the cosmos as well as a connecting thread among us. We are all subject to the same laws of the cosmos!

Here we will be looking at two categories of rhythms: *returns* and *transits*. A *return* occurs when a planet (or Node) returns to its zodiacal degree in the astrological chart in question. The Sun on your birthday is the simplest example of this—the Sun's return to its degree at your birth signifies the day on which your guardian Angel is nearest to you. *Planetary returns happen to all of us at the same temporal interval in life, in accordance with orbital speed.* There are three returns in particular that have the potential to wield the greatest influence upon us.[19]

A *transit* is a lot like a return, but less specific. It describes the movement of any planet in relation any other planet, house, or angle in the birth chart. The passage of the slower-moving planets—Jupiter, Saturn, Uranus, Neptune, and Pluto—across key points in the chart have the ability to define the arc of the personal biography. A soon as I print a chart, I scribble-in the current positions of these planets along its outer, zodiacal, edge. *Transits bring a birth chart to the present.*

I allow an orb of five degrees; in my experience, when a transiting planet is within five degrees of a planet or angle in a birth chart, its effects will be felt. Also important to consider is that the duration of a return or a transit is inversely proportional to the speed of the moving planet or node. In other words, the slower moving the planet is, the longer it will take to move out of our defined orb.

Remember: The "retrograde" movement of Mars, Jupiter, Saturn, Uranus, Neptune, and Pluto (which occurs annually) can draw out the time that these planets will be within the orb of influence. In the case of Jupiter and Saturn, a return or a transit might come and go before they go retrograde. The same is not possible for the transcendentals—whose returns and transits last *years*. The average duration of the influence of the returns and transits relevant to this study is as follows:

Moon's Nodes: six months
Jupiter: two to nine months, depending upon retrograde movement
Saturn: ten to twenty months, depending upon retrograde movement
Uranus: three years
Neptune: five years
Pluto: seven years

THE RETURNS OF THE MOON'S NODES

The invisible axis that connects the North and South Nodes of the Moon moves backward around the zodiac in eighteen years, seven months. The average individual experiences three such returns in his lifetime: at eighteen years, seven months; at thirty-seven years, two months; and at fifty-five years, nine months.[20] As the Moon sphere is the domain of the Angels, this axis signifies a portal to the angelic realm—and thus the nodal returns mark important periods in our biography. The guardian Angel has a deep interest in our karma and does everything in its power to lead us to relationships and activities that will, over time, assist us as we strive for "karmic balance." The nodal returns represent three such efforts. Steiner said:

> The nights passed during these periods are the most important nights in an individual's life. It is then that the macrocosm completes its 18 respirations (i.e., completes one minute)—and we open a window, as it were, facing quite another world.[21]

Here it is critical to consider some numbers in order to grasp the correspondence between

---

19 No transcendentals are mentioned here. This is because the speediest among them—Uranus—requires eighty-four years to complete the circuit.
20 The Moon's Nodes also complete a return as we turn 74 years, four months and 92 years, eleven months—but these returns lack the significance of the first three. Neither Steiner nor Vreede mentioned them. Additionally, we can think of age 70 as a threshold of sorts, for this is when we "age out" of the karmically ordered influence of the etheric weaving that took place in the prenatal period. During gestation, each 27.3-day revolution of the Moon influences one seven-year period in the life to come. As there are, on average, ten revolutions of the Moon between conception and birth, the reach of the etheric weaving during gestation is 70 years (7 x 10 = 70).
21 Steiner, *Astronomy and Astrology*, 192. See also CW Nr. 201.

the macrocosm and the microcosm to which Steiner is referring. The human being takes an average of 18 breaths per minute. Therefore, in one hour there will be 1080 respirations—and in 24 hours—25,920 respirations.

We know that the length of a Platonic year is 25,920 "Earth years." This is the time required for the vernal point to "precess" through all 360° of the zodiac. Steiner also refers to this period of time as the macrocosmic day, or *a great day of the heavens*, leading us to two correspondences: one between the microcosmic day (25,920 breaths) and the macrocosmic day (25,920 years); the other between the "microcosmic minute" (18 breaths) and the "macrocosmic minute" (18 years). To rephrase: *18 years—the approximate time required for a return of the Moon's Node—is analogous to one minute within one great day of the heavens.* This is one way in which the spiritual world interpenetrates our own!

The three nodal returns have different effects, but all share the quality of *destiny*. They occur so that we might be changed. We could say that at 18, the intent of the return is to prepare for our "birth" into the spiritual world. The family and environment in which we grew up were chosen by the hierarchies with care; at eighteen and seven months, a change is usually needed to bring us to our own karmic group. This return is often accompanied by a physical change in life, either through a physical challenge—even an accident—or a move to a new location. At this time, we are motivated by questions like, *What should I be doing? Am I in the right place?*

This is a time when we might begin to wonder if we are more than what we seem to be, and *idealism* is our currency. *It is as if we are standing before an open window, facing quite another world.* Our dreams, should we pay attention, will help us to answer the questions we have posed. In my own biography, I chose to attend university 3000 miles from home—an apparently random choice that led me to my husband and to my spiritual community.

The second return at 37 and two months occurs just after the midpoint of life and therefore bears the heaviness of life's cares. This return usually appears in the manner of a crisis, leading us to assess the health of our souls at that time—so that we might experience healing. This can present as an illness, a change in career, a divorce, or simply the realization that we are not living the life that has been calling to us since the last return. *The second return offers us a new opportunity to connect with our true purpose.* Within whatever crisis is before us, we can intuit the abiding love of the Son for humanity. My own experience at this time involved a grave health crisis.

At 55 and nine months, the return of the Nodes manifests in the manner of "a crisis of the spirit" that seeks to bring us into fuller harmony with the destiny of humanity. It is not unusual to experience a greater longing for the spirit in response to life's inevitable disappointments. Perhaps this is why many of us begin to bring down "the fire of the spirit" (if we haven't done so already) by stepping into our "spiritual selves": *We are finally ready to stand up!* And we do so not to satisfy personal ambitions, but to fulfill a destiny that we know will benefit others over time. At this age, I was introduced to the individual who was uniquely qualified to guide my study of astrosophy.

Like all cosmic rhythms, the returns of the Nodes offer a rich topic of shared conversation.

THE RETURNS OF JUPITER

Jupiter's returns proceed in a twelve-year rhythm, finding us at the age of 12, 24, 36, and so on. As Jupiter is the planet of wisdom, these returns tend to signify either an influx of wisdom—sometimes extraordinary—or a burst of creativity or discovery that can occur in any domain of endeavor. The Jupiter return indicates a new period in life that is expressive of personal growth. This, of course, requires effort:

> But what Jupiter reveals to the eye of spirit must be grasped with thoughtful intelligence. If a person does not himself make efforts to develop his capacities in thinking, he cannot, even if he is clairvoyant, approach the mysteries of Jupiter.[22]

We see living in the number twelve the concept of *a totality of wisdom*. We can discern this in the twelve-fold division of the zodiac, the

---

22 Ibid., 120.

twelve Bodhisattvas around the Christ, the twelve tribes of Israel, the twelve apostles of Christ, and the twelve knights of the Round Table. The archetype of this rhythm is apparent in the life of Jesus, who was twelve years old when his worried family found him teaching in the temple with remarkable erudition: his new-found grasp on an endless variety of topics astonished his family. We know from Steiner that, at this time, the Nathan Jesus had already received the "I" of Zarathustra—and was immediately transformed from a simple, loving child into the bearer of the wisdom of the ages. The youth of Nain was twelve years of age when Jesus restored his life.

A return of Jupiter, then, marks the arrival, *at a higher octave*, of wisdom and growth. It can sometimes signify introductions to others who will assist you on this path. While these returns enable us to ask more of the world, they also demand that we contribute more to it. *The fruits of our growth must be in the interest of others.*

THE RETURNS OF SATURN

Saturn bears a deep connection to the laws of destiny, holding the threads of evolution leading from the past to the present. It demands order. In its returns live profound secrets of time, connecting us with even greater time-rhythms.[23] Saturn requires 29½ years to encircle the zodiac; this means that we experience the Saturn returns in our own lives as we turn 29½ and 59. These returns actuate two of the most profound points of transition in our lives.

We associate seriousness with Saturn, as well as focus, determination, and the need to face reality. As young people, we enter our twenties having accepted the idea of a higher meaning and purpose to life. *This is the gift of the first return of the Moon's Nodes.* As we near 30, we are ready to receive insight into our individual spiritual mission. Such knowledge comes to initiates (Christ among them, who was baptized at the age of 29 and nine months) with full clarity—indeed, this is typically the time when we begin to prepare for what we know they must do, despite the sacrifices involved. For most of us, however, it comes as more of an urge to take our lives in a particular direction. The return can also be felt simply as the recognition that "party time" is over, and it is not unusual to pursue a course of action that is more "adult" at this time (e.g., marrying, buying a home, or saving for the children's future.)

When an understanding of our mission comes later in life—sometimes decades later—we are often able to look back with absolute clarity at the earlier moments *when we were called but failed to respond. That's okay!*

It is no coincidence that the first Saturn return happens *after* the completion of the first septenary of the Sun years, after which the "I" has a foothold in the emotional life, or sentient soul. The years between 21 and 28 are filled with new experiences, excitement, and discovery; the pot is at full boil! These years precede those associated with the maturity of intellectual soul,[24] during which reason and conscience are more easily integrated into our thinking capacity. William Bryant wrote:

> On the one hand, [between the ages of 28 and 30] we have the changing disposition of the psyche; on the other, the synchronistic events of the outer world that break into our lives. In countless cases, the change at 28 does not "materialize" on the surface as a visible event of some kind until 30 or thereabout. This transition is seldom comfortable and may be marked by conflict, frustration, disenchantment, and disruption. In many cases, this major turning point offers vitally significant human relationships or an adventure of some kind. Frequently a time of agitation and tension, in some respects it represents our release from the legacies of the first 30 years. It can be a new beginning, a time when we reset the rudder of the soul.[25]

The nature of the mission is illuminated by both the natal house placement and the zodiacal sign of Saturn. Looking to the birth charts of Steiner and Tomberg as examples, we find Steiner's Saturn in the 3rd house at 13° Leo, while Tomberg's is in the 11th house at 10° Sagittarius.

---

23 Sucher, *Isis Sophia: Outline of a New Star Wisdom*, 191.
24 This is also known as the "mind soul" or "rational soul."
25 Bryant, *The Veiled Pulse of Time*, 98–99.

Cosmic Tempo

Steiner's Saturn is high on the circle, indicating visibility in the world (along with the inevitable criticisms thereby engendered). The top of the wheel is seen imaginatively as *the mountaintop*, where one goes to receive the high teachings of the spiritual world. His list of accomplishments was as long as an encyclopedia (versatility is characteristic of the 3rd house), and he stood as the authority (Leo) of numerous organizations. The 3rd house, an echo of Gemini, bestowed upon him ambition, intellectual prowess, and the ability to master several different subjects concurrently.

Saturn at Tomberg's birth paints a different picture entirely. It is situated near the bottom of the chart—the least visible portion of the wheel—in the 11th house. He worked anonymously, unrecognized and bereft of a connection to the organization that he might have led forward. His mission was proceeded in obscurity and, during the Second World War, could continue only under the threat of death. Saturn in the 11th house warns of betrayals by those who might be expected to be supportive; Tomberg's ouster from the anthroposophic community might be interpreted in this light. The 11th house

Geocentric birth chart of Rudolf Steiner

Geocentric birth chart of Valentin Tomberg

is the region of the letter-Arcanum of "Temperance," wherein we might find the current of our inner life. He wrote extensively on the importance of meditation as *a means of communion between our eternal and our temporal selves*.

The second Saturn return brings to consciousness the necessity to review the extent to which we have succeeded in accomplishing our mission. Though we live in a time when 60 sounds "youngish," the second return of Saturn signals primarily the beginning of a period of reflection, during which our previous experience is meant to be *digested*. Although, for some, work may continue well past 60, it is crucial that our "activity" not be allowed to elbow "reflection" out of the way. Needless to say, this can be a challenge for those of us who have been using our elbows in this manner for decades.

When the second return of Saturn is upon us, so also is the fifth return of Jupiter. Between this Jupiter return and the next, twelve years will pass— thereby escorting us to the age of 72. (From the cosmic perspective, 72 is the number of years of an average life.) This is the span of time required for the precession of the vernal point by one degree. The vernal point is currently at 5° Pisces. This means that seventy-two years ago, it was at 6° Pisces.

Let's look at this from the other way round. As the vernal point moved from 6° Pisces to 5° Pisces, something else happened: the date at which the Sun finds 6° Pisces advanced one *calendar day*. Seventy-two years ago, the Sun was at 6° Pisces on March 21st; the Sun now reaches 6° Pisces on March 22nd.

On every birthday before we approach our 72nd year, the Sun will reach the degree of our birth on our birthday. As we approach 72 years of life, however, our birthday and the Sun's degree at our birth no longer happen on the same day. (This reminds us that the rate of the precession of the equinoxes is 1° per 72 years.) We can imagine the star shining above our heads, which follows us from one incarnation into another, always serving to magnify the particular horoscope we are currently living; *the birth Sun acts as the mediator of these spiritual forces*. If, for example, the Sun was at 4° Virgo at our birth, we can expect its zodiacal degree on our 72nd birthday to instead be 3° Virgo. This movement thus grants us two celebrations: the celebration of the *day* of our birth, and the celebration of our *cosmic* birthday. The former is a *calendar* memory, whereas the latter is a *cosmic* memory that reflects the exact degree of the Sun at the time of our birth.[26] Even if we are graced with additional years, there is much to be gained by holding in consciousness the cosmic archetype for the length of a human life upon the Earth.

Transits compare current planetary positions with elements in the birth chart: planets, Nodes, and the horizontal and vertical axes. Familiarity with transits is based upon the knowledge of where the planets are *on any given day*. This in itself is a fruitful endeavor—a habit that is enriched by nightly stargazing.

We can discern a great deal by simply knowing the current house locations of Jupiter, Saturn, Uranus, Neptune, and Pluto. Remember: jot down the current locations of these planets on the outer zodiacal ring of every chart you're asked to interpret. Transiting planets can form any of our chosen astrological aspects (conjunction, square, opposition) to a point of interest in a natal chart—but in my experience, transits need to be looked at in a different way.

Regarding transits to the astrological houses, we don't care when a planet is *opposite* the 2nd house (for example); we care that it's *in* the 8th. As an average house spans 30° of the zodiac, it is helpful to know how many *years* these planets typically remain in *one house*:

Jupiter: 1
Saturn: 2½
Uranus: 7
Neptune: 14
Pluto: 21

The same principle holds true for the angles of the chart. If Pluto is conjunct the Ascendant, it is simultaneously opposite the Descendant and square the EZ and EN. A four-in-one! We need only concern ourselves with which of these zodiacal points is being crossed (i.e., *conjuncted*) by a transiting planet. Bearing in mind the forgoing descriptions of the houses, and the meaning of the four angles of the chart (i.e., Ascendant > self, personality; EZ > stature in the world; Descendant > others; and EN > inner life), we will be left to our own imagination regarding the influence of transiting planets as they circumnavigate the chart.

When we venture into the world of transits to natal *planets*, we return to the effects of the conjunctions, squares, and oppositions described in the section on aspects. Conjunctions demand integration; squares cause disruption that renders us unable to go on as we have; and oppositions invoke the law of the Cross, whereby the two planets and their zodiacal signs must be restrained so that—with the assistance of their "opposites"—they might *expand* on a higher plane.

Regarding transits to the Nodes, it's best to look at the Nodes as a united pair (which, indeed, they are). We can surmise that a conjunction to the North Node is at the same time an opposition to the South Node—and also that a transiting planet that is square to one Node is simultaneously square to the other. *All* of these aspects are highly significant; however, square aspects to the Nodes (particularly by the transcendentals) seem to have the most disruptive

---

26 Upon turning 72, our *cosmic* birthday thus occurs on the day *after* our "regular" birthday.

effect upon our biography. Is there any way to head them off at the pass?

These transits will be more productive—and possibly less disruptive—when we do not let ourselves be ambushed. Therefore, it's important that we get used to knowing where in the zodiac they can be found. As we might imagine, the invisible transcendentals in particular are remarkably efficient at working by stealth. (Perhaps they are even amused by how easily we can be surprised!)

The transits of the transcendental planets (Uranus, Neptune, and Pluto) are different from the others, and yet similar to each other in that they lead us (through temptation) to dysfunctional behaviors—at which point they "lower an anvil" to reveal to the world our folly in having fallen for the temptation in the first place! Their effectiveness cannot be overstated. *Transits of the transcendentals are nearly always once-in-a-lifetime events*, and should be respected accordingly. We ignore them at our peril.

When a transcendental planet transits a house in the birth chart, it's difficult *not* to notice. The upheaval and disruption that they usually cause within the domain of life represented by the house have the capacity to alter our lives in profound ways. It's not the intent of the Angels to inflict suffering and pain upon us! They wish instead to make available to us the *redemption* that can result as a consequence of that suffering.

TRANSITING JUPITER

Jupiter broadens our thinking—reaching the level of true wisdom in some of us—and thus brings opportunity for expansion and growth. They key word here is *opportunity*, which is not *static*. It comes and goes. It has a rhythm, a respiration; and the movement of Jupiter is one of its markers. The area of life affected by a transit of Jupiter can seem to go smoothly—provided we avoid overextending ourselves. Jupiter can also bring an almost manic mood that gives us the optimistic feeling that anything is possible, even when it is not.

Jupiter also has a bearing on the social fabric of our lives. Its relationship to the law is one aspect of this, as laws are designed to uphold and support society. We can step this down another level and say that *Jupiter represents the community that supports* us—and in order to remain vital, it requires our attention.

It's beneficial to become attuned to the *transient possibilities* that Jupiter brings. Transiting Jupiter spends about a year in each house. That's our window! If ever there is a time to take a chance on a matter related to its house, this is it. To put this in perspective, it means that Jupiter passes each angle[27] and each house once in twelve years. So, in a typical lifetime—72 years from a cosmic standpoint—Jupiter will make only six passes through the first house, six passes across the Ascendant, etc.

But there is, of course, another side to these transits. For when the forces of Jupiter are received by a person with a lesser degree of moral development, they can result in egotism. (The person can become puffed up with a sense of self-importance.) We could say that when Jupiter comes our way, we must judge our opportunities by what benefit *others* might gain from them. In this way, we guard against Zeus's swift kick in the rear—the fall that follows pride as night follows day!

TRANSITING SATURN

Since Saturn's journey around the zodiac requires almost thirty years, the average time in a house is two and a half years. This means that in a typical lifetime, Saturn will transit a certain point in the chart only two, maybe three times.

The effect of "Saturn's scythe" can be quite depressing when its purpose is not recognized.

As we know, Saturn in the birth chart represents the nature of the spiritual mission. Because Saturn requires discipline and focus, its "scythe" is commonly felt as *the restriction and delay of personal plans*. Indeed, its transits can be seen as a whisper from Mary—one that asks us if the affairs of the house Saturn is transiting are in order. If we were to find little in disarray, the transit would pass like a spring breeze across an alpine meadow. But, because disarray is the "all too human" condition, this is seldom the case! And rest assured: If we ignore the entreaties

---

27 The Ascendant, the EZ, the Descendant, and the EN.

of Saturn now, our work in the future will be that much more difficult. Just like an unpaid electricity bill, cosmic debts compound over time.

Conscience comes to us through the Saturn (crown) chakra, and is typically experienced as *intuition*. To the extent that our intuition is at odds with the current course of our lives, the transits of Saturn bring a period of testing. The call of responsibility and duty are manifestations of transits of Saturn. And when we listen, we become more serious about what we know we must do, even though this is invariably at the expense of personal desire. Ultimately, we see these desires (if only from our upcoming journey through the planetary spheres) for what they are: distractions from a greater purpose.

During transits of Saturn, it is helpful to think of Mary — of her loving embrace and her devotion to our ideal selves (our true Names) which she will protect until we are ready to take them as our own.

TRANSITING URANUS

Uranus requires 84 years to circle the zodiac; therefore, within an average lifespan, Uranus will not have time to transit every planet, every angle, and every house. For example, a significant percentage of us will never experience Uranus transiting the Sun, and for many that do, it will occur at an age when we will be helpless to respond in any way (either by way of our youth or our advanced age). This makes many transits of Uranus once-in-a-lifetime events of great importance.

Transits of Uranus are exciting, unexpected, and agitating. They demand that we nurture our own uniqueness; but in doing so, they can also feed our egotism. One common experience of transiting Uranus is restlessness, or a desire to break free from those people and circumstances that we feel are holding us back in some way. Uranus give us ingenious ideas that tend to "break the mold." It creates an almost irresistible pull toward future possibilities, some of which might come to us in flashes of imagination. Uranus challenges us to speak without notes, and to chart a path to freedom. It illuminates the worn-out aspects of our lives and requires that we evaluate ourselves, our careers, and our friendships and partnerships in terms of their ability to carry us *forward*. (Some of these might be ripe for the old heave-ho!)

Another possibility with these transits is simply *change* — which can come out of the blue like a bolt of lightning. Most of us fear change to some degree or another, but any attachment to the status quo in our life will make the transit more challenging by far. If we feel the restlessness and dissatisfaction that are common to transits of Uranus, but *fail* to make any changes in our life, we risk greater upsets in the future.[28] Why resist the beneficial effects that fresh air and sunshine can bestow on a musty room?

TRANSITING NEPTUNE

All transits of Neptune are once-in-a-lifetime occurrences. Neptune orbits the Sun in 165 years; and so, on average, it might traverse five or six houses between birth and death. Neptune transits bring the possibility of watching something we consider to be steady and secure simply disappear into the ether in the most imperceptible way. No wonder that these transits can render us confused and unable to make decisions! Moreover, "not knowing which end is up" causes us to become especially susceptible to delusion and untruths. Neptune has been known to leave us discouraged and unsure of ourselves. When in this condition, we are more likely to allow the prevailing currents to take us where they will. We might become inclined to abandon our responsibilities, or to expect others to take care of things for us.

The domain of activity of whichever house Neptune happens to be transiting will demand *vigilance* — for the possibility of misreading individuals or circumstances is high. We might even be at risk of being taken for a ride. This is more likely to happen when we idealize something (or someone) beyond the limits of reality. When we recall that the temptation that Neptune puts before us is that of "magnetized feeling" — when feelings are guided only by what we like and dislike — we can be sure that these transits will go better when every effort is made to achieve equanimity within the soul.

---

28 An example of this is the fate of the "tower," which is the subject of the sixteenth letter-Arcanum in *Meditations on the Tarot*.

Alternatively, Neptune draws us to the spirit and inspires us to dream of how our lives could be better. Under its influence, we long to devote ourselves to those things whose value is more eternal. Neptune arouses compassion, and might therefore inspire us to give ourselves over to the needs of others and to devote our efforts toward living more in harmony with our deepest convictions. In this way, some of what Neptune may have dissolved — possessions, status, flawed relationships — is more easily put in the rear-view mirror. We will then be especially open to seeking communion with those who share our spiritual outlook.

TRANSITING PLUTO

Pluto's orbit of 248 years is erratic. It can transit as few as three houses in an average life, or as many as six. As mentioned above, Pluto transits a house for an average of 21 years — but such transits can stretch to *nearly 30*. Obviously, the house that Pluto is transiting will gain significance in proportion to the duration to its passage through it. When we know when we can expect Pluto to be swinging by, we are better able to cope with the crises that its presence can foment.

One of the most important things to understand about the nature of Pluto is that it will set in motion forces that we cannot stop — any more than we can halt the flow of lava from an active volcano! This metaphor is particularly apt, because Pluto deals with forces that exist in the darkness of the subconscious. Indeed, it is the source of nearly everything we hope to avoid. Whatever does rear its head from the depths will likely be *out of our control*, which is why Pluto can arouse fear and shame that can shake us to the core. The irony is that we often succumb to the Plutonian temptation of "will-to-power" in order to *regain* our lost control!

When we cope consciously with Pluto's upsets, we inch toward obedience to the will that is greater than our own. We see in its activity not only the forces of destruction, but also those of regeneration and transformation. Pluto can bring rebirth from the bottom up, for it summons radical transformation — requiring us to assess what is beyond repair in our lives. Furthermore, its transits can precipitate transformative events (as well as introductions to individuals who can have the same effect).

Pluto's character is not sentimental. Always inclined to get to the bottom of things, it confers intensity, depth, and ambition. Its potential to be a tremendous force for good can lead us to union with the divine, whereby the human being comes into communion with the primal love of the heavenly Father. But first we must pray: *Thy will be done.*

AFTERWORD

Two things fill the mind with ever-increasing wonder and awe,
the more often and the more intensely the mind of thought is drawn to them:
the starry heavens above me and the moral law within me.
—Immanuel Kant, *Critique of Practical Reason*

WHEN WE GAZE UPON THE starry firmament with reverent awe, we are drawn to the great cosmic story. We long to know our part within it. But this is increasingly harder to do; stargazing has become so difficult that when we find ourselves in a remote location—beneath millions of stars—we can't believe our eyes! We've never seen so many stars!

The vast expanse that exists between the Earth and the celestial sphere has been polluted by the derivatives of our industry, by electric glare (skyglow), and by invisible beams of electromagnetism that are being propagated at an alarming pace. Even if we adopt the charitable (and unrealistic) viewpoint that it was no one's *intention* to sever our connection with the stars, we can certainly see that the *effect* of these forms of pollution has been exactly that. This consequence has been magnified by our enormous appetite for the virtual life found on electronic screens.

A spiritual assessment of this mess leads us to the certain knowledge that we must engage all of our soul forces to re-establish our lost connection to the cosmos. There was a time, long ago, when clairvoyant perception was an ordinary human faculty. This capacity began to fade as the *kali yuga*, or dark age, was upon us[1]—and though humanity was thereby set adrift in the material world, it also experienced (for the first time) the freedom to establish these lost spiritual connections in a *conscious* manner. Simultaneously, humanity has been free to turn its back on the spiritual world altogether, veering ever closer to the dark future over which hangs the dire warning, "Abandon hope, all ye who enter here."

And yet, between humanity and the stars there now dwells something else: The Earth's etheric atmosphere—and the Earth herself—are now permeated by Christ. This radiant being (the "Etheric Christ") proceeds in waves from the Earth's etheric apex in the region of the South Pole. Moreover, it bears the memory of the entirety of the Incarnation, from the Baptism to the Resurrection. Through Christ's strengthening and enlivening presence, we can remain out of Ahriman's grasp. But first we must acknowledge evil with "a knowing glance," and then consciously align ourselves with Christ:

> The power of Christ is immeasurably strengthening.
> With him, one can pass through all trials and remain peaceful.
> Through him, one can endure to an extraordinary degree.
> Christ bestows great power.[2]

Sophia, too—the Daughter in the heights—can be our companion at this time. As she draws nearer to our Sun, her revelations will be increasingly perceptible to all of humanity. Sophia speaks to us in the language of the stars—astrosophy—and it is she who leads us to the living beings that dwell among the heavenly bodies. Through her intercession, our study can lead us back to the wondrous awe we once felt as we beheld the starry vault so many centuries ago. Perhaps we gazed together upon the stars of the Ram in Mesopotamia as Abraham began his long journey to Canaan. We might then have been fellow stone craftsmen at rest upon the golden sands of Giza, bearing witness to the rising of Orion. And, following the Crucifixion, perhaps we even knelt together in prayer as the Libra Full Moon shone over Golgotha. Dear fellow stargazers: may we experience many more lifetimes together!

---

[1] This 5,000-year period began in 3,102 BC and ended in 1899—when the *Satya Yuga*, or age of light, began.
[2] From Valentin Tomberg's "Meditation on the Etheric Christ."

APPENDIX 1

SIDEREAL LONGITUDES OF IMPORTANT STARS

(Asterisks indicate megastars)

Star	Sidereal Longitude	Constellation
♈ ARIES		
Mirach	5°40'	Andromeda (side of)
Scharatan	9°14'	Aries (left horn)
Hamal	12°55'	Aries (head)
Schedar*	13°3'	Cassiopeia (main)
Almaak*	19°29'	Andromeda (main)
Menkar	19°35'	Cetus (neck)
Zaurak	29°8'	Eridanus
♉ TAURUS		
Algol	1°26'	Perseus (eye of Medusa)
Alcyone*	5°15'	Taurus, Pleiades (main)
—	11°4'–12°8'	Taurus, Hyades
Ain	13°44'	Taurus (left eye)
Aldebaran	15°3'	Taurus (right eye)
Rigel*	22°5'	Orion (left foot)
Nihal	24°56'	Lepus (upper)
Bellatrix*	26°12'	Orion (left shoulder)
Arneb*	26°38'	Lepus (lower)
Capella	27°7'	Auriga (main)
Phaet	27°26'	Columba (main)
Mintaka*	27°37'	Orion (left belt)
Alnilam*	28°43'	Orion (center belt)
Meissa*	28°58'	Orion (head)
Alnitak*	29°56'	Orion (right belt)
♊ GEMINI		
Saiph*	1°40'	Orion (right foot)
Polaris*	3°50'	Ursa Minor (end of tail)
Betelgeuse*	4°1'	Orion (right shoulder)
Menkalinan	5°10'	Auriga (head)
Yildun	6°28'	Ursa Minor (tail)
Alhena	14°22'	Gemini (left foot)
Sirius	19°21'	Canis Major (neck)
Canopus*	20°13'	Carina (main)
Wasat	23°47'	Gemini
Castor	25°30'	Gemini (upper head)
Pollux	28°29'	Gemini (lower head)
♋ CANCER		
Procyon	1°3'	Canis Minor (neck)
Praesepe	12°39'	Cancer (center)
Asellus Borealis	12°48'	Cancer (above the manger)
Asellus Australis	13°59'	Cancer (below the manger)
Kocab	18°35'	Ursa Minor (shoulder)
Acubens	18°54'	Cancer (claw)
Dubhe	20°27'	Ursa Major (Mercury)
Merak	24°42'	Ursa Major (Venus)
Ras Elased Australis	25°58'	Leo (head)
Ras Elased Borealis	26°41'	Leo (head)
Pherkad*	26°52'	Ursa Minor
♌ LEO		
Alphard	2°32'	Hydra (main)
Eta Leonis*	3°10'	Leo
Regulus	5°5'	Leo (heart)
Phad	5°44'	Ursa Major (Moon)
Megrez	6°20'	Ursa Major (Sun)
Rho Leonis*	11°39'	Leo
Alioth	14°12'	Ursa Major (Mars)
Zosma	16°35'	Leo (back)
Mizar	20°58'	Ursa Major (Jupiter)
Denebola	26°53'	Leo (tail)
♍ VIRGO		
Alkaid	2°12'	Ursa Major (Saturn)
Zaniah	10°6'	Virgo
Vindemiatrix	15°12'	Virgo
Algorab	18°43'	Corvus (main)
Spica	29°6'	Virgo (wheat)
Arcturus	29°30'	Boötes (main)
♎ LIBRA		
—	17°8'–17°46'	Crux
Alphecka	17°33'	Corona Borealis
Unuk	27°20'	Serpens (head)

SCORPIO

Antares*	15°1'	Scorpio (heart)
Ras Algethi*	21°25'	Hercules (head)
Lesath*	29°16'	Scorpio (stinger)

⚹ SAGITTARIUS

Central Sun*	2°6'	Galactic Center
Etamin	3°14'	Draco (right eye)
Nunki*	17°39'	Sagittarius (shaft of arrow)
Vega	20°35'	Lyra (main)

♑ CAPRICORN

Altair	7°2'	Aquila (main)
Deneb Algedi	28°48'	Capricorn (back)

AQUARIUS

Sadr*	0°6'	Cygnus (heart)
Fomalhaut	9°7'	Piscis Austrinus (main)
Deneb*	10°35'	Cygnus (tail)
Achernar*	20°34'	Eridanus (end of)
Markab	28°45'	Pegasus (saddle)

♓ PISCES

Scheat	4°38'	Pegasus (shoulder)
Difda	7°51'	Cetus (tail)
Algenib*	14°25'	Pegasus (wing)
Alpheratz	19°34'	Andromeda (main)

APPENDIX 2

PLANETARY ASPECTS WITHIN THE CHRIST CHRONOLOGY

THE EARLIEST DATE OF THE aspects listed here is the conception of the Blessed Virgin in 22 BC; the last is her Assumption in the year AD 44. Again, *the aspects listed apply equally to both the sidereal and tropical zodiacs*, as they do not change from one zodiac to the other. However, any reference to zodiacal degrees will refer only to the original, sidereal zodiac of the Babylonians, in which each sign spans 30° of the heavens. When a planetary pair (e.g., Neptune-Pluto) or one aspect within a set is missing, it is because no major events in or surrounding Christ's life occurred under it.

☉ SUN

SUN–MOON

New Moon

Conception of Solomon Mary	8/DEC/22BC
Conception of Nathan Mary	24/OCT/18BC
Conception of John the Baptist	9/SEP/3BC
Conception of Nathan Jesus	6/MAR/2BC
Healing of three blind boys	10/MAY/31
"I Am the Resurrection…"	25/JUL/32
Raising of Lazarus	26/JUL/32
Triumphant entry into Jerusalem	19/MAR/33

First Quarter Moon

"Behold the Lamb of God" (John 1:36)	1/DEC/29
Summons of Andrew	1/DEC/29
Raising of a man at Cana	31/DEC/29
Conversation at Jacob's well	26/JUL/30
Healing of the paralyzed man	19/JAN/31
Raising of Nazor	1/SEP/32

Full Moon

Birth of Solomon Jesus	5/MAR/6BC
Raising of Essene's daughter	7/FEB/30
Teaching of baptism by fire	23/JUN/31
Healing of ten lepers	12/JUN/32
Scourging, Crowning with thorns, Death sentence, Carrying of the cross, Nailing to the cross, Raised upon the cross, Death of Nathan Jesus	3/APR/33

SUN–MERCURY

Inferior Conjunction

Summons of Philip	24/DEC/29
Walking on the water (1st)	8/DEC/30
Commissioning of the disciples	10/DEC/30
Transfiguration	4/APR/31
Healing of the man born blind	23/NOV/31

Superior Conjunction

Conception of Nathan Mary	24/OCT/18BC
Start of the forty days (Jesus Christ)	21/OCT/29
Arrival at Mount Attarus	23/OCT/29
Healing of the blind youth	6/OCT/30
Healing of the Syrophoenician woman	12/FEB/31
Blessing of the children	17/MAY/32
Raising of Nazor	1/SEP/32

SUN–VENUS

Inferior Conjunction

Death of Solomon Jesus	5/JUN/12
Triumphant entry into Jerusalem	19/MAR/33
Cursing the fig tree	20/MAR/33
Theophany (2nd)	20/MAR/33
"Woe upon the Pharisees"	24/MAR/33

Superior Conjunction

Healing of the blind youth	6/OCT/30
Summons of Judas	24/OCT/30
Summons of Thomas	29/OCT/30
Conversion of Mary Magdalene (1st)	8/NOV/30
Blessing of the children	17/MAY/32
The call of Zacchaeus	30/MAY/32
Healing of two blind men	10/JUN/32
Healing of ten lepers	12/JUN/32

SUN–MARS

Conjunction

Death of Solomon Jesus	5/JUN/12

Square

Raising of youth of Nain	13/NOV/30
Raising of Jairus's daughter (1st)	18/NOV/30
Summons of Matthew	19/NOV/30

Jesus stills the Sea of Galilee	21/NOV/30
Miraculous draught of fishes	26/NOV/30
Raising of Jairus's daughter (2nd)	1/DEC/30
Power upon the twelve	4/DEC/30
The call of Zacchaeus	30/MAY/32
Healing of two blind men	10/JUN/32
Healing of ten lepers	12/JUN/32

Opposition

Conversation at Jacob's well	26/JUL/30
Healing of Theokeno	28/SEP/32

SUN–JUPITER

Conjunction

Conception of Solomon Mary	8/DEC/22BC
Blessing of the children	17/MAY/32

Square

Birth of Nathan Jesus	6/DEC/2BC
Conversion of Mary Magdalene (2nd)	26/DEC/30

SUN–SATURN

Conjunction

Teaching of baptism by fire	23/JUN/31

Square

Adoration of the Magi	26/DEC/6BC
Raising of a pagan child	23/SEP/30
Feeding of the four thousand	15/MAR/31
Scourging through the Resurrection	3/APR/33–5/APR/33
Appearance in Emmaus	6/APR/33
Appearance to the eleven	11/APR/33

Opposition

First temptation	27/NOV/29
Second temptation	28/NOV/29
Third temptation	29/NOV/29
End of the forty days	30/NOV/29
Summons of Andrew	1/DEC/29
Commissioning of the disciples	10/DEC/30

SUN–URANUS

Conjunction

Flight into Egypt	2/MAR/5BC
Healing of the nobleman's son	3/AUG/30

Square

Conversion Mary Magdalene (1st)	8/NOV/30
Ascension	14/MAY/33

Opposition

Birth of Nathan Mary	17/JUL/17BC
Feeding of the five thousand	29/JAN/31
Walking on the water	30/JAN/31
Teaching of the bread of life	2/FEB/31

SUN–NEPTUNE

Conjunction

Healing of the paralyzed man	19/JAN/31

Opposition

Death of Solomon Jesus	5/JUN/12
"I Am the Resurrection…"	25/JUL/32
Raising of Lazarus	26/JUL/32
Death of Solomon Mary	15/AUG/44
Assumption of Virgin discovered	16/AUG/44

SUN–PLUTO

Conjunction

Conception of John the Baptist	9/SEP/3BC
First temptation	27/NOV/29
Second temptation	28/NOV/29
Third temptation	29/NOV/29
End of the forty days	30/NOV/29
Summons of Andrew	1/DEC/29
Raising of Jairus's daughter (2nd)	1/DEC/30
Power upon the twelve	4/DEC/30
Healing of demons at Gergesa	6/DEC/30

Square

Healing of Mara the Suphanite	4/SEP/30
Raising of Nazor	1/SEP/32

Opposition

Birth of Solomon Jesus	5/MAR/6BC
Flight into Egypt	2/MAR/5BC
Peter cures a lame man	2/JUN/33

☽ MOON

MOON–MERCURY

Conjunction

Birth of John the Baptist	4/JUN/2BC
Conception of Nathan Mary	24/OCT/18BC
Death of Nathan Mary	5/AUG/12
"I am the Resurrection and…"	25/JUL/32
Appearance to the five hundred	16/APR/33

Square

Conception of Solomon Jesus	7/JUN/7BC
Conversion of Mary Magdalene (1st)	8/NOV/30
Teaching of the bread of life	2/FEB/31
Raising of Nazor	1/SEP/32
"Woe upon the Pharisees"	24/MAR/33

Opposition

Conversion of Mary Magdalene (2nd)	26/DEC/30
Last anointing	1/APR/33

Planetary Aspects within the Christ Chronology

MOON–VENUS

Conjunction
Birth of Nathan Mary	17/JUL/17BC
First temptation	27/NOV/29
Healing of the Syrophoenician woman	12/FEB/31
Triumphant entry into Jerusalem	19/MAR/33
Death of Nathan Jesus	3/APR/33
Appearance to the seven	15/APR/33

Square
Baptism	23/SEP/29
"Behold the Lamb of God" (John 1:29)	7/OCT/29
Summons of Peter	19/DEC/29
Walking on the water (1st)	8/DEC/30
Death of Solomon Mary	15/AUG/44

Opposition
Feeding of the five thousand	29/JAN/31
Healing of ten lepers	12/JUN/32
Last anointing	1/APR/33

MOON–MARS

Conjunction
Birth of Nathan Mary	17/JUL/17BC
Birth of John the Baptist	4/JUN/2BC
Death of Nathan Mary	5/AUG/12
Summons of Peter	19/DEC/29

Square
Adoration of the Magi	26/DEC/6BC
Union in the temple	3/APR/12
First temptation	27/NOV/29
Cleansing of the temple	6/APR/30
Healing of Mara the Suphanite	4/SEP/30
Appearance to the seven	15/APR/33

Opposition
Healing of demons at Gergasa	6/DEC/30
Death of John the Baptist	4/JAN/31

MOON–JUPITER

Conjunction
Conception of Solomon Mary	8/DEC/22BC
"Behold the Lamb of God" (John 1:29)	7/OCT/29
End of the forty days	30/NOV/29
Turning water into wine	28/DEC/29
"Woe upon the Pharisees"	24/MAR/33

Square
Raising of a pagan child	23/SEP/30
Transfiguration	4/APR/31
Last anointing	1/APR/33
Appearance to the seven	15/APR/33

Opposition
Visitation (Nathan Mary) to Elizabeth	30/MAR/2BC
Start of the forty days (Jesus Christ)	21/OCT/29

Walking on the water (1st)	8/DEC/30
Theophany (1st)	28/MAR/31

MOON–SATURN

Conjunction
Healing of the nobleman's son	3/AUG/30
Attempted murder of Jesus Christ	12/AUG/30
Peter receives the keys	19/MAR/31
The call of Zacchaeus	30/MAY/32

Square
Birth of Solomon Mary	7/SEP/21BC
"Behold the Lamb of God" (John 1:36)	1/DEC/29
Summons of Andrew	1/DEC/29
Turning water into wine	28/DEC/29
Death of John the Baptist	4/JAN/31
Healing of the Syrophoenician woman	12/FEB/31
Enmity of the Pharisees	26/MAR/31
Cursing the fig tree	20/MAR/33
Theophany (2nd)	20/MAR/33
Descent into hell	4/APR/33
Ascension	14/MAY/33

Opposition
Death of Solomon Jesus	5/JUN/12
Teaching of baptism by fire	23/JUN/31

MOON–URANUS

Conjunction
Birth of Solomon Mary	7/SEP/21BC
Death of Solomon Mary	15/AUG/44
Power upon the twelve	4/DEC/30
Pentecost	24/MAY/33

Square
Birth of John the Baptist	4/JUN/2BC
Raising of youth of Nain	13/NOV/30
Miraculous draught of fishes	26/NOV/30
Feeding of the four thousand	15/MAR/31
Appearance in Emmaus	6/APR/33

Opposition
Summons of Matthew	19/NOV/30

MOON–NEPTUNE

Conjunction
First temptation	27/NOV/29
Raising of Jairus's daughter (1st)	18/NOV/30
Raising of Essene's daughter	7/FEB/30
Appearance to the eleven	11/APR/33

Square
Birth of Solomon Mary	7/SEP/21BC
Healing of Mara the Suphanite	4/SEP/30
Summons of Thomas	29/OCT/30
Resurrection	5/APR/33

Opposition

"I am the Resurrection and…"	25/JUL/32
Raising of Lazarus	26/JUL/32

MOON–PLUTO

Conjunction

Birth of Solomon Jesus	5/MAR/6BC
Raising of Nazor	1/SEP/32
Peter cures a lame man	2/JUN/33

Square

Union in the temple	3/APR/12
Death of Nathan Mary	5/AUG/12
"Behold the Lamb of God" (John 1:36)	1/DEC/29
Summons of Andrew	1/DEC/29
Jesus stills the Sea of Galilee	21/NOV/30
Healing of demons at Gergasa	6/DEC/30
Walking on the water	30/JAN/31
Last anointing	1/APR/33
Appearance to the seven	15/APR/33
Death of Solomon Mary	15/AUG/44

Opposition

Conversion of Mary Magdalene (2nd)	26/DEC/30

☿ MERCURY

MERCURY–VENUS

Conjunction

Conception of John the Baptist	9/SEP/3BC
Healing of Mara the Suphanite	4/SEP/30
Raising of a pagan child	23/SEP/30
Healing of the blind youth	6/OCT/30
Raising of Jairus's daughter (2nd)	1/DEC/30
Power upon the twelve	4/DEC/30
Death of Lazarus	15/JUL/32
Death of Nathan Jesus	3/APR/33
Descent into hell	4/APR/33
Resurrection	5/APR/33
Appearance in Emmaus	6/APR/33

MERCURY–MARS

Conjunction

Birth of John the Baptist	4/JUN/2BC
Death of Nathan Mary	5/AUG/12
Teaching of baptism by fire	23/JUN/31

Square

Summons of Thomas	29/OCT/30
Commissioning of the disciples	10/DEC/30
Healing of the paralyzed man	19/JAN/31
Blessing of the children	17/MAY/32
Triumphant entry into Jerusalem	19/MAR/33
Theophany (2nd)	20/MAR/33
Cursing the fig tree	20/MAR/33
"Woe upon the Pharisees"	24/MAR/33

MERCURY–JUPITER

Conjunction

Feeding of the four Thousand	15/MAR/31
Peter receives the keys	19/MAR/31
Enmity of the Pharisees	26/MAR/31
Healing of three blind boys	10/MAY/31
Blessing of the children	17/MAY/32
Pentecost	24/MAY/33

Square

Birth of Solomon Mary	7/SEP/21BC
Adoration of the Magi	26/DEC/6BC
Healing of the paralyzed man	19/JAN/31
Last anointing through the Resurrection	3/APR/33–5/APR/33

Opposition

Healing of the blind youth	6/OCT/30

MERCURY–SATURN

Conjunction

Healing of two blind men	10/JUN/32
Healing of ten lepers	12/JUN/32

Square

Birth of Nathan Mary	17/JUL/17BC
Baptism	23/SEP/29
Healing of Theokeno	28/SEP/32

Opposition

Miraculous draught of fishes	26/NOV/30
Raising of Jairus's daughter (2nd)	1/DEC/30
Power upon the twelve	4/DEC/30
Healing of demons at Gergasa	6/DEC/30
Death of John the Baptist	4/JAN/31

MERCURY–URANUS

Square

Birth of John the Baptist	4/JUN/2BC
Cleansing of the temple	6/APR/30
Conversation with Nicodemus	9/APR/30
Summons of Judas	24/OCT/30
Summons of Thomas	29/OCT/30

MERCURY–NEPTUNE

Conjunction

Raising of Essene's daughter	7/FEB/30
Feeding of the five thousand	29/JAN/31
Walking on the water	30/JAN/31

Square

Start of the forty days (Jesus Christ)	21/OCT/29
Healing of three blind boys	10/MAY/31

Planetary Aspects within the Christ Chronology

Opposition

Death of Lazarus	15/JUL/32

MERCURY–PLUTO

Conjunction

Birth of Nathan Mary	17/JUL/17BC
Raising of youth of Nain	13/NOV/30
Commissioning of the disciples	10/DEC/30
Conversion of Mary Magdalene (2nd)	26/DEC/30

Square

Death of Nathan Mary	5/AUG/12
Healing of the nobleman's son	3/AUG/30
Attempted murder of Jesus Christ	12/AUG/30
Raising of Nazor	1/SEP/32
Last anointing through the Resurrection	3/APR/33–5/APR/33

Opposition

Visitation (Nathan Mary) to Elizabeth	30/MAR/2BC

♀ VENUS

VENUS–MARS

Conjunction

Birth of Nathan Mary	17/JUL/17BC
Birth of Nathan Jesus	6/DEC/2BC
Death of Solomon Jesus	5/JUN/12
Transfiguration	4/APR/31

Square

Arrival at Mount Attarus	23/OCT/29
First temptation	27/NOV/29
Second temptation	28/NOV/29
Third temptation	29/NOV/29
End of the forty days	30/NOV/29
Summons of Andrew	1/DEC/29
Summons of Peter	19/DEC/29
Conversion of Mary Magdalene (1st)	8/NOV/30
Raising of youth of Nain	13/NOV/30
Raising of Jairus's daughter (1st)	18/NOV/30
The call of Zacchaeus	30/MAY/32
Healing of two blind men	JUN/10/32
Assumption of Virgin discovered	14/MAY/33

VENUS–JUPITER

Square

"Behold the Lamb of God" (John 1:29)	7/OCT/29
Conversation at Jacob's well	26/JUL/30
Walking on the water (1st)	8/DEC/30
Commissioning of the disciples	10/DEC/30
Teaching of baptism by fire	23/JUN/31
Appearance to the eleven	11/APR/33
Appearance to the seven	15/APR/33
Appearance to the five hundred	16/APR/33
Mary receives holy communion	17/APR/33

Opposition

Healing of the blind youth	6/OCT/30

VENUS–SATURN

Conjunction

Visitation (Nathan Mary) to Elizabeth	30/MAR/2BC

Square

Conception of Solomon Mary	8/DEC/22BC
Raising of a pagan child	23/SEP/30
Healing of the Syrophoenician woman	12/FEB/31
Pentecost	24/MAY/33
Peter cures a lame man	2/JUN/33

Opposition

Start of the forty days	21/OCT/29
Raising of Jairus's daughter (2nd)	1/DEC/30
Power upon the twelve	4/DEC/30
Healing of the demons at Gergesa	6/DEC/30
Walking on the water (1st)	8/DEC/30

VENUS–URANUS

Conjunction

Teaching of baptism by fire	23/JUN/31
"I Am the Resurrection…"	25/JUL/32
Raising of Lazarus	26/JUL/32

Square

Enmity of the Pharisees	26/MAR/31
Theophany (1st)	28/MAR/31

VENUS–NEPTUNE

Conjunction

First temptation	27/NOV/29
Second temptation	28/NOV/29
Third temptation	29/NOV/29
End of the forty days	30/NOV/29
Summons of Andrew	1/DEC/29
Summons of Peter	19/DEC/29
Summons of Philip	24/DEC/29
Turning of water into wine	28/DEC/29
Raising of a man at Cana	31/DEC/29
Conversion of Mary Magdalene (2nd)	26/DEC/30

Square

Feeding of the four thousand	15/MAR/31
Peter receives the keys	19/MAR/31

Opposition

Visitation (Nathan Mary) to Elizabeth	30/MAR/2BC
Death of Solomon Jesus	5/JUN/12
Death of Lazarus	15/JUL/32

VENUS–PLUTO

Conjunction

Jesus stills the Sea of Galilee	21/NOV/30
Miraculous draught of fishes	26/NOV/30

Square

Teaching of the bread of life	2/FEB/31

Opposition

Death of Solomon Mary	15/AUG/44
Assumption of Virgin discovered	16/AUG/44

♂ MARS

MARS–JUPITER

Conjunction

Birth of Solomon Jesus	5/MAR/6BC
Healing of the paralyzed man	19/JAN/31
Appearance to the eleven	11/APR/33
Appearance to the seven	15/APR/33
Appearance to the five hundred	16/APR/33
Mary receives holy communion	17/APR/33

Square

Conception of Nathan Jesus	6/MAR/2BC
Blessing of the children	17/MAY/32

Opposition

Conception of Solomon Jesus	7/JUN/7BC

MARS–SATURN

Conjunction

Visitation (Nathan Mary) to Elizabeth	30/MAR/2BC

Square

"Behold the Lamb of God" (John 1:29)	7/OCT/29
Conversion of Mary Magdalene (2nd)	26/DEC/30
Raising of Nazor	1/SEP/32

Opposition

Conception of Solomon Jesus	7/JUN/7BC
Union in the temple	3/APR/12
Raising of Essene's daughter	7/FEB/30

MARS–URANUS

Square

Birth of John the Baptist	4/JUN/2BC
Turning of water into wine	28/DEC/29
Raising of a man at Cana	31/DEC/29
Feeding of the four thousand	15/MAR/31

Opposition

Summons of Judas	24/OCT/30
Summons of Thomas	29/OCT/30

MARS–NEPTUNE

Conjunction

Flight into Egypt	2/MAR/5BC
Conversation at Jacob's well	26/JUL/30
Healing of the nobleman's son	3/AUG/30
Attempted murder of Jesus Christ	12/AUG/30
Healing of Mara the Suphanite	4/SEP/30

Square

End of the forty days	30/NOV/29
Summons of Andrew	1/DEC/29
Healing of the Syrophoenician woman	12/FEB/31
Healing of the man born blind	23/NOV/31

Opposition

Visitation (Nathan Mary) to Elizabeth	30/MAR/2BC
Death of Solomon Jesus	5/JUN/12

MARS–PLUTO

Conjunction

Birth of Solomon Mary	7/SEP/21BC

Square

Death of Nathan Mary	5/AUG/12
Baptism	23/SEP/29
Raising of Jairus's daughter (2nd)	1/DEC/30
Power upon the twelve	4/DEC/30
Healing of demons at Gergesa	6/DEC/30
Walking on the water (1st)	8/DEC/30
Commissioning of the disciples	10/DEC/30
The call of Zacchaeus	30/MAY/32
Healing of two blind men	10/JUN/32

Opposition

Conception of Nathan Mary	24/OCT/18BC
Appearance to the eleven	11/APR/33
Appearance to the seven	15/APR/33
Appearance to the five hundred	16/APR/33
Mary receives holy communion	17/APR/33

♃ JUPITER

JUPITER–SATURN

Conjunction

Conception of the Solomon Jesus	7/JUN/7BC

Square

Turning of water into wine	28/DEC/29
Raising of a man at Cana	31/DEC/29

JUPITER–URANUS

Square

Conception of Nathan Mary	24/OCT/18BC
Teaching of baptism by fire	23/JUN/31

Planetary Aspects within the Christ Chronology

JUPITER–NEPTUNE

Square

Death of Nathan Mary	5/AUG/12
Healing of three blind boys	10/MAY/31

JUPITER–PLUTO

Opposition

Death of Lazarus	15/JUL/32
"I Am the Resurrection…"	25/JUL/32
Raising of Lazarus	26/JUL/32
Triumphant entry into Jerusalem	19/MAR/33
Cursing of the fig tree	20/MAR/33
Theophany (2nd)	20/MAR/33
"Woe upon the Pharisees"	24/MAR/33
Last anointing through the Resurrection	1/APR/33–5/APR/33
Appearance in Emmaus	6/APR/33
Appearance to the eleven	11/APR/33
Appearance to the seven	15/APR/33
Appearance to the five hundred	16/APR/33
Mary receives holy communion	17/APR/33

♄ SATURN

SATURN–URANUS

Square

Conception of Solomon Mary	8/DEC/22BC
Birth of Solomon Mary	7/SEP/21BC

SATURN–NEPTUNE

Conjunction

Conception of Solomon Mary	8/DEC/22BC
Birth of Solomon Mary	7/SEP/21BC

Opposition

Conception of Nathan Jesus	6/MAR/2BC
Visitation (Nathan Mary) to Elizabeth	30/MAR/2BC
Healing of Theokeno	28/SEP/32

SATURN–PLUTO

Square

Birth of Nathan Mary	17/JUL/17BC

Opposition

Arrival at Mount Attarus	23/OCT/29
First temptation	27/NOV/29
Second temptation	28/NOV/29
Third temptation	29/NOV/29
End of the forty days	30/NOV/29
Summons of Andrew	1/DEC/29
Summons of Peter	19/DEC/29
Summons of Philip	24/DEC/29
Turning of water into wine	28/DEC/29
Raising of a man at Cana	31/DEC/29
Raising of Essene's daughter	7/FEB/30
Cleansing of the temple	6/APR/30
Conversation with Nicodemus	9/APR/30

♅ URANUS

URANUS–NEPTUNE

Square

Conception of Solomon Mary	8/DEC/22BC
Birth of the Solomon Mary	7/SEP/21BC

URANUS–PLUTO

Opposition

Conception of Solomon Jesus	7/JUN/7BC
Birth of Solomon Jesus	5/MAR/6BC
Flight into Egypt	2/MAR/5BC
Conception of John the Baptist	9/SEP/3BC
Conception of Nathan Jesus	6/MAR/2BC
Visitation (Nathan Mary) to Elizabeth	30/MAR/2BC
Birth of Nathan Jesus	6/DEC/2BC

APPENDIX 3

GEOCENTRIC PLANETARY POSITIONS WITHIN THE CHRIST CHRONOLOGY

☉ SUN

Event	Date	Position
Cursing the fig tree	20/MAR/33	0♈23
Theophany (2nd)	20/MAR/33	0♈33
"Woe upon the Pharisees"	24/MAR/33	4♈24
Enmity of the Pharisees	26/MAR/31	5♈52
Theophany (1st)	28/MAR/31	7♈41
Visitation (Nathan Mary) to Elizabeth	30/MAR/2BC	10♈5
Last anointing	1/APR/33	12♈22
Last supper	2/APR/33	13♈20
Gethsemane	2/APR/33	13♈26
Betrayal of Judas	2/APR/33	13♈28
Trial by Caiaphas	3/APR/33	13♈36
Peter's denial	3/APR/33	13♈41
Trial by Pontius Pilate	3/APR/33	13♈44
Scourging	3/APR/33	13♈51
Crowning with thorns	3/APR/33	13♈52
Death sentence	3/APR/33	13♈54
Carrying of the cross	3/APR/33	13♈58
Transfiguration	4/APR/31	13♈59
Nailed to cross	3/APR/33	13♈59
Raised upon the cross	3/APR/33	14♈0
Death of Nathan Jesus	3/APR/33	14♈6
Union in the temple	3/APR/12	14♈36
Descent into hell	4/APR/33	14♈57
Resurrection	5/APR/33	15♈39
Cleansing of the temple	6/APR/30	16♈29
Appearance in Emmaus	6/APR/33	17♈0
Conversation with Nicodemus	9/APR/30	19♈4
Appearance to the eleven	11/APR/33	22♈4
Appearance to the seven	15/APR/33	25♈19
Appearance to the five hundred	16/APR/33	26♈50
Mary receives holy communion	23/APR/33	2♉46
Healing of three blind boys	10/MAY/31	19♉5
Ascension of Jesus Christ	14/MAY/33	23♉19
Blessing of the children	17/MAY/32	26♉26
Pentecost	24/MAY/33	2♊35
The call of Zacchaeus	30/MAY/32	8♊49
Peter cures a lame man	2/JUN/33	11♊21
Birth of John the Baptist	4/JUN/2BC	12♊37
Death of Solomon Jesus	5/JUN/12	14♊12
Conception of Solomon Jesus	7/JUN/7BC	16♊10
Healing of two blind men	10/JUN/32	19♊17
Healing of ten lepers	12/JUN/32	21♊11
Teaching of baptism by fire	23/JUN/31	1♋7
Death of Lazarus	15/JUL/32	22♋43
Birth of Nathan Mary	17/JUL/17BC	25♋25
"I am the Resurrection and..."	25/JUL/32	2♌37
Conversation at Jacob's well	26/JUL/30	2♌50
Raising of Lazarus	26/JUL/32	3♌4
Healing of the nobleman's son	3/AUG/30	10♌36
Death of Nathan Mary	5/AUG/12	12♌36
Attempted murder of Jesus Christ	12/AUG/30	19♌37
Death of Solomon Mary	15/AUG/44	22♌46
Assumption of Virgin discovered	16/AUG/44	23♌17
Raising of Nazor	1/SEP/32	9♍28
Healing of Mara the Suphanite	4/SEP/30	11♍57
Birth of Solomon Mary	7/SEP/21BC	16♍3
Conception of John the Baptist	9/SEP/3BC	17♍3
Raising of a pagan child	23/SEP/30	0♎40
Baptism	23/SEP/29	0♎50
Healing of Theokeno	28/SEP/32	6♎3
Healing of the blind youth	6/OCT/30	13♎40
"Behold the Lamb of God" (John 1:29)	7/OCT/29	14♎48
Start of the forty days (Jesus Christ)	21/OCT/29	29♎21
Arrival at Mount Attarus	23/OCT/29	1♏22
Summons of Judas	24/OCT/30	1♏50
Conception of Nathan Mary	24/OCT/18BC	2♏23
Summons of Thomas	29/OCT/30	6♏49
Conversion of Mary Magdalene (1st)	8/NOV/30	17♏19
Raising of youth of Nain	13/NOV/30	22♏1
Raising of Jairus's daughter (1st)	18/NOV/30	27♏22
Summons of Matthew	19/NOV/30	28♏26
Jesus stills the Sea of Galilee	21/NOV/30	0♐44
Healing of the man born blind	23/NOV/31	2♐20
Miraculous draught of fishes	26/NOV/30	5♐45
First temptation	27/NOV/29	6♐51
Second temptation	28/NOV/29	7♐53
Third temptation	29/NOV/29	8♐54
End of the forty days	30/NOV/29	9♐58
"Behold the Lamb of God" (John 1:36)	1/DEC/29	10♐36
Summons of Andrew	1/DEC/29	10♐41
Raising of Jairus's daughter (2nd)	1/DEC/30	10♐46
Power upon the twelve	4/DEC/30	13♐49
Healing of demons at Gergasa	6/DEC/30	15♐37
Birth of Nathan Jesus	6/DEC/2BC	16♐4

Geocentric Planetary Positions within the Christ Chronology

Walking on the water (1st)	8/DEC/30	17♐9
Conception of Solomon Mary	8/DEC/22BC	17♐35
Commissioning of the disciples	10/DEC/30	19♐49
Summons of Peter	19/DEC/29	29♐8
Summons of Philip	24/DEC/29	4♑29
Conversion of Mary Magdalene (2nd)	26/DEC/30	6♑0
Adoration of the Magi	26/DEC/6BC	6♑15
Turning water into wine	28/DEC/29	8♑18
Raising of a man at Cana	31/DEC/29	11♑21
Death of John the Baptist	4/JAN/31	14♑39
Healing of the paralyzed man	19/JAN/31	0♒35
Feeding of the five thousand	29/JAN/31	10♒37
Walking on the water	30/JAN/31	10♒54
Teaching of the bread of life	2/FEB/31	14♒47
Raising of Essene's daughter	7/FEB/30	19♒41
Healing of the Syrophoenician woman	12/FEB/31	24♒34
Flight into Egypt	2/MAR/5BC	13♓41
Birth of Solomon Jesus	5/MAR/6BC	15♓46
Conception of Nathan Jesus	6/MAR/2BC	16♓13
Feeding of the four thousand	15/MAR/31	25♓16
Peter receives the keys	19/MAR/31	28♓41
Triumphant entry into Jerusalem	19/MAR/33	29♓24

☾ MOON

Raising of a man at Cana	31/DEC/29	9♈53
Birth of Nathan Jesus	6/DEC/2BC	11♈59
Appearance to the five hundred	16/APR/33	12♈14
Cursing the fig tree	20/MAR/33	13♈44
Theophany (2nd)	20/MAR/33	16♈12
Ascension of Jesus Christ	14/MAY/33	16♈44
Healing of Mara the Suphanite	4/SEP/30	26♈38
Summons of Thomas	29/OCT/30	29♈3
Healing of the paralyzed man	19/JAN/31	5♉9
Death of Solomon Jesus	5/JUN/12	5♉57
Feeding of the four thousand	15/MAR/31	8♉45
Miraculous draught of fishes	26/NOV/30	12♉51
Healing of three blind boys	10/MAY/31	23♉6
Conversion of Mary Magdalene (2nd)	26/DEC/30	11♊9
"Woe upon the Pharisees"	24/MAR/33	11♊43
Peter receives the keys	19/MAR/31	20♊27
Healing of the blind youth	6/OCT/30	20♊39
Attempted murder of Jesus Christ	12/AUG/30	20♊42
Birth of John the Baptist	4/JUN/2BC	3♋15
Mary receives holy communion	23/APR/33	7♋44
The call of Zacchaeus	30/MAY/32	8♋11
Raising of Jairus's daughter (2nd)	1/DEC/30	11♋9
Adoration of the Magi	26/DEC/6BC	15♋46
Death of Nathan Mary	5/AUG/12	24♋7
"I am the Resurrection and…"	25/JUL/32	29♋12
Raising of Lazarus	26/JUL/32	4♌39
Birth of Nathan Mary	17/JUL/17BC	5♌50
Healing of the man born blind	23/NOV/31	5♌51
Baptism	23/SEP/29	16♌16
Power of the twelve	4/DEC/30	18♌23
Raising of Essene's daughter	7/FEB/30	24♌20
Pentecost	24/MAY/33	24♌59
Start of the forty days (Jesus Christ)	21/OCT/29	0♍19
Conversion of Mary Magdalene (1st)	8/NOV/30	4♍45
Feeding of the five thousand	29/JAN/31	7♍2
Healing of demons at Gergasa	6/DEC/30	10♍35
Walking on the water	30/JAN/31	10♍55
Birth of Solomon Jesus	5/MAR/6BC	14♍48
Conception of John the Baptist	9/SEP/3BC	16♍32
Last anointing	1/APR/33	21♍34
Enmity of the Pharisees	26/MAR/31	23♍45
Death of John the Baptist	4/JAN/31	27♍15
Arrival at Mount Attarus	23/OCT/29	29♍46
Walking on the water (1st)	8/DEC/30	0♎47
Last supper	2/APR/33	3♎30
Gethsemane	2/APR/33	4♎45
Betrayal of Judas	2/APR/33	5♎15
Trial by Caiaphas	3/APR/33	6♎45
Cleansing of the temple	6/APR/30	7♎49
Peter's denial	3/APR/33	7♎53
Trial by Pontius Pilate	3/APR/33	8♎31
Scourging	3/APR/33	9♎53
Crowning with thorns	3/APR/33	10♎9
Death sentence	3/APR/33	10♎31
Death of Solomon Mary	15/AUG/44	10♎56
Carrying of the cross	3/APR/33	11♎24
Nailed to cross	3/APR/33	11♎39
Raised upon the cross	3/APR/33	11♎47
Conception of Solomon Jesus	7/JUN/7BC	11♎54
Death of Nathan Jesus	3/APR/33	13♎2
Assumption of Virgin discovered	16/AUG/44	17♎52
Theophany (1st)	28/MAR/31	20♎11
Descent into hell	4/APR/33	23♎41
Summons of Peter	19/DEC/29	29♎4
Resurrection	5/APR/33	2♏42
Teaching of the bread of life	2/FEB/31	3♏22
Conversation at Jacob's well	26/JUL/30	4♏2
Conception of Nathan Mary	24/OCT/18BC	4♏25
Commissioning of the disciples	10/DEC/30	8♏11
Raising of youth of Nain	13/NOV/30	11♏18
Conversation with Nicodemus	9/APR/30	18♏33
Appearance in Emmaus	6/APR/33	20♏8
Healing of two blind men	10/JUN/32	25♏40
Healing of Theokeno	28/SEP/32	3♐45
Raising of Nazor	1/SEP/32	9♐55
Conception of Solomon Mary	8/DEC/22BC	18♐47
Peter cures a lame man	2/JUN/33	19♐20

Event	Date	Position
Healing of ten lepers	12/JUN/32	24♐50
Teaching of baptism by fire	23/JUN/31	3♑4
Flight into Egypt	2/MAR/5BC	3♑26
Birth of Solomon Mary	7/SEP/21BC	4♑5
Raising of a pagan child	23/SEP/30	7♑55
Summons of Philip	24/DEC/29	14♑0
Blessing of the children	17/MAY/32	15♑2
First temptation	27/NOV/29	18♑46
Transfiguration	4/APR/31	23♑15
Raising of Jairus's daughter (1st)	18/NOV/30	29♑23
Appearance to the eleven	11/APR/33	0♒5
Visitation (Nathan Mary) to Elizabeth	30/MAR/2BC	0♒28
Second temptation	28/NOV/29	2♒7
Union in the temple	3/APR/12	2♒19
Summons of Matthew	19/NOV/30	13♒44
Third temptation	29/NOV/29	15♒4
Healing of the nobleman's son	3/AUG/30	26♒56
End of the forty days	30/NOV/29	28♒10
Summons of Judas	24/OCT/30	28♒18
"Behold the Lamb of God" (John 1:29)	7/OCT/29	1♓15
Turning water into wine	28/DEC/29	3♓24
"Behold the Lamb of God" (John 1:36)	1/DEC/29	5♓53
Summons of Andrew	1/DEC/29	6♓54
Conception of Nathan Jesus	6/MAR/2BC	12♓12
Jesus stills the Sea of Galilee	21/NOV/30	13♓13
Death of Lazarus	15/JUL/32	18♓29
Appearance to the seven	15/APR/33	18♓52
Healing of the Syrophoenician woman	12/FEB/31	21♓41
Triumphant entry into Jerusalem	19/MAR/33	28♓46

☿ MERCURY

Event	Date	Position
Conception of Nathan Jesus	6/MAR/2BC	0♈31
Appearance to the eleven	11/APR/33	2♈44
Appearance to the seven	15/APR/33	8♈42
Transfiguration	4/APR/31	11♈4
Appearance to the five hundred	16/APR/33	11♈38
Feeding of the four thousand	15/MAR/31	14♈10
Theophany (1st)	28/MAR/31	15♈1
Enmity of the Pharisees	26/MAR/31	15♈49
Peter receives the keys	19/MAR/31	16♈1
Mary receives holy communion	23/APR/33	23♈48
Healing of three blind boys	10/MAY/31	27♈29
Cleansing of the temple	6/APR/30	4♉53
Conversation with Nicodemus	9/APR/30	5♉35
Blessing of the children	17/MAY/32	28♉13
Ascension of Jesus Christ	14/MAY/33	9♊4
The call of Zacchaeus	30/MAY/32	24♊49
Pentecost	24/MAY/33	25♊20
Birth of John the Baptist	4/JUN/2BC	0♋19
Death of Solomon Jesus	5/JUN/12	1♋16
Peter cures a lame man	2/JUN/33	7♋4
Conception of Solomon Jesus	7/JUN/7BC	7♋22
Healing of two blind men	10/JUN/32	13♋50
Healing of ten lepers	12/JUN/32	15♋50
Teaching of baptism by fire	23/JUN/31	22♋30
Raising of Lazarus	26/JUL/32	23♋10
"I am the Resurrection and…"	25/JUL/32	23♋24
Death of Nathan Mary	5/AUG/12	26♋54
Death of Lazarus	15/JUL/32	1♌19
Assumption of Virgin discovered	16/AUG/44	11♌55
Death of Solomon Mary	15/AUG/44	12♌10
Birth of Nathan Mary	17/JUL/17BC	20♌56
Healing of Mara the Suphanite	4/SEP/30	25♌23
Conversation at Jacob's well	26/JUL/30	0♍1
Healing of the nobleman's son	3/AUG/30	7♍1
Conception of John the Baptist	9/SEP/3BC	7♍32
Attempted murder of Jesus Christ	12/AUG/30	9♍41
Raising of Nazor	1/SEP/32	9♍50
Baptism	23/SEP/29	12♍46
Raising of a pagan child	23/SEP/30	19♍45
Birth of Solomon Mary	7/SEP/21BC	28♍52
"Behold the Lamb of God" (John 1:29)	7/OCT/29	1♎9
Healing of the blind youth	6/OCT/30	11♎34
Healing of Theokeno	28/SEP/32	22♎51
Start of the forty days (Jesus Christ)	21/OCT/29	24♎26
Arrival at Mount Attarus	23/OCT/29	27♎37
Conception of Nathan Mary	24/OCT/18BC	29♎30
Summons of Judas	24/OCT/30	10♏8
Summons of Thomas	29/OCT/30	17♏42
Birth of Nathan Jesus	6/DEC/2BC	25♏32
Conception of Solomon Mary	8/DEC/22BC	25♏42
Healing of the man born blind	23/NOV/31	0♐59
Conversion of Mary Magdalene (1st)	8/NOV/30	3♐19
Raising of youth of Nain	13/NOV/30	10♐2
Conversion of Mary Magdalene (2nd)	26/DEC/30	11♐53
Commissioning of the disciples	10/DEC/30	15♐53
Raising of Jairus's daughter (1st)	18/NOV/30	17♐4
Summons of Matthew	19/NOV/30	18♐20
Walking on the water (1st)	8/DEC/30	19♐23
Death of John the Baptist	4/JAN/31	19♐59
Jesus stills the Sea of Galilee	21/NOV/30	20♐51
Healing of demons at Gergasa	6/DEC/30	21♐16
First temptation	27/NOV/29	22♐23
Power of the twelve	4/DEC/30	23♐9
Second temptation	28/NOV/29	23♐54
Miraculous draught of fishes	26/NOV/30	24♐45
Raising of Jairus's daughter (2nd)	1/DEC/30	25♐10
Third temptation	29/NOV/29	25♐24
End of the forty days	30/NOV/29	26♐57
Raising of a man at Cana	31/DEC/29	27♐22
"Behold the Lamb of God" (John 1:36)	1/DEC/29	27♐52

Geocentric Planetary Positions within the Christ Chronology

Event	Date	Position
Summons of Andrew	1/DEC/29	27♐59
Turning water into wine	28/DEC/29	0♑7
Summons of Philip	24/DEC/29	4♑43
Summons of Peter	19/DEC/29	10♑17
Healing of the paralyzed man	19/JAN/31	11♑8
Adoration of the Magi	26/DEC/6BC	24♑41
Feeding of the five thousand	29/JAN/31	26♑48
Walking on the water	30/JAN/31	27♑17
Raising of Essene's daughter	7/FEB/30	29♑45
Teaching of the bread of life	2/FEB/31	3♒50
Birth of Solomon Jesus	5/MAR/6BC	19♒34
Healing of the Syrophoenician woman	12/FEB/31	21♒38
Flight into Egypt	2/MAR/5BC	25♒55
Triumphant entry into Jerusalem	19/MAR/33	2♓25
Cursing the fig tree	20/MAR/33	3♓14
Theophany (2nd)	20/MAR/33	3♓22
"Woe upon the Pharisees"	24/MAR/33	7♓10
Last anointing	1/APR/33	17♓11
Last supper	2/APR/33	18♓35
Gethsemane	2/APR/33	18♓44
Betrayal of Judas	2/APR/33	18♓48
Trial by Caiaphas	3/APR/33	18♓58
Peter's denial	3/APR/33	19♓6
Trial by Pontius Pilate	3/APR/33	19♓11
Scourging	3/APR/33	19♓20
Crowning with thorns	3/APR/33	19♓22
Visitation (Nathan Mary) to Elizabeth	30/MAR/2BC	19♓24
Death sentence	3/APR/33	19♓25
Carrying of the cross	3/APR/33	19♓31
Nailed to cross	3/APR/33	19♓33
Raised upon the cross	3/APR/33	19♓34
Death of Nathan Jesus	3/APR/33	19♓43
Descent into hell	4/APR/33	20♓59
Resurrection	5/APR/33	22♓4
Union in the temple	3/APR/12	22♓38
Appearance in Emmaus	6/APR/33	24♓11

♀ VENUS

Event	Date	Position
Theophany (2nd)	20/MAR/33	2♈4
Cursing the fig tree	20/MAR/33	2♈10
Triumphant entry into Jerusalem	19/MAR/33	2♈48
Ascension of Jesus Christ	14/MAY/33	8♈45
Conception of Nathan Jesus	6/MAR/2BC	15♈34
Pentecost	24/MAY/33	17♈2
Peter cures a lame man	2/JUN/33	25♈40
Flight into Egypt	2/MAR/5BC	26♈51
Feeding of the four thousand	15/MAR/31	28♈53
Peter receives the keys	19/MAR/31	3♉3
Enmity of the Pharisees	26/MAR/31	11♉48
Theophany (1st)	28/MAR/31	14♉1
Visitation (Nathan Mary) to Elizabeth	30/MAR/2BC	14♉52
Transfiguration	4/APR/31	21♉38
Blessing of the children	17/MAY/32	22♉11
Union in the temple	3/APR/12	29♉49
The call of Zacchaeus	30/MAY/32	8♊8
Death of Solomon Jesus	5/JUN/12	15♊54
Healing of two blind men	10/JUN/32	21♊39
Healing of ten lepers	12/JUN/32	24♊17
Death of Nathan Mary	5/AUG/12	27♊8
Healing of three blind boys	10/MAY/31	2♋50
Death of Solomon Mary	15/AUG/44	7♋4
Assumption of Virgin discovered	16/AUG/44	7♋38
Conversation at Jacob's well	26/JUL/30	10♋10
Healing of the nobleman's son	3/AUG/30	20♋50
Conception of Solomon Jesus	7/JUN/7BC	20♋36
Birth of John the Baptist	4/JUN/2BC	27♋48
Birth of Solomon Mary	7/SEP/21BC	0♌26
Attempted murder of Jesus Christ	12/AUG/30	1♌26
Birth of Nathan Mary	17/JUL/17BC	4♌29
Death of Lazarus	15/JUL/32	4♌47
Teaching of baptism by fire	23/JUN/31	14♌31
"I am the Resurrection and..."	25/JUL/32	17♌29
Raising of Lazarus	26/JUL/32	18♌3
Healing of Mara the Suphanite	4/SEP/30	29♌43
Conception of John the Baptist	9/SEP/3BC	3♍40
Conception of Nathan Mary	24/OCT/18BC	16♍7
Raising of a pagan child	23/SEP/30	23♍21
Raising of Nazor	1/SEP/32	4♎11
Healing of the blind youth	6/OCT/30	9♎40
Healing of the man born blind	23/NOV/31	18♎13
Summons of Judas	24/OCT/30	2♏19
Birth of Nathan Jesus	6/DEC/2BC	2♏23
Healing of Theokeno	28/SEP/32	7♏6
Summons of Thomas	29/OCT/30	8♏31
Baptism	23/SEP/29	15♏3
Conversion of Mary Magdalene (1st)	8/NOV/30	21♏31
Raising of youth of Nain	13/NOV/30	27♏20
"Behold the Lamb of God" (John 1:29)	7/OCT/29	0♐49
Raising of Jairus's daughter (1st)	18/NOV/30	3♐56
Summons of Matthew	19/NOV/30	5♐15
Jesus stills the Sea of Galilee	21/NOV/30	8♐5
Miraculous draught of fishes	26/NOV/30	14♐15
Start of the forty days (Jesus Christ)	21/OCT/29	16♐28
Arrival at Mount Attarus	23/OCT/29	18♐34
Raising of Jairus's daughter (2nd)	1/DEC/30	20♐26
Power upon the twelve	4/DEC/30	24♐12
Healing of demons at Gergasa	6/DEC/30	26♐24
Walking on the water (1st)	8/DEC/30	28♐17
Commissioning of the disciples	10/DEC/30	1♑34
Conception of Solomon Mary	8/DEC/22BC	13♑12
Raising of Essene's daughter	7/FEB/30	13♑50

Event	Date	Position	Event	Date	Position
First temptation	27/NOV/29	19♑57	Raising of Lazarus	26/JUL/32	11♈33
Second temptation	28/NOV/29	20♑37	Feeding of the five thousand	29/JAN/31	15♈1
Third temptation	29/NOV/29	21♑15	Walking on the water	30/JAN/31	15♈12
Conversion of Mary Magdalene (2nd)	26/DEC/30	21♑28	Teaching of the bread of life	2/FEB/31	17♈41
End of the forty days	30/NOV/29	21♑54	Raising of Nazor	1/SEP/32	17♈44
"Behold the Lamb of God" (John 1:36)	1/DEC/29	22♑16	Healing of the Syrophoenician woman	12/FEB/31	24♈0
Summons of Andrew	1/DEC/29	22♑19	Union in the temple	3/APR/12	4♉36
Raising of a man at Cana	31/DEC/29	25♑4	Conception of Nathan Jesus	6/MAR/2BC	4♉46
Turning water into wine	28/DEC/29	26♑21	Feeding of the four thousand	15/MAR/31	13♉56
Summons of Philip	24/DEC/29	27♑29	Peter receives the keys	19/MAR/31	16♉10
Summons of Peter	19/DEC/29	28♑5	Visitation (Nathan Mary) to Elizabeth	30/MAR/2BC	20♉36
Death of John the Baptist	4/JAN/31	2♒5	Enmity of the Pharisees	26/MAR/31	20♉52
Birth of Solomon Jesus	5/MAR/6BC	4♒15	Theophany (1st)	28/MAR/31	22♉4
Adoration of the Magi	26/DEC/6BC	7♒1	Transfiguration	4/APR/31	26♉12
Healing of the paralyzed man	19/JAN/31	21♒42	Triumphant entry into Jerusalem	19/MAR/33	1♊14
Cleansing of the temple	6/APR/30	1♓6	Cursing the fig tree	20/MAR/33	1♊49
Conversation with Nicodemus	9/APR/30	3♓58	Theophany (2nd)	20/MAR/33	1♊55
Feeding of the five thousand	29/JAN/31	4♓2	"Woe upon the Pharisees"	24/MAR/33	4♊14
Walking on the water	30/JAN/31	4♓23	Last anointing	1/APR/33	9♊5
Teaching of the bread of life	2/FEB/31	9♓10	Last supper	2/APR/33	9♊41
Healing of the Syrophoenician woman	12/FEB/31	21♓13	Gethsemane	2/APR/33	9♊45
Appearance to the eleven	11/APR/33	23♓14	Betrayal of Judas	2/APR/33	9♊46
Appearance to the seven	15/APR/33	23♓27	Trial by Caiaphas	3/APR/33	9♊51
Appearance to the five hundred	16/APR/33	23♓41	Peter's denial	3/APR/33	9♊54
Appearance in Emmaus	6/APR/33	23♓47	Trial by Pontius Pilate	3/APR/33	9♊56
Resurrection	5/APR/33	24♓8	Scourging	3/APR/33	10♊0
Descent into hell	4/APR/33	24♓20	Crowning with thorns	3/APR/33	10♊1
Death of Nathan Jesus	3/APR/33	24♓37	Death sentence	3/APR/33	10♊2
Raised upon the cross	3/APR/33	24♓39	Carrying of the cross	3/APR/33	10♊4
Nailed to cross	3/APR/33	24♓39	Nailed to cross	3/APR/33	10♊5
Carrying of the cross	3/APR/33	24♓40	Raised upon the cross	3/APR/33	10♊5
Death sentence	3/APR/33	24♓41	Death of Nathan Jesus	3/APR/33	10♊9
Crowning with thorns	3/APR/33	24♓42	Descent into hell	4/APR/33	10♊40
Scourging	3/APR/33	24♓42	Resurrection	5/APR/33	11♊6
Trial by Pontius Pilate	3/APR/33	24♓44	Appearance in Emmaus	6/APR/33	11♊56
Peter's denial	3/APR/33	24♓46	Appearance to the eleven	11/APR/33	15♊4
Trial by Caiaphas	3/APR/33	24♓48	Death of Solomon Jesus	5/JUN/12	16♊17
Betrayal of Judas	2/APR/33	24♓50	Appearance to the seven	15/APR/33	17♊5
Gethsemane	2/APR/33	24♓51	Appearance to the five hundred	16/APR/33	18♊2
Last supper	2/APR/33	24♓53	Healing of three blind boys	10/MAY/31	19♊21
Last anointing	1/APR/33	25♓16	Mary receives holy communion	23/APR/33	21♊44
Mary receives holy communion	23/APR/33	25♓27	Birth of John the Baptist	4/JUN/2BC	2♋15
"Woe upon the Pharisees"	24/MAR/33	29♓34	Ascension of Jesus Christ	14/MAY/33	4♋46
			Pentecost	24/MAY/33	10♋42
			Peter cures a lame man	2/JUN/33	16♋22
			Teaching of baptism by fire	23/JUN/31	17♋12
			Death of Nathan Mary	5/AUG/12	25♋28

♂ MARS

Event	Date	Position
Birth of Solomon Jesus	5/MAR/6BC	4♈56
Death of Lazarus	15/JUL/32	7♈3
Healing of the paralyzed man	19/JAN/31	8♈36
Healing of Theokeno	28/SEP/32	11♈0
"I am the Resurrection and..."	25/JUL/32	11♈23

Death of Solomon Mary	15/AUG/44	4♌44
Assumption of Virgin discovered	16/AUG/44	5♌4
Birth of Nathan Mary	17/JUL/17BC	5♌18
Birth of Solomon Mary	7/SEP/21BC	14♌21

Baptism	23/SEP/29	4♍2
"Behold the Lamb of God" (John 1:29)	7/OCT/29	12♍58
Start of the forty days (Jesus Christ)	21/OCT/29	22♍13
Conception of Solomon Jesus	7/JUN/7BC	23♍1
Arrival at Mount Attarus	23/OCT/29	23♍31
Adoration of the Magi	26/DEC/6BC	13♎20
First temptation	27/NOV/29	15♎58
Second temptation	28/NOV/29	16♎37
Third temptation	29/NOV/29	17♎15
End of the forty days	30/NOV/29	17♎56
"Behold the Lamb of God" (John 1:36)	1/DEC/29	18♎20
Summons of Andrew	1/DEC/29	18♎23
Healing of the man born blind	23/NOV/31	27♎22
Summons of Peter	19/DEC/29	0♏2
Birth of Nathan Jesus	6/DEC/2BC	3♏24
Summons of Philip	24/DEC/29	3♏25
Turning water into wine	28/DEC/29	5♏50
Raising of a man at Cana	31/DEC/29	7♏46
Flight into Egypt	2/MAR/5BC	10♏33
Raising of Essene's daughter	7/FEB/30	2♐1
Cleansing of the temple	6/APR/30	6♑58
Conversation with Nicodemus	9/APR/30	8♑28
Conception of John the Baptist	9/SEP/3BC	14♑52
Attempted murder of Jesus Christ	12/AUG/30	25♑0
Healing of Mara the Suphanite	4/SEP/30	25♑46
Healing of the nobleman's son	3/AUG/30	26♑33
Conversation at Jacob's well	26/JUL/30	28♑29
Raising of a pagan child	23/SEP/30	0♒59
Conception of Solomon Mary	8/DEC/22BC	5♒14
Healing of the blind youth	6/OCT/30	6♒19
Summons of Judas	24/OCT/30	15♒14
Summons of Thomas	29/OCT/30	17♒54
Conception of Nathan Mary	24/OCT/18BC	21♒47
Conversion of Mary Magdalene (1st)	8/NOV/30	23♒44
Raising of youth of Nain	13/NOV/30	26♒25
Raising of Jairus's daughter (1st)	18/NOV/30	29♒32
Summons of Matthew	19/NOV/30	0♓10
Jesus stills the Sea of Galilee	21/NOV/30	1♓31
Blessing of the children	17/MAY/32	2♓4
Miraculous draught of fishes	26/NOV/30	4♓30
Raising of Jairus's daughter (2nd)	1/DEC/30	7♓31
Power upon the twelve	4/DEC/30	9♓22
Healing of demons at Gergasa	6/DEC/30	10♓28
The call of Zacchaeus	30/MAY/32	10♓43
Walking on the water (1st)	8/DEC/30	11♓24
Commissioning of the disciples	10/DEC/30	13♓2
Healing of two blind men	10/JUN/32	17♓44
Healing of ten lepers	12/JUN/32	18♓59
Conversion of Mary Magdalene (2nd)	26/DEC/30	23♓4
Death of John the Baptist	4/JAN/31	28♓29

 JUPITER

Miraculous draught of fishes	26/NOV/30	2♈52
Raising of Jairus's daughter (2nd)	1/DEC/30	2♈54
Jesus stills the Sea of Galilee	21/NOV/30	2♈55
Power upon the twelve	4/DEC/30	2♈57
Summons of Matthew	19/NOV/30	2♈58
Raising of Jairus's daughter (1st)	18/NOV/30	3♈0
Healing of demons at Gergasa	6/DEC/30	3♈0
Walking on the water (1st)	8/DEC/30	3♈3
Commissioning of the disciples	10/DEC/30	3♈10
Raising of youth of Nain	13/NOV/30	3♈13
Conversion of Mary Magdalene (1st)	8/NOV/30	3♈28
Conversion of Mary Magdalene (2nd)	26/DEC/30	4♈16
Summons of Thomas	29/OCT/30	4♈18
Birth of Solomon Jesus	5/MAR/6BC	4♈32
Summons of Judas	24/OCT/30	4♈47
Death of John the Baptist	4/JAN/31	5♈11
Healing of the blind youth	6/OCT/30	7♈0
Healing of the paralyzed man	19/JAN/31	7♈21
Raising of a pagan child	23/SEP/30	8♈45
Feeding of the five thousand	29/JAN/31	8♈59
Walking on the water	30/JAN/31	9♈3
Teaching of the bread of life	2/FEB/31	9♈44
Healing of Mara the Suphanite	4/SEP/30	11♈2
Healing of the Syrophoenician woman	12/FEB/31	11♈36
Attempted murder of Jesus Christ	12/AUG/30	12♈40
Conversation at Jacob's well	26/JUL/30	12♈48
Healing of the nobleman's son	3/AUG/30	12♈52
Feeding of the four thousand	15/MAR/31	18♈15
Peter receives the keys	19/MAR/31	19♈3
Enmity of the Pharisees	26/MAR/31	20♈45
Theophany (1st)	28/MAR/31	21♈11
Transfiguration	4/APR/31	22♈42
Conception of Nathan Mary	24/OCT/18BC	22♈47
Adoration of the Magi	26/DEC/6BC	24♈4
Healing of three blind boys	10/MAY/31	1♉16
Flight into Egypt	2/MAR/5BC	2♉11
Teaching of baptism by fire	23/JUN/31	10♉36
Healing of the man born blind	23/NOV/31	11♉5
Birth of Nathan Mary	17/JUL/17BC	27♉55
Blessing of the children	17/MAY/32	29♉38
The call of Zacchaeus	30/MAY/32	2♊36
Healing of two blind men	10/JUN/32	5♊6
Healing of ten lepers	12/JUN/32	5♊32
Death of Lazarus	15/JUL/32	12♊34
"I am the Resurrection and..."	25/JUL/32	14♊33
Raising of Lazarus	26/JUL/32	14♊38
Triumphant entry into Jerusalem	19/MAR/33	15♊9
Cursing the fig tree	20/MAR/33	15♊16
Theophany (2nd)	20/MAR/33	15♊18

Event	Date	Position
"Woe upon the Pharisees"	24/MAR/33	15♊48
Last anointing	1/APR/33	16♊57
Last supper	2/APR/33	17♊6
Gethsemane	2/APR/33	17♊7
Betrayal of Judas	2/APR/33	17♊8
Trial by Caiaphas	3/APR/33	17♊9
Peter's denial	3/APR/33	17♊10
Trial by Pontius Pilate	3/APR/33	17♊10
Scourging	3/APR/33	17♊11
Crowning with thorns	3/APR/33	17♊11
Death sentence	3/APR/33	17♊12
Carrying of the cross	3/APR/33	17♊12
Nailed to cross	3/APR/33	17♊12
Raised upon the cross	3/APR/33	17♊12
Death of Nathan Jesus	3/APR/33	17♊13
Descent into hell	4/APR/33	17♊21
Resurrection	5/APR/33	17♊28
Appearance in Emmaus	6/APR/33	17♊41
Appearance to the eleven	11/APR/33	18♊32
Appearance to the seven	15/APR/33	19♊6
Appearance to the five hundred	16/APR/33	19♊23
Raising of Nazor	1/SEP/32	20♊19
Mary receives holy communion	23/APR/33	20♊29
Death of Solomon Mary	15/AUG/44	21♊54
Assumption of Virgin discovered	16/AUG/44	21♊59
Healing of Theokeno	28/SEP/32	22♊21
Ascension of Jesus Christ	14/MAY/33	24♊40
Pentecost	24/MAY/33	26♊42
Peter cures a lame man	2/JUN/33	28♊41
Visitation (Nathan Mary) to Elizabeth	30/MAR/2BC	2♌50
Conception of Nathan Jesus	6/MAR/2BC	3♌39
Conception of John the Baptist	9/SEP/3BC	4♌18
Birth of John the Baptist	4/JUN/2BC	8♌46
Union in the temple	3/APR/12	8♍33
Death of Solomon Jesus	5/JUN/12	8♍48
Birth of Nathan Jesus	6/DEC/2BC	12♍22
Death of Nathan Mary	5/AUG/12	18♍0
Conception of Solomon Mary	8/DEC/22BC	18♐27
Birth of Solomon Mary	7/SEP/21BC	1♑4
Start of the forty days (Jesus Christ)	21/OCT/29	26♒21
Arrival at Mount Attarus	23/OCT/29	26♒22
"Behold the Lamb of God" (John 1:29)	7/OCT/29	26♒43
Baptism	23/SEP/29	27♒42
First temptation	27/NOV/29	28♒37
Second temptation	28/NOV/29	28♒44
Third temptation	29/NOV/29	28♒51
End of the forty days	30/NOV/29	28♒59
"Behold the Lamb of God" (John 1:36)	1/DEC/29	29♒3
Summons of Andrew	1/DEC/29	29♒4
Summons of Peter	19/DEC/29	1♓45
Summons of Philip	24/DEC/29	2♓40
Turning water into wine	28/DEC/29	3♓21
Raising of a man at Cana	31/DEC/29	3♓55
Raising of Essene's daughter	7/FEB/30	12♓4
Conception of Solomon Jesus	7/JUN/7BC	25♓14
Cleansing of the temple	6/APR/30	25♓48
Conversation with Nicodemus	9/APR/30	26♓25

♄ SATURN

Event	Date	Position
Adoration of the Magi	26/DEC/6BC	2♈29
Flight into Egypt	2/MAR/5BC	8♈28
Conception of Nathan Jesus	6/MAR/2BC	16♉33
Visitation (Nathan Mary) to Elizabeth	30/MAR/2BC	18♉59
Conception of John the Baptist	9/SEP/3BC	21♉8
Birth of John the Baptist	4/JUN/2BC	27♉14
Birth of Nathan Jesus	6/DEC/2BC	0♊54
Raising of Essene's daughter	7/FEB/30	6♊23
Raising of a man at Cana	31/DEC/29	7♊32
Turning water into wine	28/DEC/29	7♊44
Summons of Philip	24/DEC/29	7♊59
Summons of Peter	19/DEC/29	8♊21
Cleansing of the temple	6/APR/30	9♊30
Conversation with Nicodemus	9/APR/30	9♊45
Summons of Andrew	1/DEC/29	9♊48
"Behold the Lamb of God" (John 1:36)	1/DEC/29	9♊49
End of the forty days	30/NOV/29	9♊52
Third temptation	29/NOV/29	9♊57
Second temptation	28/NOV/29	10♊2
First temptation	27/NOV/29	10♊7
Arrival at Mount Attarus	23/OCT/29	12♊36
Start of the forty days (Jesus Christ)	21/OCT/29	12♊42
"Behold the Lamb of God" (John 1:29)	7/OCT/29	13♊13
Baptism	23/SEP/29	13♊22
Healing of the Syrophoenician woman	12/FEB/31	20♊42
Teaching of the bread of life	2/FEB/31	20♊55
Walking on the water	30/JAN/31	21♊3
Feeding of the five thousand	29/JAN/31	21♊4
Feeding of the four thousand	15/MAR/31	21♊10
Peter receives the keys	19/MAR/31	21♊20
Healing of the paralyzed man	19/JAN/31	21♊31
Enmity of the Pharisees	26/MAR/31	21♊44
Theophany (1st)	28/MAR/31	21♊51
Transfiguration	4/APR/31	22♊18
Death of John the Baptist	4/JAN/31	22♊32
Conversation at Jacob's well	26/JUL/30	22♊58
Conversion of Mary Magdalene (2nd)	26/DEC/30	23♊11
Healing of the nobleman's son	3/AUG/30	23♊49
Commissioning of the disciples	10/DEC/30	24♊30
Walking on the water (1st)	8/DEC/30	24♊43
Attempted murder of Jesus Christ	12/AUG/30	24♊44
Healing of demons at Gergasa	6/DEC/30	24♊50

Event	Date	Position
Power upon the twelve	4/DEC/30	24♊58
Raising of Jairus's daughter (2nd)	1/DEC/30	25♊13
Miraculous draught of fishes	26/NOV/30	25♊35
Healing of three blind boys	10/MAY/31	25♊46
Jesus stills the Sea of Galilee	21/NOV/30	25♊57
Summons of Matthew	19/NOV/30	26♊6
Raising of Jairus's daughter (1st)	18/NOV/30	26♊10
Raising of youth of Nain	13/NOV/30	26♊30
Healing of Mara the Suphanite	4/SEP/30	26♊31
Conversion of Mary Magdalene (1st)	8/NOV/30	26♊46
Summons of Thomas	29/OCT/30	27♊14
Raising of a pagan child	23/SEP/30	27♊23
Summons of Judas	24/OCT/30	27♊24
Healing of the blind youth	6/OCT/30	27♊37
Teaching of baptism by fire	23/JUN/31	1♋14
Blessing of the children	17/MAY/32	9♋3
The call of Zacchaeus	30/MAY/32	10♋30
Healing of the man born blind	23/NOV/31	10♋47
Healing of two blind men	10/JUN/32	11♋48
Healing of ten lepers	12/JUN/32	12♋3
Death of Lazarus	15/JUL/32	16♋15
"I am the Resurrection and…"	25/JUL/32	17♋33
Raising of Lazarus	26/JUL/32	17♋37
Triumphant entry into Jerusalem	19/MAR/33	18♋33
Cursing the fig tree	20/MAR/33	18♋33
Theophany (2nd)	20/MAR/33	18♋33
"Woe upon the Pharisees"	24/MAR/33	18♋34
Last anointing	1/APR/33	18♋42
Last supper	2/APR/33	18♋43
Gethsemane	2/APR/33	18♋44
Betrayal of Judas	2/APR/33	18♋44
Trial by Caiaphas	3/APR/33	18♋44
Peter's denial	3/APR/33	18♋44
Trial by Pontius Pilate	3/APR/33	18♋44
Scourging	3/APR/33	18♋44
Crowning with thorns	3/APR/33	18♋44
Death sentence	3/APR/33	18♋44
Carrying of the cross	3/APR/33	18♋44
Nailed to cross	3/APR/33	18♋44
Raised upon the cross	3/APR/33	18♋45
Death of Nathan Jesus	3/APR/33	18♋45
Descent into hell	4/APR/33	18♋46
Resurrection	5/APR/33	18♋47
Appearance in Emmaus	6/APR/33	18♋50
Appearance to the eleven	11/APR/33	19♋1
Appearance to the seven	15/APR/33	19♋10
Appearance to the five hundred	16/APR/33	19♋14
Mary receives holy communion	23/APR/33	19♋34
Ascension of Jesus Christ	14/MAY/33	21♋7
Raising of Nazor	1/SEP/32	21♋55
Pentecost	24/MAY/33	22♋1
Peter cures a lame man	2/JUN/33	22♋57
Healing of Theokeno	28/SEP/32	24♋10
Conception of Solomon Mary	8/DEC/22BC	8♎45
Birth of Solomon Mary	7/SEP/21BC	9♎39
Death of Nathan Mary	5/AUG/12	3♏22
Death of Solomon Jesus	5/JUN/12	3♏26
Union in the temple	3/APR/12	7♏35
Conception of Nathan Mary	24/OCT/18BC	15♏16
Birth of Nathan Mary	17/JUL/17BC	19♏11
Death of Solomon Mary	15/AUG/44	1♐35
Assumption of Virgin discovered	16/AUG/44	1♐35
Conception of Solomon Jesus	7/JUN/7BC	26♓47
Birth of Solomon Jesus	5/MAR/6BC	29♓15

♅ URANUS

Event	Date	Position
Union in the temple	3/APR/12	16♉30
Death of Solomon Jesus	5/JUN/12	20♉2
Death of Nathan Mary	5/AUG/12	22♉28
Conversation with Nicodemus	9/APR/30	5♌43
Cleansing of the temple	6/APR/30	5♌44
Raising of Essene's daughter	7/FEB/30	7♌19
Baptism	23/SEP/29	8♌40
Raising of a man at Cana	31/DEC/29	8♌55
Turning water into wine	28/DEC/29	9♌1
Summons of Philip	24/DEC/29	9♌9
"Behold the Lamb of God" (John 1:29)	7/OCT/29	9♌12
Summons of Peter	19/DEC/29	9♌19
Start of the forty days (Jesus Christ)	21/OCT/29	9♌37
Arrival at Mount Attarus	23/OCT/29	9♌39
Summons of Andrew	1/DEC/29	9♌44
"Behold the Lamb of God" (John 1:36)	1/DEC/29	9♌44
End of the forty days	30/NOV/29	9♌45
Conversation at Jacob's well	26/JUL/30	9♌45
Third temptation	29/NOV/29	9♌45
Second temptation	28/NOV/29	9♌46
First temptation	27/NOV/29	9♌47
Healing of the nobleman's son	3/AUG/30	10♌15
Transfiguration	4/APR/31	10♌32
Theophany (1st)	28/MAR/31	10♌38
Enmity of the Pharisees	26/MAR/31	10♌40
Healing of three blind boys	10/MAY/31	10♌41
Attempted murder of Jesus Christ	12/AUG/30	10♌50
Peter receives the keys	19/MAR/31	10♌50
Feeding of the four thousand	15/MAR/31	10♌55
Healing of the Syrophoenician woman	12/FEB/31	12♌2
Healing of Mara the Suphanite	4/SEP/30	12♌11
Teaching of baptism by fire	23/JUN/31	12♌18
Teaching of the bread of life	2/FEB/31	12♌28
Walking on the water	30/JAN/31	12♌38
Feeding of the five thousand	29/JAN/31	12♌39

Event	Date	Position
Healing of the paralyzed man	19/JAN/31	13♌5
Raising of a pagan child	23/SEP/30	13♌10
Death of John the Baptist	4/JAN/31	13♌42
Healing of the blind youth	6/OCT/30	13♌44
Conversion of Mary Magdalene (2nd)	26/DEC/30	13♌59
Summons of Judas	24/OCT/30	14♌18
Commissioning of the disciples	10/DEC/30	14♌24
Summons of Thomas	29/OCT/30	14♌24
Walking on the water (1st)	8/DEC/30	14♌26
Healing of demons at Gergasa	6/DEC/30	14♌28
Power upon the twelve	4/DEC/30	14♌29
Raising of Jairus's daughter (2nd)	1/DEC/30	14♌32
Conversion of Mary Magdalene (1st)	8/NOV/30	14♌33
Miraculous draught of fishes	26/NOV/30	14♌35
Raising of youth of Nain	13/NOV/30	14♌35
Jesus stills the Sea of Galilee	21/NOV/30	14♌36
Raising of Jairus's daughter (1st)	18/NOV/30	14♌36
Summons of Matthew	19/NOV/30	14♌36
Blessing of the children	17/MAY/32	15♌29
The call of Zacchaeus	30/MAY/32	15♌51
Healing of two blind men	10/JUN/32	16♌15
Healing of ten lepers	12/JUN/32	16♌20
Death of Lazarus	15/JUL/32	18♌21
"I am the Resurrection and…"	25/JUL/32	18♌38
Raising of Lazarus	26/JUL/32	18♌39
Healing of the man born blind	23/NOV/31	19♌21
Mary receives holy communion	23/APR/33	19♌58
Appearance to the five hundred	16/APR/33	20♌0
Appearance to the seven	15/APR/33	20♌1
Appearance to the eleven	11/APR/33	20♌4
Ascension of Jesus Christ	14/MAY/33	20♌6
Appearance in Emmaus	6/APR/33	20♌9
Resurrection	5/APR/33	20♌10
Descent into hell	4/APR/33	20♌11
Death of Nathan Jesus	3/APR/33	20♌12
Raised upon the cross	3/APR/33	20♌12
Nailed to cross	3/APR/33	20♌12
Carrying of the cross	3/APR/33	20♌12
Death sentence	3/APR/33	20♌12
Crowning with thorns	3/APR/33	20♌12
Scourging	3/APR/33	20♌12
Trial by Pontius Pilate	3/APR/33	20♌12
Peter's denial	3/APR/33	20♌12
Trial by Caiaphas	3/APR/33	20♌13
Betrayal of Judas	2/APR/33	20♌13
Gethsemane	2/APR/33	20♌13
Last supper	2/APR/33	20♌13
Last anointing	1/APR/33	20♌14
Pentecost	24/MAY/33	20♌17
"Woe upon the Pharisees"	24/MAR/33	20♌26
Peter cures a lame man	2/JUN/33	20♌32
Theophany (2nd)	20/MAR/33	20♌33
Cursing the fig tree	20/MAR/33	20♌33
Triumphant entry into Jerusalem	19/MAR/33	20♌35
Raising of Nazor	1/SEP/32	20♌59
Healing of Theokeno	28/SEP/32	22♌28
Death of Solomon Mary	15/AUG/44	13♎17
Assumption of Virgin discovered	16/AUG/44	13♎18
Conception of Solomon Mary	8/DEC/22BC	7♑48
Birth of Solomon Mary	7/SEP/21BC	9♑11
Conception of Nathan Mary	24/OCT/18BC	21♑34
Birth of Nathan Mary	17/JUL/17BC	27♑22
Conception of Solomon Jesus	7/JUN/7BC	8♓59
Birth of Solomon Jesus	5/MAR/6BC	9♓20
Adoration of the Magi	26/DEC/6BC	9♓42
Flight into Egypt	2/MAR/5BC	12♓58
Conception of John the Baptist	9/SEP/3BC	23♓11
Conception of Nathan Jesus	6/MAR/2BC	24♓23
Birth of Nathan Jesus	6/DEC/2BC	24♓59
Visitation (Nathan Mary) to Elizabeth	30/MAR/2BC	25♓46
Birth of John the Baptist	4/JUN/2BC	28♓34

♆ NEPTUNE

Event	Date	Position
Birth of Solomon Mary	7/SEP/21BC	7♎10
Conception of Solomon Mary	8/DEC/22BC	7♎59
Birth of Nathan Mary	17/JUL/17BC	14♎15
Conception of Nathan Mary	24/OCT/18BC	15♎7
Conception of Solomon Jesus	7/JUN/7BC	6♏9
Birth of Solomon Jesus	5/MAR/6BC	10♏32
Adoration of the Magi	26/DEC/6BC	12♏13
Flight into Egypt	2/MAR/5BC	12♏44
Conception of John the Baptist	9/SEP/3BC	14♏55
Birth of John the Baptist	4/JUN/2BC	17♏17
Visitation (Nathan Mary) to Elizabeth	30/MAR/2BC	18♏55
Conception of Nathan Jesus	6/MAR/2BC	19♏16
Birth of Nathan Jesus	6/DEC/2BC	20♏0
Death of Nathan Mary	5/AUG/12	14♐52
Death of Solomon Jesus	5/JUN/12	16♐11
Union in the temple	3/APR/12	17♐27
"Behold the Lamb of God" (John 1:29)	7/OCT/29	21♑54
Baptism	23/SEP/29	21♑55
Start of the forty days (Jesus Christ)	21/OCT/29	21♑59
Arrival at Mount Attarus	23/OCT/29	22♑1
First temptation	27/NOV/29	22♑44
Second temptation	28/NOV/29	22♑46
Third temptation	29/NOV/29	22♑47
End of the forty days	30/NOV/29	22♑49
"Behold the Lamb of God" (John 1:36)	1/DEC/29	22♑50
Summons of Andrew	1/DEC/29	22♑50
Summons of Peter	19/DEC/29	23♑26
Summons of Philip	24/DEC/29	23♑37

Geocentric Planetary Positions within the Christ Chronology

Turning water into wine	28/DEC/29	23♑45
Raising of a man at Cana	31/DEC/29	23♑52
Healing of the blind youth	6/OCT/30	24♑6
Raising of a pagan child	23/SEP/30	24♑8
Summons of Judas	24/OCT/30	24♑12
Summons of Thomas	29/OCT/30	24♑15
Healing of Mara the Suphanite	4/SEP/30	24♑21
Conversion of Mary Magdalene (1st)	8/NOV/30	24♑25
Raising of youth of Nain	13/NOV/30	24♑31
Raising of Jairus's daughter (1st)	18/NOV/30	24♑38
Summons of Matthew	19/NOV/30	24♑39
Jesus stills the Sea of Galilee	21/NOV/30	24♑43
Attempted murder of Jesus Christ	12/AUG/30	24♑49
Miraculous draught of fishes	26/NOV/30	24♑50
Raising of Jairus's daughter (2nd)	1/DEC/30	24♑59
Healing of the nobleman's son	3/AUG/30	25♑3
Power upon the twelve	4/DEC/30	25♑4
Healing of demons at Gergasa	6/DEC/30	25♑7
Walking on the water (1st)	8/DEC/30	25♑10
Commissioning of the disciples	10/DEC/30	25♑15
Conversation at Jacob's well	26/JUL/30	25♑16
Raising of Essene's daughter	7/FEB/30	25♑17
Conversion of Mary Magdalene (2nd)	26/DEC/30	25♑48
Death of John the Baptist	4/JAN/31	26♑6
Healing of the paralyzed man	19/JAN/31	26♑42
Cleansing of the temple	6/APR/30	26♑45
Conversation with Nicodemus	9/APR/30	26♑47
Healing of the man born blind	23/NOV/31	26♑54
Feeding of the five thousand	29/JAN/31	27♑5
Walking on the water	30/JAN/31	27♑5
Teaching of the bread of life	2/FEB/31	27♑14
Healing of the Syrophoenician woman	12/FEB/31	27♑35
Teaching of baptism by fire	23/JUN/31	28♑24
Feeding of the four thousand	15/MAR/31	28♑30
Healing of Theokeno	28/SEP/32	28♑32
Peter receives the keys	19/MAR/31	28♑35
Enmity of the Pharisees	26/MAR/31	28♑44
Theophany (1st)	28/MAR/31	28♑46
Raising of Nazor	1/SEP/32	28♑53
Transfiguration	4/APR/31	28♑53
Healing of three blind boys	10/MAY/31	29♑4
Raising of Lazarus	26/JUL/32	29♑47
"I am the Resurrection and…"	25/JUL/32	29♑48
Death of Lazarus	15/JUL/32	0♒5
Healing of ten lepers	12/JUN/32	0♒52
Healing of two blind men	10/JUN/32	0♒55
The call of Zacchaeus	30/MAY/32	1♒5
Blessing of the children	17/MAY/32	1♒14
Triumphant entry into Jerusalem	19/MAR/33	2♒54
Cursing the fig tree	20/MAR/33	2♒55
Theophany (2nd)	20/MAR/33	2♒56
"Woe upon the Pharisees"	24/MAR/33	3♒1
Last anointing	1/APR/33	3♒11
Last supper	2/APR/33	3♒12
Gethsemane	2/APR/33	3♒12
Betrayal of Judas	2/APR/33	3♒12
Trial by Caiaphas	3/APR/33	3♒12
Peter's denial	3/APR/33	3♒12
Trial by Pontius Pilate	3/APR/33	3♒12
Scourging	3/APR/33	3♒12
Crowning with thorns	3/APR/33	3♒12
Death sentence	3/APR/33	3♒12
Carrying of the cross	3/APR/33	3♒13
Nailed to cross	3/APR/33	3♒13
Raised upon the cross	3/APR/33	3♒13
Death of Nathan Jesus	3/APR/33	3♒13
Descent into hell	4/APR/33	3♒14
Resurrection	5/APR/33	3♒14
Appearance in Emmaus	6/APR/33	3♒16
Peter cures a lame man	2/JUN/33	3♒17
Appearance to the eleven	11/APR/33	3♒20
Appearance to the seven	15/APR/33	3♒22
Appearance to the five hundred	16/APR/33	3♒23
Pentecost	24/MAY/33	3♒24
Mary receives holy communion	23/APR/33	3♒27
Ascension of Jesus Christ	14/MAY/33	3♒28
Assumption of Virgin discovered	16/AUG/44	26♒28
Death of Solomon Mary	15/AUG/44	26♒29

♇ PLUTO

Conception of Solomon Mary	8/DEC/22BC	12♌25
Birth of Solomon Mary	7/SEP/21BC	13♌25
Birth of Nathan Mary	17/JUL/17BC	19♌29
Conception of Nathan Mary	24/OCT/18BC	20♌25
Conception of Solomon Jesus	7/JUN/7BC	10♍28
Birth of Solomon Jesus	5/MAR/6BC	14♍10
Flight into Egypt	2/MAR/5BC	16♍45
Adoration of the Magi	26/DEC/6BC	18♍1
Conception of John the Baptist	9/SEP/3BC	22♍41
Birth of John the Baptist	4/JUN/2BC	22♍44
Visitation (Nathan Mary) to Elizabeth	30/MAR/2BC	23♍42
Conception of Nathan Jesus	6/MAR/2BC	24♍23
Birth of Nathan Jesus	6/DEC/2BC	27♍55
Death of Nathan Mary	5/AUG/12	26♎34
Death of Solomon Jesus	5/JUN/12	26♎34
Union in the temple	3/APR/12	28♎7
Baptism	23/SEP/29	6♐53
"Behold the Lamb of God" (John 1:29)	7/OCT/29	7♐11
Start of the forty days (Jesus Christ)	21/OCT/29	7♐35
Arrival at Mount Attarus	23/OCT/29	7♐39
Attempted murder of Jesus Christ	12/AUG/30	8♐40

Event	Date	Ref
Healing of Mara the Suphanite	4/SEP/30	8♐42
Healing of the nobleman's son	3/AUG/30	8♐43
Conversation at Jacob's well	26/JUL/30	8♐48
First temptation	27/NOV/29	8♐50
Second temptation	28/NOV/29	8♐53
Third temptation	29/NOV/29	8♐55
Raising of a pagan child	23/SEP/30	8♐57
End of the forty days	30/NOV/29	8♐57
"Behold the Lamb of God" (John 1:36)	1/DEC/29	8♐58
Summons of Andrew	1/DEC/29	8♐59
Healing of the blind youth	6/OCT/30	9♐13
Summons of Peter	19/DEC/29	9♐37
Summons of Judas	24/OCT/30	9♐42
Summons of Philip	24/DEC/29	9♐48
Summons of Thomas	29/OCT/30	9♐51
Turning water into wine	28/DEC/29	9♐56
Raising of a man at Cana	31/DEC/29	10♐1
Conversion of Mary Magdalene (1st)	8/NOV/30	10♐11
Raising of youth of Nain	13/NOV/30	10♐20
Raising of Jairus's daughter (1st)	18/NOV/30	10♐31
Summons of Matthew	19/NOV/30	10♐33
Jesus stills the Sea of Galilee	21/NOV/30	10♐38
Miraculous draught of fishes	26/NOV/30	10♐49
Raising of Essene's daughter	7/FEB/30	10♐59
Raising of Jairus's daughter (2nd)	1/DEC/30	10♐59
Power upon the twelve	4/DEC/30	11♐6
Conversation with Nicodemus	9/APR/30	11♐6
Cleansing of the temple	6/APR/30	11♐8
Healing of demons at Gergasa	6/DEC/30	11♐10
Walking on the water (1st)	8/DEC/30	11♐13
Commissioning of the disciples	10/DEC/30	11♐19
Teaching of baptism by fire	23/JUN/31	11♐33
Conversion of Mary Magdalene (2nd)	26/DEC/30	11♐52
Death of John the Baptist	4/JAN/31	12♐8
Healing of the paralyzed man	19/JAN/31	12♐36
Healing of three blind boys	10/MAY/31	12♐38
Healing of the man born blind	23/NOV/31	12♐41
Raising of Nazor	1/SEP/32	12♐47
Feeding of the five thousand	29/JAN/31	12♐50
Walking on the water	30/JAN/31	12♐51
Teaching of the bread of life	2/FEB/31	12♐56
Raising of Lazarus	26/JUL/32	12♐59
"I am the Resurrection and…"	25/JUL/32	12♐59
Healing of Theokeno	28/SEP/32	13♐5
Healing of the Syrophoenician woman	12/FEB/31	13♐6
Death of Lazarus	15/JUL/32	13♐9
Transfiguration	4/APR/31	13♐15
Theophany (1st)	28/MAR/31	13♐18
Enmity of the Pharisees	26/MAR/31	13♐19
Peter receives the keys	19/MAR/31	13♐21
Feeding of the four thousand	15/MAR/31	13♐21
Healing of ten lepers	12/JUN/32	13♐53
Healing of two blind men	10/JUN/32	13♐56
The call of Zacchaeus	30/MAY/32	14♐13
Blessing of the children	17/MAY/32	14♐32
Peter cures a lame man	2/JUN/33	16♐13
Pentecost	24/MAY/33	16♐27
Ascension of Jesus Christ	14/MAY/33	16♐40
Mary receives holy communion	23/APR/33	17♐6
Appearance to the five hundred	16/APR/33	17♐11
Appearance to the seven	15/APR/33	17♐12
Appearance to the eleven	11/APR/33	17♐15
Appearance in Emmaus	6/APR/33	17♐18
Resurrection	5/APR/33	17♐19
Descent into hell	4/APR/33	17♐19
Death of Nathan Jesus	3/APR/33	17♐20
Raised upon the cross	3/APR/33	17♐20
Nailed to cross	3/APR/33	17♐20
Carrying the cross	3/APR/33	17♐20
Death sentence	3/APR/33	17♐20
Crowning with thorns	3/APR/33	17♐20
Scourging	3/APR/33	17♐20
Trial by Pontius Pilate	3/APR/33	17♐20
Peter's denial	3/APR/33	17♐20
Trial by Caiaphas	3/APR/33	17♐20
Betrayal of Judas	2/APR/33	17♐20
Gethsemane	2/APR/33	17♐20
Last supper	2/APR/33	17♐20
Last anointing	1/APR/33	17♐20
"Woe upon the Pharisees"	24/MAR/33	17♐23
Theophany (2nd)	20/MAR/33	17♐23
Cursing the fig tree	20/MAR/33	17♐23
Triumphant entry into Jerusalem	19/MAR/33	17♐23
Assumption of Virgin discovered	16/AUG/44	5♑27
Death of Solomon Mary	15/AUG/44	5♑28

AN ABBREVIATED BIBLIOGRAPHY

WE MIGHT SAY THAT TRUE astrosophy was known to the ancients through the faculty of clairvoyance. Long ago, humanity was unable to imagine itself as separate from nature and from the cosmos; we lived in shared rhythm with both. As the grip of materialism tightened, our connection to the stars became more tenuous.

Underlying the great body of work of Rudolf Steiner (1861-1925) was a return to the spiritual life of the cosmos. *Astronomy and Astrology, At Home in the Universe: Exploring Our Suprasensory Nature*, and *Life between Death and Rebirth* offer the most readable collections of lectures on our relationship to the cosmos; those brave souls who long to dive into the deep end of the pool might also want to read his two *Cosmosophy* volumes.

Elisabeth Vreede (1879-1943) met Steiner in 1903 and worked closely with him. She went on to help him establish the Anthroposophical Society, as well as the first Goetheanum (in Dornach, Switzerland). *Anthroposophy and Astrology*, a collection of lectures given by Vreede between 1927 and 1930, elaborates on many of Steiner's themes with a clarity that renders them approachable to the star novice. Beginning in 1923, Vreede served as an original member of the Vorstand (board of directors) of the Anthroposophical Society, heading its Mathematical-Astronomical Section for twelve years. A Platonist among Aristotelians[1], she was ousted from the Vorstand in 1935 (along with Ita Wegman, leader of the Medical Section).[2] And because Vreede (alone, to my knowledge, within the leadership of the Anthroposophical Society) supported and nurtured the work of both Valentin Tomberg and Willi Sucher, we are left wondering "what might have been."

Valentin Tomberg (1900-1973) was a protégé of Elisabeth Vreede. Upon meeting Tomberg, Vreede immediately recognized him as a fellow Platonist, and she identified him as an individual capable of carrying on spiritual research commensurate with Steiner's own. Seeking to bridge the perceived chasm between the Aristotelians and the Platonists (Steiner had insisted that they must learn to work together), she arranged for Tomberg to lecture extensively. In 1930, Vreede gave a set of two lectures entitled "The Bodhisattva Question."

Tomberg was deeply moved by Steiner's work and began corresponding with him at an early age (though the two never met). Because of Vreede's ouster from the Vorstand, Tomberg worked and wrote in relative obscurity for the rest of his life. Few were familiar with his work before 1985, when Tarcher/Penguin published Robert Powell's English translation of *Meditations on the Tarot* (completed by Tomberg in 1965). *Lazarus, Come Forth!* (written between 1967 and 1970) was posthumously published, also in 1985.[3] Though the first English translation of Tomberg's anthroposophical meditations on the Old Testament appeared in 1939 (with an introduction by Vreede), they were republished in 2006 by SteinerBooks within a volume entitled *Christ and Sophia*—which included his later meditations on the New Testament and the Apocalypse.

As a young man, Willi Sucher (1902-1985) had an abiding interest in the cosmic world and in our relationship to it. Having heard Rudolf Steiner lecture, he became so inspired that he devoted his life to the development of a new star wisdom (or, astrosophy). His book *Cosmic Christianity* was published in 1970, followed by *Isis Sophia: Outline of a New Star Wisdom* in 1985, the year of his death. It was Sucher who developed the study of astrological biography, whereby planetary events in an individual's gestational period were shown to correspond

---

1 The overuse of these designations has bred confusion and a large degree of infighting since Steiner's death. In simplistic terms, we could say that Aristotelians labor for knowledge and wisdom, while Platonists receive it through revelation. For a contemporary treatise on the subject, see Joel Park's November 2018 article—"Moving Beyond Aristotle and Plato"—on his website (treehouse.live).
2 After Steiner's death in 1925, tension arose among the Council members regarding the future direction of the Anthroposophical Society.
3 The first section of *Lazarus, Come Forth!*—comprising the seven archetypal healing miracles of Christ, and their effect upon humanity—was reprinted in 2022 by Angelico Press under the title *Lazarus: The Miracle of Resurrection in World History*.

to the unfolding of the life to come. In 1927, Sucher had attended one of Vreede's lectures on the cosmos and felt the lightning bolt of profound wisdom. He came to know Vreede through a warm correspondence that led to an invitation to meet with her in Dornach; he also attended an important conference in Wales (in 1938) that was facilitated by Vreede. The speaker was Valentin Tomberg.

It was Willi Sucher who began the *Monthly Star Journal* in 1965. By 1974, the Journal changed its name (to *Mercury Star Journal*), its rhythm (it was published quarterly), and its editor (Sucher, aged seventy-two, had handed it over to Robert Powell when Powell was just twenty-seven). Any one of Robert Powell's accomplishments is able to stand alone within an enormous body of his work that will be carried across time; among these are the development of Choreocosmos (sacred dance and movement in accordance with the heavens), the careful selection of music for those dances, his karmic research based upon the indications of Steiner, and his pioneering work in "astrogeographia" (whereby correspondences between the starry firmament and the Earth can be established). But what concerns us here is his work in Christian Hermetic astrology, contained in two *Hermetic Astrology* volumes, as well as in another that bears the title *Christian Hermetic Astrology. The Christ Mystery* is not to be missed, either.

Here it is important to remember that the *Astrofire* computer program (created by Peter Treadgold), was inspired by the mathematical toiling of Willi Sucher! As a result, one of the unique features of *Astrofire* is its ability to study the prenatal period for the purpose of astrological biography. Additionally, *Astrofire* contains a database of planetary positions for the events within and peripheral to the life of Christ. Powell's mathematical genius, paired with his painstaking study of the visions of Anne Catherine Emmerich, led to the creation of this database within *Astrofire*.

The *Mercury Star Journal* ended publication in 1980. By the time the Journal had metamorphosed into the annual *Christian Star Calendar* in 1991, it had received a new impulse. For it was during this time that the planetary data of the life of Christ had been revealed. The *Christian Star Calendar* was last published in 2009. Though it featured articles by many accomplished astrosophers (William Bento, Brian Gray, Robert Schiappacasse, and David Tresemer among them), its calendar aspect was (in my opinion) somewhat dry, and difficult to "sink one's teeth into."

The *Christian Star Calendar* evolved further in 2010. Renamed the *Journal for Star Wisdom*, it then featured the addition of *commentaries* to the planetary and stellar data for the year. Though the commentaries began as a shared responsibility, it quickly fell solely to Claudia McLaren Lainson to write the remarks that would bring to readers not only the ability to "follow" the movements of the heavens, but also to take into their hearts the correspondences of these movements to the life of Christ. Lainson contributed her commentaries — as well as her brilliant articles — for ten years, at which time she stepped into an advisory capacity. Her final commentaries appeared in the 2019 edition of the *Journal*. In 2016 she published *The Circle of Twelve and the Legacy of Valentin Tomberg*. This was followed in 2020 by *The Hermit, the Minotaur, and the Shadow of Evil*. Lainson's profound insights into the stellar world, her devotion to Christian Hermeticism, and her uncanny ability to read any situation with clarity (and love) have touched a great many people.

The final change of scene in our drama occurred in 2018. This was the year of the last *Journal for Star Wisdom* that Robert Powell would edit, and in that issue was an article by Joel Matthew Park bearing the title "The Cosmic Communion of Fish: The Rhythm of the New Jerusalem." Two years previously, Park had established a website (treehouse.live) that had caught the attention of Lainson. Within these two forums, Park has explored anthroposophical, Christian Hermetic, and astrosophical topics with astounding depth; these include essays on the mysteries of Joseph, the Kalki Avatar, and Revelation — as well as an extensive and profound series on the sacrifices of Christ. In 2019 (the year Powell turned seventy-two), the editorship of the *Journal* was turned over to Park. Now presented under different titles (each yearly edition bears the subtitle *Star Wisdom*), it can be distinguished by its many international (and younger) authors. *Star Wisdom* is nurturing the seed of true globalism.

An Abbreviated Bibliography

WORKS CITED

"Asclepius to King Ammon," *Corpus Hermeticum* XVI, 7, trsl. W. Scott, [*Hermetica*, Oxford, 1924; repr. Boulder, 1982, p. 267] as cited in *Hermetic Astrology*, vol. 1.

Bryant, William. *The Veiled Pulse of Time* (Gt Barrington, MA: Lindisfarne Books, 1993).

Charbonneau-Lassay, Louis. *The Bestiary of Christ* (Harmondsworth, UK: Penguin Books, 1991).

Copernicus, Nicholas, *De revolutionibus orbium coelestium* I, 10, trsl. E. Rosen, [*On the Revolutions*, Cracow-London, 1978, p. 22] as cited in *Hermetic Astrology*, vol. 1.

Dorsan, Jacques. *The Clockwise House System* (Gt Barrington, MA: Lindisfarne Books, 2011).

Dorsan, Jacques. *Retour au Zodiaque des Étoiles: Vous n'êtes pas né sous le signe que vous croyez* [*Return to the Stellar Zodiac: You're Not the Sign You Think You Are*] (Paris: Dervy-Livres, 1986).

Gray, Brian. "Anthroposophic Foundations for a Renewal of Astrology," *Journal for Star Wisdom* (Gt Barrington, MA: SteinerBooks/Anthroposophic Press, 2012).

Lainson, Claudia McLaren. *The Circle of Twelve and the Legacy of Valentin Tomberg* (Boulder, CO: WindRoseAcademyPress, 3rd edition, 2021).

Lainson, Claudia McLaren. *The Hermit, the Minotaur, and the Shadow of Evil* (self-published, 2020).

Park, Joel Matthew Park. "Saturn in Cancer: Returning to the Origin of the Houses, Part I," *Star Wisdom*, vol. 2 (Hudson NY: Lindisfarne Books, 2020).

Park, Joel Matthew Park. "The Tree of Life: Returning to the Origin of the Houses, Part II," *Star Wisdom*, vol. 3 (Hudson, NY: Lindisfarne Books, 2021).

Park, Joel Matthew. "The Archetypal Language: Returning to the Origin of the Houses, Part III," *Star Wisdom*, vol. 4 (Hudson, NY: Lindisfarne Books, 2022).

Paul, Laquanna and Powell, Robert. *Cosmic Dances of the Zodiac* (San Rafael, CA: Sophia Foundation Press, 2003).

Paul, Laquanna and Powell, Robert. *Cosmic Dances of the Planets* (San Rafael, CA: Sophia Foundation Press, 2007).

Powell, Robert and Dann, Kevin. *The Astrological Revolution* (Gt Barrington, MA: Lindisfarne Books, 2010).

Powell, Robert. *The Christ Mystery* (Fair Oaks, CA: Rudolf Steiner College Press, 1999.)

Powell, Robert. *Chronicle of the Living Christ* (Hudson, NY: Anthroposophic Press, 1996).

Powell, Robert. *Elijah Come Again* (Gt Barrington, MA: Lindisfarne Books, 2009).

Powell, Robert. *Hermetic Astrology*, vol. 1. (San Rafael, CA: Sophia Foundation Press, 1987).

Powell, Robert. *Hermetic Astrology*, vol. 2. (San Rafael, CA: Sophia Foundation Press, 1989).

Powell, Robert. *History of the Houses* (Epping, NH: ACS Publications, 1996).

Rael, Leyla and Rudhyar, Dane. *Astrological Aspects: A Process Oriented Approach* (Santa Fe, NM: Aurora Press, 1980).

Rivers, Karen. *Love and the Evolution of Consciousness* (Gt Barrington, MA: Lindisfarne Books, 2016).

Scott, Randall. *The Christos Sun Meditations: Following the Eightfold Path Through the Decans of the Zodiac* (San Rafael, CA: LogoSophia Press, 2009).

Steiner. Rudolf. *The Ahrimanic Deception* (October 27, 1919), CW Nr. 193.

Steiner, Rudolf. *Astronomy and Astrology* (Forest Row, UK: Rudolf Steiner Press, 2009).

Steiner, Rudolf. *Christian Rosenkreutz — the Mystery, Teaching and Mission of a Master* (Forest Row, UK: Sophia Books, 2001).

Steiner, Rudolf. *The Fifth Gospel* (Forest Row, UK: Rudolf Steiner Press, 1995).

Steiner, Rudolf. *Life between Death and Rebirth* (United States: Anthroposophic Press, 1968).

Steiner, Rudolf. *The Spiritual Foundation of Morality* (Hudson, NY: Anthroposophic Press, 1995).

Steiner, Rudolf. *The Spiritual Hierarchies and the Physical World* (Gt Barrington, MA: SteinerBooks, 2008).

Steiner, Rudolf. *The Spiritual Guidance of the Individual and Humanity* (United States: Anthroposophic Press, 1991).

Steiner, Rudolf. *Verses & Meditations*, transl. George and Mary Adams (Forest Row, UK: Rudolf Steiner Press, 2004).

Sucher, Willi. *Cosmic Christianity & The Changing Countenance of Cosmology* (Hudson, NY: Anthroposophic Press, 1985).

Sucher, Willi. *Isis Sophia: Outline of a New Star Wisdom* (Meadow Vista, CA: Astrosophy Research Center, 1985).

Tarnas, Richard. *Cosmos and Psyche* (New York, NY: Penguin, 2006).

Tomberg, Valentin. *Christ and Sophia: Anthroposophic Meditations on the Old Testament, New Testament, and Apocalypse* (Gt Barrington, MA: SteinerBooks, 2006).

Tomberg, Valentin. *Lazarus: The Miracle of Resurrection in World History* (Brooklyn, NY: Angelico Press, 2022).

Tomberg, Valentin. *Meditations on the Tarot: A Journey into Christian Hermeticism* (Brooklyn, NY: Angelico Press, 2019).

Tomberg, Valentin. *Proclamation on Sinai: Covenant and Commandments* (Brooklyn, NY: Angelico Press, 2022).

Tomberg, Valentin. *Russian Spirituality & Other Essays* (San Rafael, CA: LogoSophia, 2010).

Tomberg, Valentin. *The Wandering Fool* (San Rafael, CA: LogoSophia, 2009).

Von Halle, Judith. *Descent into the Depths of the Earth* (Forest Row, UK: Temple Lodge Publishing, 2011).

Vreede, Elisabeth. *Anthroposophy and Astrology* (Gt Barrington, MA: Anthroposophic Press, 2001).

ACKNOWLEDGMENTS

I MARVEL DAILY THAT—THANKS TO Cecille Greenleaf and Karen Rivers—I crossed paths with Robert Powell in 2009. From that point onward, my happy but secular life took a bold turn into the unknown and my true acquaintance with the stars began. There is not a single part of my life that has not been touched by his work.

Though I managed to tread water while reading Powell's *Hermetic Astrology* volumes, I remained a hermit without a lamp who often found herself lost in a dark wood. This changed when I made the acquaintance of Claudia Lainson, who quickly offered to act as my mentor, even inviting me to assist her with some of her work. It was she who encouraged me to begin to write about the stars. Her suggestions for *Awakening to the Spiritual Archetypes within the Birth Chart* invariably made the book much better than it would have otherwise been.

This project could not have materialized without the steady guidance and support of my editor, Richard Bloedon, who had an imaginative picture of the book long before I did. Throughout the process, I was sustained by his (inexplicably) unwavering confidence in my ability to pull it off.

Several other individuals provided input and suggestions that proved invaluable to the quality of the result: Robert Powell, Joel Park, Kevin Dann, and Brian Gray. Many heartfelt thanks to you all!

ABOUT THE AUTHOR

JULIE HUMPHREYS has been a contributor to *Star Wisdom*, the annual publication formerly known as the *Journal for Star Wisdom*. An early interest in astrology lay dormant for more than three decades until she was introduced to the sidereal system, the works of Robert Powell and Valentin Tomberg, and the visions of Anne Catherine Emmerich. Julie offers a weekly "star letter" that appears in the substack version of *Starlight*, the newsletter and journal of the Sophia Foundation of North America.

www.ingramcontent.com/pod-product-compliance
Lightning Source LLC
Chambersburg PA
CBHW080448170426
43196CB00016B/2719